Monica Jahner...

The self starting tireless worker from North West Initiative Program... AARO (Advocacy Re-Entry Resources Outreach).

You bring all the ideals of the greatest generation to your life:

STRENGTH
COURAGE
TEAMWORK
SERVICE TO OTHERS
AND
COMPASSION.

STAY STRONG. LIVE LONG.

Fred Lauck

COMPLIMENTS OF RUSSELL VAIL

Children
of the
Greatest Generation

An Emotional History

Children
of the
Greatest Generation

—◦◦◦—

An Emotional History

By

Frederick W. Lauck

ISBN# 978-0-615-51084-2

Text and Cover Design by Susan Leonard/Rose Island Bookworks
Printed in the United States of America

"On Children" from The Prophet by Kahlil Gibran, copyright 1923 by
Kahlil Gibran and renewed 1951 by Administrators C.T.A. of Kahlil
Gibran Estate and Mary G. Gibran. Used by permission of Alfred A.
Knopf, a division of Random House, Inc.

Acknowledgments

Twenty years ago, my dear Irish friend, Jack Harrington, suggested that I write a history of the West Side of Detroit: "Lauck, *Free Press* writer, Neal Shine, covers the colorful anecdotes of the East Side of Detroit, but nobody covers the West Side… so Lauck, why don't you write the story of the West Side?" That seed Jack Harrington planted

Jack Harrington and Fred Lauck

those many years ago eventually grew into a plan of action, and out of that plan came three books of the "*Children of the Greatest Generation.*" Thanks for the great suggestion Jack. And, hats off to your "Greatest Generation" father, Patrick Joseph Harrington (January 24, 1904 to July 13, 1986),

that giant of a gentleman with the softest of voices and the warmest of smiles – a true Irishman from Castletownbere, Deenish Island, County Cork, Ireland who came to America in 1928 and worked at the Ford Rouge Steel Plant in Dearborn, Michigan for almost forty years, and… in between, "flipped a few steaks" for us in his small kitchen on

Patrick Joseph
Harrington

Dalby Street in Redford, Michigan after Jack and I returned from some "all nighters" at the "blind pigs" (aka "after hours joints"). Jack later brought his own great sense of integrity and compassion to his career as a probation officer both in Wayne County and Oakland County.

And, thanks to another great Irishman and St. Scholastica classmate, Judge Jimmy "Cash and Carry" Sheehy, for the story of Caveman Lee which he brought to my attention, and which I rewrote for my book (with his permission). I also owe a great debt of gratitude to my compatriots Rick Rashid, Esquire, Frank "Designated Hitter" Demers, Johnny "Pizza" DiBella, Brian Lavan, Esquire, and Professor Colin Michael Bryce for their colorful expressions, uncanny insights and unique views which helped me formulate my concepts of life, law and philosophy. These fine men took up where my own genius father, Frederick Valentine Lauck, with his ninth grade education left off when he died in my home on December 11, 1982.

Fred and Debra Lauck
1999

And, most importantly, thanks to my beloved wife, Debra Economy Sandoval, who pushed me to understand that the differences in each person and their own uniqueness is good – not threatening. Debra, you are a good wife and a terrific mother. Thanks for being there for me during the good and the bad, through sickness and health and for enduring my rapid-fire staccato, verbalization of ideas and concepts as I habitually thought out loud in technicolor – or, as my "Greatest

Generation" Father would say: "Lauck, do you ever have a thought that you don't verbalize?"

Finally, thanks to the "Greatest Generation." Thanks for your legacy of daily lessons in courage as we watched you struggle to survive and humbly live your lives in quiet, routine fashion leaving us with a smile and a gentle word of encouragement when it came our time to go forth in the world. Thanks for teaching us how to entertain one another with a good story told on the porch during the summer, or acted out at the kitchen table during the winter, or with a song, sung along with the radio when, as was usually the case, there was no money for movies, concerts or dining out. Although my generation will never be known as the "Greatest Generation," we are not too far removed from the strength, loyalty, work ethic and the ideals of our "Greatest Generation" parents.

Jean Lauck and baby Fred 1943
"Luxurious Accomodations"

Val and Fred
1972

Jessie and Fred
Kingsville, Ontario 2001

Frances in Milford, MI
2003

Debra, Frances, and Jessie
2002

Jessie Valentine Lauck

Frances Sandoval Lauck

Val and Fred
Jackson Hole, WY 1986

Val, Fred, Debra, Jessie and Frances 2006

Dedication...
The Next Generation

Frederick Valentine Lauck... d.o.b. March 7, 1970
Jessie Valentine Lauck... d.o.b. July 27, 2000
Frances Sandoval Lauck... d.o.b. July 31, 2002

Congratulations, Congratulations, Congratulations!!
You Did It!! You Got Born!!

Now the world opens up for you. Take all the new challenges that life has to offer. The only way successful people separate themselves from the crowd is by accepting the difficult challenges. Going out on a limb and being able to live with that scary feeling of being out of your comfort zone is **your key** to success. And, even though you may feel uncomfortable or overwhelmed when you are out on a limb, it's nice to know that there is a **key**. And, it's also nice to know that with hard work and determination you can conquer your fears and find a place of comfort in an otherwise chaotic world.

Life is a big wonderful adventure filled with so many unique individuals and personalities. Working your way through those personalities is one of life's biggest challenges. But, don't just fake it, and don't just put up with those diverse personalities. As your mother taught me, learn to appreciate and even love the uniqueness and differences of various personalities – even when they upset you. But, above all… **BE YOURSELF**, and do not compromise the **essence** of who you are.

For me (but not necessarily for you because we are all unique, different creatures)… for me, my credo was: "stand out above the horizon, stand out above the crowd, stand out front and center, so you are distinguishable from the background of humanity." The psychologists would say "not so." The theologians would say "not so." For, as they would say, your birthright alone makes you unique, or, as 80-year-old Maude said to 15-year-old Harold in the movie *Harold and Maude*:

> "No, Harold, those daisies are not all the same. They are all unique and different in so many subtle ways. Some turn to the left, some to the right; some look up, some look down; some say hello to the sun in the morning, while others say goodnight in the evening. So no two daisies and no two human beings are the same, Harold."

I agree, and I think Maude's view of daisies and people and their uniqueness is the foundation for respect for life (daisies and people) – a respect for life that clamors for world peace.

In the end, kids of mine, I have to answer for myself… as you will have to answer for yourselves. My constant companion was a burning desire to have my uniqueness stand out in accomplishment. That's just my desire and my chosen path, and I have no fault to find with those whose paths are different. But, isn't it ironic that, no matter what path we choose to express our own uniqueness, the actual accomplishment in all of our lives is the same; it's the "journey," – the inevitable journey each of us take up in following our own path and our own star. It is the journey much more than the success or even the failure that writes our story in the night sky as our epitaph of who we were in our short span of years on this earth. So enjoy the journey because… well, because… you are the journey and the journey is you.

Thank you, kids of the next generation for all the joy you gave me! First, you saw the world through my eyes. Then, I saw the world through yours. And, now, in the pages of these three volumes, you will see the world through my eyes one more time.

Book I: "Children of the Greatest Generation"…
    "The Marathon Begins"

Book II: "Children of the Greatest Generation"…
    "We Danced with Life"

Book III: "Children of the Greatest Generation"…
    "Winding Down… Losing Our World"

And, within these three books, you will find a philosophy of life told in story form – a philosophy of life that will answer your question: **"Who was my father?"**

Table of Contents

Introduction to

Book III: Winding Down.. Losing Our World **306**

THE MARATHON BEGINS

BOOK I
The Marathon Begins

CHILDHOOD...
Shooting stars of wonder, anticipation and a thousand possibilities in a world that is endlessly new.

UNRAVELS INTO ADOLESCENCE...
Sobering awareness of inadequacy, fear and a thousand limitations of "less than the rest."

REVERSAL OF FORTUNE
Some of the kids of the Greatest Generation were born with gifts... **others not**. Some arrived in life as rising stars... **others not**. Some just knew how to run, dance, sing and play the game... **others not**. Some were blessed with natural beauty, confidence and an outgoing style... **others not**.

This is the story of the "**others not**" – those Children of the Greatest Generation who claimed the heritage of their parents' emotional strength, courage and work ethic to overcome self doubt, inadequacy and "less than the rest"... those who, eventually, outdistanced their gifted peers during the Marathon of Life.

CHAPTER 1

In The Beginning

Ah... I remember it well.

It was in the beginning when it began. Everybody was waiting for it to begin, but it wasn't beginning or beganning. Nothing was happening. It was dark and cold as a witches' bosom. There was a sea of featureless faces, but nobody was saying anything. Everybody was bored. Everybody was just listlessly hanging out waiting for it to begin, but nothing was happening. It wasn't beginning. It wasn't the best of times, and it wasn't the worst of times; it was just "no times" – nothing happening for the longest time.

Suddenly, "Bang!" It all began, and we were hurtling head long at the speed of light, expanding from the beginning through an eon of time, and into an unbounded universe. But, it must have been a false start because, other than hurtling through space, nothing was happening. Then, long after the "Big Bang" birth of the Universe, it finally happened. Our generation slipped through a seam in a parallel universe into our own universe, and headed straight toward the Hood in Northwest Detroit.

There were five births in the first wave, all occurring simultaneously at Mt. Carmel Hospital (southwest corner of Schaefer and West Outer Drive) on July 4, 1943. Bang! Bang! Bang! Bang! and Bang! At 5:05 a.m. on the 5th day of the week, 5 newborns, each weighing 5 lbs. 5 oz, burst forth like roman candles exploding onto the Detroit Scene – bare naked, and all unrelenting in the echoing cacophony of their vocal chorus:

> "We are Scholasticans, Scholasticans
> And loyal we will be to Cell Block 203."

Five babies born simultaneously to five different mothers, while the fathers, who barely survived the Great Depression and the Dust Bowl of the 1930s, were off fighting World War II – the war to end all wars where over 50 million people, mostly civilians, were killed. Bang! Hello, Valentina Frances Victory! Bang! Hello, Tom Terrific! Bang! Hello, Brigetta BeBop! Bang! Hello, Sammy Slow! Bang! Hello, Brenda Blah! It took you long enough to get here, but "welcome to the Hood."

All the grandparents, the aunts, uncles, cousins, brothers, sisters and other well wishers lined up at the nursery room window, smoking cigars to help stimulate the kids' new lungs, and wondered out loud: "What will Valentina Frances Victory become?" "What will Tom Terrific become?" "Brigetta BeBop?" "Sammy Slow?" "Brenda Blah?" At this wondrous moment, while relatives of the newborns pondered what greatness the future would hold for their new arrivals, Dr. Nathan Goodfellow magically appeared out of a puff of cigar smoke. Dr. Goodfellow, admiring his deliveries, overheard the relatives' dreams and ambitions for each new infant's future. Dr. Goodfellow, a wise and caring man, shook his head and cautioned one and all:

"Above all, the individual uniqueness of each infant must be recognized and appreciated, a uniqueness which must be turned loose into the world to find its own star, its own course, its own dream, and fulfill its own destiny, unburdened by the well-intentioned, but counter-productive, expectations of family members and well wishers."

Dr. Goodfellow wisely counseled one and all: "Each child is blessed with different gifts. So, sit back and watch patiently for years and decades as each child's own unique gifts magically unfold over life's marathon." Or, as the wise Lebanese poet, Khalil Gibran, so elegantly put it:

On Children

"Your children are not your children.
They are the sons and daughters of Life's longing
        for itself.
They come through you but not from you,
And, though they are with you yet they belong
        not to you.
You may give them your love but not your thoughts,
For they have their own thoughts.
You may house their bodies but not their souls,
For their souls dwell in the house of tomorrow,
Which you cannot visit, not even in your dreams.
You may strive to be like them, but seek not to make
        them like you.
For life goes not backward nor tarries with yesterday.
You are the bows from which your children as living
        arrows are sent forth."

Heading Home

After a few days of hanging out in the nursery, the Five Bangs left the hospital and each went to their own home in the Northwest Detroit Hood. Heredity, a.k.a. nature, was a fait accompli, but nurture, a.k.a. environment, lurked around the corner, concealed in the shadow of uncertainty, and waited to make its imprint on the lives and souls of the Five Bangs and the rest of us kids in the Hood – perhaps a magical imprint, perhaps a devastating imprint. Who knows? Time will tell. The question of what these new lives would become was left to the great uncharted, human journey into an uncertain future.

The initial years bounced along with varying experiences. Some of the kids in the Hood saw love, peace, joy, gentleness, kindness, understanding, thought provoking kitchen-table discussions and encouragement with their parents realizing their own lives were on hold for the unfolding development of the next generation. Others less fortunate saw anxiousness, fear, harshness, excessive discipline, criticism and shouting matches with parents unable to break from the strong environmental link of their own harsh past. But, for the most part, the environment and nurture in the Hood was a combination of good news – bad news, painted by parents who were a patchwork of all of life's emotions. The lucky ones, however, grew up in households where the good of nurture outweighed the bad – homes where the new, young souls would be given a peaceful, protected place to live as they started to take baby steps toward their physical, emotional and spiritual development.

Off to School

On September 5, 1949, after six years of living in the cocoon of parental protection, the Five Bangs and the rest of us in the Hood started our first day of first grade at St. Scholastica at $20.00 a semester – the cost of a parochial education with teaching nuns. On the first day of class, we all dutifully followed our parents over to St.

St. Scholastica Grade School

Scholastica Grade School at the corner of Southfield and Outer Drive in Northwest Detroit – a magnificent corner which would later be affectionately called the "Holy Corner:" Little Sisters of the Poor, home for the aged, on the northeast corner; Mercy College, that grand edifice of unparalleled architectural beauty run by the Sisters of Mercy, on the northwest corner; St. Scholastica Grade School run by St. Scholastica's successors, the Adrian Dominicans, in full nun regalia, on the southwest corner; and, later in the 1950s, Benedictine High School on the southeast corner.

St. Scholastica parish was run by the Benedictine priests, right off the boat from Italy, and offering the Sacrament of Confession in English or Italian, or, if you could get away with it, you could give your confession in "Pig Latin" to an Italian immigrant priest still struggling to understand the vagaries of the English language. Pig Latin worked for 6-year-old Valentina Frances Victory who, with her best Pig Latin, confessed to adultery (Oh Boy – You talk about a case of scruples!). But, she's the same kid who shocked the dinner table as a 4-year-old by telling her father: "You ain't the boss of me, you sum of bitch."

So formal education began for the Five Bangs and the rest of us children of the Greatest Generation. In the fall of 1949, we were split up into two first grade classes of sixty plus students in each class – one class taught by Sister Joan Cecil and the other by Sister Kathleen. The very first day started with an impressive lesson in discipline. The pastor and one of the founders of St. Scholastica Grade School, Father

Boniface Lucci, stopped by to offer a kind and reassuring first grade "hello" to the 6-year-old newcomers. Every kid's name was printed on a card that sat upright at the front of each desk. Father Boniface,

Father Boniface, OSB
First Pastor of
St. Scholastica

in flowing black robes, proudly strode down the aisle – all 5' 4" of him, and asked Tom Terrific what the sign on his desk said, to which Tom Terrific shyly replied: "I don't know Father; I can't read." **SMASH!** A quick, devastating back hand found Tom Terrific's jaw, and he almost went down for the count. Thank heaven that rattling noise inside his mouth were his baby teeth. Tom Terrific's head was just beginning to clear when he heard Father Boniface shout: **"That-a sign-a says-eh 'Tom-a Terrific.' REMEMBER THAT!"** Father Boniface advanced to the next desk and asked Sammy Slow the same question: "Hey boy, what-a does-eh that-a sign-a on your desk-eh say?" With a certain "learning-on-the-run" trepidation, Sammy Slow quickly responded with what he just learned: "The sign says 'Tom Terrific,' Father." **SMASH!** another shot to the head. All eyes now on Father Boniface, the well-intentioned precursor of Darth Vader, with each pair of eyes starting to cry in unison: "I want my Momma."

Well, those days with Momma are over, kids. Welcome to Catholic School Discipline 101. From now on, you will learn firsthand the strength, discipline and courage that it took for the Greatest Generation to survive economic disasters like the Great Depression, world threats to security like Pearl Harbor, Adolph Hitler, Joseph Stalin and the intense teamwork it took to evacuate Dunkirk during World War II. It will be a brief childhood, but you will learn Discipline 101 and Survival 101 as well as the route to the nearest Cold War, air raid shelter. And so it begins.

St. Scholastica Second Grade Class 1951
Teaching the Unteachables

CHAPTER 2

Grade School...
Magic Of The 1950s

With half of the first grade over, it was now 1950. Each first grade day was a new learning experience as the drudgery of getting an education began: Catechism 101 "God is Love," Arts and Crafts 101 with a cigar box filled with crayons, scissors, glue and an oil cloth,

Sister Katie
1953

Reading 101 from our "Dick and Jane Reader:" "See Dick Jump." "See Spot Run," as we learn to read by separating syllables and sounding out phonetic segments of words. There were also the significant events of spiritual celebration – First Communions in second grade with Sister Kathleen, with the boys in white shirts, white ties, white pants, white socks and girls in white veils, all of us worked up to a fever pitch, and looking forward to picking up some "cash" in a card. There were first kisses in the third grade. Why not? It may have been too early for the big hormonal bang, but that kissing stuff was made for me and that blond "Cutie Pie," Diane Zarza. Diane and I were single-handedly (or is it double-handedly?) responsible for the nuns partitioning the playground – boys on the north side, girls on the south side, leaving me with the lingering thought that the nuns were taking this discipline thing too seriously.

There was Confirmation in fourth grade with the Bishop's ring kissed, sponsor Jim Gribbin, the Great Irishman, to stand behind me and a new name for everyone ("James" for me, of course), followed by dinner at Nate Manzo's Italian restaurant on Six Mile and my first watch which I never wore because there were only two time zones for me: "Light – Play ball," and "Dark – Go to sleep." There was the fourth grade classroom in the unfinished basement, boiler room with Sister Ricardo, an aging Dominican nun, who had her hands full with the likes of me and my classmates. Yeah, the same boiler room where we learned to dance to Bill Haley and the Comets' Rockabilly Classic "Rock Around the Clock" – **Now that's what I'm talking about!**

There were the first lay teachers in the fifth grade (looking back, the first sign that the nuns weren't going to last forever) – Miss Wheeler (the wild redhead) and Miss Oldani (a reserved brunette), and a new concept, "changing classes." There was fifth and sixth grade football and baseball with Father Livius Paoli at the helm, assisted by Mr. Steele, Mr. Quinn and Rip Collins – a former fighter pilot in the Korean War and long time equipment manager for the Detroit Lions, and later visiting club house manager for major league baseball teams visiting Tiger Stadium. Talk about a feisty Irishman!

The Boston-Irish Gang

There was the seventh and eighth grade football team under Coach Frank Bowler, an Irishman from Boston, who played college football for four years in Boston in the 1920s, and then moved to

Detroit to attend the University of Detroit Law School playing three more years of college football along with his Boston area friends – including Thomas "Tiger" Thornton, later a Federal Court judge in Detroit. Twenty years later, Judge "Tiger" Thornton would grant my request for a Restraining Order against the United States Army when the Army tried to court martial my law school classmate, John J. Conlon, son of the owner of the "Blarney Rose Bar" in New York City.

"Just Makin' a Livin'... Your Honor"

Another football player from that 1920s era who came to Detroit from the Boston area to go to law school and play three more years of football at the University of Detroit was Judge Joe Gillis, a 300 pounder in the 1920s when the average lineman weighed 160 lbs. – the very

The Honorable
Joe Gillis

same Judge Gillis who in the 1950s acquitted my father of being a "bookie" in Detroit's Recorder's Court. The cops saw my father hide his bet slips in the hubcap of his car, and, when my father went back into his bookie joint to get his hat, the cops loosened his hubcap, and then "tailed" my father until the hubcap came off, and bet slips blew everywhere. The cops stopped my father for littering, and upped the ante to illegal gambling when they confirmed the bet slips, and then hauled my father before the tough Judge Gillis. After the cops told their side of the story, my father admitted he had no defense: "It's like the police officer said, Your Honor." Judge Gillis, obviously feeling sorry for my defenseless father, and a betting man himself, asked my father if he had any kids. My father responded: "Yes, a kid at Catholic Central High School and two daughters at St. Scholastica." An elated and very Catholic Judge Gillis blurted out:

The Honorable Bookie
Fred Lauck

The Honorable
Jerome Cavanagh

"Okay, now we got something to work with," and promptly dismissed the case on the grounds that my father was a "working stiff" – not a criminal.

This is the very same Judge Gillis who was summoned to testify before Attorney General Bobby Kennedy's Federal Grand Jury in Detroit in the 1960s. Judge Gillis was represented by Oliver Nelson (tough lawyer and Dartmouth Football Star) and Jerome Cavanagh (later 29-year-old whiz kid Mayor of the City of Detroit). At the Federal Court building in Detroit, Judge Gillis confronted Bobby Kennedy: "Why the hell was I subpoenaed?" Bobby Kennedy responded that there were **"rumors"** that Detroit Police officers who were charged with crimes were waiving jury trials before Judge Gillis, and were being regularly acquitted by Judge Gillis. Judge Gillis then blasted Bobby Kennedy with the rumor that Kennedy's father (Rose Kennedy's husband), the legendary Joseph "Bootleg" Kennedy, was rumored to be keeping company with *Sunset Boulevard* starlet Gloria Swanson – "so how much faith do you want to put in rumors, Bobby?"

This is also the very same Judge Gillis, who upon catching court officer Cornelius Flynn taking a St. Patrick's Day "nip" with the court staff, told officer Flynn that: "If this were Ireland, you would not be drinking alcohol on St. Patrick's Day," to which Officer Flynn retorted in an uninhibited moment: "Your Honor, if this were Ireland, you wouldn't even be a Magistrate." Needless to say, there were consequences to be paid. Officer Flynn lost his cushy job as court officer, and went back to patrol duties, and his son, my St.

**Court Officer
Cornelius Flynn**

Scholastica classmate, Neil Flynn, lost his high-paying, customer-of-one job cutting the Honorable Joseph Gillis' lawn. Judge Gillis and Officer Flynn were both good men, but their dispute is a classic example of an Irish misdemeanor – a technical violation of the social decorum, but perpetuated with the best of excuses. The lesson... when you take on the government with an act of "civil disobedience," or with an Irish misdemeanor, there are consequences to pay, so the issue better be one that's worth fighting over.

The Flight of the Pumpkin

Meanwhile, back in the Hood, the beat was going on. Sister Gertrude Mary for sixth grade – a grand lady who could get the most out of you because she conveyed the message that she cared about you. Sister Gertrude Mary walked into our second floor, sixth grade classroom on a blue-gray, October day in 1954 and took one look at the crumbling visage of our carved pumpkin on the window ledge, and instantly knew that something was up. In reality, it was Rodney Gibbons' fault. He didn't do what I told him to do. I told him to go down to the first floor, and catch the pumpkin when I threw it out the second story window. As soon as I toss the pumpkin out the window, Rodney starts turning in circles trying to surround the free-falling pumpkin. The inevitable happened. Rodney never even got his glove on the pumpkin. Rodney, a rather unathletic albino guy, let the pumpkin play him, and it bounced off his skinny head and hit the ground taking on a Humpty-Dumpty likeness. Upstairs comes Rodney with the pumpkin pieces. Despite my best effort to reshape that out-of-whack pumpkin, and put it back on the window ledge before Sister Gertrude Mary arrived, that pumpkin didn't look the same. The pumpkin looked like it took a few shots to the (pumpkin) head. Even at a casual glance, it just didn't look right.

To make matters worse, Rodney crumbled a second time under pressure. When Sister Gertrude Mary entered the room and came face to face with that Humpty-Dumpty looking pumpkin, she turned to the class with fire in her eyes. I was always one of the "usual suspects," but, when her eyes met mine, I put on one of my best "Oh, nothing!" looks. But, when her eyes met Rodney's eyes, Rodney crumbled like the pumpkin, and gave it all away, blurting out (before the interrogation even began): "Fred Lauck threw the pumpkin out the window, Sister." So, I took it on the chin, but the reality is that, if Rodney doesn't blow my plan, and, if he makes the two story catch of the free falling pumpkin, Sister Gertrude Mary doesn't know a thing, and we're both daring heroes of the day and reigning champs at next year's "throw the pumpkin out the window" caper. I vowed that next year I was going to replace Rodney with Frank Demers. Demers couldn't see a lick, but he had soft hands, and, most importantly, he wouldn't panic under pressure and squeal. If push came to shove, Frank would take it on the chin (both the pumpkin and the interrogation), and Sister Gertrude Mary would be none the wiser for my role, and I would skate.

Death Sneaks In...

In the sixth grade, humor was replaced by tragedy as life began to take its toll. My very likeable classmate, Tom Wills, lost his three young nephews in a house fire. Their small bodies were carried out on stretchers while both parents survived. Survived to what? 17-year-old Paul Massaron drowned in Lake Erie off Pointe Pelee, Ontario. I was haunted as I kept seeing his face every time I closed my eyes – especially as I lay sleepless at night… trying to comprehend young death. My Mother's youngest sister Charlene LaTour's son, my cousin Jimmy LaTour, drowned in Lake Huron. The other LaTour children rushed to their rented cottage to tell my Aunt Charlene that Jimmy was out in the deep water, and they couldn't get him in. Aunt Charlene rushed to the shoreline and saw Jimmy's red bathing suit, and, a parent's worst nightmare – 7-year-old Jimmy, lifeless and floating face down. During rescue attempts, Jimmy's lifeless blue lips began to bleed, and Aunt Charlene had a moment of hope. Where there's blood, there's life! But, it was not to be. Seven-year-old Jimmy was gone.

All the young were buried out of Ted C. Sullivan's Funeral Home on the North Side of Six Mile (a.k.a. McNichols), half way between Hubbell and Schaeffer. Little Jimmy LaTour was buried in a small white casket, the Mass of the Angels. How do the parents absorb such tragedy and carry on? Perhaps, it was their faith in Christianity, their faith in Jesus, or, perhaps, it was just the need to take care of the rest of their children. But, the reality – there were no other options. Later in life, at age 39, I would bury my 66-year-old father on December 15, 1982, and start a major trial the very next day in Wayne County Circuit Court before Judge Paul Teranes – a gentleman and a great jurist. Later in life, in June 2007, at age 64, (close to the age of my father when he died), I tried a most difficult first degree murder case in Wayne County Circuit court by day, and attended funeral homes at night to bury sister-in-law, Anne Stoner O'Kane, to bury my St. Scholastica mentor, confessor, coach and barber, 94-year-old Father Livius Paoli O.S.B., and to bury 36-year-old Billy Wertheimer who, like my cousin Jimmy LaTour, drowned in Lake Huron. And, during the first week of trial, my brother Marty Lahti was put in the care of hospice and lived for another thirty-three days, finally succumbing

15

to lung cancer – a victim of second hand smoke. Still later, on June 1, 2010, I gave the eulogy for (almost) 90-year-old Lena Butera DiBella, and the next day appeared in a most contentious three day hearing working with one of Michigan's finest trial lawyers, Elbert Hatchet, a contemporary of mine from the Pontiac Hood. But, through all the bad news, funerals and wakes, my focus in the courtroom was riveted beyond belief, almost supernatural – a "twilight zone" experience, probably part gift from the Holy Spirit and part gift from the Greatest Generation who shared their strength, focus and determination with their children.

Fr. Livius Paoli, OSB	Billy Wertheimer	Lena Butera DiBella
Spiritual Mentor	A Great Kid	A Special Woman

From eulogies to opening statements and closing arguments, from spiritual judgment by God to temporal judgment by a jury, you can't adjourn death. I could have adjourned the trials, but a client is entitled to have their legal matter finalized without unnecessary delay. The real issue… I had to prove to my ever present critic (myself) that I was as strong as my parents' Greatest Generation. Bury your dead on the lone prairie, brush off the dust, kick aside the tumbleweed, and get up and go on to the next day, as the next day turns into the next month, the next year, the next decade until you eventually make your own exit from this vale of tears, and, perhaps, embrace your dead in another form of life's eternal existence.

Rockin' in the Hood

But, even with the first experiences of death, life had an undeniable greatness in the 1950s. Each day, life exploded with the freshness of brand new events, experiences and possibilities. In 1955, Elvis Presley burst onto the scene from Tupelo, Mississippi. Before we had television sets, our radios blared out with Elvis' rockabilly classics: "That's Alright Momma," "Heartbreak Hotel" and "Don't Be Cruel." Others quickly followed: Buddy Holly with "Peggy Sue" and "That'll Be the Day;" Jerry Lee Lewis with "Great Balls of Fire," his career derailed when he married his 13-year-old first cousin; Johnnie Ray with "Walkin' My Baby Back Home" and "The Little White Cloud That Cried," his career derailed when he was arrested on a morals charge during a Detroit performance by my classmate Frank Demers' father, Detroit Police Vice Cop, Sgt. Frank Demers.

Sgt. Frank Demers Sr., Detroit P.D.
Busted Crooner Johnnie Ray in the 1950s.

The music moved us all. It wasn't the extraordinary musicianship of the Big Band sound of the Greatest Generation by bandleaders Glenn Miller, Guy Lombardo, Artie Shaw, brothers Jimmy and Tommy Dorsey, Duke Ellington, Benny Goodman, Harry James, Cab Calloway and the rest, but it was our music and our identity, and, when we walked out the door of our houses and headed to the corner, it was "Let's go – get it on," singing on the corner with our own homegrown group, Johnny MaGoo and the Hoody "Dank Coons."

Besides Rockabilly, there was Doo Wop and Rhythm and Blues all the way from the crowded street corners of New York and Philadelphia to our own Northwest Detroit Hood: Frankie Lymon and the Teenagers with "Why do Fools Fall in Love," the "Peppermint

Twist" by Joey D and the Starlighters, "Runaround Sue" and the "Wanderer" by Dion and the Belmonts, "Loco-Motion" by Little Eva, "The Great Pretender" by the Platters, "Save the Last Dance for Me," "There Goes My Baby" and "Under the Boardwalk" by the Drifters, and many others. And how about that crazy Little Richard ("Bop bopa-a-lu a whop bam boo" – they don't write meaningful lyrics like that any more), with Pat Boone, the white kid with the smooth voice and white bucks, stealing Little Richard's songs (but not his thunder) by singing a cover version of Little Richard's bombastic hit "Tutti Fruitti" – all sanitized by the clean cut, all American white recording industry (pre Berry Gordy's "Hitsville" on Grand Blvd. and "Motown" records). And ditto for cutie pie white singer, "Her Nibs," Miss Georgia Gibbs' cover of one of the best love songs I ever heard, "Tweedle Dee, Tweedle Dee… Give it up, Give it up, Give your love to me," originally sung by that great black vocalist LaVern Baker.

There was also local boy, the Greek Adonis, Jamie Coe, formerly known as George Colovas, an all-state point guard on Dearborn Fordson High's State Basketball Championship team of 1953. Jamie Coe was the front man for the "Gigolos" – "Jamie Coe and the Gigolos," the house band at Mickey Chiado's "Gay Haven" Night Club (when "gay" meant "happy") located on the north side of Warren just east of Greenfield. Bobby Darin (who performed at the Gay Haven before he hit the charts with "Splish Splash, I was Takin' a Bath," and his cover of Louie Armstrong's "Mack the Knife" from the *Three Penny Opera*) promoted Jamie Coe's career, and put Jamie on the national charts with "Green Back Dollar," "How Low is Low" and my favorite, "Drink to a Fool." Jamie died of a heart attack on January 27, 2007 at the age of 71, as he drove home after finishing his umpteenth performance at his own bar, "Jamie's." And, don't forget the girls' favorite "gigolo," Vic Olsen, the blond sex machine who lit it up vocally with "The 7th Son of a 7th Son," and his hook, "I Want to **rowh** with ya Baby" – perhaps a verb derived from "rowdy," but, whatever it's actual meaning, the girls seemed to understand the sensual message Gigolo Vic was putting out. And, what about my favorite, Mr. Chiado's beautiful daughter Teri who worked at her father's club, the Gay Haven.

Jaime Coe
1965

Mickey Chiado and Johnny Rivers

Vic Olsen
1965

Teri Chiado and Barbara Bouchie
"Styling in the 1960s"

Teri Chiado was there when Bobby Darin got the hook at the Gay Haven from Teri's father who ran Bobby Darin out of town, telling Bobby he would never amount to anything. Bobby died early at age 37 of a congenital heart condition, but his popularity and his career as a great vocalist was already well established. So, just think

Teri, had you been available, and if your father wasn't so protective, you could have been Bobby Darin's widow, still taking in those huge royalties. "Move over Sandra Dee, I'm here to pick up some overdue royalty checks."

Saxe's Ride Flew the Coop

Later, in the 60s when I hit drinking age, I was at the Gay Haven to see Chuck Berry, the Everly Brothers and Johnny Rivers, fresh off his live performances at "The Whiskey A-Go-Go" in Los Angeles. It was at one of those performances at the Gay Haven that the Dearborn Police impounded my St. Scholastica classmate Fred Saxe's "ride" for illegal parking, and what a surprise the Dearborn cops must have had when they went to their own police pound the next day, and discovered that

**Fred Lauck and Fred Saxe
Who Stole Our "Ride?"**

someone sawed the chain lock off the police impound gate, and drove off with Saxe's impounded ride! Did Saxe file a missing vehicle report the next day? No! Did Saxe go back to the Dearborn Police to complain that someone stole his "ride" out of the police pound? No! For further incriminating details contact Larry Brogan and Ned Bowler (son of

our first football coach Frank Bowler). That's the same Ned Bowler who, with Michael "Mickey" Farkas (son of NFL Hall of Famer Andy Farkas), elevated the Irish misdemeanor of "joy riding" to an art form, getting oil changes, tune-ups, and even liability insurance on other people's "rides" that Ned (shall we say) "borrowed." Anyway, no further investigation is warranted because the statute of limitations on Fred Saxe's caper ran out forty years ago, and my pal Fred Saxe died in 1999. But, whenever it came down to a game of wits between Saxe and the cops, my money was on Saxe.

There was also Jack Scott, Hazel Park Michigan's own Rockabilly legend, singing "What in the World's Come over You?," "Baby, Baby" and "Burning Bridges" on Dick Clark's "American Bandstand" – a midday 1950s television show that, in my world, marked the midway point between baseball double headers at Greenview Park (at Greenview and Curtis). Greenview Park was the Hood's summer home. I remember John DiBella and I watching 16-year-old blond bombshell Barbara Schotz bounce (and I mean bounce) through a forty-yard dash as she raced against some dark haired beauty at Greenview Park. The gorgeous Barbara later married local Greek boy entrepreneur, Peter Karmanos, who graduated from Henry Ford High School in the Hood, and later founded his most successful "Compuware" business and the Barbara Karmanos Cancer Center, named after the beautiful Barbara who died of cancer in her prime. Peter Karmanos knows, as we all do, that the success stories of our generation were bought and paid for by the sacrifices of the Greatest Generation who opened the doors to an abundance of opportunities for their children.

Endlessly New

Those endless summers in Greenview Park in the 1950s playing baseball or just hanging out left a ton of rich memories. Bobby Tambornini (may he rest) flawlessly scooped up every ground ball at shortstop until he cut his throat open on the cyclone fence while chasing a foul ball. I'll never forget watching 80-year-old Mr. Greishammer stop the flow of Bobby's blood with black electrical tape. Bobby survived that incident, and later set a state record for the most goals scored in a Michigan High School hockey game – thirteen goals.

Bobby Tambornini
Record Holder
from 1961

Doug Vannier
"Spiritual Leader" of
Greenview Park

That record still stands fifty plus years later. And, who could forget our main man Doug Vannier borrowing a page from Detroit Tiger announcer Van Patrick, "Going, going, gone!," as Doug hit imaginary home runs to the bullpen in Yankee Stadium. And, who could forget Frank Demers starting off as a spring phenom, hitting line drives to all fields until his eyes gave out in the hot weather as the Dog Days of summer dragged on. And how about "Black Boy" who would patrol the outfield for us after leaving Alabama and coming north to the industrial complex of Detroit during the summer. He never talked, but he was one of us during those warm, endless summers in the 1950s in the Hood. Did anybody know his real name or where his dusky complexion came from? And who could ever forget "Kid Gilbert" who worked on his 12 to 6 o'clock curveball in between hustling "chicks" and experimenting with intoxicants, or "Whitey" Erger, our white version of Jackie Wilson's "Mr. Excitement," or Jimmy Krausman who was so cool he dare not talk to or dance with a chick, and risk the possibility of damaging his "oh so cool" image.

During the mid-1950s in the Hood at St. Scholastica, there was real talent playing out. There were science fairs, story writing, spelling bees, and stage productions at the Cow Palace starring everyone except Frank Demers who had a lifelong ambition to be a stage hand, and hold hands with Mary Michaud. "Oh you love-sick kids," said the nun. Well Sister, it beats a shot to the head from Father Boniface, and at least Frank wasn't encroaching on my "squeezes." There was the *Frosty the Snow Man* song and dance production, *Tony "The-*

Balloon-Man" by John DiBella, *Yankee Doodle Dandy*, my lead role given to me by Sister Roslyn who obviously felt guilty for knocking my orthodontic braces off center once a week with her own bony "backhands." Move over George M. Cohan, and let the toothy kid with the buck teeth shine!

And, as young as we all were in the early and mid-1950s, nobody in the Hood was immune from work. Would you expect anything less than a strong work ethic from the children of the Greatest Generation? The Greatest Generation fought pitched battles against all odds just to survive, and the Greatest Generation made sure their children adopted that same rigorous mental attitude. As a 9-year-old in 1952, I pedaled my *Detroit Times* paper route, lying to the Station Master, telling him I was 12 – another Irish misdemeanor which my mother Jean, one of ten children and a child of survival, fully backed up – "Yeah, the kid's a young and puny-looking 12-year-old." I had sixty customers and made $12.00 a week – a ton of purchasing power in those days. When I collected on Saturdays, I would treat myself to a cheeseburger, fries and a chocolate malt while I put nickels into the juke box to hear "See the Pyramids Along the Nile" and "Shrimp Boats" by Jo Stafford, "They often call me Speedo but my real name is Mr. Earl" by the Cadillacs, "Tennessee Waltz" and "Mockin' Bird Hill" by Patti Page, and "Goodnight Irene" by the Weavers (and, God please never forget to bless the Weavers' Greatest Generation vocalist-banjo player and long-time social activist Pete Seeger – a tireless peace activist and labor supporter and a protégé of Woody Guthrie). There was also "Dance With Me Henry" by Miss Georgia Gibbs, "See You Later Alligator" and "Rock Around the Clock" by Bill Haley and His Comets, "Love is Strange" by Mickey and Sylvia, "Eh Cumpari" by Julius LaRosa, and "Mambo Italiano" and "Come Ona My Houseah" by Rosemary Clooney and on and on… with endless new hits hitting the radio waves every day.

23

It doesn't get any better! I had youthful exuberance, a thirst to discover life, a job, coins jingling in my pocket, paper money folded in my wallet, a cheeseburger, french fries, a Reese's Peanut Butter Cup or a Hostess Cupcake for my physical survival, music for my spiritual needs, and an expansive view of the Hood at Seven Mile and Evergreen Road at the end of my paper route as I ate, listened to the sounds of life, and peered out condensation-streaked windows into the short, cold days of winter, wondering what the next moment would bring.

Then, there was the beauty of change. The long, cold, dark days of winter and the deprivation of the Lenten Season, Good Friday, and Tre Ore Service at Lady Scholastica, all turned to Easter Sunday and Spring with the promise of resurrection, renewal, spring rains, flowers, First Communions and the crowning of the Blessed Mother in

**Marilyn Versaci
Crowning the
Blessed Mother**

May – "Oh Mary we crown thee Queen of the May… " and "Immaculate Mary our hearts are on fire… " with classes in front of mine graduating year after year until, finally, in 1957, it was time for my class to graduate. As eight years of grade school at St. Scholastica came to an end, I was at the eighth grade dance with my midget girlfriend, Barbara Schroeder, who pulled me down toward her for each "cheek to cheek" dance, bending my posture out of shape and ruining my pitching arm for a week. I never realized until the eighth grade that dancing was a full contact sport. But I'm not complaining. Getting a girl to go to the dance with me was no easy task, and Barbara was gorgeous and vivacious. Where are you now dear Barbara?

Eight grades of education was over. Our gang graduated from St. Scholastica surpassing the formal education of many of our parents and relatives of the Greatest Generation. Eight years of growth and experience concluded, and now new challenges awaited on the horizon of life. Some of my classmates would disappear, die and be buried without a trace. Some would disappear and resurface thirty, forty or even fifty years later. Fifty years later, you could walk right by a St. Scholastica classmate, and have no idea who they were, but, if you stopped and listened to them speak, you'd recognize the voice, and then you could look at the unrecognizable face of age and match the voice to the youthful face you once knew.

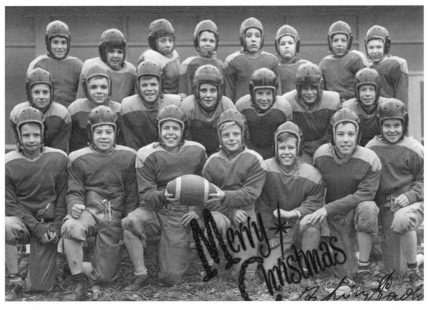

St. Scholastica Fifth and Sixth Grade Football Team 1955

CHAPTER 3

Vicissitudes Of High School

Eight long, arduous years of education at St. Scholastica were over. Eight years of playing cat and mouse with the nuns, and eight years of innocence and joy were over. But, grade school is not that much of an accomplishment. It merely develops the tools you need (reading, writing and computation of numbers) for a real education. You literally graduate from grade school to the starting point of your education. Looking back, it amazes me how long it takes to obtain an education, and how much longer it takes to develop an agile, analytical mind and fluid verbal ability. I'm not talking about the storehouse of knowledge that you commit to memory, and that you are tested on in a formal educational setting. I'm not talking about winning the spelling bee or even the ability to memorize the meaning of hundreds of vocabulary words. If that's all there was to education, a "savant" like Raymond from the movie *Rain Man* would graduate at the top of his class each year. What am I talking about? I am talking about the benchmark of an educated man or woman (self taught or otherwise).

I'm talking about the analytical agility and fluid verbal ability you see in the art of human conversation when it reaches its highest level – a benchmark that generally takes forty years of life to develop and another ten to twenty years to fully develop.

Learning to Think

Fluid, high level human communication is truly a masterpiece of art. You hear or read the words of others – their thoughts, their ideas, their concepts. Then, with the speed of light, you process what you heard or read by instantly check-listing against your pre-existing storehouse of knowledge to determine whether you just heard (or read) old familiar words, thoughts and concepts, or new words, thoughts and concepts, and, if new, whether they are truly new or analogously similar to your pre-existing storehouse of knowledge. After such an exhaustive, yet instantaneous check list evaluation of the words, thoughts and concepts of others, you then select a response in an instant – a response that is relevant to and most appropriate for the particular context or social setting you find yourself in, after which you then articulate your response, basically agreeing, disagreeing or expanding on the words, thoughts and concepts of others… **all done effortlessly in a millisecond.**

That kind of speed-of-light analytical agility and fluid verbal ability are not taught in most schools. Organizing and mastering new information is what's taught in a formal classroom setting, or what you might learn informally in life's classroom. Organizing and mastering new information may be great exercise for the brain, but it does not, in and of itself, give you the analytical agility and verbal ability that you see in the masterpiece of human communication at its highest and most fluid level. Organizing and mastering new information is, however, the first step in developing an analytically agile mind and fluid verbal ability because it gives you a readily retrievable storehouse of knowledge which must be immediately accessible in check list fashion as step number one in developing an analytically, agile mind and fluid verbal ability.

But, it's only when there is **"Challenge"** to the new information you're attempting to organize and master that you begin to develop analytical agility and verbal ability. The **"Challenge"** approach is often referred to as the "Socratic Method" – an approach which teaches new information by laying out and organizing the new information, memorizing the details of the new information, and then challenging the classroom student (or the student of life) to either defend the correctness and viability of the new information or attack its correctness and viability. That "no holds barred" mental and verbal challenge not only breathes life into learning and rivets attention, but, most importantly, it's that challenge that forces the classroom student (or the student of life) to **"think"** – not just memorize and repeat on a test. It's that **"challenge"** and the critical **"thinking"** under fire, which begins the slow, decades-long process of developing an agile, analytical mind and the verbal ability that eventually earns you an informal degree as a master and fluid communicator of language – thoughts, words and concepts.

Well, as I said, it was 1957, and eight years of formal education at St. Scholastica were over. It was fourteen years since the July 4, 1943 births of the Five Bangs: Valentina Frances Victory, Tom Terrific, Brigetta BeBop, Sammy Slow and Brenda Blah, and all of them, and all of us, were now headed to Benedictine Catholic Central High School in the fall of 1957. And, just as Dr. Goodfellow had predicted, all of them, and all of us, were slowly developing, each according to plan, and according to the unique gifts God had given to each of us.

Valentina Frances Victory

Valentina Frances Victory was tall and lean, and walked with the grace of a gazelle. She had the lines of classic beauty: almond shaped green eyes, high cheek bones (a tribute to her American Indian heritage) and a strong jaw line, topped by a crown of dark auburn hair that flew in the wind when she was running the 100 meter dash faster than anyone else in the City of Detroit. In addition to her athletic gifts, she was a singer, dancer, piano player and actress, and, even at the tender age of 14, she was also a prolific writer of drama-filled short stories. Valentina Frances Victory was kind of an artistic prodigy. She was the darling of summer stock theatre in Augusta, Michigan. During her summer vacation, she would sing and act, and emotionally move people toward swelling crescendos, pathos and precipitous emotional drop-offs. To boot, she became one of the top ten students in her high school class at Benedictine Catholic Central. She was a leader who belonged to no clique. She was her own clique. All her classmates counted with her and she befriended them – one and all. It came as no surprise that she was unanimously elected as president of her class each year at Benedictine Catholic Central.

Valentina's God-given talents presented numerous options for her future, provided she put in the effort and sacrifice to develop her talents, her mental agility and her verbal ability, and provided she worked hard to avoid the Catch 22 short term relief from human stress and anxiety that drugs and alcohol offer... before they wear off the next day leaving you deeper in the inexorable emotional dump of increased depression, anxiousness and paranoia. In order to fulfill the promise of her childhood ability and to reach her lofty goal of future success, Valentina Frances Victory, like the rest of us, would have to live with the stress of high expectation, cold turkey, and she would have to avoid the Catch 22 of short term relief that alcohol and drugs offer. Valentina had to keep her gorgeous, almond shaped green eyes steadfastly fixed on her long term goals.

Valentina Frances Victory intuitively knew that she could get high on life by smoking the competition in a 100 meter dash, "catch me if you can," or by bringing out an emotional connection in another human being with the pathos of her songs, her acting and her short stories. Yes, Valentina Frances had received God's gifts in abundance, but now she had to understand how much sacrifice was expected of her to develop her natural gifts to the highest level possible. Valentina Frances had to understand and accept that "to whom much is given, much is expected" – including a true humility that recognizes her gifts were not earned, but bestowed by a higher power, and including the realization that many gifted persons fail to reach their potential because, paradoxically, their gifts get in the way of developing their potential.

Because God's gifts make it easy to compete in life early on, sometimes those gifts stand in the way of developing a work ethic and discipline. When you are gifted, you don't have to work hard in the early years. It comes easy. But, eventually, it won't come easy anymore as gifted kids are finally matched up with other gifted kids across the city, the state, the country or even the world. And, when it doesn't come easy any more, and the competitors climb toward the top of life's pyramid, the gifted kids that pull ahead from the other gifted kids are the ones who developed a work ethic and discipline early on in life despite their gifts. Or, maybe (just maybe), a good work ethic is itself a gift – a gift of **"determination"** that opens the door for those without an abundance of natural gifts.

Whether a gift or not, those with less natural gifts have no choice but to develop a strong work ethic if they are going to compete with the gifted. Those with less natural gifts who refuse to bemoan their fate, and just take up the challenge of hard work many times, over time, overcome and overtake the gifted ones just on the basis of a determined work ethic that perseveres one slow step at a time over the course of years and decades – while those blessed with natural gifts become accustomed to succeeding without effort and without a work ethic until, perhaps, it's too late to acquire a work ethic when they eventually face stiffer competition later on in life.

So, Valentina Frances Victory looked good coming off the starting line of life, but life is not a 100 meter dash. Life is a marathon where a flash in the pan sprinter can catch fire quickly, but burn out just as quickly and fade to the back of the pack as the hardworking, determined tortoise rejects the allure of instant gratification, and takes up the cross of the long term sacrifice required for accomplishment and success. Anyway, 14-year-old, gifted Valentina Frances Victory, despite the sage advice of the adult kingdom, would probably have to learn life's lessons on her own as she began to project her own image on the screen of life and discover who she was, what her goals were and how important those goals were to her. Most importantly, she would have to decide whether she was willing to leave the safety of the sidelines of life, embrace vulnerability and jump high out over the dangerous chasm of life with no safety net to... hopefully, catch the brass ring.

The older generation gives advice and warnings so the younger generation won't misstep in the minefield of life, and make the same mistakes the older generation did. That advice, sage and relevant as it might be, seldom works – at least the first time around. Most times, the advice of the adult kingdom becomes intelligible to the younger generation only after they misstep and blow up. Then, after learning the hard way, the advice becomes "their truth" – the younger generation's truth. Sad to say, the most indelible lessons in life come not from advice, but from our own mistakes in failing to heed the older generation's advice. Invariably, therefore, mistakes are going to be made and advice ignored, but, just as invariably, what separates out the successful in life's race is simply the ability to learn from mistakes.

The advice from the older generation, though unheeded at first, nevertheless plays an important role in teaching the younger generation to learn from their mistakes. Being forewarned helps the younger generation to learn from life's inevitable mistakes because, after you misstep and blow up in the minefield of life, you don't have to ask what went wrong. You already know. You were forewarned and fore-advised, and now the past warning is no longer theoretical. Now, the past warning has a real world context which moves the past warning from the theoretical world of "Yeah! Yeah!" to the real world of failure. Failure is inevitable. It's part of the genetic code of all life – animal, vegetable and human. But, as Charles Darwin would say, nature selects out for survival (and success) those living organisms that learn from and adapt to their failures. As my own father would say: "It's 'trial and error' baby, but you gotta be paying attention." As I would say: "Winners fail without excuses… Losers because of them."

Tom Terrific

Tom Terrific also seemed to have an abundance of natural gifts. At 15 he was 6' 3" tall, a skinny 195 lbs., with a lean, muscular body, and he could run like the wind, stop on a dime, give you change and leave you in his wake. As a 15-year-old sophomore, he was a starter on the Benedictine Catholic Central varsity football team, playing in the same league with such football powerhouses as Grand Rapids Catholic Central, Saginaw Valley, Bay City Central, St. Mary's of Redford, U of D High School, Monroe Catholic Central, Muskegon Central

Catholic, Shrine of the Little Flower, Boys Town, St. Anthony, St. Ambrose, Notre Dame High School, Salesian, Cathedral, DeLaSalle, St. Thomas of Detroit, Austin Prep and Lansing Resurrection. There was an abundance of competition in the Catholic League, but Benedictine Catholic Central, affectionately known as "We are… CC!" was a team that everyone took seriously, year in and year out.

Despite the talent in the Catholic League in the mid 1950s and early 1960s, Tom Terrific was a man among boys. (With a little help from Glenn "Pretty Boy" Bennett, "Bucky" Hagen, Mickey Farkas, John "Hode-it" Lombardi, "Massive" Don Quinn, "Quick" Don Quick, Frankie "Big Man" Wendt, "Gorgeous George" Steintrager, Frank "Hitman" Demers, "Togo" Kozlowski, Billy "The Dancer" Downs, Paul "The Sheik" Daugherty, "Pistol Pete" Sullivan, "Mad Dog" Johnny Banich, Tony "Mr. T." Mooter, John "Pizza Man" DiBella, Stuart "The Stew" Mahler, "Two Gun" Johnny Rioux, Eddie "Haymaker" Hammacher and others), Tom Terrific could light it up at any moment. He was a threat to score every time he touched the ball. He could run by you for 100 yards, around you for 100 yards or through you. It didn't matter to him. In fact, his first choice was usually to run you over because… well… well, just because he could.

John "Hode-it" Lombardi   Frankie "Big Man" Wendt   Billy "Dancer" Downs   "Two Gun" Johnny Rioux

Pin the Tail on the Donkey

Tom Terrific's run-you-over philosophy taught him a valuable lesson one day in the Fall of 1958. It was late in the fourth quarter of Benedictine Catholic Central's mythical state Championship game against St. Mary's of Redford. The score was tied 14 to 14, but C.C. had the ball and was marching toward a late winning score. C.C.'s coach, "Wild Bill" Foley, called for a "Y-out Counter" – a fake hand-off to Barry Schonfeld to the right, with Tom Terrific stutter stepping in unison with Schonfeld to the right, and then instantly countering back against the grain to the left and taking the hand off, and slashing over the left side of C.C.'s offensive line. At least that was the play coach Foley sent in, and that was the play called in the C.C. huddle. But St. Mary's must have been sitting in C.C.'s huddle when the play was called because St. Mary's defense, led by future NFL greats Fred Arbanas and Norm Masters, overloaded on the left side of C.C.'s line shutting any running lane on that side.

C.C.'s quarterback, Paul O'Brien, seeing the overload, changed the play at the line of scrimmage with an audible, took the center from Wendt, and quick-pitched to his right to Tom Terrific. Tom Terrific turned the corner with great acceleration. He was off to the races, with only a scared jack rabbit, defensive back for St. Mary's between him and a last minute touchdown victory for C.C. But, rather than outrun the lone St. Mary's defensive back to win the game, as he easily could have done, Tom Terrific wanted to put an exclamation point to his winning touchdown by running over the lone minor obstacle to victory – the St. Mary's 150 lb. jack rabbit, defensive back. Tom Terrific diverted from the sideline and a sure touchdown, and ran toward the middle of the field putting the St. Mary's 150 lb. jack rabbit in his sights. The jack rabbit turned into a deer in the headlights and froze. Two feet away from the jack rabbit, Tom Terrific dropped his shoulder, let out a blood-curdling growl, and threw all 6′3″, 195 lbs. of his train wreck self right into the jack rabbit… but… but wait… what? – nothing there but air. The jack rabbit, his eyes as big as saucers and his hair standing on end inside his helmet, ducked out of the way of the impending collision, and hooked the football free as Tom Terrific sailed forward into thin air without resistance, and tumbled ignominiously down onto the ground and bounced along, his tough-guy, anticipated collision with the jack rabbit evaporating into thin air.

Now the football is bouncing helter-skelter (now this way, now that way) all over the field with time running out. In a flash, an embarrassed and now humbled Tom Terrific ("Oh, God! Please don't let this be happening to me") was up off the ground, and in hot pursuit of the bounding football. Tom Terrific ignominiously bent over at the waist, reaching to his right as the ball bounded left, and then to his left as the ball bounded right, and then forward and backward, and then left and right again in futile, hot pursuit of the elusive football… having gone from gazelle to goof in one horrifying moment. Tom Terrific, now hyper-ventilating, passed out and fell on the ground head first, frozen in time, looking like a bridge with only the top of his helmet and the tips of his toes touching the ground, semi-conscious in his precariously perched position. The ever alert Bert, the-Jack-Rabbit from St. Mary's scooped up the ball, and ran it back for a touchdown, sealing a last minute victory for St. Mary's in the 1958 mythical State Championship game. Game over. The game clock was at zero – no time left. St. Mary's won it all on that last, ill-conceived, fatal play by a "struttin-his-stuff" Tom Terrific.

The St. Mary's fans stormed the field in victory and tore down the goal posts, all the while carefully walking around Tom Terrific, still face first and head and toes only down on the field, precariously perched in his semi-comatose position, barely breathing and strung

"Hitman" Demers

"Pizza" DiBella

out in an altered sense of consciousness of self-inflicted failure. As the crestfallen Benedictine Catholic Central team headed to the team bus, they filed by their fallen hero Tom Terrific. "Hitman" Frank Demers commented: "Put a saddle on his ass and send him down to Mickey Gilley's joint in Texas and let the 'urban cowboys' use him for bull riding practice." Teammate John "Pizza" DiBella quickly corrected him... "Make that 'donkey riding' for that donkey SOB."

Finally Tom Terrific involuntarily exhaled, gave off a seizure-like tremble, and crumbled all the way down, flat out onto the ground, imploding for the second time. It would be two long years later before Benedictine Catholic Central would have another shot at the title – two long years in which Tom Terrific could hopefully learn from his failure by contemplating the meaning of "take what life gives you; it will be enough" and the meaning of "the exalted shall be deflated and the deflated shall be exalted."

Brigetta BeBop

Brigetta BeBop. Now there's an enigma. She had it all, but then again she had nothing. She had more natural ability than any of the Five Bangs or anybody in her grade school class at St. Scholastica or in her high school class at Benedictine Catholic Central. She probably had more natural intellectual, athletic and artistic ability than anyone who ever attended those schools, and, perhaps, more than any other child of the Greatest Generation who grew up in the Northwest Detroit Hood. But, like many others with God-given talent, she wasn't destined to succeed because she lacked maturity, discipline, and determination. She was satisfied with letting her God-given talents take her as far as they could on their own, without any effort on her part to develop those talents or get the most out of them. What came without effort allowed her to shine, but, when effort was needed to extend her natural ability, she fell down. Was it just laziness? Was it that she just didn't care? Was it that she simply wasn't motivated? Was it fear of failure? Was it because there were no challenges early on in grade school with course work, athletics, singing and dancing coming so easy for her?

For whatever reason, Brigetta never learned that ultimate lesson of life that "struggle" is the inseparable ingredient of all life. Life is struggle. Struggle is life. Look at an organism that is struggling, and you know it's alive. Look at an organism that's not struggling, and you know it's dead. And, it is also just as certain that struggle is indispensable for all long term accomplishment. Brigetta BeBop wasn't aware of that truism, or, if she was, it never mattered to her. She just didn't understand that there comes a point in life when all the gifted people in their own Hoods move on to that larger stage of life, and leave the Hood to meet and compete on a citywide, statewide, nationwide or worldwide level. Brigetta BeBop never embraced the truism that those who combine God-given talent with a disciplined work ethic are the ones who are able to compete in that extended geographical area that eventually takes everyone out of their own Hood and out of their own comfort zone. In the last analysis, competition on life's large stage is reserved for those long-struggling souls who perfect whatever gifts their birthright gave them with large doses of discipline and commitment, and with, perhaps, the biggest gift of all – "**determination**."

Oh, "determination… !" Where does it come from? Is determination just another one of God's gifts? Does it come from the struggle to survive for those who are challenged to survive in the early years of their lives? Is it a learned behavior coming out of that feeling of self worth you get when the adult world praises you for accomplishment in the early years of life? Whether inherited biologically, whether an evolutionary predisposition of personality or whether acquired in an encouraging or challenging environment, "determination" is probably the most important ingredient to keep you on your feet in the ten round "Main Event" or in the twenty-six mile "Marathon of Life." No doubt, relentless determination over the years and decades of life separates the doers from the talkers. In fact, determination may trump all the other gifts – a mystery captured in *The Tortoise and The Hare* fable and in President Calvin Coolidge's words:

> "Nothing in the world can take the place of persistence.
> Talent will not; nothing is more common than
>   unsuccessful men with talent.
> Genius will not; unrewarded genius is almost a proverb.
> Education will not; the world is full of educated derelicts.
> Persistence and determination alone are omnipotent."

Whatever it was, poor Brigetta BeBop, with all her God-given ability, never had the determination to do anything with her gifts. She lived each day of high school content with whatever her natural talent brought her, never reaching out of her comfort zone to dare to rise above her natural ability. She was satisfied to be the Big Fish in a small pond, starring in the high school basketball games, soccer and baseball games, and starring in high school leading roles as a singer and dancer. She was living life exactly as she envisioned it for herself, and, in the end, she was just being true to herself. But, poor Brigetta BeBop still lived with the dream of becoming a professional singer, naively disconnected from the reality that she would never make it because her lack of determination and focus doomed her to a life of mediocrity well below where her natural talents could have taken her. Yeah… "could have."

Could it be that Brigetta's ample natural gifts simply made things so easy for her early in life that she didn't have to develop determination and discipline? Did her early natural gifts undo her and divert her from developing determination? Did her God given ability consign her natural gifts to the discount bargain bin of mediocrity? Or was her lack of determination and discipline related to the deeper roots of unfathomable evolutionary phenomena or perhaps unintelligible psychological factors? Who knows? But paraphrasing Marlon Brando from the movie *On the Waterfront* – "She could have been somebody." Yeah, "**Could** have been."

Sammy Slow and Brenda Blah

And what about Sammy Slow and Brenda Blah? What was going on with them? What was going on was that there was a marked difference in personality and gifts between those two and the Dynamic Trio of Valentina Frances Victory, Tom Terrific and Brigetta BeBop. Sammy Slow and Brenda Blah didn't move their classmates. They didn't light up a room when they walked in. They were just part of the barely visible background of white noise at Benedictine Catholic Central. Neither, it seemed, had any gifts, natural or otherwise. They couldn't even project their voices in a classroom, let alone burst out in song. They couldn't gracefully flow through the school hallways, let alone spin through flowing dance moves or accelerate past an opponent in an athletic event. In a crowd, they verbally kept to themselves – happy not to be called upon or challenged. In grade school at St. Scholastica, they were just part of a loving group of their classmates – happy and content to be part of the class and part of the

Hood. But, in high school, there was a growing separation between Sammy Slow, Brenda Blah and the Dynamic Trio of Valentina Frances Victory, Tom Terrific and Brigetta BeBop.

Tom Terrific lived next door to Sammy Slow, and, during grade school, they walked to St. Scholastica together every day with Tom sensing a true appreciation from his pal Sammy, and Sammy sensing a true acceptance from his gifted buddy Tom Terrific. Sammy Slow had no bigger fan, no bigger promoter and no better protector than Tom Terrific. No bully in the neighborhood was going to touch Sammy Slow because the price of messing with Sammy had to be paid to his debt collector, Tom Terrific – a price you would rather not pay... if you had a choice.

Likewise Brenda Blah and Brigetta BeBop were connected at the hip in grade school at St. Scholastica. Brenda was Brigetta's biggest fan. Brenda Blah was happy to live vicariously through her pal Brigetta BeBop. Brenda Blah watched and admired Brigetta and cheered her on, content to live in the very large shadow that Brigetta cast as Brigetta played hoops at the side of the garage during those long, sweet, seemingly endless days of the summers of their youth, or as Brigetta captained the St. Scholastica's 1957 CYO Basketball Championship Team, scoring nineteen points in the Girl's Championship victory over Gesu, or as Brigetta starred in leading roles in St. Scholastica's plays, *Moon for the Misbegotten* and *Showboat* in blackface, or as Brigetta effortlessly won singing and dancing competitions, or as they both walked down Curtis Boulevard in the Hood when Brigetta BeBop would spontaneously burst into the "forbidden fruit" of LaVern Baker's risqué song "Tweedly Dee" ("Give it up, give it up, give your love to me") with each of them hysterically giggling themselves silly, or when Brigetta BeBop would confide in Brenda about her secret crushes on dream boats Elvis, Paul Anka, Fabian, Troy Donahue,

Hazel Park's Jack Scott, or even local pretty boys Glenn Frundel, Glenn Bennett and Charley Uzelac, the swashbuckling Serbian.

But the innocence and lightheartedness of childhood camaraderie changed overnight. When the Five Bangs got to Benedictine Catholic Central High School in the fall of 1957, the pressure to be "cool" took its toll, and put distance between the gifted ones, Tom Terrific, Brigetta BeBop and the lesser lights of Sammy Slow and Brenda Blah. Sammy Slow and Brenda Blah became excess baggage that slowed Tom Terrific and Brigetta BeBop down, as their gifts accelerated them into the fast lane of growing social lives and burgeoning recognition and acclaim at the local high school level. Valentina Frances Victory, on the other hand, drew on a maturity beyond her years, and handled her success and her growing resume of accomplishments in stride, deftly maintaining her sense of self and her humility, and never comparing herself to others. Valentina Frances Victory realized at a very young age that all of her classmates were unique children of God, and that high school was only mile three in the twenty-six mile marathon of life.

The last social event that Brenda Blah attended with Brigetta BeBop was the 1958 Homecoming Dance at Benedictine Catholic Central's dance emporium, affectionately known in the Hood as the "Cow Palace" (located on the southwest corner of Outer Drive and Southfield). Brigetta danced every dance – twenty-seven straight dances, eclipsing her classmate Kathy Hankins record of twenty-five straight dances. The last dance was "Mr. Blue" by the Fleetwoods, as Brenda Blah sat in the bleachers and looked on, blue to the core with an empty dance card, sitting next to a forlorn and all-alone Sammy Slow. That night both Sammy Slow and Brenda Blah made a silent vow that they would never put themselves through that image-shattering experience again. And, true to their vow, that was the last high school dance for either of them – no prom and no social life, with the void filled with gainful employment and academic pursuits. At least Sammy and Brenda had wonderful parental support for their academic pursuits. It wasn't the life they wanted. It wasn't the life they would choose. It wasn't a life of praise and adulation with a sense of being somebody, but it was their fate by forfeit, and, although they didn't know it at the time, their life of quiet desperation would forge a strength that would later allow them to overcome all obstacles, and find the key to their own future greatness.

Both Sammy Slow and Brenda Blah led a no frills life. Thank heaven for Catholic School uniforms. If it weren't for the forest green shirts with gray pants and a black tie for the boys, and navy pleated skirts with white blouses, buster brown collars and navy beanies for the girls, both Sammy and Brenda would have been conspicuously underdressed in high school as second class citizens, wearing clothes from Federals Department Store, Robert Hall and Epps Navy Surplus while some of their classmates would have been dressed in fashion-plate style with classy outfits from the latest-style stores at the new Northland Mega Shopping Mall.

With the benefit of 20-20 hindsight, it is now apparent that the nuns and priests had it right-on with the uniform requirement. The kids from the well-to-do families in Rosedale Park, who lived in two-story colonials just south of Six Mile (McNichols), and the middle class kids who lived in two bedroom, brick bungalows just north of Six Mile and the poorer kids who lived in the wooden shacks on the east side of Southfield Road, all dressed and looked alike in those uniforms without any social class distinction as we all thought of ourselves (for the most part) as just "Kids from the Hood."

Brenda Blah, the oldest of the family, lived her life as a second mother to five brothers and four sisters. Her (best-time-of-your-life) high school years were spent caring for brothers and sisters, and studying English, Writing, History, Latin, Math, Chemistry and

Physics. Sammy Slow, also coming from a working class family, spent his time studying as well as working any job he could get his hands on to help his family: sweeping up the floor of Dempsey's Barber Shop or Tanino's Shoemaker Shop, *Detroit Times* paper route, night *Free Press* route in the Rosedale Park area (where the well-to-do of the Hood like L. Brook Patterson, Wesley Ellis, The Teagons, the Stellas, the Whites, the Madigans and the Cregars lived in colonials with garages and with new cars), or hawking *Free Press* newspapers on Saturday night while standing in the street on the southeast corner of Grand River and Outer Drive in front of Cregar's Restaurant.

Other more financially fortunate classmates enjoyed their high school youth, driving right by Sammy's Saturday night *Free Press*, street corner job in 1955 Fords and Chevys, sporting a throaty rumble with glass pack exhaust systems, heading to Richards Drive-In on Six Mile and Grand River, or to Geiger's Drive-In further down Grand River near Seven Mile or to the Telway Drive-In at Grand River and Telegraph – windows open wide while radios blared out the "Book of Love" by the Monotones, "That'll Be the Day" by Buddy Holly, "Come Dance With Me" by Eddie Quinteros, "Happy Organ" by Dave "Baby" Cortez and "Bongo Rock" by Preston Epps – all presented by Detroit DJs, "Jack the Bell Boy," Mickey Shore (who signed off with Buddy Morrow's "Night Train"), and Lee Allen "On the Horn" (who signed off with Frank Sinatra's "I Can't Get Started"). But that music, that emotion, that spirit, that youth and those best-days-of-your-life belonged to somebody else's world, not Sammy's world. Sammy just watched and listened as a spectator on the sidelines of life, focusing his energy on any job he could find to help defray the financial needs of his family or studiously focusing on homework assignments when he wasn't working.

Senior Year

The good old days of youth were speeding by faster than Buddy Morrow's "Night Train" and, in September of 1960, the Five Bangs entered their senior year at Benedictine Catholic Central, their twelfth straight year of parochial school education together. But, subliminally pulsating and ebbing and flowing throughout the St. Scholastica-Benedictine Catholic Central Hood were the almost-forgotten words of Dr. Goodfellow, spoken seventeen years before, on the July 4, 1943 births of the Five Bangs:

> "Each child is blessed with different gifts. So, sit back, and watch patiently for years and decades as each child's own unique gifts magically unfold over life's marathon."

And, what a senior year it was at Benedictine Catholic Central High School for the Class of 1961. Tom Terrific, still haunted by the 1958 Championship loss to St. Mary's of Redford on the last disastrous play of the game, learned the lesson to "take what life gives you; it will be enough." He returned for his senior year bigger, stronger and faster, ready to run through a wall… or, on second thought, ready to sidestep the wall so he didn't lose sight of the goal line. Benedictine Catholic Central, under head coach Wild Billy "The Irishman" Foley and assistant coaches, Mike Toth, Chuck "One Punch" McHenry, "Screamer" John Cullen and "Bullet Bob" Riley were highly rated pre-season favorites to win it all. If the luck of the Irish had anything to do with it, their Irish coaching staff couldn't hurt.

Some of the players from the 1958 runner-up team had graduated, but there were new large bodies to take their place. The awesome nucleus at Benedictine Catholic Central included returning lettermen designated "Hit Man" Frank Demers, Frank Wendt at 190 lbs., the

Danny "Togo"
Kozlowski
1960

Paul "Sheik"
Daugherty
1960

David Vitali
St. Ambrose

Frank Orlando
St. Thomas

biggest player, John "Don't Shoot Me" DiBella, aka the "Pizza Man," Danny "Togo" Kozlowski, Mickey "Strong Man" Farkas, Brian "Tall Man" Motter, Paul "The Sheik" Daugherty, Johnny "Two Gun" Rioux, Dennis "Zipper" Fedorinchik, George "Smash" Smrtka, Don "Quick Man" Quick, "Rockin' Ronnie" and big brother Vince Rotole, George "Crazy Legs" Popham (the only running back who could run two minutes off the clock going sideways and backwards and eventually get a two yard gain), Mike "Cut-it-Back-Against-the-Grain" Nally, Danny "The Wyoming Kid" Prevo, Pete "The Plumber" Lind, "Dancin'" Billy Downs, "Two Gun" Johnny Rioux, "Steady Eddie" Hammacher, "Gorgeous George" Steintrager, Ronnie "The Head" Ross and Glenn "Heart Throb" Bennett, with Johnny "Mad Dog" Banich and "Pistol Pete" Sullivan lost for the season, but keeping in shape with workouts at the Detroit House of Correction while hanging out with Cathedral Central's "Bad Boy," Bob "The Knife" Hines – a slashing, running back and a slicing street fighter who was a third cousin, twice removed to "Mack the Knife."

In the fall of 1960, the Benedictine Catholic Central team took no prisoners. They lived up to expectations, rolling over all comers: Jack Harrington and Tim Lafferty's St. Agatha Aggies; Bob Burghart's Notre Dame's Fighting Irish; Father Flannigan's Boys Town Cowboys from Nebraska; David Vitali, Mike Currie, Tom Beer and Joey D'Angelo's St. Ambrose; Joe Henze and Rick Johnson's St. Catherine; Paul Ewing, Paul Caligaro, and Phil Stackpoole's U of

D High; John Everly, Mike Randall, Chuck Lowther, and John and Herb Seymour's Shrine High School; Tom Smith, Steve Mass and Bob Plumpe's Austin Friars; Frank Orlando and the Bankey brothers of

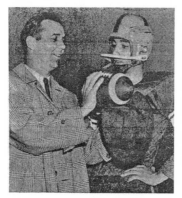

**Supportive Father
Frederick Valentine Lauck
1958**

St. Thomas; and the toughest game of all, a close 7 to 6 victory over "The Judge" Bob Ziolkowski's DeLaSalle Pilots at DeLaSalle's home stadium, where the planes took off and landed next door at the Detroit City Airport while the game was played below the soaring wings of flight (and where my own father, Frederick Valentine Lauck, paced up and down in his signature fedora in front of a dark stadium as the Catholic Central team bus pulled up to drop off our C.C. team – his way early presence, long before game time, signaling the most visible message of love and support I ever received in my life).

Catholic Central 1960
Back row: Grzywacz,Kozlowski,O'Brien and Downs
Front row: Brink,Lombardi,Lauck,Wendt,Hagen,Daugherty and Mahler

C.C. beats Shrine for Catholic League Championship.
November 5, 1960

CHAPTER 4

The Big Game

The showdown for the mythical 1960 State Championship (before the state playoff format) was scheduled for Friday November 18, 1960 at Tiger Stadium – home to the Detroit Tigers and Detroit Lions. And, what a night it was for football – a clear, crisp, cool night with 39,000 plus fans in attendance to watch a high school football showdown with Tom Terrific's Benedictine Catholic Central Shamrocks squaring off against Lansing Resurrection High School with their star running back Rick "The Phoeni-

Tiger Stadium
Goodfellow Game... November 18, 1960

cian" Rashid. Rashid was Lansing Resurrection's answer to Benedictine Catholic Central's Tom Terrific – another strong, fast and fearless warrior shouting his ever present message: "Let's get it on!"

Opening Salvos

Game time 8:00 p.m. Game time temperature 48 degrees. Game time excitement… off the charts. Benedictine Catholic Central won the coin toss and elected to receive. Valentina Frances Victory sang the National Anthem, and, in honor of our friends across the river, "O Canada!" Thirty-nine thousand plus fans continued to stand as the foot hit the ball and the game was on. And, what an unbelievable beginning it was as Benedictine Catholic Central's Tom Terrific grabbed the opening kickoff out of the night sky, and brought the house down… running the football back ninety-five yards, getting knocked out of bounds just five yards short of the goal line by a jarring tackle, courtesy of Lansing Resurrection's Tom LaTour, who saved the day for Lansing Resurrection… but only for a moment. One play later, Tom Terrific picked up a picture-perfect trap block from his right guard, Frank Demers, and exploded into the end zone for first blood. Benedictine Catholic Central fans went crazy. But, lost in the frenzy… Tom Terrific limped off the field, noticeably favoring his right knee while the marching band played a rousing touchdown, victory version of "Hold that Tiger." Sammy Slow, huddled in the end zone seats alone, celebrated quietly by himself and smiled broadly as he saw his old buddy, Tom Terrific, light it up just seconds into the game. But Sammy's smile turned to concern as he noticed Tom Terrific's painful limp to the sidelines.

The Benedictine Catholic Central fans knew the game was going to be a route for their team… but… but… wait! C.C.'s fans had barely finished their opening salvo, touchdown celebration when they were quickly silenced. Unbelievably, on the very next kick off, Lansing Resurrection's Rick Rashid matched Tom Terrific's kickoff return stride for stride with his own ninety-five yard return for a "take that!," counter punch reply. On that return, Lansing Resurrection's kickoff team was able to set up a wall on C.C.'s sideline, and the Resurrection receiving team was picking off and leveling Benedictine Catholic Central players with bone jarring cross body blocks as the Rashid kid put on a clinic on broken field running, finally hitting the two yard line with "Two Gun" Rioux on his back, but Rashid surged forward into the end zone for the touchdown. The stadium was going wild, each team scoring a knockdown in the first round. A good old fashioned shootout was unfolding with the score tied 7 to 7 with less than a minute played in the first quarter.

Tom Terrific or Rick Rashid? One in the same… interchangeable parts

The shootout was not to be, however. Both teams settled down, and the stellar defensive units took over and controlled the game. As Coach Foley always said… "I'll take my eleven best athletes and put 'em on defense, and build my team from there." The game resembled a tug of war with bone jarring collision after bone jarring collision as neither team penetrated inside the other team's thirty yard line. But… disadvantage C.C! Sammy Slow was quick to note that his old buddy Tom Terrific was hobbled. Tom Terrific's right knee was obviously bothering him. He just didn't have his old explosiveness and ability to accelerate and change directions on a dime. Tom Terrific was still in the game, but his "shake and bake" trademark moves and his straight ahead explosiveness were noticeably missing. For the rest of the first half and into the third and fourth quarter neither team's offense could put together any sustained drive, and the 7 to 7 tie remained right into the last minute of the game.

Finally, with just forty seconds left on the game clock, Lansing Resurrection had the ball on their own twenty yard line, with a third down and ten to go. Hoping to free Rashid up for some broken field running and a shot at a touchdown, Resurrection's quarterback, Tom

LaTour, threw a last minute desperation screen pass to Rashid on the left sideline. Benedictine Catholic Central's linebackers "Hit Man" Demers and "Pizza" DiBella smelled out the screen pass, and took on and took out the right side of Lansing Resurrection's offensive line on the very sideline where the screen pass was set up. Resurrection's Rashid, sprinting to the sideline, stumbled over the falling bodies of his own linemen while instinctively reaching for LaTour's screen pass. Rashid got one hand on the ball, and balanced it on the tip of his right hand. Suddenly, Tom Terrific came out of nowhere, and,

with his trademark lightening reflexes, he snatched the ball out of Rashid's extended hand and made a twenty-yard "midnight express," b-line to the end zone and the C.C. fans went crazy. But C.C. missed the extra point. Benedictine Catholic Central 13 – Lansing Resurrection 7 with just fifteen seconds left on the gameclock. Benedictine Catholic Central stole the lead with just fifteen seconds left. Tom Terrific lit it up again, redeeming himself from his bonehead debacle of two years ago against St. Mary's of Redford. Sammy Slow, alone and bundled up in the Benedictine Catholic Central end zone, smiled silently to himself.

You Won't Believe It!!!

With fifteen seconds left on the game clock, Benedictine Catholic Central kicker Glenn Bennett thought that, with the slight wind assist he had that night, he could kick the ensuing kickoff right over Lansing Resurrection's Rick "The Phoenician" Rashid's head and through the end zone to insure there would be no run back by the ever dangerous

Rashid. After all, what player in his right mind, with fifteen seconds on the game clock, would put the game's outcome in the hands of a Phoenician genetically linked to Hannibal... the superman from Carthage who, during the Punic Wars, crossed the Alps on an elephant to surprise and destroy the Roman legions. When the game is on the line, you don't kick the ball to Rashid, Hannibal or any other Phoenician. But Glenn "Pretty Boy" Bennett, his ever over-confident self, boomed the kickoff high into the night sky above the Tiger Stadium playing field and straight toward Lansing Resurrection's end zone.

The football sailed effortlessly high above the fans and was seen coming out of the night sky magically floating at first, and then flying toward and then through the end zone – all according to plan. But wait! What was that crazy Phoenician Rashid doing? Running away from the field of play with his back to the on-rushing Benedictine Catholic Central kickoff team, Rashid cleanly fielded the football over his left shoulder, running full speed away from the field of play, almost sprinting out of his own end zone. Just as Rashid caught the ball on a dead run away from the field of play, he slammed on the brakes a foot short of his own out-of-bounds end zone line. Then, 110 yards away from Benedictine Catholic Central's goal line, Rashid turned back around into the face and jaws of C.C.'s on-rushing kickoff team which, by now, was flying downfield, closing in on him at 100 miles per hour.

"No touchback with a first down on the twenty yard line," Rashid thought to himself. "No time for that now!" Rashid instinctively knew he had only one chance, and that was to make a run for it. Rashid started to head up field with the fate of the game in his hands. After a ten yard sprint, Rashid reached his own goal line, still 100 yards away from pay dirt. Suddenly Rashid's emotional and physical state was strangely altered, almost frozen in a surreal moment. With the Benedictine Catholic Central kickoff team bearing down on him like a scene out of a latter day "Attila the Hun," Rashid magically, almost supernaturally, reined in his emotions, refocused his view of the playing field, and, with telescopic tunnel vision, he saw the bright lights of stardom beckoning him to the Benedictine Catholic Central goal line 100 yards away. At the same time, Rashid became acutely aware of his own incessant heart beat, crescendoing rhythmically in slow motion. Swish-boom. Swish-boom. Swish-boom. Swish-boom. In his altered state of consciousness, Rashid felt himself running in slow motion. As he scanned the entire 100 yard field that lay before him and his destiny, he could see, but not hear, the loud echoing sound of each inhaled and exhaled vaporized breath on the separate, distorted faces and lips of 39,000 fans – all silently screaming in slow motion directly under the game clock that was frozen in time with fifteen seconds on it. "But what will it be?" Rashid thought to himself – fifteen seconds of heroic adrenaline rush and a rendezvous with immortality, or fifteen seconds of failure and ignominious defeat?

"So this is what it all comes down to," Rashid thought to himself. All the years of the pursuit of excellence. All the sacrifices. All the denials of social pleasures. All the endless practices. All the summer workouts. All the winter and spring workouts. All the years of determination. All the injuries, pain and past disappointments. And, now, it all comes down to this fifteen second period of life. In that freeze-frame reality, Rashid knew that this moment, this very strange moment of twisted reality, was the very the moment he was born to live out. In that surreal moment, Rashid knew that this night, at "Tiger Stadium," at the corner of Michigan Avenue and Trumbull, on a cool November evening in the fall of 1960… he had a rendezvous with destiny.

As Rashid crossed his own goal line 100 yards away from fame and glory, the pent-up energy from the distorted, slow motion faces and lips of 39,000 screaming fans coalesced into a single sonic boom that crescendoed from those slow motion, featureless faces directly back into the rhythm of Rashid's own heartbeat and the explosion shook the stadium. In that explosive instant, the Championship Game and

Let it Rip

life itself sped back to real time. One hundred difficult, obstacle-course yards and a determined Benedictine Catholic Central kickoff team lay between the speedy Phoenician and heroic immortality. For a single moment, Rashid indulged himself with a faint smile thinking: "Let's get it on."

Rashid quickly accelerated to his own ten yard line, picked up a crushing, knock-down block on the right sideline, accelerated to the twenty, to the thirty and then saw an opening on the far sideline. Without conscious thought, Rashid instinctively cut back across the grain and headed toward the far sideline, accelerating past the over-pursuing Benedictine Catholic Central kickoff team. Rashid now saw daylight with just fifty yards to go. Tom Terrific took up the chase. Making allowances for his hobbled knee, Tom Terrific picked the exact angle of pursuit that would pick Rashid off right before Rashid hit the Benedictine Catholic Central end zone. And Sammy Slow, still huddled alone in the Benedictine Catholic Central end zone, and fighting the temptation to cover his eyes, instinctively held his breath and willed a favorable ending: "Go Tom! Go! Go! Cut him off! Cut him off! You gotta cut Rashid off!"

Rashid was at full fly, gobbling up a full yard per stride, but Tom Terrific was still in hot pursuit on his calculated angle of collision just short of the Benedictine Catholic Central goal line. Now time seemed to shift into slow motion for Tom Terrific. With each stride, Tom Terrific heard his own heartbeat exploding in his eardrums and his breathing echoing loudly in his head. His right knee was giving out on him, and he began to hyperventilate as Rashid hit full stride, crossing mid-field with fifty more yards to go. Rashid to the forty, the thirty-five, the thirty, the twenty-five, with Tom Terrific still in pursuit on his chosen angle toward the sideline, trying to cut Rashid off at the pass before he scored the winning touchdown. Tom Terrific was

Rick Rashid… heading toward the goal line

Benedictine Catholic Central's last chance to stop Rashid and save the day for C.C. But, as Tom Terrific's knee began to give out, he heard a familiar echo from the all-too-familiar refrain from his last championship debacle of two years ago: "Oh God, please don't let this be happening to me!"

Rashid to the twenty, the fifteen, the ten, and then with every ounce of strength and energy he had left, Tom Terrific's brain instantly sped back to real time as he exploded into Rashid's churning, cement-mixer legs knocking Rashid out of bounds just three yards short of the Benedictine Catholic Central end zone. Tom Terrific jumped up and thrust his fist in the night air in triumph, "I did it! I did it!" But… but… wait. As Tom Terrific was visually searching the field for his celebrating teammates, he finally realized… it wasn't over. At the last moment, as Rashid was flying out of bounds from Tom Terrific's bone-jarring tackle, Rashid lateraled the ball to his own teammate, Tom LaTour, who was now in the middle of the field trying to get the last three yards for the touchdown. When Tom Terrific saw LaTour about to score, he was overwhelmed with emotion and a sense of defeat, and, looking into the face of a gloating Rick Rashid, Tom Terrific reflexively struck out at him and punched Rashid in the face mask, knocking Rashid off his feet. What happened next is one for the ages… although very few witnesses are still alive who could give a first hand account of that final, climactic moment.

Rashid jumped up from the ground, and instantly retaliated against Tom Terrific. **POW!** A counter punch by Rashid found Tom Terrific's helmet. Rashid followed with an overhand, pummeling forearm that knocked Tom Terrific right off his feet and on to his back, after which Resurrection's Tom LaTour stepped over the goal line scoring the winning touchdown, winning the State Championship for Lansing Resurrection.

But wait! Hold on! The referee threw a flag on Lansing Resurrection. The referee did not see Tom Terrific's smash to Rashid's facemask, but the ref couldn't miss Rashid's retaliatory overhand blow that knocked Tom Terrific off his feet. Therefore, instead of off-setting penalties against both teams that would have allowed LaTour's touchdown to stand, and that would have won the State Championship for Lansing Resurrection with no time left on the clock, Resurrection's touchdown was nullified by Rashid's unsportsman-like conduct penalty, and, with no time left on the game clock, Benedictine Catholic Central snatched victory from the jaws of defeat, winning the mythical State High School Football Championship for the year 1960. With the fog of Rashid's blow starting to clear, Tom Terrific finally realized that Benedictine Catholic Central had won it all on his game-saving, heroic tackle, and Tom Terrific hearkened back in time to the lesson he learned two years before in the 1958 State Championship debacle against Redford St. Mary's: "Take what life gives you; it will be enough."

—◦◦◦—

Sammy Slow, sitting in the spectator section of the Field of Dreams, smiled and left the game alone to work his late night dishwashing job at Mt. Carmel Hospital while his classmates left Tiger Stadium in jubilation to attend the victory party at the Cow Palace at Outer Drive and Southfield. On the way out of the stadium, Sammy saw Brigetta BeBop and Valentina Frances Victory running down the steps toward the victory celebration on the field. Brigetta BeBop almost knocked Sammy down as she blew past him without acknowledging him, but the ever sensitive and compassionate Valentina Frances Victory stopped, hugged Sammy and had a victory moment with him. It helped alleviate some of Sammy's all-aloneness. In fact, it made his evening: a victory for Benedictine Catholic Central, with Sammy's old buddy, Tom Terrific, the unorthodox hero, and… someone who cared enough about him to spend a moment validating his existence.

It wasn't a lot, but he could live on that acknowledgment for a couple of days.

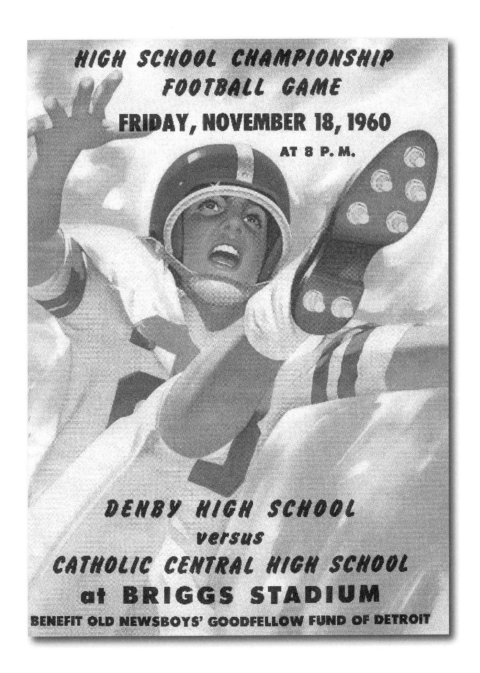

HERE IS THE DENBY HIGH LINE-UP which coach Ed Rutherford will open with Friday night. The unbeaten Tars' line will consist of (left to right): Frank Locricchio, George Haislip, Dave Garden, Jesse Shick, Al Letrock, Rich Easton and Ray Anderson. In the backfield will be Dave Cooper, Paul Danforth, Bob Schram and Phil Pitters.

Photo Courtesy of The Detroit Free Press

CATHOLIC CENTRAL'S PROBABLE STARTING LINE-UP FOR THE GOODFELLOW'S GAME (left to right): Line—Tom Brink (left end), John Lombardi (left tackle), Fred Lauck (left guard), Frank Wendt (center), Bill Hagen (right guard), Paul Daugherty (right tackle), Stu Mahler (right end). In the backfield will be Jerome Grzywacz (left half), Paul O'Brien (quaterback), Dan Kozlowski (full back), and Bill Downs (right half).

Photo Courtesy The Detroit News

CHAPTER 5

The Game of Life

Afterglow Drudgery

Sammy Slow arrived at his dishwashing job at Mt. Carmel Hospital at 11:15 in the evening… fifteen minutes late. He didn't need to be berated by his boss for being late, but he was. He didn't want to be in the noisy kitchen, hosing down dishes and flatware, but he was. He didn't need to have his mind continually playing out the Benedictine Catholic Central victory party going on without him, but he couldn't shut it off. Water running from the faucet became the party-goers running conversation of victory. Food washing clean off the plates became the clean sweep of victory in Benedictine Catholic Central's 12-0 season. Swirling water and soap bubbles became the rhythm and popping beat of the dancers at the victory party in a world that wasn't Sammy's.

As the night wore on, Sammy began to understand and accept that the victory party wasn't for him anyway. It wasn't for guys like Sammy Slow. It was for guys like the football players who accomplished something with their lives. The victory party was for athletic guys, cool guys, guys who were somebody, dudes – not duds like him. That night his heart, at the tender age of 17, longed for the good old days. Good old days when he and Tom Terrific were inseparable buddies, good old days when ignorance was bliss, and he didn't realize that he lived vicariously on the fringes of life – a life of energy created only by the gifted of God's children. Sammy longed for the good old days of grade school when the poignant pain of separation from his classmates was not felt. Good old days when looking in the mirror only presented Sammy with a simple reflection of himself, not the complex outcast he now saw himself to be. After four tiring hours of endless monotony at the hospital's huge kitchen sink, Sammy left the basement kitchen and tiredly shuffled up the "Employees Only" stairway to the first floor for his fifteen minute break. The "Employees Only" door opened out into the fresh air of a 3:00 a.m., early-fall morning in the Northwest Detroit Hood, and Sammy found a bench to sit on just outside the emergency room, not knowing that he was about to witness an event that would let him catch a glimpse of his future destiny.

Game On… Life vs. Death

As Sammy lingered on his bench, lost in the reverie of exhaustion, he suddenly noticed a 1957 Ford Galaxy rushing up to the emergency room main entrance with a woman at the wheel. The front passenger door opened, and a man in obvious distress stumbled out the door and staggered toward the main entrance of the emergency room while the woman parked the car right near the entrance, and helped two young girls out of the back seat. Sammy's first impulse was to help. He got off his bench, and, acting on reflex, started to rush toward the staggering man. But Sammy didn't have a clue what to do. The man stumbled into the emergency room foyer as Sammy cautiously approached. He saw that the woman was visibly upset with tears in her eyes, but she was trying to control her emotions so that the two little girls with her weren't more upset and alarmed than they already were. Before the woman could catch up with the man, the man stumbled and collapsed head long into the wheel chairs ringing the foyer. The little girls began to panic. Sammy instinctively reached toward the man to help him up thinking in simple terms that, if he could get the man up on his feet again, the man would be alright.

Suddenly, out of nowhere, Sammy saw a young doctor bend over the man and yell out "Code Blue!" "Code Blue!" Within seconds, four nurses were with the doctor, and the doctor was bent over the man pressing his thumb and index finger at the top of the man's throat as if he were trying to straighten out the man's windpipe. "We need an airway!" yelled the doctor, and then calmly asked the man: "Give me a history; what happened?" "Everything is black," the man feebly replied. "I'm losing it. I'm going toward the darkness." The woman blurted out: "He was swarmed by bees and he's having a difficult time breathing." "Anaphylactic shock!" yelled the doctor. "Get a gurney, oxygen, Effeneferin, Prednisone and warm blankets." The two little girls were sobbing. Their fragile little minds could not process anything other than terror as they saw the strongest man in their world, their father, going down helplessly. Sammy was also overwhelmed by the life and death struggle he stumbled upon, but, even in his own state of shock, he couldn't help but admire the leadership of the take-control, cool headed, young doctor that everyone in the Northwest Detroit Hood now looked up to... to take charge of a medical emergency that, to Sammy's eye, seemed to be quickly marching toward a final, fatal outcome. In that same moment, Sammy clearly realized that only the cool-headed young doctor stood between life and death in the struggle which the man seemed to be losing.

The gurney arrived. Sammy was commandeered into action by the doctor, and, with one coordinated effort, the man was lifted up and onto the gurney as the medical team continued their heroic response. Sammy heard the young doctor's assessment in real time as the doctor worked and directed the "Code Blue" medical team: "Blood Pressure 70 over 40, very low;" "Heart rate 190, racing," "Oxygen levels fair – that's good; pump the Effeneferin in the patient **STAT**; hook up an IV with Prednisone **STAT**; put the warm blankets on the patient and wheel him into the emergency room."

The man's legs appeared to convulse in reaction to the shots. The two young girls were almost hysterical while the woman with them was trying to soothe their aching, trembling hearts. The doctor then turned to the woman as the man was being pushed away on the gurney. "Who is this man?" asked the doctor. "He is my husband, Fred Victory, and the father of the 4-year-old and the 2-year-old girls who are with me. We have another daughter Valentina Frances, but she's staying with friends tonight." Sammy Slow, standing within earshot, gasped. The man in the life and death struggle was his dear friend Valentina Frances Victory's father. "Unbelievable," he thought as his mind repeated Charles Dickens words from the *Tale of Two Cities*, "It was the best of times; it was the worst of times." From championship victories and a hug from Valentina Frances Victory to witnessing the life and death struggle of her father while Valentina Frances, asleep in another part of the city, was blissfully unaware of her father's struggle to live, and to survive the devastating effects of anaphylactic shock.

As Mrs. Victory responded to the doctor's question, "Who is he?," the doctor reached out and lifted the 4-year-old up in his arms while the mother held her 2-year-old. "What's going to happen doctor? Is my Daddy going to die?," asked the 4-year-old. Sammy felt his throat tighten. He felt his heart race and felt anxiety running away with him, knowing that Valentina's father was probably convulsing in the last moments of his life. At that moment, Sammy comforted himself with the silent refrain from a popular song:

> "Did an angel suddenly appear and hold you close and
> whisper in your ear and take away your fear in those
> long... last... moments?"

Sammy closed his eyes and silently wept as he heard the doctor say: "Mrs. Victory, there are no certainties in life, but I think your husband is going to be okay. He suffered a major allergic reaction to bee venom. Medically, the general term is 'anaphylactic shock' which means a major allergic reaction. 'Anaphylactic shock' can be caused by anything that a person is allergic to: bee venom, wasp venom, peanut butter, penicillin or any other medication or any other substance that a human being is exposed to. You got your husband to the hospital just in time. He was in stage II 'anaphylactic shock' when he collapsed into the wheelchairs." The young doctor continued: "As part of the allergic reaction, your husband's blood pressure dropped dangerously low in reaction to the bee venom, and, as a result, his heart's ability to pump blood and oxygen to all parts of his body was severely compromised by the dangerously low blood pressure. In stage I your husband's anaphylactic shock compromised the oxygen supply to his extremities because his blood pressure wasn't strong enough to pump oxygen enriched blood to all parts of the body. So your husband's legs, feet, arms and hands were not receiving the volume of oxygen they should have received. Next, your husband entered stage II anaphylactic shock when the body's control center, the brain, realized there wasn't enough oxygen enriched blood to go around so the brain executed two commands: command one, increase heart rate, the heart's pumping power, to the maximum, and command two, cut off blood pressure and blood flow to all parts of the body except the major organs. If your husband would have arrived in the emergency room later than he did, he would have been in anaphylactic shock Stage III where his brain would have executed a more drastic command, telling his heart to pump oxygen enriched blood to the brain only. Thank heaven your husband did not get to Stage III where his medical outcome would have been much more uncertain."

Mrs. Victory, already overwhelmed, was now on medical overload, but she focused on the positive aspects of the young doctor's medical presentation. The young doctor continued: "When you arrived at the hospital, your husband had probably just entered stage II anaphylactic shock with his brain telling his heart to go faster and faster to compensate for the low blood pressure and with his brain also telling his body to compensate for the loss of oxygen levels by pumping oxygen enriched blood to the major body organs only. We administered Effeneferin – an antihistamine to slow down the body's production of histamines so we could decrease the cascading role of the body's own histamines in triggering further allergic reactions. We also administered Prednisone, a strong anti-inflammatory steroid, to directly combat the allergic reaction and keep your husband's airway open. Had you brought your husband to the hospital ten minutes later," the doctor continued, "he probably would have been in stage III where his throat would have swollen, limiting his ability to breathe, and, even if we would have intubated him on a ventilator to give him oxygen support, his body functions would have cascaded out of control, and he probably would have entered stage IV – ARDS, Adult Respiratory Distress Syndrome." The young doctor continued: "With ARDS, it's a coin flip whether your husband survives. But I think you got your husband here just in time and, although I have no crystal ball, I expect your husband will make a full recovery."

Sammy couldn't believe his ears. He just heard a medical school lecture in Allergic Reactions 101 and he was not only mesmerized, but he understood every word – especially the part that said Valentina Frances Victory's father was going to "make a full recovery." Mrs. Victory, not quite assured yet, asked the doctor why her husband's legs seemed to shake and convulse if he's going to be okay. Now, a crestfallen Sammy silently joined in the question. The young doctor then allayed all fears when he told Mrs. Victory that "the shaking legs were just the simple and expected reaction to the adrenaline administered to your husband." The doctor kissed 4-year-old Jessie Victory on the cheek, telling her: "I'm going to take care of your daddy; everything is going to be fine." Then the young doctor turned away, disappearing as quickly as he first appeared.

Celebration of Another Kind

The good news finally sank in. Mrs. Victory took her two young daughters into her arms and told those beautiful girls that their father was going to be okay, and all three sobbed in one huge, just-dodged-a-bullet, indistinguishable mass of humanity. Sammy, still standing nearby, could not shut off his own silent tears copiously flowing down his cheeks. Although he wanted to join in the family hug, he did not approach. If anyone knew his boundaries, it was Sammy, who stayed out of life's limelight and lived in the shadow that other lives cast over his life.

Sammy retreated from the outside world and from the life and death struggle he just witnessed, and returned down the steps to the monotonous, underground world of dishwashing. But Sammy was still on his own adrenaline high. His dear friend Valentina Frances Victory's father had been spared. No funeral homes with emotionally battered children looking in disbelief at the last remains of their father, no funeral masses, no rites of the dead, no widows and no fatherless children left to fend for themselves without a strong male figure.

As Sammy returned to his dishwashing job, the symbolism of his world changed. Water running from the faucet was no longer the running conversation at the victory party. The running water was now the symbol of blood pressure with oxygen enriched blood – the source of all life. The freshly cleaned plates were no longer the clean sweep of victory, but were now the symbol of a fresh start for a life snatched from the jaws of death. The swirling water and soap bubbles were no longer the rhythm and popping beat of the dancers at the victory party, but were now the symbol of the endless flow and rhythm of the human heart and life itself.

Sammy finished up his midnight shift at 7:00 a.m. and walked up the same "Employees Only" stairway he used four hours earlier. Sammy exited the "Employees Only" door just in time to catch a glimpse of Mr. Fred Victory shuffling out of the emergency room, moving gingerly toward a waiting automobile, a little worn out from his flirt with death, but very much alive. Mr. Victory walked hand in hand with his wife while Sammy's classmate, Valentina Frances Victory, who had just hugged Sammy at the end of the championship football game hours before, now appeared, rubbing sleep from her eyes while holding the hand of her 4-year-old sister Jessie and carrying her sleeping 2-year-old sister Frances. The family entered the same 1957 Ford Galaxy that just four hours before, in hearse-like fashion, with the Grim Reaper riding shotgun, carried a life and death drama to the front door of the emergency room. Again, Sammy kept his distance. He made no acknowledgement. But, he did let out an audible sigh of relief. And, as Valentina Frances Victory's family drove away, Sammy spotted the Grim Reaper sitting on a nearby curb – the game of life and death postponed for now. As the Victory's family car pulled out onto Schaefer Road, Sammy heard a distinct clang, and, as he looked up, he swore he saw the Grim Reaper's scythe being flung out the rear window of the Victory family's 1957 Ford Galaxy and bound down the roadway and onto a grassy knoll.

The Grim Reaper never moved from the curb and Sammy saw no need to engage the symbol of death. Sammy had enough excitement for the night. Afraid of both possibilities: one, that he would find the Grim Reaper's scythe, or, the other, that he wouldn't find that scythe that he clearly saw flung out the 1957 Ford Galaxy car window, Sammy purposely avoided Schaefer and went north on the hospital grounds, walking along the sweeping veranda that led to the front entrance of Mt. Carmel Hospital on Outer Drive. Sammy hit Outer Drive and headed westbound on foot. A couple of miles later he passed the early crowd heading into the St. Scholastica Fall Fair. Still traveling westbound, he crossed Southfield Road, passing right by St. Scholastica's infamous Cow Palace where last night's State Championship victory party was held.

The irony of the last twelve hours wasn't lost on Sammy as he thought to himself… "Friday, November 18, 1960, a State Championship Victory of Benedictine Catholic Central over Lansing Resurrection led by unorthodox hero Tom Terrific, in front of 39,000 plus screaming fans, and just five hours later, on Saturday morning, November 19, 1960, a victory of another sort – a victory of life over death led by ????? – led by Doctor ????? Shall we say led by Dr. Hero" – a victory played out in front of a faint hearted crowd of one, disconnected kid, Sammy Slow. The Saturday edition of the *Detroit Free Press* and *Detroit News* carried front page photos and multiple stories of the big, down-to-the-wire, State Championship football game, but nary a mention of Dr. Hero's heroic, take-charge, saving-of-the-day effort for Valentina Frances Victory's family.

Finally, Sammy arrived home for his Saturday morning sleep as the rest of his household was just beginning to stir. Sammy was too exhausted to talk. He stumbled to his room, and, as Sammy laid his tired body down to rest at 8:30 Saturday morning, he clearly realized that Tom Terrific was but the hero of a game, and, on a world scale, a hero of a rather meaningless event with no real life consequence while, on the other hand, Dr. Hero was the unsung hero in a human drama where life and death fought a pitched, no-holds-barred battle for supremacy – a dramatic battle that had real life and death consequences, a battle that made real life-long differences in real peoples' lives. In contrast to Dr. Hero's victory of life over death, Benedictine Catholic Central's State Championship paled significantly. Sammy also knew, in his fog of exhaustion, and in some not-yet-fully-realized way that the events of the last twelve hours would impact his life forever. But he wasn't sure how or when. Sammy fell into a pleasurable coma of rest and slept ten hours in the warm bosom of the Lord, safe from the exigent vicissitudes and vagaries of life. Restorative sleep. Deep sleep. Sleep free from anxiety or fear – a gift from heaven that blesses both the conscious and the subconscious minds.

As Sammy slept in a cocoon of exhaustion, he never moved, and, therefore, never awoke even partially to catch a glimpse of his grandiose "rapid eye movement" dreams that come out of ascending stage two sleep. Those dreams were dreamed, but, due to Sammy's deep, deep sleep, those grandiose "rapid eye movement" dreams were irretrievable lost, forever, and we are only left to guess what the themes of Sammy's dreams were. What grandiose images ran through Sammy's sleeping psyche and played out on the big-dream screen of his subconscious mind? Were they dreams of simple confusion – not being able to put the pieces of the subconscious mind together in the logical sequence of the conscious mind? Were they dreams of the monotony of washing dish after dish or some other detail after detail? Were they dreams reliving bits and pieces and glimpses of the strange twists and heroics of the championship game? Were they dreams of bits and pieces of medical emergencies with heroic intervention? Were they dreams of depression and rejection for being shut out as a participant in life's heroic or magic moments? No one, including Sammy, will ever know. The content of Sammy's dreams are gone forever, but, as we know, the emotional impact of those unremembered dreams will still subconsciously influence Sammy's emotional feelings from the moment he awakes and throughout the rest of his day's activities.

What we do know for sure is that everyone dreams every night, but the sounder you sleep, the less chance you have for any patchwork recall of your dreams. And, we also know for sure that we spin our dreams right out of our subconscious, unaware mind – dreams that tell a story of our life's struggles and our life's longings, struggles and longings that we may not be consciously aware of in our waking life. And, we also know for sure that the themes of the dreams we create in our sleep can give us great insight into the unknown or partially known struggles and longings that live within our subconscious, unaware minds. Therefore, we should learn as much about dream interpretation as we can so we can gain insight into the repressed thoughts, influences, longings and struggles that live in our subconscious minds because, once the dream plays out in our sleeping, unaware, subconscious mind, the dream will, upon awakening, influence our feelings thereafter whether we recall our dream or not. That's why some days we awake happy and ready to go without understanding why, while, on other days, we awake sad and forlorn in a state of malaise, again without understanding why. Maybe Benedictine Catholic Central teacher Father "Tunney" Hathaway's ten second homily had it right: "When you awake, you have just ten seconds to decide whether you are going to have a happy day or a sad day."

Oh, yes. The eternal dilemma – how to overcome the rut of our emotionally entrenched feelings with the spirituality of free will. How to actually do it rather than talk about it, and how to do it in some lasting way. Perhaps the answer to how to do it is to "live in the moment" by enjoying, or at least embracing, each moment – the happy, the mundane and even the sad, because the moment is all we ever have… as each moment, once spent, is gone forever as it turns into the next moment, then the next moment until there are no more moments left in this vale of tears. Perhaps, we could not only live in the moment, but, perhaps, embrace that moment, whatever it is, because the sum total of our moments writes our own epitaph, and tells the world who we are or, when gone, who we were.

An Awakening

Sammy awoke, consciously dreamless, but hungry, and he could smell Saturday night's dinner. "What time was it?," he thought. The clock said 6:30 p.m. He didn't have to be at Cregar's Restaurant on Grand River and Outer Drive to hawk the *Detroit Free Press* newspapers in the street until 8 o'clock. So he had time to enjoy dinner and he was starving. He bounded out of bed refreshed, and then stopped in his tracks, suddenly remembering the heroics on the gridiron and the heroics at Mt. Carmel Hospital Emergency Room. What a great day they must be having at Valentina Frances Victory's house – endless group hugs around the living room, celebrating the victory of life over near death. What an overwhelming sense of joy and peace there must be in the Victory household with each new recognition that life itself and physical health were restored to a husband and a father. No doubt, they are living in the moment. It's undeniable that nothing makes a person feel more alive and alert than being in the presence of near death or impending death, provided, I guess, it isn't your own death. Sammy was sure the Benedictine Central Championship Game was not the topic of conversation at Valentina Frances Victory's household, and he was sure the group hugs would go on for days as the Victory household truly lived in the moment, and all the anticipated moments still left to play out in Mr. Victory's life, because Dr. Hero beat the Grim Reaper one to nothing in a close game of life and death – a game with real life consequences.

As Sammy approached the dinner table, he saw a gray-haired man sitting with his family. Recognition came a moment later. It was the doctor who brought him into the world. It was Dr. Nathan Goodfellow. "Good morning Dr. Goodfellow." "And, good evening to you, Sammy," responded Dr. Goodfellow. Sammy blushed. "Sorry. I guess I missed a day." "Congratulations on Benedictine Catholic Central's State Championship," said a jubilant Dr. Goodfellow. Sammy felt no need to respond to that bit of overdone, yesterday's news. Sammy was still locked in mentally, emotionally and spiritually to last night's medical drama. That's what he needed to talk out and talk about. That's what he needed to emotionally resolve, and what better opportunity was there than right now with a medical doctor sitting at the dinner table.

Sammy got right to the point: "Dr. Goodfellow, I saw a doctor save Valentina Frances Victory's father last night at Mt. Carmel Hospital. He almost died from an allergic reaction to bee stings. I think they called it 'Flactic Shock'," Dr. Goodfellow's eyebrows raised. "I know all about that Sammy. It's called 'anaphylactic shock.' But I can't tell you what I know because Mr. Victory's medical history or anybody's medical history is privileged and protected from disclosure." But Dr. Goodfellow, always an astute student of life, saw Sammy's need to

73

emotionally talk through what Sammy saw last night. Dr. Goodfellow therefore continued: "But Sammy, you are free to tell me what you saw and heard." Sammy's parents and his brothers and sisters looked dumbfounded. Apparently there was some extraordinary life and death news that Sammy and Dr. Goodfellow knew, with the rest of Sammy's family in the dark.

All eyes and ears were on Sammy as he explained in detail last night's lesson of allergic reaction, "code blue," "anaphylactic shock," falling blood pressure, compensating increase in heartbeat, re-routing of blood flow to the major organs and then to the brain only, neutralizing of histamines with Effeneferin, adrenaline boost and the administration of the life-saving steroid, miracle drug Prednisone. Sammy told the story of last night's medical miracle in all its detail right down to the scythe being thrown out of Mr. Victory's car, bounding down Schaeffer Avenue as Valentina Frances Victory's family drove off from Mt. Carmel Hospital – the family unit still intact.

All eyes were fixed on "the story-teller," Sammy. There were no yawns, patronizing glances or interruptions. Sammy's dramatic life and death account flowed to eager ears with Sammy realizing for the first time in his life that others were listening to him. Others cared what he had to say, and others were truly interested in him and his story. Sammy saw, for the first time, that he counted, and that he was the center of rapt attention. All eyes were on Sammy, and everyone at that dinner table was mesmerized by his story and his delivery. It was a moment frozen in time, a magical moment where awareness meets destiny, a moment of self-recognition where a subtle, but not-yet-fully-realized message, appeared in Sammy's psyche: "Sammy, you can be somebody. Sammy, you are not confined to the sidelines of life... you are a meaningful participant in life." Sammy acknowledged the message silently to himself, but continued with the flow of his riveting story.

When Sammy finished his extraordinary tale, there was complete silence. No one moved, and no one said anything. To Sammy, ever struggling with his low self image, the silence haunted him. He must have blown it. Sammy, instinctively waiting for the inevitable recoil of criticism, was caught off guard when Dr. Goodfellow was the first to respond: "Sammy, that was one mesmerizing story, filled with fear, suspense, anticipation and the denouement of dramatic unraveling, triumph, happy ending and all." That denouement part certainly wasn't clear to Sammy, but it sounded like… "A" okay. The mere sound of the word "denouement" evoked a pleasant feeling of artistic accomplishment, and Sammy accepted the word as positive reinforcement. Sammy's low self image receded and his ears perked up, and a genuine, irrepressible smile brightened his Huckleberry Finn face – truly a Norman-Rockwell-meets-Mark-Twain moment, a moment fit for the cover of the *Saturday Evening Post*.

Everyone at the dinner table smiled and nodded approvingly as Dr. Goodfellow continued: "Sammy, I would say you are on the horns of a pleasant dilemma," another uncertain but nice sounding "A" okay phrase. "Your riveting story of Mr. Victory's life and death struggle had all the highlights of a great oral argument to a jury in a court of law. You told a story that gripped the listener, entertained, took them on an emotional roller coaster, and held their attention while allowing your listeners to comfortably handle and understand the complex medical science of 'anaphylactic shock.' You took the complex, ever-expanding universe of medicine, reduced it to the size of a basketball, and put it comfortably into the laps of the listeners."

"My own father was a great trial lawyer, Sammy. He was afraid of nothing. He went to bat for the blue collar, working class guy and for those who found themselves in the unrelenting grip of the establishment – insurance companies, government, law enforcement, drug companies and corporate America – that five percent of the world who constantly strive to control the lives of the other ninety-five percent of the world." Dr. Goodfellow continued: "Sammy, I see in you the potential to be a great trial lawyer like my father. Sammy, if you are willing to continue the same sacrifices you make everyday, working two jobs and helping your family, studying, developing analytical agility and verbal ability, I'm sure you could eventually become a great trial lawyer. You could develop those same attributes that made my father a successful trail lawyer – the killer instinct of a street fighter, the polished social etiquette of a diplomat, the conditioning and endurance of a marathon runner who, despite fatigue, does not hit the wall physically or emotionally, an analytical agility, verbal ability, total command of the language, postponed gratification and, above all else, a courageous commitment to the cause of social justice for the common man." Sammy had never heard such laudatory encouragement. He couldn't keep that Huckleberry Finn smile off his face – the same bemused smile of wonderment he also noticed on the faces of his mother and father, whose faces read like a book: "Is Dr. Goodfellow talking about our Sammy?"

Preparing to be "Lucky"

Dr. Goodfellow continued: "As I say Sammy, you have a dilemma… kind of a 'to-be-or-not-to-be' choice. In addition to law, you have a great potential for medicine. Sammy, your ability to handle complex medical concepts tells me you may be headed to medical school. The doctor who saved Valentina's Victory's father, Dr. John Ronayne, was one of my best students in medical school and the best intern at Mt. Carmel Hospital. He is bright, courageous and calm under pressure. Pretty soon Dr. Ronayne will be in his residency for training as a surgeon. It certainly was Mr. Victory's lucky day that Dr. Ronayne was rotating through the emergency department of Mt.

Dr. "Hero"
John Ronayne M.D.

Carmel the night Mr. Victory ended up in the emergency room with 'anaphylactic shock.' Another doctor with less skill... well, who knows, Sammy. With another doctor could have come another result that I don't even want to think about Sammy." Dr. Goodfellow, now on a soap box and in full philosophical "windup," continued to deliver his pitch: "Not all doctors are equal Sammy, and sometimes the difference between a successful medical result and an unsuccessful one, lies only in the skill, competence and analytical ability of the individual doctor. After all, Sammy, the doctor who graduates last in his medical school class is still called 'doctor.' So Sammy, it really was Mr. Victory's lucky day that Dr. Ronayne was manning the emergency room when Mr. Victory's medical emergency came crashing head first into the emergency room wheel chairs."

"But Sammy," continued Dr. Goodfellow: "'Luck' is one of those deceptive words that can fool you and undo your will to succeed if you are not careful. Looking at life from the eyes of Mr. Victory, it was his lucky day because it was just random luck of the draw that a doctor as skillful and cool-headed as young Dr. Ronayne was on duty at the Mt. Carmel Mercy Hospital Emergency Room to save his life. But, if you look at that same life saving event through the eyes of Dr. Ronayne, there was no luck involved because Dr. Ronayne's saving of Mr. Victory was not dependent on the random event of luck-of-the-draw, but rather was the result of Dr. Ronayne's lifetime work ethic of pushing himself to be the best he could be, day in and day out, and, each day, every day, preparing himself to win the battle of life's unexpected medical emergencies. So luck in saving Mr. Victory's life involved two separate concepts of luck, Sammy. For Mr. Victory, his life was saved through the random luck of the draw that he just happened to have a medical emergency on Dr. Ronayne's shift. But, for Dr. Ronayne, saving Mr. Victory was not based upon luck; it was based on Dr. Ronayne's years of sacrifice and preparation that enabled Dr. Ronayne to step up to a desperate situation when the moment presented itself, and pull Mr. Victory's life away from the grip of death. So Sammy, luck is a truly random event that Mr. Victory had no control over, but when any of us get lucky in the success of life, it usually has nothing to do with random events, but rather it has to do with 'preparation' and 'opportunity' coming together at the same time. When opportunity presents itself, Sammy, only the prepared will be lucky. But, whether you call it luck or whether you call it 'preparation meeting opportunity,' Mr. Victory should thank his lucky stars or, better yet, offer a prayer of thanksgiving that his life was spared. Maybe it just wasn't his time. And Sammy, maybe you shouldn't breeze around that incident of the Grim Reaper's scythe coming out of Mr. Victory's car and bounding down Schaefer Avenue. After all Sammy, you were tired and pumped up with your own adrenaline surge, and, one day, you might have to explain that incredible, other-world incident to the Medical Board or to the Character and Fitness Committee of the State Bar." Sammy got Dr. Goodfellow's drift, but Sammy knew he saw what he saw and heard what he heard.

Dr. Goodfellow finally ran out of air. He was after all, 67 years old now. Dr. Goodfellow shook Sammy's hand. "It's up to you now, Sammy," and he left. Sammy's mother and father, still beaming, turned to Sammy. "We are so proud of you, Sammy." – something Sammy never heard before, and, at that moment, the universe echoed back Dr. Nathan Goodfellow's words from the day Sammy was born on July 4, 1943:

> "Above all, the individual uniqueness of each infant must be recognized and appreciated, a uniqueness which must be turned loose into the world to find its own star, its own course, its own dream, and fulfill its own destiny, unburdened by the well-intentioned, but counter-productive expectations of family members and well-wishers. Each child is blessed with different gifts. So sit back, and watch patiently for years and decades, as each child's own unique gifts magically unfold over life's marathon."

And the universe echoed back the crescendoing words of Khalil Gibran:

> "You may strive to be like them,
> but seek not to make them like you."

Sammy hurried from the dinner table, left the house, and went to work hawking the bulldog Sunday edition of the *Detroit Free Press* at Grand River and Outer Drive in front of Cregar's Restaurant. Sammy gave nary a thought to Tom Terrific and the gridiron exploits of the Benedictine Catholic Central's football championship game. His mind was preoccupied with college, medical school and the heroic exploits of Dr. Ronayne – heroic exploits that would someday be his. Even in his state of euphoria, he knew postponed gratification would be the key, but he was willing to pay that price because, for the first time in his life, he knew it was his destiny to move from the sidelines of life to the medical field of play and on to heroic, save-the-day, deeds of his own.

As Sammy was hawking newspapers to the cars heading down Grand River, Sammy's dream-like state of euphoria almost cost him his life when he came within an inch of a 60 mph automobile speeding through the red light on east bound Grand River. Sammy thought to himself: "I hope that 'Grim Reaper' guy isn't still in the Hood." And the universe echoed back the answer Dr. Finn gave to my own mother, Jean Lauck, at Mt. Carmel hospital hospice in September 1988 when she asked Dr. Finn if she was going to die: "We are all going to die Jean, but not tonight."

CHAPTER 6

Life...
Levels The Playing Field

The Girls Bring it Home

The autumn days of 1960 flew by as fall turned to winter with our radios lamenting Johnny Mercer's love-lost: "autumn leaves of red and gold and sunburned hands he used to hold." Just as successful as Benedictine Catholic Central State Championship football team was, so also was the girl's basketball team, anchored by the fast-darting, quick-dribbling, hot-shot darling of the hardwood court, Brigetta BeBop. She had all the gifts. She didn't have to work at technique. She didn't have to work at shooting. She didn't have to work at defense. She didn't have to develop a work ethic. Brigetta could sing, dance and play hoops with the best of them, and it was all so effortless.

Valentina Frances Victory was also gifted. And she was tough. She dominated the boards, and she jammed you with defense, defense and more defense. Despite her charming nature and her gentle, likeable ways, Valentina Frances feared no one, and backed up (or down) to no one except to allow a little light of glory to fall on her teammates – including power forward and a beauty of a young lady, Kathleen Hankins. Kathleen's talent and natural beauty complemented Brigetta and Valentina Frances perfectly. The starting five for the Benedictine Catholic Central Ravenettes was rounded out with "No Nonsense" Roseanne Moran and "Cutie Pie" Mary Brozek ("I may be cute but I'll break your nose if I have to"). These hoop girls were overwhelming and amazing.

In their senior year opener, the Ravenettes of Benedictine Catholic Central knocked off St. Alphonsus 8 to 6 in something less than a shootout (Hey, no one had their shooting eye that early in the season). They rolled past St. Mary's 41 to 9 (now somebody is throwing the ball up to the hoop), St. Gregory 42 to 11, St. Theresa 11 to 6 (ok, the Ravenettes went cold or maybe it was an outside game in the snow – I honestly don't recall). The Ravenettes beat southwest Detroit's Holy Redeemer 23 to 14 and vanquished numerous other foes who felt the sting of defeat. When you face the Ravenettes, there's always something macabre or something from the occult going on:

> "And the silken, sad uncertain curtains
> filled me with terror never felt before.
> So that now to still the beating of my heart, I stood repeating
> Tis some visitor entreating entrance at my chamber door;
> Tis only this and nothing more.
> But the silence was unbroken and the stillness gave no token
> And the only word there spoken was the whispered word 'Lenore?'
> This I whispered and nothing more."

Well it wasn't just any visitor at Edgar Allen Poe's portal. No, it was... you guessed it – a raven. Well, if a raven fills you "with terror never felt before," just imagine what the female of the species, a Ravenette, brings to the game: 42 points pumped over your head, St. Gregory the Dragon Slayer. Bang – all net. Take that St. Gregory! 41 points over, through and around you St. Marys of Redford. Bang. Swoosh! All net, baby. Take that St. Marys! No clunkers or clangers or bricks. This ain't horseshoes. All net baby! Don't mess with the Ravenettes.

Head coach Mary Preda, knew she had a special group. The only blemish on Benedictine Catholic Central's record was a 21 to 21 tie with Mercy High School led by the debonair and graceful Helen Ivory. That's right, a tie. Don't ask me. I was up in the corner of the Cow Palace in the cheap seats with the charter members of the "Curtis Gang": DiBella, Demers, Quick, Fedorinchik, Hoody McGoo and our lead vocalist, Danny Mac – "When are you coming back?" We were working on our Buddy Holly lyrics: "Rave on that crazy feeling cuz I know you got me reeling." Get it? "Rave on" for the Ravens. Well, anyway, none of us remember a tie, but the historical record speaks for itself. The Hood don't lie.

That strange tie aside, the Ravenettes won 'em all, and met Immaculata High School in the City Championship game at the University of Detroit Memorial Building (now Calihan Hall – named after U of D's All American basketball player, legendary coach and Irish gentleman Bob Calihan). Like Benedictine Catholic Central's football championship, the City Championship basketball game went down to the wire. Benedictine Catholic Central was down one point with 10 seconds to go, and Immaculata had the ball. Their power forward, the "Leaping Latvian," Christine Golting, took the ball with the shot clock at three seconds and the game clock at nine seconds. Immaculata's Christine Golting knew she had to go to the basket.

She knew she couldn't let the shot clock run out and turn the ball over to Benedictine Catholic Central with only a one point lead and six seconds left on the game clock. Golting, always a hard charger, picked her moment, and drove to the basket as the shot clock and the game clock ran down… nine seconds, eight seconds, seven seconds. Benedictine Catholic Central's Valentina Frances Victory's "all-over-you-step-for-step" defensive coverage forced Immaculata's Leaping Latvian to abort her drive to the basket, pull up short and throw up a desperation jump shot. Valentina Frances Victory seized the moment, and with the impeccable timing she learned as a dancer, went up with Golting and stripped the ball from Golting, and, in one powerful, graceful motion, Valentina Frances fed an overhead, arcing, floating pass to fast-breaking Brigetta BeBop who grabbed the ball out of the air, drove the length of the court… three seconds, two seconds, one second for a two point jam giving Benedictine Catholic Central the City Championship as the game clock hit zero and the horn sounded. That's what I'm talking about!

In one anxious moment, classmates, parents, supporters and friends of Benedictine Catholic Central's girl's basketball team went from shallow breathing silence and anticipation of doom to a slow motion jumping up and down followed by bursting euphoria with fists clenched and arms thrust upward, punctuating Benedictine Catholic

Central's nail biting Championship victory. It was over, and the Championship trophy was all but in Benedictine Catholic Central's trophy case, even though the Leaping Latvian's father and prominent lawyer, Eric Golting, was threatening a lawsuit claiming Valentina

Kathy Hankins and the Ravenettes Celebrate 1960

Frances Victory's mauling defensive coverage of his daughter, Christine, was a flagrant foul that the blind referee, Billy Oldani, missed. In short order, even trial lawyer Golting realized that the "bang bang" competition of a photo finish would be better left undisturbed in the record book and in the hearts and minds of Detroiters than to be endlessly litigated, dissected and replayed over and over for years in a courtroom setting – especially where referee Billy Oldani's Irish uncle, Michael Cotter, was rumored to be an enforcer for the Curtis Gang, the Dank Coons, the Dirty Thirty and the Detroit Mob.

In the stands, a quiet, smiling Brenda Blah felt happy for her old friend, Brigetta BeBop. Brenda Blah walked onto the court as Brigetta BeBop was hoisted on the shoulders of her teammates to cut down the net. Brenda tried to congratulate her old friend Brigetta, but Brigetta looked right past her as the adoring fans and flash bulbs mobbed Brigetta. Valentina Frances Victory, however, never one to be overcome by short term victories, and never one to overlook long term relationships, saw the hurt in Brenda Blah's eyes, and went out of her way to greet and embrace Brenda and share a moment of victory with her. Brigetta BeBop, ever the gifted hero, couldn't find a moment away from her adoring fans to reach out and touch her old friend Brenda Blah.

Forlorn Brenda Blah

The victory party at Benedictine Catholic Central's Cow Palace went on late into the night, but a forlorn Brenda Blah went home that night feeling as blah as her name and as colorless as her white pale complexion. Was there no place in this world for her? She finished her endless chores at home by bathing her little sisters and brothers and putting them to bed while her mother was finishing her double shift as a waitress at Kim's Gardens Cantonese Restaurant on Six Mile, and while her father was just beginning the monotony of the night shift at a noisy, semi-lit, parts shop, "Arrowsmith," on the north side of Eight Mile Road in Southfield, Michigan.

Brenda thought about the victory party at the Cow Palace, and felt the emotional sting of not belonging and not being someone. While her classmates were celebrating at the victory party, she was going to bed. She washed her makeup-less face and glanced in the mirror, but, strangely, her reflection was not there. Was she so inconspicuous in life that her mirror couldn't see her? Was she as bereft of the world as Robert Frost was?

> "Out on the porch's sagging floor.
> Leaves got up in a coil and hissed,
> Blindly struck at my knee and missed.
> Something sinister in the tone
> Told me my secret must be known;
> Word I was in the house alone
> Somehow must have gotten abroad,
> Word I was in my life alone,
> Word I had no one left but God."

Unvalidated, unnoticed and exhausted, she collapsed into her bed and fell into a fitful sleep. She dreamed that she ran away to join the carnival, but the distorted, misfit faces of the carney workers screamed when they saw her and ran away from her. She dreamed that she went to church alone, and, as she walked into the church, the congregation got up and walked out on her. She then knelt in prayerful submission, finally looked up toward the altar where she saw a sign that read: "God is tending to others Brenda; please call back another time." At that very moment, someone got the drop on her from behind, and she felt forceful hands on her throat... squeezing the life out of her as she struggled to breathe. She was slipping into unconsciousness as she struggled against the frozen muscle paralysis of her deep sleep rapid eye movement dream stage. Finally, she awoke sobbing in despair, only to find her mother consoling her and reassuring her that it was only a dream. But Brenda, even at 17 years of age, knew that her dreams of disconnection and self-bereavement, captured symbolically in the struggle of her subconscious, sleeping mind, were a true echo of the actual struggle of solitary isolation in her real life. Brenda's subconscious mind, bubbling over in her dreams and playing out in gaudy, symbolic imagery on the silver dream-screen of her sleeping mind, told Brenda what she already knew in her conscious, awake mind – she was a "no count."

The Road to Recovery

Brenda's family also knew intuitively that all was not well with Brenda. Although she was a great kid, very helpful to the family, and, although she was an excellent student and never complained, Brenda was a loner, and she lacked the carefree nature of youth. Worse yet, she seemed to be drowning in a river of tears. Finally, Brenda's parents could deny it no longer. Brenda was literally told that she was going to see a psychotherapist. Brenda, the ever-obliging, good daughter, dragged her low self image over to the psychotherapist's office next to the Ted C. Sullivan Funeral Home on Six Mile Road. "How appropriate... " she thought. "Her dead-end life was now supposedly going to be resurrected by a therapist, or, failing that, officially put to rest next door at Ted Sullivan's Funeral Home among the real dead, or is it really, the really dead?" The reluctant, good girl, Brenda Blah, did her best to cooperate with her parents' wishes to find the elusive bubble of happiness, or at least contentedness, with weekly psychotherapy visits with psychologist, Dr. Getbetter Ph.D.

The Minnesota Multiphasic Personality Inventory (MMPI) test that Dr. Getbetter administered to Brenda pointed toward a depressive disorder, anger and a general lack of trust of intimate relationship, also referred to as "paranoia" by her psychologist. Brenda couldn't help but laugh to herself about the lack-of-trust-of-intimate-relationship diagnosis. No one found her attractive. She never had a boyfriend, so how could anyone or any test tell her she would be non-trusting in such non-existent relationships? Brenda was soon to learn, however, that her "paranoia" was real, and that a paranoid horse-of-distrust was pulling her cart away from the possibility of any personal relationships. Brenda was soon to learn that her low self esteem sent an out-loud, clear message, "for her ears only," that she was "unworthy" of being loved. Therefore, as Brenda constructed her own self image in the world, anyone who approached her for a relationship certainly had some agenda other than the need to be around her own worthless self. "Who could ever love worthless Brenda" became her self defeating mantra – a projection of herself that her high school classmates just did not have the energy or skill to take on or fight through to get to know the real Brenda. But, Brenda's therapist was hopeful that Brenda could eventually gain insight into and understand that her own low self image and her projection of unworthiness was really the force that kept others away.

If Brenda was not worthy of love, as she truly believed, then anyone trying to reach out to her for any kind of relationship must be acting out of, and motivated by, a hidden agenda cloaked by the not-to-be-trusted facade of "lets be friends." Unwittingly and unknowingly, Brenda confirmed her own paranoia and lack of trust on a daily basis as she interpreted the neutral, non-significant actions of others as confirmation that they were rejecting her. True, Brenda wasn't the gifted darling of her age group like the ever-popular Brigetta BeBop, but the insignificant actions of others weren't always rejecting her either. Brenda Blah was living proof of what the great German author Goethe believed… that we tend to find what we're looking for. And, each day, every day, Brenda found what her preconceived low self image expected to find – rejection.

Strange how we evaluate new information each day, and yet find the same old thing. We find what our preconceived notions expect to find which, in Brenda's case, was rejection. A little too deep or convoluted you say. Well, then, take a close look at the vagueness, ambiguity and subtle nuance of your own fragile emotions living in the grey areas of your psyche where, everyday, what you know to be true in your intellect is overruled or trumped by your emotional rorschach. Or, as the great Dutch impressionist painter, van Gogh, said: " …small emotions are great captains of our lives." Yes, we are all a patchwork of emotions which contradict our stated beliefs. We are all living contradictions, partly truth and partly fiction. And, when you are 17, like our poor Brenda Blah, you are governed by the undeniable, emotional impression that your life is already written in stone, and your die irretrievably cast. You are either a winner like the gifted Brigetta BeBop, or you are defective like Brenda Blah saw herself to be… for the rest of her life. Poor kid. Good kid. Brenda struggles and suffers, thinking the "Story of Her Life" is already written, and that she has already been cast into the discount bargain bin until death will mercifully release her from her emotional pain on earth to… to… to what? To the great unknown.

Although faith may comfort us, nobody really knows about life after death so we better make the most of this life on earth. And, even if our faith and belief in eternal life is a reality, still we must strive to get the most out of our time in this vale of tears on earth because the concept of eternal life undeniably means our time on earth is also a part of our eternal life. Yet, each day, every day, our patchwork of emotions rejects or discounts the value of the moment as we undo ourselves, constantly wishing for a different moment. True, we must have long term goals, but we must also struggle to find a way to live in the moment, each and every moment, the good, the bad and the indifferent moment – for the sum total of those moments are who we are and who we are becoming. And, if we really don't like the moment, if we really don't like who we are or who we are becoming in the moment, then we must seize that moment and embrace it as impetus for change, a motivation to avoid that kind of moment in the future – not a change we can make overnight, but something we can work toward accomplishing eventually, even if it takes years of emotional baby steps to start to get there.

So Dr. Getbetter had her work cut out for her if she was going to provide an emotional way out for Brenda Blah from Brenda's past accumulated and present moments of depression, or, more precisely, if she was going to find a way for Brenda Blah to discover insight so that Brenda could see that her "Book Of Life" was on target, and was being written slowly and deliberately as it was supposed to be – even with a painful precision that would eventually allow Brenda to develop her own unique talents over life's marathon.

Well, I'm happy to report the story of success and recovery had by Brenda Blah. The Hood rejoices in Brenda's recovery. Due to her intellectual ability to comprehend the analytical underpinnings of psychotherapy, due to her courage to put truthful labels on her demons and face them head on, due to her family support, and, in no small part, due to her willingness to throw out her erroneous preconceived notions of life, Brenda grew emotionally, obtained insight into her self-defeating paranoia, and began to find self worth. After six months of weekly psychotherapy visits with Dr. Getbetter, Brenda was on her feet emotionally, and, each month thereafter, she grew in the comfort that the "Story of her Life" was only in the first chapter, and that she was building her foundation academically and emotionally for a strong and resilient character, and, more importantly, that she had the power to create and write each new chapter of her life according to her own unique gifts. Brenda finally accepted the truth that she had control over her future. Brenda finally accepted the truth that the time and effort she put into developing her own unique gifts in the present moment would, in large measure, determine just how future moments and future chapters of her life would be written – either as failures of quiet desperation from not having control over her own destiny, or, alternatively, as success stories that Brenda herself would write on the blank pages of a future that awaited her pen.

As the fresh light of a new emotional day in the rest of her life dawned on Brenda in 1961, just in time for the end of her senior year, Brenda heard the echo of Dr. Nathan Goodfellow's on-target advice given on the day of her birth almost eighteen years ago:

> "Each child is blessed with different gifts. So, sit back and watch patiently for years and decades, as each child's own unique gifts magically unfold over life's marathon."

Brenda's therapist, a woman and a role model, breathed life into Dr. Goodfellow's words. At the end of her senior year as Brenda graduated from Benedictine Catholic Central High School, she had a new lease on life, a new beginning and hopeful anticipation for the future. Thank heaven Brenda's parents didn't subscribe to the conventional wisdom of the 1950s and 1960s that "only crazy people go to shrinks," or "don't go to a shrink because people will think you're crazy."

How many other kids in the Hood could have, and should have, been saved from long, inherited cycles of dysfunction and debilitating ignorance that is passed on to each new generation by well-intentioned, but dysfunctional, parents and grandparents. How many other kids from the Hood could have, and should have, been saved from the tsunami of dysfunction and ignorance that rolls over each succeeding generation... over and over and over again like a family curse? How many other kids in the Hood did we lose because the older generation passed on the baton of dysfunction and crippling ignorance to each new generation? The problem is captured in the imponderable paradox: "Is there life after birth?" Who knows? My money says, "Yes." But, there is an awful lot of inertia, gravity and knee jerk philosophy from our family backgrounds that presents all of us with the great challenge of trying to pry open our minds to new possibilities and insist that our free will make changes. But, if you don't take on that challenge, you will never (for emphasis, never) become your own man or your own woman. And, if you do take on that challenge, maybe... , just maybe, you will stop the non-stop carousel of inherited ignorance and dysfunction for yourself and for future generations – hopefully, without any false sense of betraying those who came before you.

From the Sidelines... to the Game of Life

Dr. Goodfellow was right on all counts. Delayed gratification, sacrifice and the decades-long pursuit of education, and the decades long development of analytical agility and verbal ability is the key to future success. That strategy of discipline moved both Sammy Slow and Brenda Blah from the discount bargain bin and from the side-lines of life to the professional ranks. Sammy Slow graduated from the University of Michigan medical school and became a renowned sports medicine surgeon, working with all four professional sports teams in Detroit: the Lions, Tigers, Pistons, and the Red Wings. And who do you guess was his favorite patient? Correcto mundo! Tom

Terrific, who dropped off the college football team at Notre Dame because an unstable knee, first injured in the mythical State Championship game in the fall of 1960. Tom Terrific's injured knee would not withstand the rigors of college football. But, Dr. Sammy Slow, borrowing a page from Dr. John "The Hero" Ronayne, became Tom Terrific's hero when he salvaged Tom's career by flawlessly reconstructing Tom Terrific's knee, allowing Tom to return to Notre Dame at a later time and become an "All American" and graduate from Notre Dame. After a belated college career with the "Fighting Irish," Tom Terrific was drafted in the first round of the National Football League draft, and then spent nine years as an all-pro defensive back in the National Football League. Guess who Tom Terrific's lifetime hero is? Again, correcto mundo, the Mt. Carmel dishwasher, Sammy Slow, who moved from the basement of Mt. Carmel Hospital to the Super Bowl of sports medicine.

And Brenda Blah? Brenda Blah, moved by Dr. Getbetter's psychotherapy that so dramatically altered the course of her own life, made a commitment to spend her life helping others. In 1971, Brenda Blah obtained her Ph.D. from Northwestern University in clinical and behavioral psychology, writing her doctoral thesis on "The Non-Performance of the Gifted." And, her favorite patient? Correcto mundo, again, Brigetta BeBop. Dr. Brenda Blah eventually mentored her dear old friend Brigetta BeBop after Brigetta's attempted musical career as a pop vocalist failed – no surprise, because Brigetta BeBop, generally content to go only as far as her natural talents would take her, lacked the disciplined work ethic and focus to succeed in the very competitive arena of professional music. Without any commitment or sustained effort on her part, Brigetta BeBop was the proverbial "finish-out-of-the-money" performer.

Eventually, Brigetta swallowed her pride and called upon her old friend, Dr. Brenda Blah. Brigetta threw all of her trust and confidence into her old friend. After one year of intense psychotherapy, under the guiding hand of Dr. Brenda Blah, Brigetta BeBop was finally able to gain insight into her personality, finding out, ironically, that it was her lifetime fear of failure that kept her from maximizing her God-given talents.

As Brigetta found and confronted the demons in her subconscious mind, she gained insight into her own subtle, self-defeating defense mechanisms. For some, fear of failure motivates them to succeed, but, for Brigetta, fear of failure doomed her to fail. Brigetta's flawed reasoning told her that, if she did nothing to perfect her God-given talents, she couldn't be a failure because she could always fall back on her defense that she didn't fail; she just didn't care whether she succeeded or not. In the last analysis, Brigetta's feigned "I-don't-care" defense mechanism soothed and comforted her present fear of failure. But, predictably, Brigetta's defense mechanism, with its lack of disciplined focus and work ethic, also became a self-fulfilling prescription for future failure.

Brigetta concealed any desire to succeed with a blasé cover: "Who cares?" So, for Brigetta, there was no personal failure because she pretended she just didn't care. On the other hand, if Brigetta showed that she was invested in or cared about success, and, if she worked hard to perfect her God-given talents and still finished out of the money, then she would have no excuse, no cover, and the whole world would see that her best effort resulted in failure. It was this possibility of failing despite a concentrated effort and focus to succeed that gave birth to Brigetta's worst emotional nightmare, and, ultimately, became the emotional obstacle that kept Brigetta from developing a strong work ethic to perfect her God given talents.

With the experienced, guiding hand of her lifelong friend, Dr. Brenda Blah, Brigetta BeBop was finally able to see that life's only true failures are the ones that don't try, the ones that don't give their all, or the ones who are simply content to be spectators rather than run the risk of failure. Brigetta BeBop, with the painstaking patience, help and care of Dr. Brenda Blah, was finally able to understand the wisdom that the only ones who truly fail are the ones whose fear of failure keeps them from fully engaging in the pursuit of life:

"It is not the critic that counts
It is not the one who points out how the strong man or
    woman stumbled
Or where the doer of deeds could have done them better.
The credit belongs to the man and the woman in the arena
Whose faces are marred with dust and sweat and blood,
Who strive valiantly and who err and come up short,
    again and again.
But who, if they fail, at least fail while daring greatly
So that their place will never be among those cold
    and timid souls
Who know neither defeat nor victory." (Anonymous)

Once again, it's the journey of life that counts. For whether you win or lose, all that truly matters in the end is the journey you took – for you are the journey and the journey is you. As the poet says: "It matters not whether you won or lost, but how you played the game."

Paul Simon's song, "I am a Rock; I am an Island," says: "If I never loved, I never would have lost." But, through Dr. Brenda Blah's analytical approach and great insight, Brigetta BeBop was finally able to understand the fallacy of Paul Simon's two dimensional world of winners and losers, and finally able to see that the real world is a three dimensional world where the only losers are the spectators who refuse to emotionally invest in the game of life because of their fear of failure. On the other hand, those who invest fully in the pursuit of life and in the pursuit of their dreams will never fail because, even if they lose, "their place will never be among those cold and timid souls that know neither defeat nor victory." Brigetta BeBop got the picture, and went on to a great recording and stage career, and Dr. Brenda Blah looked into the mirror of life, and, this time, she saw her own worthwhile, courageous image smiling back at her.

A Story Yet to be Told

Valentina Frances Victory's story has yet to be written. She graduated from law school Summa Cum Laude, number one in her class, and threw herself headlong into politics, bringing the voice of reason and sanity to an otherwise insane profession and world. She built a political platform on the quest for world peace, and she quietly, but authoritatively, shut down the hypocrisy of any religious group that would condone violence and preemptive military strikes against another nation or group in the name of God. Valentina Frances promoted the sometimes unpopular universal message of seeing ourselves in the faces of all our neighbors across the globe. Or, as Valentina Frances would say:

> "We are children of God first, and
> a member of a religious organization second.
> We are citizens of the world first, and
> a member of some nation or tribe second."

And being a child of God first and a Christian second, Valentina Frances Victory would steadfastly proclaim a political reality rooted in the universality of the message of Jesus – a message that asks us to see ourselves in the plight of others:

"When I was hungry, you gave me to eat,
Thirsty you gave me to drink,
Imprisoned as an outcast, you visited me."

And, in the Sermon on the Mount:

"Blessed are the meek for they shall inherit the earth
Blessed are the peacemakers, for they shall be called
    Children of God
Blessed are the merciful for they shall obtain mercy."

In a country and a world so devoid of strong leaders, we look to you, Valentina Frances Victory, to secure our civil rights and liberties, to secure social justice for us, to secure the politics of reason and sanity, to follow the light of truth and justice, and to secure the victory of peace over war in any small way or, God willing, in a large way, worldwide. I know you will have the courage to speak the truth others need to hear. Your sincerity and your transparency will be refreshing, and will win you more votes than you lose, or, if not, so what? You will sleep like a baby in the bosom of the Lord knowing that you charted the correct course and did the right thing.

CHAPTER 7

Graduation... Going Forth

*You can't be all things
to all people
But you can be you...
to yourself*

The Moment

Let's live in the moment for a moment. Truly live in the moment for a moment. Congratulations Catholic Central's Class of 2008. You are about to graduate from one of the finest college preparatory schools in the world. For four long years, you have invested in life, you have marshaled your time, your energy, your discipline and your commitment. For four long years, you have withstood the rigors of emotional challenges, physical challenges and academic challenges. Now, in this moment in time, you stand here today basking in the glory of accomplishment and success. Treasure this moment. For you know how it feels to be a "winner" in the competition of life.

Catholic Central Class of 2008, please rise to your feet. President, Father Richard Elmer, Principal, Father Richard Ranalletti, Basilian

Priests, lay teaching staff, guidance staff, administrative staff, support staff, distinguished Guests, and especially family members and friends… from 1928, when Catholic Central High School first opened its doors, to 2008, I give you eighty years of Basilian tradition in education. I give you Catholic Central's Graduating Class of 2008.

Class of 2008 let's stay in the moment for another moment. You deserved that ovation. But, you didn't make it to this successful moment in time all on your own. You made it to this successful moment in time because of the love, support and encouragement you received from others. You made it to this very successful moment in time because of the emotional sacrifices, spiritual sacrifices and financial sacrifices of your parents, your family and the sacrifices of Catholic Central's fine staff. You are like an American, jet fighter pilot. You now know the thrill of "high flight," but only because you have a great support team that has helped put you in that stratosphere. Catholic Central's Class of 2008… please stand again and recognize and show your appreciation for your parents, your family members, your friends, and the Catholic Central family – whose dedication to you and whose sacrifice for you have made this very successful moment in time, a reality.

The Journey… Be Yourself

Let's leave the moment for a moment… and look to the future. After all, the "commencement" which we celebrate today means "to begin… " as today you begin your unrelenting march into the future. As you embark on that unrelenting march into the uncharted world of the future, I want to leave you with one message and one message only – a message that gives you your best option for a rewarding life.

The message – **"BE YOURSELF."** I repeat – **"BE YOURSELF."** That's it! So simply stated… but oh so very difficult to achieve –

especially at 18 years of age when you don't yet know who you are. And, if you don't know who you are, then it is impossible to "be yourself."

To "be yourself" is part paradox and part riddle. Some might say you will "find yourself" as you live your life. I don't agree. Catholic Central Class of 2008, you don't need to find yourself. You're not lost. You are right on target. You are right where you should be.

Some might say you will "discover yourself" as you journey through life. I don't agree. I say it is not possible to passively discover yourself in this world of overwhelming chaos. It is not possible to passively discover yourself in this world so influenced by greed and power. It is not possible to passively discover yourself in this world so fraught with violence and death... both the random violence of criminal acts and the organized violence of military and para military groups with partisans and foes on all sides shouting "God is on our side" as they kill and maim one another. No! In this world of chaos, temptation and distracting influence, the roll-of-dice, random chance of passively discovering yourself is at best slim, and, in reality, probably nonexistent.

But, today is your graduation and I bring you a gift – a gift that you can put in your pocket today, count on tomorrow and each day thereafter, and carry with you through life. The gift I give you is a key – a key that will unlock the paradox and solve the riddle of "being yourself." The key to "being yourself" is... to... literally "invent yourself." I repeat for emphasis... the key to "being yourself" is to literally "invent yourself." And, here's a three-step formula you can count on to invent yourself – a three step formula that will allow you to free yourself to truly "be yourself."

Step one: get in touch with the idealistic side of your nature. I'm not talking about power, position or wealth. I'm talking about "ideals." As President John F. Kennedy said in the 1960s: "A man or a woman may die, nations rise and fall, but an ideal lives on." You were exposed to ideals in your family life. You were exposed to ideals at Catholic Central. In large part that's why you were sent to Catholic Central. But, a word of caution. The ideals you get in touch with in step one of being yourself must, and I repeat for emphasis, must be the **ideals you choose**. No one can choose the ideals you get in touch with except you. You must choose the ideals – not your mother, not your father and not Catholic Central, even though the ideals you choose might, by happenstance, coincide with their ideals. If you do not choose your own ideals, you will never truly reach the goal of "being yourself." You will never truly free yourself to "be yourself."

Step two: After you get in touch with the idealistic side of your nature, look into the "mirror of life," and ask yourself what reflection you want to see looking back at you in the "mirror of life." What do you want to see in the "mirror of life" when you see yourself? What do you want the world to see when the world sees you?

When you realize what you want to see when you look into the "mirror of life" and what you want the world to see when the world sees you, then step three… you invent the idealist person you want to see looking back at you in the "mirror of life." You literally invent the person you want the world to see. You literally create yourself by creating the "impression" you want the world to see… painstakingly nurturing your emerging "impression" over the next ten, twenty or thirty years of life's marathon until that emerging impression becomes the reality of who your are. Now "being yourself" is automatic, as well as rewarding, because you have literally invented the person you are out of the potential you saw in yourself. Now it is easy to "be yourself" because you have invented yourself; you have authored yourself. You are your own book because you wrote each and every chapter of your book over the marathon of life.

One note of caution. As you nurture your emerging perception toward reality over the marathon of life, always, always, keep an open mind for discovering new truths… because "truth" frees us all. Always keep an open mind toward the opinions of others. With a mind open for new information and new truths, you will become the sculpture, ready to resculpture and subtly redefine who you are as your journey continues over life's marathon.

What is the bottom line of being yourself? Be proactive. Be self reliant. Don't wait for an invitation into the game of life. Don't wait for the coach to call your number. Don't wait for someone to ask you to dance with life. Acknowledge your vulnerability, but jump out over the chasm and reach for the brass ring. Don't be afraid to fail. And, if you fail, get up and reposition yourself for another go-round with that brass ring. Never let fear of failure stop you… for the road to success is paved with failure and… ultimately, the lessons learned from failure. And even if you fail, always remember, that at least: "you failed while daring greatly so that your place will never be among those cold and timid souls that know neither defeat nor victory." And, remember that winners fail without excuses… losers because of them.

The Greatest Generation

Let's leave the future for a moment… and look at the past for the past can provide you with a "context" for your own present and for the future that is waiting up ahead for you.

My parents' generation was known as the "Greatest Generation." The Greatest Generation was born into the flu pandemics of 1918 and 1919 that killed millions worldwide. Those of the Greatest Generation who survived the flu pandemics then found themselves thrust headlong into the "hopelessness" of the Dust Bowl and the "hopelessness" of the Great Depression that began in 1929, a year after Catholic Central first opened its doors – the Great Depression that was, ostensibly, triggered by the stock market crash of October 29, 1929 which, overnight, made paupers out of the rich and brought malnutrition and starvation to the huddling masses who stood in soup lines and around barrel fires to keep warm.

After enduring the long, bleak, hopeless years of the Dust Bowl and the Great Depression, the Greatest Generation then put their lives on hold and marched full speed ahead and, as the popular World War II song said, they "passed the ammunition" to stop the Arian, Nazi genocide, war machine of Adolph Hitler, and to respond to the Japanese preemptive, "sneak attack" air strike at Pearl Harbor.

That Greatest Generation gave us the teenage soldiers, your age, who stormed the beaches at Normandy, France in 1945 on D-Day enduring overwhelming losses of life. As the allied forces hit the beaches at Normandy on D-Day, young soldier warriors courageously huddled in fear in the launch boats praying with Chaplains, rosary beads in hand, knowing full well that at least half their numbers were doomed. Many of those young warrior soldiers were killed right in their launch boats from German artillery dug in on the bluffs above the beaches. Many left the boats and tried to wade ashore only to be cut down by enemy fire in the water or to drown, weighed down by their heavy equipment. Those who survived the initial surge onto the beaches at Normandy were unmercifully pinned down by German artillery raining hellfire down on them from the steep bluffs above. Hours and days passed by as young warrior soldiers your age fought to advance five yards, then ten yards, twenty yards, and on toward the base of the bluffs. Those young heroes, fighting for days in the salt air stench of death and suffering, finally ascended the bluffs and routed the Germans, and then fought their way through the French countryside and victoriously entered Paris, kissed the young Parisian ladies, liberated France, and then put the face of war back on, and fought on to Germany to defeat the Nazi war machine and celebrate VE Day – Victory in Europe.

A half a world away, on a completely separate front, the Greatest Generation also gave their all to beat back the preemptive, "sneak-attack" airstrike of the Japanese at Pearl Harbor. On the decks of battleships and carriers, the Greatest Generation launched fighter planes and fought off kamikaze pilots who were sentenced by the Japanese emperor, Hirohito, to fly missions of mass suicide against the American Navy. That greatly outnumbered Greatest Generation left their blood in the hot, humid South Pacific Islands of the Philippines during the "Bataan death march," and as they fought pitched battles in hell itself in places named Guadalcanal, Midway, Okinawa, and Iwo Jima, finally celebrating VJ Day – Victory in Japan – and witnessing the unconditional surrender of the Japanese Emperor, Hirohito, and his empire.

That Greatest Generation, after providing a safer world for my generation, then returned home and raised families and sent their children to schools like "Salesian" housed in the original Catholic Central building at Harper and Woodward, "Cathedral," housed in the second Catholic Central building at Belmont and Woodward and "Catholic Central of Detroit" at 6565 West Outer Drive in Northwest Detroit – where my father, in 1957 on the athletic fields behind the school, paid Father Gerard French his long overdue 1930 tuition from my father's depression era Sophomore year at Catholic Central – my father's last year of formal high school education.

Children of the Greatest Generation

Eventually, my generation, "The Children of the Greatest Generation," took our place on the front lines of life. Borrowing a page from the woman's suffrage movement where women strenuously protested and fought for the right to vote, and borrowing a page from American workers who gave their all to organize labor unions for fair wages and safe working conditions, my generation took to the streets and protested for civil rights for all Americans and protested against injustice in America. The ideal was peaceful, **"non violent"** protest. We followed the peaceful "non violent" protest philosophy of Jesus of Nazareth and the early Christians. We followed the peaceful "non violent" protest philosophy of India's great statesman, Mahatma Gandhi, and the great American poet, Henry David Thoreau, and the great Baptist minister, Dr. Martin Luther King, and others. Although violence sometimes found its way into peaceful protest, those in-the-know knew that violence of any kind had to be denounced whether it was violence by protestors or the reactionary violence of white segregationists or the violence of overzealous law enforcement agents. Violence ultimately wins only one thing – more violence.

Like the founding patriots of our county, my generation was influenced by the English philosopher John Locke's *Social Contract* with its "age of enlightenment" philosophy that all rights and powers not given to the government remain the rights and powers of "We the People," free from interference by our government. Although we renounced violence in our social protests, we stood by the principles of America's founding fathers that, as true patriots, "We the People" in a true Democracy were obligated to protest against our own government's hypocrisy and injustice because, like America's founders, we intuitively knew "bad things happen when good people remain silent." We brought our founding father's philosophy to the streets of America for all to see because we also intuitively knew that the more robust the ideological debate in the American market place of ideas, the greater the chance America had to make the right decisions, follow the right path, and take the right course of action.

Where we saw injustice and hypocrisy, "We the People" of my generation held a mirror up to the face of America and demanded change. America's 200-year-old political promise set forth in the Declaration of Independence forcefully proclaimed that it was "self evident" that "all men are born equal." Yet in the 1950s and the 1960s of my youth, the right of "We the People" to vote was taken away from millions of American citizens, mostly black and mostly the poor and uneducated, because those American citizens could not afford to pay a poll tax to vote or because those American citizens couldn't pass a literacy test as a prerequisite to casting their vote. With President John F. Kennedy and later President Lyndon Johnson, the Children of the Greatest Generation changed that.

Our protests also opened up the door of public accommodations of restaurants, hotels, and public parks to all Americans regardless of race, color or creed. The Children of the Greatest Generation, derisively called "Peaceniks" (actually a compliment) also protested against the American war machine to make it accountable to "We the People." As Children of the Greatest Generation, we never lost sight of the fact that we protested against the bellicose attitude of our older generation leaders and never against those poor, young souls that were making the soldiers' sacrifice on the frozen tundra of Korea or in the jungles of Vietnam.

And, perhaps, the greatest legacy of the Children of the Greatest Generation... after fifty years living in the shadow of a nuclear holocaust, we won the "Cold War" against communist Russia without bloodshed. I repeat for emphasis **without bloodshed**. For fifty years of the "Cold War," Communist Russia and America stared down the barrel of annihilation at one another (especially during the "Cuban Missile Crisis"), each with their fingertips on doomsday weapons. Finally, Communist Russia blinked, as it was financially bankrupted by the military arms race. Communist Russia economically self destructed, and America won the fifty year old "cold war" without firing a single shot. The Berlin wall, the symbol of the cold war and the symbol of communism, which was put up in the summer of 1961 when I graduated from Catholic Central, was torn down in 1989. In your own lifetime, Class of 2008, the decaying symbol of oppression, totalitarianism and communism, the Berlin Wall, was torn down without a single American casualty.

Your Turn

Now it's time for your generation to be heard. Your time has come. Get in touch with the idealistic side of your nature and invent yourself over the next ten, twenty, thirty years of life's marathon, and keep an open mind and resculpture yourselves as new truths emerge in your field of vision. Invent and create the image of yourself that you want to see and the image you want the world to see when they look at you. Go forth, you young, tough, courageous Catholic Central Graduates of 2008 and "be yourself," and, over the marathon of life, leave your footprints and your ideals in our world so that the generation that follows you can find their way.

As the great Irish, Capuchin Priest, Father Solanus Casey, Detroit's "Porter of St. Bonaventure," said:

"Do not pray for easy lives;
Pray to be strong.
Do not pray for tasks equal to your
    power;
Pray for powers equal to your tasks
Then the doing of your life's work shall
    be no miracle;
You shall be the miracle."

Fr. Solanus Casey
"Porter of St. Bonaventure"

Epilogue

As the children of the Greatest Generation left high school heading out into a larger world, they saw mile marker five in the twenty-six mile marathon of life, and they heard the universe echo back the words of Dr. Nathan Goodfellow spoken eighteen years earlier on the date of their birth:

> "The individual uniqueness of each infant must be recognized and appreciated, a uniqueness which must be turned loose into the world to find its own star, its own course, its own dream, and fulfill its own destiny, So sit back and watch patiently for years and decades as each child's own unique gifts magically unfold over life's marathon."

WE DANCED WITH LIFE... WITH FLAIR

WE DANCED WITH LIFE... WITH HEART

BOOK II
We Danced With Life

THE MENTALITY... "LET'S GET IT ON"
For some... not all... nothing in this world equals "head to head," "face to face," "mano a mano" challenges amongst brave-hearted competitors of life who roll the dice and dare to be great... if only for a quickly fading, perhaps, forgotten moment in time.

THE ARENAS
"We Danced With Life" follows the lives and times of these brave-hearted competitors who competed mightily on the Detroit sandlots, in the Major Leagues, in the National Football League, in the fields of Art, Medicine, Psychology, Psychiatry, Politics and in the whacked-out world of Bar Brawlers and professional Prize Fighters and in the high-stakes battles between courtroom gladiators who slug it out in the Halls of Justice in a 'war of words'... where the agile, lightning-quick reflexes of the articulate shine while the inarticulate stumble and descend into obscurity along with their cause."

THE JOURNEY
Join us for a journey into the daring, and, often comical, world of "mano a mano."

CHAPTER 8

Al "The Kid" Moran...
Major League Ballplayer

S ome from the Hood became Major League ballplayers...
like **AL "SWIVEL HIPS" MORAN**.

If you like drama, you'll like the story of our beloved friend, Al Moran – one of the Hood's gifted athletes. The story begins on December 5, 1938. Richard Alan Moran is the first of eight children born to Edward Moran and his lovely Irish bride Rosemary McMichael Moran. Into this crazy world of diverse talents, Al inherits special physical gifts of balance, agility, quickness and great hand-eye coordination, and, best of all, an ever present, but partially subdued, smile just waiting for an excuse to bubble over into full-blown laughter.

Let me take you back to the mid-1950s in Detroit. As a fourth grader, I sit on a snow bank at the edge of a make-shift ice pond at Southfield and Outer Drive in Northwest Detroit, waiting my turn to play, as the seventh and eighth graders dominate the hockey rink while the skinny Irish kid, Al Moran, dominates the seventh and eighth graders – **a man among boys.**

Al Moran plays out his time as a grade-schooler in Northwest Detroit at St. Scholastica School. My friends, John Dibella, Jack Gilbert, Frank Demers, and I watch the skinny Irish kid, and we marvel at his athletic gifts. In between confessions and communion, Father Livius showcased Al's talents as a shortstop on the baseball team. In between phonics, reading, spelling and arithmetic, Coach Frank Bowler showcased Al's talents as a halfback on the seventh and eighth grade CYO football team. With teammates Danny Hedberg, Bob Dacoff, Brooks Patterson, Steve Patterson, Bob Lebo, Tom Girard, Tom Peligrin, Bunns Monroe, Rudy Seichter and others, the St. Scholastica Ravens dominated. Al set the CYO scoring record in 1952 – a record that remains unbroken today, more than fifty years later:

> "Al Moran swivel-hipped merchant... has scampered to fourteen touchdowns and seven extra points for ninety-one points in three games."
>
> *Detroit Free Press* October 9, 1952

Life Moves On

Life moves on for Al Moran. Parochial grade school education turns into high school, and, in the Fall of 1953, the reddish-complected, skinny Irish kid with the **Norman Rockwell poster boy looks** joins the tradition laden Catholic Central Shamrocks. New challenges academically. New challenges athletically. In the Fall of 1954, as a sixth grader, I sit huddled in field-level seats with my mother, father and sisters at Briggs Stadium (later Tiger Stadium) – everybody sick with the flu. We watch in awe as Coach Johnny Hackett's Catholic Central Shamrock machine runs the gauntlet against Father Flannigan's Boystown Cowboys from Nebraska. Shamrock's Don Muntz, Bob

Russo, Bob Handloser, Don Rambiesa, Tom King, Leonard Else, Ray Chomicz, Tom Jozwiak, Dan Collins, Art Gariepy, Ed Ryder and others, and, in their midst, 15-year-old sophomore, Al Moran, starting in the defensive backfield – now a boy among men… but only for a moment.

Time moves on and head coach Johnny Hackett relinquishes the reins to new head coach, Irish Bill Foley, the wild man with the glass eye and the hard nosed enthusiasm. In the mid-1950s, the Shamrocks travel to Rochester, New York to play Aquinas, to Chicago to play Mt. Carmel, to Dayton, Ohio to play Chaminad and just down the road to the University of Detroit Stadium to play their toughest opponent of all, the Rustics of St. Marys of Redford, led by future NFL All Pro, local boy, Fred Arbanas. As a 13-year-old, my Father positions me at the entrance gate to U of D Stadium, close enough to touch number 77, Catholic Central's Al Moran, and close enough to look into the eyes of big, bad Fred Arbanas of St. Marys. I desperately want into the action, but I'm still a 13-year-old boy among men. My time will come. Al Moran's time is now.

Seasons fly by. Years fly by. In one year, Al earns four letters at Catholic Central – football, basketball, hockey and baseball. In his senior, year Al scores seventeen touchdowns on his way to an All State selection. In baseball, under coach Father Joe Miller, Al is selected as a National Hearst All Star, and plays in the high school All Star game at the Polo Grounds in New York City. Al's natural gifts, exploits and courage have caught the attention of the college football coaches and professional baseball scouts everywhere.

Life moves on again for 18-year-old Al Moran. From a Catholic Central Shamrock to Michigan State Spartan football player – full scholarship. In the Fall of 1957, Al joins the Michigan State legends, Athletic Director Biggie Munn and Coach Duffy Daugherty ("Dancing is a contact sport; football is a collision sport"). Those were glory days for the Spartans who were still reveling in their 1956 Rose Bowl victory over UCLA – 17 to 14 on Dave Kowalczyk's last minute field goal and their 1954 Rose Bowl victory over UCLA on the strength of Michigan State's "pony backfield." Al Moran, the skinny Irish kid from Northwest Detroit, is slotted to carry on the tradition of the Spartan's **but… but… wait** – professional baseball scouts lurking behind the scenes were advancing with huge bonus offers tempting Al back to his first love – **BASEBALL.**

Professional Baseball

Detroit multi-sport star, Al Moran, signs with the Boston Red Sox for (at that time) one of the largest bonuses ever paid to a "bonus baby." In the era before expansion baseball, in the era before the talent pool was watered down by numerous new major league franchises, the skinny Irish kid from Northwest Detroit starts out with high expectations playing high minor league ball with the Memphis Chicks in double A, going five for five in his first game. But, professional sports is a shell game that sets up hopeful, young athletes for broken hearts by giving them just enough talent and success to keep the dream alive, and keep them coming back for "just one more year"… each and every year.

After coming out of the chute like a potential Hall of Famer, Al levels off and gets demoted to the low minor leagues, but Al quietly and perseveringly goes about the business of learning his craft as a professional ballplayer. Al pays his dues with monotonous, endless bus trips, playing for such teams as Allentown, Pennsylvania, the Minneapolis Millers, Raleigh North Carolina, Dallas Texas and Vancouver – playing side by side with future major leaguers Dick Radatz, Carl Yastrzemski, Jake Gibbs, Bill Monbouquet, Jim Fregosi, Galen Sisco, and nameless other forgotten souls whose dreams of a big league career die a slow, frustrating death… as they eventually walk away to face an uncertain future without the benefit of an education.

Casey Stengel

New York Mets manager and baseball legend, Casey Stengel, gives now-23-year-old Kid Moran the break he has been looking for since 1957. In the Spring of 1962, as a non-roster invitee to the big league camp, Al Moran wins the starting shortstop position for Casey Stengel's "Amazin' Mets."

Yogi Berra and Casey Stengel "Casey… What The Hell We Talking About?"

Casey Stengel? Need you ask? After eight years of Dominican nuns at St. Scholastica, and, after four years of Basilian priests at Catholic Central, both driving home the complex structure and use of the English language, Al must have been as cross-eyed as the "Aflack Duck" when he first heard manager Casey Stengel's "conversation by obfuscation." When it came to the spoken language, Casey was a master of linguistic disaster. He could stupefy and bewilder the most proficient interpreters of double-speak. Casey was the originator of the Yogi Berra malapropism method of communication – "if you come to a fork in the road, take it" or "a verbal contract is not worth the paper it's written on" or, "if you think you're going to hit a double play, strike out" or "if you fall in love with a homeless woman, don't move in with her." I'm sure Casey's verbal instruction to Kid Moran didn't help the Kid's focus at the bat or in the field. This was the same Casey Stengel who undertook the impossible task of teaching home run slugger, Marv Throneberry, the art of catching a fly ball. With Throneberry standing alongside the master in left field, 70-year-old Casey was showing Marv how to catch fly balls. When Casey got hit in the head by successive fly balls that bounced off Casey's glove and noggin, an embarrassed and enraged Casey screamed at the clueless Throneberry: "You got left field so screwed up, no one can play it."

Surviving "Bullet Bob" Gibson

The skinny Irish kid from Northwest Detroit sidles up behind the batting cage at Busch Stadium in St. Louis, Missouri watching future Hall of Famer Stan "The Man" Musial taking batting practice.

"Stan the Man" finishes his cuts, walks behind the batting cage, and sticks out his hand to Al – "Hello, I'm Stan Musial" says the legend. After recovering his senses, Al reflects on what a cordial group these big leaguers are.

Game time temperature 96 degrees. Humidity 90 percent. What else did you expect in St. Louis, Missouri in the summer? Starting pitcher for St. Louis, "Bullet Bob" Gibson, the intimidator's intimidator, with the ninety-eight mile per hour fast ball – another legend and certainly another cordial human being. **RIGHT?... WRONG!!!**

Second inning. Scoreless tie. "Bullet Bob" Gibson finishes his last warm up throw. The St. Louis catcher throws a strike to second, and the ball goes around the horn and back to Gibson again. "Batter up" barks the ump, and the skinny Irish kid, Al Moran, emotionally steps off his porch in Northwest Detroit and into the batters box at Busch Stadium in front of 30,000 screaming fans. Gibson winds and delivers. **"LOOK OUT!"** The Kid is down, flat down – laying in the dirt at home plate. Was he hit?... No! Just ball one. Gibson purposely threw his ninety-eight mile per hour fast ball at the Kid's head, and missed... by an inch. One more inch – end of career and a permanent trip to life's disabled list. Gibson yells in to Kid Moran: "If you want to dig in against me, I'll give you something to think about" – "Yea," Kid Moran says to himself: "like whether I want to live or die." So much for cordiality. Welcome to the big leagues kid. Let's see what you're made of. In a defining moment of **"TO BE OR NOT TO BE"** a major leaguer, Al draws upon all the courage he learned as a kid growing up in Northwest Detroit, gets up, dusts himself off and steps back into the lion's den with 30,000 fans screaming for his blood. Kid Moran survives St. Louis.

But, Bullet Bob Gibson isn't the only wild man Al and his teammates must face on this road trip. Al and his teammates, Duke Snider, Gil Hodges, Jimmy Piersal, Ron Hunt, Roger Craig and the rest will criss-cross the country, and will face Johnny Padres, Sandy Koufax, Don Drysdale, Juan Marichal, Joe Nuxall and Jim Bunning. 0 for 4? "Hell, that ain't nuthin" – facing those flame throwers a kid could go for the "0 for the whole road trip."

Surviving Roberto Clemente

Kid Moran sizzles a one hop single to right field, takes a wide turn and bluffs to second as Pittsburgh's future Hall of Fame right fielder, Roberto Clemente, comes up with the ball, looks towards second, and throws a bullet to first behind Kid Moran, picking the Kid off first base from right field. The roar of the crowd wakes up Mets Manager, Casey Stengel, and, upon learning the news that the Kid was challenging Clemente's legendary throwing arm, Casey goes ballistic. Who the hell is this skinny, Irish kid rookie to challenge the strongest arm in all of baseball? Unbelievably, Clemente does it again to Kid Moran in the same game, after which Al sheepishly takes his place in Stengel's doghouse for a week of atonement on the bench.

Crafty Lefthander Warren Spahn

Crafty left handed veteran, Warren Spahn, on the mound for Milwaukee – winner of 363 major league games over a twenty year career from 1946 to 1965, and future Hall of Fame shoo in. The skinny Irish kid from Northwest Detroit takes Spahn deep into the count. Spahn tries to cross the Kid up with a screwball on a 3-2 count. Kid Moran drives the ball hard toward the right field stands. In the words of the old Detroit Tiger announcer, Van Patrick, "GOING, GOING, GONE." In the words of the Detroit legendary announcer Ernie Harwell, "LONG GONE!" In modern parlance, "GOODBYE BASEBALL." Al hits the facing of the upper deck, and the ball bounces back onto the playing field. As Al rounds the bases with his first major league home run, Milwaukee's outfielder Hank Aaron (the most prolific pre-steroid home run hitter in the history of baseball, and the only player to hit more home runs than the legendary Babe Ruth – before the steroid juice killed statistics), retrieves the ball and delivers it to Al – a memento of his first home run.

Fireballer Sandy Koufax

Sandy Koufax, one of the most dominating left handers in the history

Jim Hickman, Al Moran and "Duke" Snider 1962

of baseball, gets the start for the Los Angeles Dodgers in Chaves Ravine ballpark. Koufax takes his no hitter into the seventh inning. Just staying alive, Kid Moran fouls off the best Koufax has to offer. A classic duel. The Jewish super star pitching against the skinny, Irish Catholic from Northwest Detroit. Kid Moran hangs tough, but he barely stays alive at the plate. This day obviously belongs to Koufax –

as most days do – **RIGHT?... WRONG!!!** Kid Moran drills a single to right and Koufax's "No hitter" total will forever remain one less than it would have been... thanks to the skinny, Irish kid from the Northwest Detroit Hood.

The "Say Hey" Kid

Last day of a grueling season at the Polo Grounds in New York. San Francisco Giant, Willie the "Say Hey" Kid Mays, is locked in a death grip, struggle for the batting title with Pittsburgh's All Star shortstop, Dick Groat. On the last day of the season, only fractions of decimal points separate Mays and Groat. In the ninth inning, Mays' digs in for his last at bat of the season. A base hit guarantees the National League batting title for Willie. Willie attacks a diving curve ball on the inside part of the plate driving a shot into the hole between third and short. The skinny Irish kid, Al Moran, at shortstop, darts into the hole like a flash, and (with those same "swivel hips" first described in a 1952 *Free Press* article) backhands the ball, plants, swivels, and fires a bullet to first. A bang-bang play, "YOU'RE OUT!" screams the first base umpire, and Willie Mays wins one less batting championship in his legendary Hall of Fame career... thanks to the skinny, Irish kid from Northwest Detroit.

Yogi Challenges God

The governor's game – a yearly exhibition game between the American League Yankees and the National League New York Mets. Mets center fielder, Jimmy "Fear Strikes Out" Piersal, steps up to the plate, and, in his usual fashion, makes the sign of the cross. Yogi Berra, the Yankee's future Hall of Fame catcher, calls time-out, steps out of his crouch, steps toward the mound, and then wheels around, now facing Jimmy Piersal. Yogi makes the sign of the cross in front of Piersal asking: "Who's God gonna favor now, Jimmy?" The answer… God's going to favor Kid Moran because God feels sorry for an Irishman.

The Kid in Us

Kid Moran returned to Northwest Detroit after his big league career, and coached football at his Alma Mater, St. Scholastica Grade School. Among others, he taught the fundamentals of football to Greg Marx, another Catholic Central legend who was an All American at Notre Dame, and drafted in the first round by the Atlanta Falcons. Later, Al rejoined the Shamrocks, and taught the fundamentals of baseball at Catholic Central. Coach John Salter and Al Moran brought home state baseball championships to Catholic Central in 1987 and in 1999. Kid Moran's circle is complete: from St. Scholastica to Catholic Central to Michigan State, to the minor leagues, to the major leagues, and then back to his roots at St. Scholastica and Catholic Central.

1961 Champs
St. Scholastica Seventh and Eighth Grade
Team Coached by Al Moran (center top row)

Greg Marx

Come with me to the baseball diamond at Catholic Central. At the end of the day, the dust from the diamond begins to settle, and we see that familiar face, red hair now flecked with gray, but that same reddish complexion, that same toothy grin and that same half-subdued smile always waiting for any excuse to bubble over into full blown laughter. The skinny Irishman, dignified in age and hobbled by a gimpy knee, is just wrapping up another baseball practice, dragging a bat bag across the shortstop position he once played with such enthusiasm. Some might say that Kid Moran has settled into restive retirement, nurtured by past glories. But, they would be wrong. Our beloved, gifted athlete, Al Moran, has just reached the high point in his life and in his career as he gives to each new generation the joy and exhilaration of no-holds-barred competition. Our very competitive, beloved Irish champion, Kid Moran, has gone from the big leagues of baseball to the league of ultimate influence – guiding and teaching young Catholic Central athletes about the intricacies of baseball, the tenacity of competition and the necessity of team work.

Al Moran was not just a gifted athlete. Al is a spiritual leader for all of us. Whatever talents God gave to Al, he has utilized those talents to their fullest. His legacy for us is his joyful spirit, his devilish grin, his contagious sense of humor and his non-judgmental acceptance of others. Today, in our graying years, Kid Al Moran is a reminder of the kid that used to live in all of us. Cherish Kid Al Moran and cherish the kid in yourself.

CHAPTER 9

Detroit Sandlots...
To The Big Leagues

No one, except a baseball player, can truly appreciate how difficult and challenging the game of baseball is, and how tenuous a grip a ballplayer has on the art of catching, throwing and hitting a baseball. One day, for inexplicable reasons, you just have it, while, the very next day, for the same, inexplicable reasons, you don't.

It's a long way from sandlot baseball for 18-year-olds to the major leagues. In biblical terms: "many are called but few are chosen." It is extremely rare that a high school kid is able to make the long jump from the sandlots directly to the big leagues, but that's what Al "the Kid" Kaline did when he was signed off the Baltimore sandlots at age 18 in the early 1950s by Detroit Tiger super scout Ed Katalinas, who lived in our Northwest Detroit Hood. As an 18-year-old, Kaline played right field for the Tigers for much of the season. As a 19-year-old in 1955, Kaline won the American League batting championship, and, after a long, productive career, all with the Detroit Tigers, Kaline rose to a peak salary of an-unheard-of $100,000 a year, and became a shoo-in for the Hall of Fame on the first ballot. But, for the rest, it's a long, hard journey from the sandlots to the big leagues – a journey that only a handful out of millions of aspiring ballplayers ever make.

Aside from girls, baseball was my first big challenge in life. I remember when I was 13, striking out in my first twenty times at bat. But, I refused to walk away. The coaches, feeling my frustration, suggested I choke up on the bat and separate my hands like Detroit Tiger Hall of Famer, Ty Cobb (the "Georgia Peach"), or like "Wee Willie" Keeler, who "hit 'em where they ain't." But, my own father counseled against that short, punch stroke, telling me I had a beautiful arcing swing like Al Kaline so: "just keep swinging and you'll catch up to the ball eventually" – my Father's usual approach of sacrificing short term gain for long term benefit. Despite my early failure, I would not take "no" for an answer.

I intensely studied the art of hitting a baseball, year-round, for almost a decade, swinging at tennis balls thrown to me by my Father

Father Fred Lauck Age 17
1933

during the winter months in Greenview Park across the street from my home at 18627 Curtis in Detroit, and also swinging a weighted, training bat year-round in my unfinished, cinder block basement, hitting imaginary fastballs, curveballs and change-ups in all parts of the strike-zone while listening to radio D.J.s: "Rockin Robin," "Jack the Bell Boy," Mickey Shorr and Lee Allen – "On the horn." Finally, after years of perseverance, I was good enough to play in the American Legion All Star Game in Tiger Stadium in 1960 as a 17-year-old, driving a shot to the left field wall. The next year, 1961, as an 18-year-old, I played for Brown Insulation and edged out my teammate, former Detroit Tiger, Willie "Superman" Horton, for the Class D, Detroit Amateur

Baseball Federation Batting Championship – the same six-team league where many future major leaguers competed . . . first and  foremost my teammate, Detroit Tiger Willie Horton, a clutch hitting, power hitter, who was on the Tigers 1968 World Championship team. Willie claimed his place in baseball folklore in the 1968 World Series when he "emotionally" catapulted the Tigers to the 1968 World Championship. Hopelessly down 3 games to 1, the Tigers faced elimination in game five. St. Louis was on the attack in game five, and poised to win it all when Willie stopped a Cardinal's rally by firing a bullet from left field to home plate to throw out St. Louis Cardinal speedster and base stealing phenom, Lou Brock. Willie's defensive gem lit an emotional fuse in the Tigers, and they rallied from that 3 game to 1 deficit to win the 1968 World Championship. Willie Horton was one of the most loved professional athletes ever in Detroit. Willie's bronze statue now decorates the Detroit Tiger's new "Comerica" ballpark.

Willie "Superman" Horton

As a "Brown Insulation" teammate of Willie Horton in the 18-year-old sandlot leagues in 1961, I can tell you first hand that nobody (I repeat nobody) hit them harder or farther than Willie "Superman" Horton. As a 16-year-old sophomore for Northwestern High School, Willie hit an opposite field home run to the upper deck right field bleachers in Tiger Stadium (with a wooden bat) in the 1959 Public School championship game. Two years later, as an 18-year-old, playing in the Detroit sandlots, Willie hit one even further off my former Catholic Central teammate, Vince Grainor.

In the summer of 1961, Vince was pitching for K.B. Shell, and Willie and I were playing for Brown Insulation. As Vince's K.B. Shell team warmed up, Vince told me he was going to strike out both

Willie and me with his "dark one." In the first inning, I was in on the "on deck" circle while Willie dug in against Vince. Willie picked up Vince's first "dark one" and launched one for the ages. Vince's "dark one" not only flew over the left field fence, but it flew over the

Vince Grainor 1961 Catholic Central Master of the Disappearing "Dark One"

roadway, over the Kelsey Hayes parking lot, over all of the cars in the parking lot, over the trees, over the Cuckoo's Nest and into the wall of the Kelsey Hayes factory. If it wasn't for the building ricocheting Willie's blast back into the parking lot, Willie would have launched America's first satellite.

But, as Willie and I both know from personal experience . . . hitting a baseball is a difficult and tenuous art. One day you unconsciously have it, the next day you don't. Willie proved that point a few days after he launched his satellite shot off Vince Grainor when, at Northwestern diamond number one with a short left field porch onto Grand River Avenue, Willie struck out swinging, four times on fastballs by the then 18-year-old left handed flame-thrower, Larry Jaster, from Midland, Michigan.

Larry Jaster St. Louis Cardinals

Larry Jaster made it to the Big Leagues, and was brought in from the St. Louis Cardinals bullpen to pitch against the Detroit Tigers in the 1968 World Series game six, pitching to three batters without getting anyone out, giving up a grand slam home run to Tiger's outfielder Jim Northrup. But, Larry Jaster had his major league success. When Jaster first came up to the big leagues in 1965, he pitched three complete game victories in his first three starts. In 1966, Jaster won eleven games and shut out the pennant-bound Dodgers five times that season.

Also playing on my Brown Insulation sandlot team in the Summer of 1961 was our shortstop, Rich Billings, who graduated from Trenton High School, played at Michigan State, and was then drafted by the Washington Senators in the twenty-fifth round in 1965. Billings made it to the big leagues as a catcher for the Washington Senators in 1968, and later played for the Texas Rangers under manager Ted Williams, the "Splendid Splinter," – baseball's greatest natural hitter. Billings finished his career in 1975 with the St. Louis Cardinals – a lifetime .227 hitter.

One of the most overlooked, least remembered and most talented of my sandlot contemporaries was Alex Johnson. Alex was Willie

Alex Johnson
California Angels

Horton's classmate at Northwestern High School. He played for "Walleys" in the Class D Federation League in the Summer of 1961, and signed with Philadelphia the same year. Alex played for thirteen years in the big leagues, and capped his career by winning the American League batting championship in 1970 with a .329 average for the California Angels.

Denny McLain
31 Game Winner

Also playing in the same sandlot leagues in Detroit was Bill Freehan, Tiger All Star catcher, who played with Willie Horton on the Detroit Tigers 1968 World Championship team. That was one of the best World Series ever. Hopelessly down three games to one, Detroit came back to win it, beating St. Louis' "Bullet Bob" Gibson in the seventh game of the World Series in St Louis – the year "Bullet Bob" Gibson's ERA was 1.12 per game. In that 1968 World Series, Tigers thirty-one game winner, "Bad Boy" Denny McLain, flopped while crafty, sinker-baller, Mickey Lolich, won three of the Tigers' four victories, including his victory over "Bullet Bob" Gibson in game seven of the World Series in St. Louis to bring the World Championship to Detroit.

Speaking of "Bad Boy" convict, Denny McLain... who would have guessed then in the fall of 1968, while I was listening to the Tigers win the World Series and plowing through my senior year in law school that one day, in 1990, I would be in a courtroom putting Denny McLain through a rigorous and necessary cross examination. My Canadian client, Leonard Martin, an over-the-road truck driver, was charged with manslaughter in the death of McLain's daughter, Kristen, in a horrific, fiery crash on westbound M-59 just east of Bogie Lake Road in Highland Township. McLain, having already served his prison term number one for drug trafficking, deftly landed back on his feet as a star radio talk show host on WXYZ. McLain, true to his usual devious form, tried to hijack the State Police's accident investigation by hiring his own, vigilante investigative team, who found witnesses that provided false testimony that could have convicted an innocent man. Rigorous preparation uncovered the false testimony, and my innocent, Canadian truck driver client, Leonard Martin, walked free – no thanks to Denny McLain's larger than life ego, and his attack broadcasts against me and my client on his WXYZ radio talk show. But Denny couldn't hold on to his radio show, and he was soon back in prison again – this time for looting the employee pension fund of a meat packing company he bought in Northern Michigan.

Back to the sandlots. Honorable mention goes to Larry Jaster's 18-year-old teammate from Livonia, Greg Bolo, who played for Al "Favros" Detroit sandlot team in the Summer of 1961 and who threw harder than anyone and intimidated everyone. Bolo signed with Cleveland, but never made a big impact. And, how about their teammate, shortstop Russ Nelson, from Redford Union High School. Nelson had the fielding skills of a big league shortstop at age 18. He signed, but never made it to "The Show." Same for my teammate and third baseman Stan Jaciuk, one of many Jaciuk brothers from the Downriver area of Detroit. My teammate, Wes Danyo, a great kid from Melvindale High School, a hard-scrabble suburb of Detroit, was an excellent pitcher, but he drove into a train Downriver one night, and that was the end of him. Another one of my Brown Insulation teammates, pitcher Stan Krogulecki, from St. Mary's of Orchard Lake High School, was outstanding, but he hung up the spikes and became a priest. Stan was "The Man."

But, along with Willie "Superman" Horton, my other favorite contemporary was the multi-talented John Paciorek from St. Ladislaus

**John Paciorek
Houston Colt .45s**

**Tom Paciorek
Chicago White Sox**

High School in Hamtramck. John Paciorek came up to the big leagues with the Houston Colt .45s, (now the Astros) on September 29, 1963 at age 20. John had three at bats and three hits, got hurt and never played again, retiring with a perfect 1.000 batting average. John Paciorek could have been a professional athlete in any sport, or a movie star, matinee idol or even a diplomat. John had all the gifts, including a great sense of kindness and humility. John's younger brother, Tom Paciorek, played football with me in 1964 at the University of Detroit. When U of D dropped football in 1964, Tom transferred to the University of Houston, becoming an All-American defensive back. Tom was drafted by baseball's Los Angeles Dodgers in the fifth round in 1968, and played for six teams over an eighteen-year big league career, finishing with a very respectable .282 lifetime batting average. Tom Paciorek later became a baseball color analyst for the Chicago White Sox. The youngest brother, Jim Paciorek, also made it to the big leagues with the Milwaukee Brewers and finished his career in Japan. Hey, what did Momma Paciorek feed those kids? I wish I would have been invited over for dinner.

There were many other major leaguers who came out of the Detroit Hood both before and after my time: Highland Park's Billy Pierce, who was traded by Detroit to the Chicago White Sox in the 1950s where he became the pitching ace of Chicago's staff; Art Houtteman and John McHale from my Detroit Catholic Central High School who both played for the Detroit Tigers; John Maybury from Northwestern High School who played first base for the Kansas City Royals in the 1980s and whose son is now in the big leagues; Ted Simmons, a switch-hitting, All-Star catcher out of Southfield High School, who caught numerous years for the St. Louis Cardinals; Jim Essian out of St. Martin's High School (one of thirteen children), who signed with Philadelphia in 1969, and who was a big league catcher for twelve seasons, finishing with a .244 lifetime average when he retired in 1984, later managing the Chicago Cubs for a year.

One day when Jimmy Essian was catching, strongman Reggie Jackson got hit by the pitch and charged the mound. Jimmy Essian's role was to protect his pitcher, but he wasn't quick enough to get out in front of a hard-charging Reggie, so Essian did the only thing he could. He jumped on Reggie's back, and sixty feet six inches later, Reggie Jackson arrived at the mound and pummeled Essian's pitcher while Essian was still on his back – "Thanks for the ride, Reggie." But, as everyone knows, Jimmy's sister, Barbara Essian, was the real star of the Essian family. And hats off to their Armenian father, Sarkis Essian, who tried to teach me the art of drinking "Mustika" and "talking to God." Hey, with thirteen kids, I think it makes sense to drink "Mustika," and maybe see if you can talk to God. I gave it my best try, but I couldn't quite get to that Armenian "vision quest." I got lost in the haze of alcohol, and the patriarch, Mr. Essian, left me behind, hopelessly lost in the fog while he was (as he claimed) "talking to God." And, who am I to doubt him. But, still, it was good to see him come back from his sojourn with God, safe, if not sound.

Jimmy Essian   **Barbara Essian**   **Sarkis Essian**

Also out of Catholic Central High School, there was Chris "Popeye" Sabo who played for Cincinnati and made an All Star Game (quick hands with the bat), and Frank Tanana, a Catholic Central standout athlete and left handed fireballer, who pitched for the California Angels in the mid-1970s when the Angels had the best one-two punch, pitching staffs in all of baseball with Frank Tanana bringing it to you from the left side and his teammate, Nolan "Heat" Ryan, bringing it to you from the right side on back to back days. Frank Tanana finished his outstanding career with the Detroit Tigers. His father, a member of the Greatest Generation, out of St. Andrews High School in Detroit, and a Detroit cop, is considered by many of his Greatest Generation peers to be the best athlete ever to come out of the City of Detroit. But, for my money, that "best-ever"-athlete-to-come-out-of-Detroit, distinction must go to Dave Debusschere of Austin High School and the University of Detroit, who pitched for the Chicago White Sox in the summer and played in the NBA (National Basketball Association) in the winter.

This baseball journey cannot end without an honorable mention to my Catholic Central teammate, Bill Collins. Bill was a left handed pitcher whose Greatest Generation father owned Collins Irish Bar on Schaefer, just north of Six Mile in Detroit where our team went for free, delicious burgers. Bill signed a professional contract, and

Billy Collins
Catholic Central
1961

was assigned to the Class D minor leagues (the lowest rung of professional baseball). Bill was a relief pitching specialist so he never got to bat. But, one night, Bill was pitching relief in a long winded fifteen inning night game under poor quality, silhouette lighting when his team ran out of eligible players. Bill was forced to bat against Nolan Ryan, some unknown, wild-as-the-wind, 18-year-old, right handed, flame thrower who could throw the ball through a wall. Collins, hitting from the left side, certainly was not going to dig in against this fearsome, flame throwing, wild, young right hander. First pitch… Collins bails out, walking right out of the batter's box before the ball gets there. "Strike one," barks the ump. Second pitch and Collins bails out of the batter's box again, as Nolan Ryan is just starting to throw to home plate. "Strike two," barks the ump. Third pitch, same routine, with Collins already walking back to his dugout as Ryan's fast ball flys toward the plate and over everyone's head. "Ball one," barks the ump, who yells over to a quickly retreating Collins: "Hey Collins, where are you going? That was ball one," to which Collins replies while still walking away: "That was close enough, ump"… "no mas."

And, all this baseball history in the Hood simply because I had the misfortune of striking out twenty times in a row as a 13-year-old. As I say, it's not the success or the failure of life that counts. It's the **"journey."** The journey is us and we are the journey. And what a rich landscape of stories that journey leaves for all of us.

CHAPTER 10

John Argenta...
Major League Artist

S ome from the Hood became major league artists...
like **JOHN P. ARGENTA** – The Master of Artistic Design.

In the story you are about to hear, two old worlds of the Greatest Generation collided and a new world was born. Giovanni Argenta's world of 1918 collided with the 1928 world of the Basilian priests, and the cosmic energy released from that collision ultimately inspired a work of art. As the dust from that brilliant stellar collision began to settle on the horizon of the twenty-first century, the silhouette of John Argenta's new world Catholic Central High School campus in Novi, Michigan began to emerge and take it's place among the great artistic accomplishments by the children of the Greatest Generation.

Old World Wayfarers

1918 – it was the middle of the flu pandemic. Fifty million people would die worldwide of influenza. In the village of Zebadessi, Italy, the province of Piedmonte, 12-year-old Giovanni Argenta was cold, hungry and malnourished. Driven by a strong instinct of survival, Giovanni left his parents' home, alone, and boarded a ship for the New World, hitching a ride on a perilous, trans-Atlantic crossing to Ellis Island... the gateway to the American dream. At the same time, his brother, Stefano, boarded a different ship... destination Buenos Aires, Argentina. Two kids, without education or fortune, said good-bye... never to see one another again. But, a man does what a man has to do to survive, or, in this instance, a kid of 12 does what a kid of 12 has to do to survive.

Giovanni Argenta did, indeed, survive the rough waters of the Atlantic Ocean and the arduous, trans-Atlantic crossing. Imagine what wonder filled young Giovanni's eyes and heart as his ship finally completed the journey, and slid into the quiet waters of the New York Harbor, past that enduring landmark, that great symbol of New-World freedom... the Statue of Liberty.

After what seemed like an endless wait in the harbor, the word got out, and spread throughout the ship with great excitement and anticipation: "We're next, we're next!" Giovanni Argenta left the ship, his second last connection to the Old World, and moved onto Ellis Island and toward the great Administration Hall. Filled with both expectation and trepidation, 12-year-old Giovanni watched the door to the Great Hall open, and he stepped into the overwhelming din. He was pulled along by a cacophony of unfamiliar, discordant sounds and languages that echoed, reverberated and crescendoed off the sturdy walls of the Great Hall – a hall that had seen it all.

As he entered the dreaded room where physical exams were administered, Giovanni's already overwhelmed heart began to beat faster and faster... swish boom, swish boom, swish boom. Giovanni had heard the talk on the ship, and he knew that a cough, a rash, a high temperature or any other tell-tale physical sign would undo the entire voyage, and those forlorn immigrants who failed their physical exam would be sent back to the ship to be returned to their point of origin and re-endure the perilous, trans-Atlantic crossing – yesterday's hope dashed by broken dreams and a sense of failure. But, Giovanni Argenta was one of the lucky ones. He passed his physical and walked out into the sunlight of new world America, leaving behind the last vestige of his old world. Young 12-year-old Giovanni left Ellis Island, and walked out onto American soil as "John" Argenta.

Giovanni Argenta was one of 28,867 immigrants who entered America through Ellis Island in 1918, down significantly from 1.2 million immigrants in 1914. He was one of 5.2 million Italian immigrants who entered America over a 158 year period from 1820 to 1978 – a half a million more than the Irish immigrants. Giovanni Argenta joined the ranks of such notable immigrants as: Frank Capra, the great Italian movie director; Knute Rockne from Norway, the storied Notre Dame football coach – Knute "win one for the Gipper" Rockne; Al "Blackface" Jolson, the "Jazz Singer" from Russia; Father Edward Flanagan, the Irish Priest who established Boystown in Nebraska on the slogan that: "There is no such thing as a bad kid;" and Irving "God Bless America" Berlin from Russia.

Twelve-year-old Giovanni Argenta adjusted to a new language and a new culture and, eventually, moved to Detroit, Michigan, and

Amalia Marchesotti Argenta and Giovanni Argenta 1940

married the lovely Amalia Marchesotti from his own hometown village of Zebadessi. On August 4, 1940, Amalia Argenta gave birth to her first child, John Argenta. On the evening of John's birth, the star of his father's Greatest Generation's **tenacity** aligned with the star of **opportunity**, and it was written in the pages of destiny that son John Argenta, one of the children of the Greatest Generation, would, in his time, leave large artistic imprints on the shores of the New World.

"New Order" Priests

1928 – **"The Basilians are coming! The Basilians are coming! The Basilians are coming!"** The word was out in Detroit's Medbury Park (Now I-94 and Woodward). The word was out at the corner of Harper and Woodward. The word was out in the Holy Rosary Parish. The word was out in the Hood. "The Basilians are coming! The Basilians are coming!" The Basilian priests were coming from Canada to start a new school, "Detroit Catholic Central."

The word was out, but my 12-year-old father, Frederick Valentine Lauck, and his school classmates at Holy Rosary wondered out loud: "Who are these Basilians?" And, the nuns at Holy Rosary, never missing an opportunity to control behavior through fear and intimidation, quickly let the Holy Rosary grade school boys know what was inexorably closing in on them from a distant horizon. The Basilians had been sent to install a spiritual version of Martial Law known as "Discipline" 101, followed by "Discipline" 102, followed by "Discipline" 103, etc., etc., until, eventually, "Discipline" became second nature, and the young students became living "testaments" to Basilian "Discipline." For, the Basilians knew in 1928 that which they still know today, eighty plus years later – discipline is the only true path to freedom. Once the foundation of discipline is set in place and becomes second nature, the student is free to live life in an artistic and extemporaneous fashion.

The Basilians were arriving to establish a new social order, and word had it that they will brook no dissent from the likes of the half boy, half man, Oliver Twist urchins they planned on educating. The Basilians are the masters; the students are the novices. The Basilians are the teachers; they teach, and the students' shut off the ongoing, nonending, dialogue in their minds and listen. The Basilians will lead the students into the first Catholic Central High School. The students don't lead; they follow. The students march to the beat of the Basilian drum, or they march out of town. The choice is theirs. The Basilians will brook no dissent. The students can walk away if they choose, but, before they do so, the students need to understand just what the Basilians have to offer.

The Basilians offer the key to the students' future. The students can work with the Basilians, and use that key to unlock the door to their futures. If they work with the Basilians, and buy into "goodness, discipline and knowledge," the students will eventually take control of their lives, and they will become captains of their own fate, and they will chart their own course in life. Work against the Basilians and work against "goodness, discipline and knowledge," and the students will flounder like rudderless ships on the shoals of life, and be buffeted about endlessly by the vagaries of uncertainty. Work with the Basilians, and the students' prospects for "quality of life" through the pursuit of excellence are… endless.

"The Basilians are coming! The Basilians are coming!" was the echo heard throughout the Hood in the summer of 1928. Then, the long-feared day of reckoning finally arrived in late summer 1928. The first day the "larger-than-life Basilians" appeared in the Hood, my 12-year-old father and the rest of his boys left the pool tables at Nate's Confectionary and poured out onto the north side of Harper Avenue, ninety feet east of Woodward. Nervously hovering between fight and flight, my father and his pals in the Hood kept a safe and respectful distance, suspiciously eyeing the caravan of black cars arriving with priests in black cassocks: Father Daniel L. Dillon, Catholic Central's first principal, Father J. Wilfred Dore, Father Francis L. Burns, Father Charles P. Donovan, Father James W. Embser, Father J. Stanley

Murphy, Father E. Leonard Rush, Father Francis S. Ruth, Father Wilfred C. Sharpe and Mr. Frank McIlhargey.

As these Darth Vader, larger-than-life characters exited their vehicles, one of the Basilians accidentally had his hand slammed in a car door, and he screamed out in pain. My father's friend turned to my father, his eyes wide as saucers and outlined with excitement and fear, and blurted out **"They're human! They're human!"** And so they were. Those very human Basilians, those men of humanity, humility and goodness, discipline, knowledge and compassion, started the nine decade odyssey that continues to this very day at Detroit Catholic Central High School in Novi. During seventy-seven of those years, the Basilians were akin to nomads and homeless missionaries wandering the streets of Detroit, going from temporary home to temporary home – from Harper and Woodward, to Belmont and Woodward, to Hubbell and Outer Drive, to Breakfast Drive in Redford, and finally to… well let's not get ahead of our story.

Children of the Greatest Generation

Giovanni Argenta's family now numbered three sons: John, the first

**Robert, Louis, and
John Argenta 1948**

born, Louis, later to become one of the world's foremost cranio-plastic surgeons helping to restore symmetry to the faces and heads of children born with serious cranial defects, and Robert, later to become one of our area's top flight dentists. The family finally settled down in a small Italian enclave in Northwest Detroit, St. Scholastica Parish, where confessions were heard in English and Italian by such priests as Father Boniface Lucci, Father Leo Cornelli and

Father Livius Paoli. My friends, John DiBella and Frank Demers, and I attended St. Scholastica Grade School with the Argenta middle son, Dr. Lou Argenta, but we always looked up to the older kids who graduated from St. Scholastica, and went on to Catholic Central High School: four-sport star Al Moran who later played shortstop for the "amazin'" New York Mets under legendary Casey Stengel; Ronnie Ross who captained Catholic Central's football team that I played on as a 15-year-old sophomore in the fall of 1958, and who later played at Michigan State under Duffy Daugherty; and Rudy Seichter, one of Catholic Central's outstanding hockey players in the late 1950s under the legendary coach Father James Enright.

But, we didn't quite know what to make of that quiet, studious kid, John Argenta, who carried a load of schoolbooks on his hip as he came out of St. Scholastica, and later as he came out of Catholic Central walking down Outer Drive westbound to the family's home at 17133 Warwick next to the alleyway just a house north of Six Mile (a.k.a. McNichols). As our magical and innocent years of the 1950s were running away from us, nobody guessed that this quiet, studious kid, John Argenta, would later have a rendezvous with destiny, and leave large artistic imprints on the shores of the new world of America.

John Argenta's family never took a vacation. John's father didn't survive the arduous trip to new world America as a hungry 12-year-old just to hang around Crystal Pool on Eight Mile Rd. and catch a suntan and talk to the chicks, or just to head over to Brennan Pools and practice his diving off the ten meter board, or to head up to Rosedale Drug Store, and hang around the counter and drink chocolate phosphates and listen to the juke box playing "Johnny B. Goode." For John's father, construction work and the survival of his family were a full time job, day in and day out, seven days a week, year after year. Finally, when son John was a junior at Catholic Central in 1956, the Argenta boys, with a concentrated effort: "Please, Please, Please,

Mr. Postman," (a hit song of the day), finally inveigled their Greatest Generation father to take a weekend vacation, his first vacation – a Friday (go), Saturday (vacation) and Sunday (come back), to see the big Mackinac Bridge which was just built to connect Michigan's upper and lower peninsulas. The family enticed their father to take that three-day vacation based on his interest in concrete construction. At that time, the Mackinac Bridge structure had more cubic feet of concrete than any other structure east of the Great Divide.

Driving hard all the way for ten hours to the Mackinac Bridge in the era before super freeways, they arrived, drove over the bridge and drove back again. Now you see it, now you don't, and now we go home. Wow! Was that a great vacation or what! The "Greatest Generation" really know how to live it up, don't they? On the way home, then 16-year-old John was driving his father's car on Woodward Avenue when he stopped at a light. "Crash!," he was rear-ended. After the Argenta family picked themselves up from the floor and off the dashboard, old man Argenta, not missing a beat, let his feelings be known: "See what I told you? Nothing good happens when you go on vacation!"

John The Architect

Mr. Argenta's great survival ethic was not lost on any of his three sons. Son John graduated from Catholic Central in 1958, and, taking full advantage of the opportunity that had eluded his father's Greatest Generation, John started college at the University of Detroit. Of the 205 hopefuls that started the architectural-engineering program at the University of Detroit in the fall of 1958, John and five others eventually graduated six years later in 1964.

After graduation from the University of Detroit, John Argenta continued to capitalize on the opportunities that eluded his father's generation. With his father's work ethic and the blessing of opportunity, John perfected his scientific craft as an engineer, perfected his "art" as an architect, and he became an artist in the tradition of the great Italian Renaissance masters. John's artistic canvas is the landscape – earth, air and skyline. On his pallet, John has mortar, bricks, stone, and marble, and John uses his architectural brush to paint the ultimate piece of interactive artwork – a building that pulsates from within with human activity that occupies a living space that John so artistically creates.

Over the years, John completed numerous successful projects for many Detroit area schools including DeLaSalle, Brother Rice, Ladywood and Marian as well as numerous public schools, receiving the accolades of his peers. But, eventually, the 1918 old world village of Zebadessi, Italy collided with the 1928 old world arrival of the Basilian priests in Detroit Michigan, and the Basilians' seventy-seven year wandering in the desert ended as the Basilian priests entrusted one of their own graduates, John Argenta, to design and build them a new school... a permanent home for Catholic Central High School. And John, displaying the same courage as his 12-year-old father before him, accepted that overwhelming challenge knowing that anything less than total success would be an "also ran" failure.

The Challenge

Although a prophet is never known in his own land or in his own time, the Basilians were savvy enough to know that John Argenta was the man they needed to design their new, permanent Catholic Central home. The idea, the impetus and the fund raising stamina of the project was that of long time Basilian priest, Father Richard Elmer. The land was the gift of Frank and Colleen Pellerito. The major donor was Pat Nesbitt, Catholic Central Class of 1962. But, despite the efforts of others, there would be no new Catholic Central High School campus until an artist like John Argenta accepted the challenge, picked up a brush and painted and constructed the new Catholic Central building and campus on the landscape of life.

And… what was John's biggest challenge in designing and building the new Catholic Central High School: **"building a school that perpetuates the tradition of Catholic Central."** That challenge seemed insurmountable. First, how do you identify a "tradition" that spans more than eighty years, over numerous generations? Then, how do you architecturally design a building that somehow mirrors and reflects that intangible "tradition"?

What is this **tradition** that the new Catholic Central High School was supposed to reflect? Was there a tradition for my father and his classmates in the late 1920s, and, if so, what was it? What was the tradition from the 1930s when the worldwide "Great Depression" demoralized both the capitalists and the working class? What was the tradition for the 1940s when the Japanese preemptively struck Pearl Harbor throwing us headlong into World War II, the war to end all wars, that raged across the European continent and in the Pacific? What was the tradition in the early 1950s when the Korean War was fought? What was the tradition of the mid to late 1950s when John and his brothers and our classmates were attending Catholic Central? What was the tradition of the 1960s when the Vietnam War divided a nation? What was the tradition of the 1970s when Watergate was uncovered and an elected president, Richard Nixon, left office under a cloud of deceit just to avoid certain impeachment? What was the tradition of John's nephews and my son Frederick Valentine Lauck and their classmates who attended Catholic Central in the 1980s? What was the tradition of John's son, John Argenta Jr., and his classmates in the 1990s, and what is the tradition now, in this, the twenty-first century? What is the common tradition for all these diverse generations spanning eighty plus years? As John thought about it, the question began to reveal the answer. The answer did not lie in the mysteries of faith. The answer did not lie in the rituals of religion. The answer lay in the fundamental human precepts of the eighty plus year tradition of the Basilian priests at Catholic Central **to nurture the mind, the body and the souls of young men.**

Mission Accomplished

Thanks to John Argenta, the architectural design mission to capture Catholic Central's tradition was accomplished! The 1918 world of Giovanni Argenta collided with the 1928 world of the Basilians, and the cosmic energy from that stellar collision gave birth to John Argenta's new world, Detroit Catholic Central High School campus in Novi, Michigan. John Argenta did indeed capture and perpetuate Catholic Central's eighty plus year tradition in his artistic design of the new Catholic Central High School. Are you ready to see it? Let me take you on a "virtual tour" of the new Catholic Central High School.

As you drive into the secluded, tree-lined campus of the new Catholic Central High School, you see a beautiful fortress-like

Catholic Central 2005

building that speaks of strength and stability. Open the front door from the outside, and enter John Argenta's Catholic Central High School. As you do, you immediately enter into a spiritual space. As you go through the door, the architectural line-of-sight that John designed directs your eye into the distance where you see the tabernacle sitting on the altar in an expansive, 300 seat chapel. John Argenta's line-of-sight beckons you to move forward, toward the chapel. As you move forward into that spiritual line of space, the stained glass figure of the risen Christ (salvaged from Catholic Central's third home at Hubble and Outer Drive), moves into view, and you see that stained glass figure of the risen Christ as it seems to ascend upward to the heavens.

Just before you arrive at the chapel door, you find yourself at the axis of the building. Your eye is directed down to the floor where you see a mosaic of the Catholic Central crest with the words "Goodness, Discipline and Knowledge" traversing the circumference of the crest...

Catholic Central High School The Crest

The Chapel

designed into the floor. It is here, at the axis, that John Argenta perpetuates the eighty-year tradition of Catholic Central with three options of movement. Move straight ahead, and you enter the chapel, perpetuating Catholic Central's eighty-year tradition of nurturing a young man's **soul through goodness**. Go left, and you enter the Academic Wing, perpetuating Catholic Central's eighty-year tradition of nurturing a young man's **mind through knowledge**. Go right, and you enter the Athletic Wing, perpetuating Catholic Central's eighty-year tradition of nurturing a young man's **body through discipline**. There it is. Mission accomplished for John Argenta and Catholic Central. John's artistic design of the new Catholic Central High School is truly a mirror which reflects and perpetuates the eighty plus year tradition of Catholic Central High School and Basilian principles of nurturing young men's souls through goodness, their minds through knowledge and their bodies through discipline. John's Catholic Central High School is, in essence, an artistic, architectural masterpiece that mirrors the strength of

John's own father and the strength of the Basilian priests, both of whom came, saw and conquered the New World with a spirit of "goodness, discipline, knowledge," compassion and love.

Designing "Mood"

But, I have yet to mention John Argenta's greatest artistic accomplishment in designing Catholic Central's new world, high school. John not only used the medium of mortar, brick, stone and marble to create a fortress that reflects the eighty plus year tradition of Catholic

**Catholic Central High School
Front Entrance**

Central High School, but John also created a fourth dimension of **"mood."** As soon as you enter John Argenta's Catholic Central High School, John's magical artistry with light and space lifts you emotionally and spiritually. John has merged light, space and the "timelessness of time" to create the **fourth dimension of mood** – a mood of "well being," an uplifting mood that descends upon all wayfarers who enter the portals of Catholic Central's new world home whispering to them: "All is well" and "all will be well."

That uplifting mood John so masterfully created by artistically merging light, space and the "timelessness of time," reflects "Faith" itself – a trust that everything will be okay. For, what is faith, if not a sense that "all is well," and "all will be well" – the same faith that allowed early Christians to persevere through 300 years of persecution, the same faith that allowed the Greatest Generation to persevere through the financial calamity of an economic wasteland during the Great Depression and through a World War fought on two fronts a world apart, and the same faith that tells the Catholic Central student and teacher alike that they can and will make it through the daily rigors of "goodness, discipline and knowledge."

So walk into John Argenta's new world Catholic Central High School, and let John's line-of-sight guide you through Catholic Central's eighty plus year tradition of "Goodness, Discipline and Knowledge." But, more importantly, walk into John's new world Catholic Central High School, and give your troubles over to the fourth dimension of mood... that spirituality and faith of "well being" that John has so mystically and artistically created.

In my day and in John Argenta's day, graduation from high school was a crowning success that put us head and shoulders over

Fred Lauck and John Argenta
2007

our parents' academic accomplishments. When we bought our first new automobile, we were head and shoulders over our parents' material accomplishments. In our lifetimes, small accomplishments created large successes. But, today's Catholic Central students, over-burdened as they are with the expectations of their successful parents and with the high expectations of their teachers and mentors, suffer from an intense competition that John and I were spared in our simpler, age-of-innocence lives of the 1950s. But, thanks to John Argenta, today's Catholic Central students will be spiritually and emotionally centered each day as they walk through the front door of Catholic Central. The daily challenge of their overly competitive lives, and the daily challenge of the ambitious expectations of their parents and mentors will give way to, and find peaceful acceptance in, John Argenta's architecturally designed gift of mood that **"all is well"** – a mood that today's students and future students can draw upon to give them the faith that they will make it through one of the most rigorous and demanding college prep high schools in America.

Catholic Central's new world high school was John Argenta's architectural baby, and I suspect John will be caring for his prodigy until he takes his last breath. John had the "opportunity" that eluded the Greatest Generation, and he made the most of it. John combined his generation's "opportunity" with the Greatest Generation's tenacity and strong survival instinct, and with the Basilians' tradition of "Goodness, Discipline and Knowledge," and, in doing so, John Argenta left his own, very large artistic imprints on the shores of the New World.

Catholic Central Campus
"New World Art"

CHAPTER 11

Ode To The Basilians

Speaking of opportunity through education, the Basilians have had an admirably long-lasting impact on education in the Hood since 1928 – a blink of the eye, and soon it will be a century of Basilian education.

From the Great Depression and the Dust Bowl to Boys Town and the Boys Bowl, from Henry Ford's Highland Park Assembly Line at $1.00 a day to websites, Bill Gates, NASDAQ and million dollar contracts. And, through it all, the Basilians have been there educating and mentoring young men at Catholic Central for eighty years. The more things change, the more they remain the same.

From the rise and fall of the Third Reich to VE Day and VJ Day, from original Catholic Central on Harper Avenue and on to Belmont and Woodward, from the post WWII building boom and the Korean conflict to Jack Kerouac, the Beat Generation and on to

C.C. home number three at 6565 West Outer Drive, from gunshots on a tragic November day in Dallas in 1963, and from Lyndon Johnson and Vietnam and napalm to home number four on Breakfast Drive and portable classrooms bursting at the seams, and finally on to a $30 million state of the art campus in Novi. And, through it all, the Basilians have been there educating and mentoring young men at Catholic Central for eighty years. The more things change, the more they remain the same.

From Louie Armstrong, Count Basie, Duke Ellington, Benny Goodman and Dave Bruebeck, from Irving Berlin, Cole Porter, Johnny Mercer, George Gershwin and Rogers and Hammerstein, from Elvis, the Four Tops, the Supremes, Bob Dylan, Aretha Franklin, Bob Seger and Eminem to Catholic Central's Band of Renown under maestros Bill Watts and Greg Normandin, from ragtime and swing and show tunes to rock, bebop, doo-wop, Kid Rock, and hip hop. And, through it all, the Basilians have been there educating and mentoring young men at Catholic Central for eighty years. The more things change, the more they remain the same.

From rolling cross country trains to a man on the moon, from Charles Lindberg's solo transatlantic flight to Paris on the Concorde in three hours, from the golden age of radio to Howdy Doody and Milton Berle on black and white TV to 100 channels of cable, from manual typewriters to laptop computers, from Roosevelt's New Deal to Regan's Star Wars to Obama's Health Care, from Steinbeck's *Grapes Of Wrath* to Kerouac's *On The Road* to Tom Brokaw's *Greatest Generation*. And, through it all, the Basilians have been there educating and mentoring young men at Catholic Central. The more things change, the more they remain the same.

From championships on every athletic field to national Quiz Bowl and merit scholars, from the lean years to the dynasty years, one generation passes to another, one decade to another, one century to another, and one millennium to another, through seven popes from Pius XI through Benedict XVI, and through nineteen principals from Father Daniel Dillion in 1928 to Father John Huber in 2010. And, through it all, the Basilians have been educating and mentoring young men at Catholic Central, including my father in the 1930s and my son in the 1980s. The more things change, the more they stay the same.

From the tintinnabulation of the recess bell to the explosive collisions on the football field, from the cadence count and melodious strains of the marching band to the bang, bang double play – around the horn and back again, to the bounding, bounding ball on the hardwood court or for any other shamrock sport, there's always been a Basilian teaching the fundamentals or working nearby.

I close my eyes and I see Father Gerard French, Father Ned Donoher (Fifty years at Catholic Central), Father Joe Miller, Father James Martin, Father William Stoba, Father Cy Bergeron, Father Norbert Clemens (my personal inspiration), Father Charlie Christopher, Father John Menner, Father Frank Bredeweg, Father John Ward, Father Dennis Andrews, and Father James Enright – teaching… coaching… or just cutting the grass on the back forty.

Inspirational Priests

 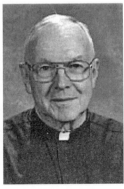 

Fr. Gerard French   Fr. Ned Donoher   Fr. Norbert Clemens

I open my eyes and I see a diminishing group of Basilians: Father Richard Elmer, Father "Tunny" Hathaway, Father John Wheeler, Father Ray Paramo, Father Mike Buentello, Father Joe Redican, Father Dennis Nolke, Father Richard Ranalletti, Father John Huber, and near-Basilians – Dr. John Ronayne and his son, John Ronayne Esquire.

The sacrifice... a Basilian vocation
For a young man's education,
The very foundation of Christian belief,
One life given for another.

Enter – a fragile, insecure and timid 14-year-old
    adolescent freshman;
Exit – four years later – a strong, self confident
    graduating senior;
Ready to take on the world – tomorrow's leader.

Fr. Richard Elmer

Generation after generation of young men, sent through the revolving door of "goodness, discipline and knowledge." Thanks to the Basilian tradition, the more things change, the more they remain the same.

CHAPTER 12

Michigan Marty...
Charismatic Tough Guy

S ome from the Hood became charismatic characters... like **"MICHIGAN MARTY"** aka Martin Kent Lahti – my big brother.

"Bandana Bob" Polander's 1960's book of poems *Tales from the Other Side of Life* describes "Michigan Marty" as **"conceived in the crucible of victory and born of partisans and foes."** I describe Brother Marty as a "man among men" with a crashious right hand that dispatched all comers to the land of nod, from which they eventually awoke with a new found respect for the one and only "Michigan Marty." Michigan Marty was a living, breathing, walking, talking prototype of Tennessee Ernie Ford's Song "Sixteen Tons":

> "One fist of iron.
> One fist of steel.
> If the right one don't get you,
> then the left one will."

The Gift of Bloodlines

Where did it all begin? It all began on July 7, 1936. Martin Kent Lahti was the first child of a good-looking, strong-willed Irish mother, Jean "McKelvy" Montroy, and tall, handsome, hard-drinking Finlander father, Harold Lahti. Marty Lahti was born into the 1936 Detroit Hood's hottest heat wave, and was cooled in the maternity ward by pre-1950 air conditioning – fans blowing over blocks of ice. Right from an oppressively hot start, life demanded that Michigan Marty become a survivor.

On Michigan Marty's mother's side, there was a host of dysfunctional characters – each one portending that Michigan Marty's life would probably be (shall we say) challenging. Michigan Marty's maternal grandmother, Mary McKelvy, was born in Eau Clair, Wisconsin on November 12, 1878, one of twelve children of John McKelvy and Catherine Monaghan – these Monaghans from Fermagh County, Ireland. The Monaghans left Ireland in the 1850s when the staple crop of the Irish, potatoes, failed for successive years resulting in mass starvation, or, if you were lucky, an arduous trans-Atlantic crossing to the New World in search of food and survival.

All of Marty's great aunts on the McKelvy side married Irish: the Kellys, the Courtneys, the Weadocks and the Dentons, leaving a legacy of Irish descendants and noteworthy characters, but losing the "McKelvy" namesake in the process. Marty's great uncles, "Black Jack" McKelvy and Larry McKelvy, themselves both bigger than life characters, left the Midwest and wander-lusted it to Truckee, California near the northern tip of Lake Tahoe, busted up Truckee and themselves, got rich as land speculators, got broke when the land bubble burst, and died leaving… who knows?

Marty's grandmother, Mary McKelvy, didn't marry Irish. She married a Frenchman, "Good Time Charlie" Montroy, a ladies' man, who was born in Port Dover, Ontario on March 27, 1870 shortly after the American Civil War ended. Marty's grandmother McKelvy and

grandfather, "Good Time Charlie" Montroy had ten children including Marty's uncle, Sherwood Montroy, who died in a logging accident at age 17 and was buried on the cold, wind swept plains of northern Minnesota, and including Marty's uncles, Jack and Larry Montroy, who grew up big, strong and fast and played football at Notre Dame in the 1920s under legendary Notre Dame football coach Knute, "Win One for the Gipper," Rockne, and including Marty's mother, Jean Montroy, who could have taught Rockne and the

Uncle Jack Montroy
Univ. of Notre Dame
Coach Knute Rockne
1926

whole dysfunctional bunch something about determination, fortitude and dysfunction.

Michigan Marty himself was named after two of his other Montroy uncles – Marty Montroy, a very successful business man in California who walked away from it all, a victim of alcoholism, but who fought his way off the "bowery" twice to become a financial success in San Diego, California, and Marty's uncle, Kent Montroy, an energized character who was also a victim of the drink, and who became a Broadway actor, eventually dying in New York City in 1996 at the ripe old age of 88. I remember well watching Uncle Kent play a bit part of an extra on the grainy picture on our black and white Philco TV. "There's Uncle Kent! There's Uncle Kent!"

Michigan Marty's Irish, French and Finlander heritage, his line of descent from many larger than life characters and adventurers, and his gene pool of relatives who invariably stood their ground, often fortified with distilled spirits, clearly signaled that Michigan Marty's life would not be ordinary, and, certainly, would not be lived in "quiet desperation" following orders or walking to the beat of "the man."

But, just what kind of life would it be for Martin Kent Lahti? Would it be a life of evolutionary progress? – a life of social refinement, sophistication and achievement, or would it be a helter-skelter, "roll-of-the-dice" life that would go one step forward dancing to the beat of the Prince of Serendipity and two steps backwards dancing to the erratic rhythm of the Duke of Destruction? "Cha, cha, cha" and duck. Turn! "Cha, cha, cha" and punch. Let me tell you the story of Michigan Marty, and you be the judge.

Early Family Lessons in "Civility"

Michigan Marty – "born of partisans and foes." How apropos. Marty's first memory of life was a tumultuous incident involving his

Mother Jean
Vulnerable by Nature
Strong by Necessity

Irish mother, Jean McKelvy Montroy, and his Finlander Grandmother Lahti squaring off in a small apartment near the Grand Boulevard and Trumbull in Detroit. Apparently, during their skirmish, Grandmother Lahti got hit (shall we say) "inadvertently" in the head with the telephone while she was threatening to call the police to resolve her dispute with Marty's mother, Jean. And, I can just hear mother Jean yelling: "We don't need any cops in here." But, alas, and over the protest of mother Jean, the local Gendarmes appeared and took mother Jean, the loudest combatant, off in handcuffs while telling 3-year-old Marty to be careful not to walk over the broken glassware and plates strewn about the kitchen floor – the residue from the "mano a mano," "save the last dance for me" incident between Mother Jean and Grandma Lahti. It almost makes you want to have a drink.

"Born of Partisans and Foes." How apropos. Mother Jean being escorted out the apartment door by law enforcement, handcuffed, and charged with an "Irish misdemeanor" – a technical violation of the law but committed with the best of excuses. I too remember being locked up at the Palmer Park Precinct on Seven Mile near Woodward with Mother Jean and my St. Scholastica classmate, John DiBella, in 1966 when I was 23 years old. We had a pretty good party going on at the Saxe Club on McNichols (Six Mile) just west of Woodward… at least until some loud mouth, or as my mother Jean called him, a "flannel mouth," started trouble. That trouble sailed out onto Six Mile Road and blocked traffic, including a Detroit city bus whose riders spilled out onto Six Mile and joined in the festivities, or, as the "Fighting" Irish say: "Is this a private fight or can anyone get in?" The cops soon arrived, and then we had a real "incident" on our hands. Mother Jean was then 51 years old, but she hadn't lost that old Irish spunk as she took on the cops, and the injustice of the false arrest of her other son… me (or, if you will allow me to take back my old persona, that would be "Downtown Freddie," son of "Uptown Freddie" and younger brother to "Michigan Marty").

Early Battles

But, this story is neither about me nor mother Jean. It's about Michigan Marty – "born of partisans and foes" and raised in the shadow of St. Gregory's Catholic Church at Fenkell (Five Mile) and Livernois. Marty's first prime time fight was in that very Hood. It was a one rounder on his home street, Quincy Ave, or, to be more precise, it was a one punch fight with Dennis O'Malley. Nine-year-old Marty had just moved into the neighborhood, and was standing on the sidewalk in front of his new rental home on Quincy next door to the junk yard, just looking around and taking in a visual of his new surroundings when some other kid appeared on the same sidewalk a few houses down the block just staring at Marty. So 9-year-old Marty, in a sign of rather unsophisticated social interaction, just thumbed his nose at the other kid. The other kid then pretended to go into his house, but really went to the back of his house to the alley and through the alley, down to Marty's house, and came out between houses and snuck up behind Marty.

Marty, blissfully unaware of his vulnerability, was still staring down the street where the other kid was last seen, waiting for the kid to resurface. But, it was a preemptive, Pearl Harbor "sneak attack" by 10-year-old Dennis O'Malley (one of ten Irish kids) who blasted the back of Marty's 9-year-old head with a right hand shot. It was a one punch knock down of Michigan Marty who started off (what would later become an illustrious career) with an 0-1 record – a victim of a technical knockout or, as they say in the fight game, a TKO. The next day Dennis and Marty became friends – a friendship that lasted a lifetime. What a break!… Marty hooking up with an Irish mentor, Dennis O'Malley, and learning to carry his early, in-home lessons of "disorderly person" and "civil disobedience" into the street arena in his own Hood.

"Born of Partisans and Foes." Over the years, Michigan Marty got bigger, stronger and quicker. He boxed C.Y.O. and Golden Gloves. He defeated many a fighter including a close win over Father French's Catholic Central Golden Boy, Jimmy Rioux, (may he rest). In the early 1950s, Marty fought for the West Side/East Side Championship of Detroit against left hook power house and knock out artist, "Ducky" Deitz. "Ducky" later became a professional boxer in the Rocky Marciano stable of promising, young prize fighters. But, apparently, "Ducky," a rather unruly character, wouldn't train. Still, "Ducky" never lost that awesome left hook, and, one night, decades later, he used it to knock out Detroit Lions Hall of Fame linebacker, Joe Schmidt, in Joe's own place, the "Golden Lion" Restaurant.

Michigan Marty also fought the older, infamous giant, St. Gregory's George Ridella, to a draw in the parking lot of McInerny's "Spotlite" bar in the local Fenkell, Livernois Hood. It all started with a young, skinny 17-year-old Marty Lahti telling George "King Kong" Ridella: "I know who you are and I'm not a-scared of you." And, George "King Kong" Ridella telling Marty: "well, in about a minute, you will be." Out to the parking lot they went. Once outside, Marty put his back on the cinder block bar wall and covered up in a turtle-like, defensive shell while big, bad George Ridella, with meaty fists two times the size of any other man, was T-ing off on Marty's coconut spending all his energy and oxygen trying to K.O. Marty. Finally big, bad George Ridella ran out of wind. The so-called fight was over, with George Ridella admonishing Marty between deep gulps of air… "don't" (breathe George)… "you be telling… " (breathe again George)… "anyone" (breathe again George)… "anyone" (breathe again)… "you kicked my ass" to which a young, skinny Marty replied: "and don't you be telling anyone you kicked my ass." That truce lasted for a life time of friendship.

The Music Scene

Second only to fighting, Michigan Marty had a love of music. It was the early to mid 1950's, and teenager Michigan Marty and his boys in the Hood were musically influenced by the "Bebop" era with its new Bebop jazz sensations: trumpeters Miles Davis and John Coltrane, saxophonist, Charlie "Bird" Parker, pianist Oscar Peterson, Dave "Take Five" Brubeck with tenor saxophonist, Paul Desmond, and the apparent spiritual leader of the Bebop movement, "Dizzy" (the crooked trumpet) Gillespie, who once stabbed the "heidi-ho" man, Cab Calloway, because Cab told Dizzy his new Bebop was "Chinese music."

It was also the era of "beat" poet, Allen Ginsberg, and the "Hep Cat" era of "beat" writer Jack Kerouac and his attention grabbing, sensational novel *On The Road* – a narration of endless travel and impromptu lifestyle that exhorted all restless young men of the 1950s to leave the "structure" of life behind, and get on with the "adventure" of life:

> "The only people for me are the mad ones, mad to talk, mad to be saved, desirous of saying everything at the same time, the ones who never yawn or say common place things, the ones that burn, burn, burn like the fabulous, yellow roman candles exploding like spiders across the night sky."

Goodbye structure! Hello adventure! "Count me in," said Michigan Marty. Kerouac's *On the Road* invitation to Marty and his boys in the Hood was met with a choral response: "RSVP – Yo! I'm in." And, Marty and his boys were, indeed, in. They changed direction and reinvented themselves. School was out with nine years of formal education finished as Michigan Marty and his boys in the Hood walked out the doors of Cooley High School on Hubble and Fenkell (Five Mile). School was out and life was in. After all, Kerouac, the spokesman for a generation of restless youths, just told everyone life is to be lived, not studied, analyzed or contemplated.

So, Michigan Marty and his boys all bought saxophones, trumpets, clarinets and trombones, took a few lessons, and drove through the Hood on Fenkell and Livernois in old convertibles "honking" on those horns. That outrageous "scene" was something to behold: youthful characters searching to establish an identity, riding through the Hood at Livernois and Fenkell, blaring out a cacophony of discordant sounds that reverberated off store front windows and into the endless summer nights of the mid-1950s, and on up to the Milky Way Galaxy, and then on up to the very ears of God – the creator of "free will" that opened the door for this discordant symphony of restless youth. Let's have another cocktail.

Marty's friend and fellow tough guy "Black Mike" Nigohsian could really "Honk." Michigan Marty, as he admitted to me later, desperately wanted to play that sax, down on his knees, "honking" from here to eternity with all the ladies worked up to a fevered pitch: "Go Marty Go – Go, Go, Go, Marty Be Good!" But when Marty stared straight into the challenging notation of real sheet music and music charts, and, when he tried to uncover the intricate rhythm of a dotted eighth note in four-four time, a perplexed Michigan Marty thought maybe he might sell the sax, and leave saxophonist Jerry Mulligan and "Take Five" behind, and reinvent himself once more.

Changing Direction

And, indeed, Michigan Marty changed direction. Fresh off the heels of the James Dean movie, *Rebel Without a Cause*, Marty and his boys went to see the Marlon Brando, Lee Marvin movie, *The Wild One*,

Michigan Marty
"The Wild One"

based on a true story of the Hell's Angel's motorcycle gang's take over of Hollister, California in the early 1950s. During the movie, Marty heard a muted voice calling him. That voice soon crescendoed into an epiphany when the Chief of Police's daughter asked Marlon Brando's character: "Johnny what are you rebelling against?," and Brando, in stylized, glib fashion replied: "Whatdaya got?" That was it. In that moment, Michigan Marty knew where he belonged. He sold the saxophone, bought a Bonneville Triumph Motorcycle, joined the "Highwayman" motorcycle club, and headed straight back to the life of bravado that was meant for him all along. But, as an endless reminder of his music days, Marty always requested "Harlem Nocturne," the anthem of a tenor sax player, at every live music venue he ever attended. But, the sax was out and the motorcycle persona was in, and Michigan Marty was back in the rough and tumble game of "mano a mano."

"Born of Partisans and Foes." Michigan Marty got bigger, stronger, faster and more socially astute, soon discovering the absolute joy of the distilled spirits. After a short stint with the "Highwaymen" motorcycle club and few odd jobs at sweat shops and landscape services, Michigan Marty soon discovered that his natural charm, good looks and his uncanny sense of humor was catapulting him to fame and acclaim on the local nightclub "scene" and bar circuit. Marty then left the landscape jobs, the dead end factory jobs and the union halls behind, and became a card carrying member of the local "Brotherhood of Saloon and Nightclub Goers," a union of offbeat, misfit characters that had no chain of command, but who rallied around the unmistakable slogan: "Let the Party Begin!"

After a couple of years, Michigan Marty was well on his way to becoming a legendary tough guy on the saloon circuit. Marty embraced life, danced vigorously with it, and left no human emotion untouched, and, in the process, Marty established a reputation as a man for all seasons – hilarious character, ladies man, loyal friend and legendary tough guy who stepped aside for no man. Repeat "no man!"

Have Fists... Will Travel

After establishing who he was in the Detroit Hood, Michigan Marty and some of his boys from the Hood, including sax player extraordinaire, "Black Mike" Nigohsian, Jimmy McGrain, "Jewish" Jimmie Ruby and others went over to the neighboring Hood in

Highland Park for some running territorial battles with Highland Park legendary tough guys Madio and Raymond Carradi and their boys. After wearing out their knuckles and their faces on one another, the Highland Park tough guys and Marty became (you guessed it) good friends for a lifetime.

Later, in 1967, at the old "Manzo's Italian Restaurant" on McNichols (Six Mile) just a few blocks east of Southfield (then known as the "Apollo Lounge"), Marty ran into sister Katie's lowlife, abusive, ex-boyfriend Raymond McKamie. There was bad blood between Michigan Marty and Raymond McKamie dating back to an earlier incident at the Kenwood Lounge on Five Mile and Telegraph on April 22, 1966 that ended with "Jack Rabbit," Raymond McKamie sprinting out the front door of the Kenwood Lounge, away from Michigan Marty, dashing eastbound across Telegraph and getting hit by three cars. McKamie looked like Wiley Coyote bouncing over car hoods and roofs with Michigan Marty in hot pursuit. Coincidentally, Marty's friend, "Fat Charlie," without an inkling of what was going on, just happened to be driving by, and was the second vehicle to strike Raymond McKamie. Raymond was scooped up by the EMS and transported to a local hospital where he later discharged himself down the back steps of the hospital to a secret hiding place where he holed up and licked his wounds just to avoid Michigan Marty nailing him again in his hospital bed. After all, McKamie, despite his punching bag condition, still overheard Marty ask the EMS attendant: "what hospital they would be transporting McKamie to?" That Kenwood Lounge incident was a precursor of what was to be.

Back to the later incident at the "Apollo Lounge" on Six Mile. It was early in the evening, and the energy of the nightclub circuit hadn't even started to heat up yet. As Marty, John Banich (the "Mad Croatian") and Highland Park tough guy Raymond Carradi entered the Apollo, Raymond McKamie immediately took notice, sizing up his impending danger. As soon as Michigan Marty saw Raymond McKamie, it was on. Raymond McKamie pulled his piece and fired at Marty, but missed and hit Marty's friend Raymond Carradi. Raymond Carradi was taken out in an ambulance and died a few weeks later, but not before calling Michigan Marty from his hospital bed so Marty could listen to "Hey Jude" by the Beatles. Raymond heard his favorite song, "Hey Jude." Marty heard nothing on his end of the phone. Raymond died from a bullet meant for Marty, and then Raymond heard nothing. Marty lived. No one was prosecuted.

Forty years later, in August of 2007, Raymond Carradi's Brother, Madio, disclosed to me that the only reason he didn't take out Raymond McKamie was because he had to support both his own family and his brother Raymond's family. And, support those two families Madio did, becoming a very successful entrepreneur and owner of "National Ladder." Madio stayed Marty's loyal friend to the very end.

"Born of Partisans and Foes." Michigan Marty soon became "K. O. Marty" on the bar circuit. In the mid-1960s and 1970s Marty was "The Man" at numerous watering holes – none more infamous than the mid 1960s "Joe Bathey's" on Wyoming south of Fenkell (Five Mile). As bikini girls danced in the elevated cages (what the heck was that about?), "Randy C and the Valiants" played the Rolling Stones "Can't Get No Satisfaction," James Brown's "I Feel Good," Junior Walker and the All Star's, "Shot Gun," Jackie Wilson's "Higher and Higher" and "Reet Petite," Johnny Rivers' "Poor Side of Town," the Temptations, Four Tops, Martha and the Vandellas' "Dancin in the Streets" and numerous other Motown artists.

At the same time, in the 1960s, my boys and I were just beginning to tune into San Francisco's Haight-Ashbury's "Summer of Love" scene and into Peter Fonda and Dennis Hopper's *Easy Rider* movie, and into our generation's greatest poet, Bob Dylan: "Blowin' in the Wind," "Positively, Fourth Street," "Mr. Tambourine Man" covered by the "Byrds" (on second thought... hold the cocktail; "Mr. Tambo-rine Man" has a new idea) and "Like a Rolling Stone":

> "You ride on your horse with your diplomat
> who carried on his shoulder a Siamese cat.
> Ain't it hard when you discover that
> he really wasn't where it's at, after he took from you
> everything he could steal."

Michigan Marty was also the man at the "Club Cliché" on John R. south of Eight Mile Road where the "Sunliners" (later the Motown group "Rare Earth") revved it up: saxophonist Gil Bridges,

Jack "Kid" Gilbert
Where's the Party?

Conga drums by Eduardo "Eddie" Guzman and percussion and vocals by Pete ("Riviera") Horlbeck of my of St. Scholastica grade school who did the lead vocals on their great cover, "Get Ready Cuz Here I Come." All the while "Kid Gilbert," my St. Scholastica Classmate, and Donnie "Mad Dog" Monroe (may he rest) sat in the "Peanut Gallery" keeping their own syncopated beat alongside Howdy Doody, Buffalo Bob, Tinker Bell and Phineas T. Bluster. Yeah, "Kid" Gilbert and "the Dog" were the leaders in a brand new concept: "An altered state of consciousness."

As the music blared and the dancers twirled, and as the cool dudes hustled the cool chicks, Michigan Marty would regularly tap out a few tough guys and some whackos – many times with a supporting cast that included former Catholic Central Football stars, the "Mad Croatian," Johnny "Don't Panic" Banich, and the infamous wild Irishman, "Peter James" Sullivan who once knocked out Frank Sinatra's off-duty-Southfield-cop bodyguard, and then put his business card in the off duty cop's pocket in case the cop eventually woke up and wanted some more of "Peter James" Sullivan. When the Southfield cop eventually came to, and found "Peter James'" business card, he and five other uniform Southfield Police Officers paid a visit

to "Peter James" Sullivan at Hoot McInerny's car dealership – a rather awkward situation for used-car salesman extraordinaire, Peter Sullivan, to talk his way out of, but he did. They don't call him "smooth Peter James" for nothing.

Also included in Marty's entourage was a notable list of Damon Runyan characters that included: Johnny "The Flake" Hill, who ran the

"Peter James" Sullivan

Blind Pigs; Bobby McDonough, four time loser stick-up man (hey Bobby did you ever get away with a single heist?); unlucky "Lucky" Barton whose last moments were spent alone bleeding to death in a dumpster on Thanksgiving Day, all because the Caldeans at Seven Mile and Woodward took umbrage at Lucky taunting them after he beat them in arm wrestling; Pete Katranis whose battered body was found in the trunk of a car for sticking up mob card games (he must have had

Jack Harrington

a death wish); St. Agatha's Jack Harrington who could have easily lost his life at John Flake's blind pig one night in the mid 1960s because Jack couldn't keep track of the name of his newly introduced acquaintance, Jim, Tim, or Slim. But, the blind pig's sergeant-at-arms, Michigan Marty, saved Jack Harrington from a knife wielding Jim, Tim, Slim or whoever that wacko was. There was also John "Pizza" DiBella and Frank "Designated Hitter" Demers, my St. Scholastica classmates, who, one night in the early morning hours, found themselves staring straight into the short barrel of Luis "Louie" Herrara's "Saturday Night Special" as Michigan Marty was attempting to fulfill his promise to take them to Herrara's "blind pig," even if it meant knocking down the front door to Louie's joint. Whoever

John DiBella

said: "Nothing good happens after midnight" was right on. Rounding out Michigan Marty's entourage was Danny Tingle, the 6′ 6″ tough guy who was big on size but short on physical explosiveness when a "beef" jumped off, dramatic Jimmy Ruby, the hoods own James Dean, the Jewish contingent: Bruce "The Clothier" Goldman, Rodney "Money Man" Shacket, David "Floorman" Silver, Sheldon "Dr. Boogie" Boardlove and many other Damon Runyan and "moon-for-the-misbegotten" characters.

Frank Demers

Michigan Marty's irrepressible sense of humor was on high alert at any time, any place. One night during the summer of 1965, I was a 23-year-old working the door at the Joe Bathey's Club as Michigan Marty's "Junior Bouncer." "Randy C and the Valiants" were driving it home with the Bobby Fuller Fours' "I Fought the Law and the Law Won." I was as revved up as the music, and I threw some muscle head, assaultive trouble maker down the steps and out the door. Then, as I shut the door, the guy bounced right back in – "Boing." So I threw him out a second time, but he bounced right back in again – "Boing." I looked at Marty in disbelief. Marty's instant assessment: "Brother Fred, you're putting to much 'English' on that guy." I listened to Marty and it worked. The third time I launched

Brother Fred
"Bouncer in Training"
1966

the guy, I cut down on the spin and down the stairs he bounced, out the door and then south bound down Wyoming and never "boinged" back. I was learning on the run as I heard Marty proclaim: "You can't beat experience Brother Fred," and, with seven years on me, Marty, at age 30, certainly had more experience in all fields of life than I did.

Michigan Marty also handled the action at "La Chambres" on Schoolcraft and Telegraph in Detroit where I witnessed him direct two overhand rights to the jaws of two different customers standing side by side – generating two knockouts in three seconds. And who can forget the "Side Door" on Telegraph and Michigan Ave. in Dearborn where Michigan Marty, shall we say, "borrowed" a security cop's gun to shoot up the engine block of a departing Corvette that was pulling out of valet parking with a couple of "mouthy" occupants – an incident that had numerous follow-up beefs, hospitalizations and legal repercussions, much to Marty's surprise. Oh the fog of the spirits! But, even without the spirits, Michigan Marty was a man of action who was quick to jump into character at a moment's notice. He was never a man of contemplation and analysis, never a man who concerned himself with consequences – even less so while under the influence of the "diminished inhibition" that walks hand in hand with the libation of distilled spirits.

Michigan Marty also covered the action at "Bimbos" at Seven Mile and Woodward. During those warm, balmy, endless Midwest summers of the 1970s, we would all sit at Michigan Marty's big round table, securely located in the corner, everyone drinking fruity Sangria wine, and everyone engaged in high energy socializing as we talked, talked and talked some more – all uninhibited, youthful, social exuberance with no one listening and with no exchange of ideas. One night at "Bimbos" as Jim Croce sang "Bad, Bad Leroy Brown," some guy, Andre, pulled his piece, cocked it and pointed at Michigan Marty, and, apparently, was about to shoot when a friend of Marty's seeing the episode go down, pulled, cocked, pointed and discharged his own piece into Andre, dispatching Andre to the great beyond – one of Detroit's still unsolved (justified) homicides.

But, the 1960s and 1970s were not shoot-out eras. For the most part, Michigan Marty's "born of partisans and foes" persona played out in one-on-one fist fights, "mano a mano," with a few all out rumbles and riots sprinkled in. The venues were usually, but not always, Marty's place of employment. Who could ever forget the Anthony House West on Plymouth Road where Peter Besso got shot in the butt? How ignominious and inglorious true life can be. Peter Besso was not the only one to take a slug in the gluteus maximus. John Flake got shot in the butt in the Red Dog Saloon in the Cass Corridor as the Flake Man was diving head first under the pool table, unable to squeeze his big-buck derriere out of harm's way. Lucky Barton took a slug in the wrist in the same episode, and the shooter, Jerry Price, walked in self defense. I'll give you odds, John Wayne, Randolph Scott, Gary Cooper, Hopalong Cassidy and Gene Autry or even Clint Eastwood never got shot in the butt. Oh – the shame of it all!

Merry Christmas Everyone

And, who could ever forget the Vertigo next to Larcos on Six Mile and Livernois where on Christmas Eve 1967, during my junior year in law school, "Quick" Don Quick and I witnessed and participated in part two of Michigan Marty's classic two-fight Christmas Eve brawl with Wendell Johnson who just got out of Jackson Prison on parole for (of all things) "good behavior." I worked that Christmas Eve at the "Olympia" in Detroit as an usher for the Detroit Red Wings hockey game. After the game, my ride, "Quick" Don Quick, drove us both over to the Vertigo for a joyous Christmas drink with Brother Marty. We arrived just in time to join in Marty's second Christmas

Eve dance of the night with Wendell Johnson and his boys. I broke a hand during the dance, but luckily avoided death-by-suffocation in the pile up. Thanks to a ride by "Quick" Don Quick, I ended up in some medical clinic on Grand River west of Seven Mile with a pretend doctor trying to stick a real needle in my really broken hand to freeze it so he could set my hand (hey – who else but a "pretend" doctor would be working Christmas Eve?). Refusing to lay down, I sat on a gurney and extended my broken paw to the pretend doctor. As the needle went in, "Quick" Don Quick, my ride, quickly fainted and crashed headlong on the floor. The pretend doctor left me to hold the needle in my own hand while he rallied to save the unconscious "Quick Man."

In that same Christmas Eve brawl, Marty also broke his hand and almost lost a piece of his nose to a bite. The missing piece of his nose was sewed back on. And, someone ran over the antagonist, Wendell Johnson, in the parking lot breaking his femur in two places. Michigan Marty, Wendell Johnson and I, with my ride, "Quick Man,"

all ended up at different hospitals as the radio played "We Wish You a Merry Christmas," "Peace on Earth, Good Will to Men" and that brand new instant Christmas classic, "Marty the Red Nose Bouncer." As William Shakespeare said: "All's well that ends well," but it sure was difficult taking those law school exams in January 1968 with that cast on my writing hand.

Marty was nicked up by New Years Eve 1967

Traumatic? Not really – just another day in the life of... Dramatic? Perhaps. But, for me, it was just "life" evolving from one day to the next in some fashion or another. But, then again, I spent a night in jail during my first week of law school, and another night in jail the very day I passed the bar exam, both false arrests, but, ironically, a bookend symmetry to my law school career or, in the bigger picture of life, perhaps a bookend symbol of the "deprivation of freedom" that comes with both the pursuit of dysfunction and the pursuit of formal education.

So, I was fully aware of how "life" in my family generally evolved in ways that other people thought was traumatic, but that for me and my family was just one day evolving into the next in some dramatic fashion or another. Brother Marty is fighting for the heavyweight championship of Jackson Prison, and then returns to the free world to fight his way through life many times without pay and sometimes for pay – earning wages as a "bouncer extraordinaire." I'm emotionally fighting my way through life one way or another, and fighting my way through law school and broke most of the time. My 16-year-old sister, Jeanne Valentine, is getting married, in my first week of law school in the Fall of 1966, and I'm taking the place of my father walking her down the aisle of St. Scholastica to give her away to 18-year-old Bob Burns. Mother Jean is exhausted working double shifts as a waitress at the Grecian Gardens Restaurant in Greektown to pay for the wedding reception. Sister Katie and I are going to the Wayne County morgue in the fall of 1971 to identify her dead husband Lonnie, as the white sheet is pulled off his corpse, and she silently weeps on my shoulder. My dear Irish mother, fighting through the loss of her marriage to my father, is sadly making it through life on her own, trying to hold the family together and cooking family meals between split shifts as a waitress. And, for me, it's just... **"life is tough,"** everyone was depressed (although we didn't know it), and one day just evolved into the next day, and so, today, on Christmas Eve, I fought my way off the bottom of the pile to avoid death by suffocation, and I also broke a hand and Marty broke a hand and lost a piece of his nose. But, okay, I'm still alive, and Marty is still alive – so what's next on our agenda? And, next on the agenda was my mother Jean telling my brother

Marty and me that we were not allowed to hang around with each other anymore. Huh?

Other Michigan Marty bouncer venues included "Bad Bobby" Tiano's "Other Place" bar in Livonia (with a very financially successful Bobby Tiano becoming one of Marty's best friends), "Starvin' Marvin's" Downriver Disco, the "Webb Wood" and the "Caravan" in Highland Park (where the odds of getting nicked up or sliced up was an even money bet), "Gold Diggers" on Michigan and Lonyo (now "Crazy Horse," owned by my dear friend and client, Southwest Detroit's 6' 6" inch Dr. Tom, the "gentle giant," Moses), the "Library Bar" on the east side, and the memorable "Clock Restaurant" in Hamtramck – absolutely the toughest after hours restaurant in the Greater Detroit area where you didn't need silverware because everyone brought their own knife to a 3:00 a.m. breakfast after a night of heavy drinking. The only sober customers were the Albanians who lived in the area. They weren't that big on drinking, but they were that big on fighting. What the Albanians gained in sobriety, they lost in temperament. Albanians, Yugoslavs, Greeks, Hillbillies, Polocks, Italians and Irish – most fueled by "firewater," and all protected by the "invincibility of youth." And, you wonder why there were so many brawls. But, Michigan Marty persevered through each and every dangerous, perverse, wacked-out night as "bouncer extraordinaire" at the Clock Restaurant in Hamtramck.

Last, but not least, there was Tommy Fertney's "Mr. F's Motown Revue and Supper Club" at Fourteen Mile Road and Van Dyke in Sterling Heights – the venue where the classic rumble with the Selfridge Air Force Base took place. Again, the biggest, baddest and most aggressive airman heard the bugle play taps as Michigan Marty bopped and tapped him to fare-thee-well. The big airman's followers, having lost their appetite for dinner with Michigan Marty at Fertney's Supper Club, cancelled their dinner reservation, and headed back to their own reservation at Selfridge Air Force Base. That same night, right after the Air Force brawl, Marty drove to Northwest Detroit to help me negotiate a very dangerous altercation that my Catholic Central High School buddy, Bob Rekiel, and I were having with the "Highwaymen" motorcycle club at Joe Bathey's. Thanks to some quick action by Joe Bathey owner, Hymie Greenblatt, I was saved from the knife wielding "Highwaymen." It was a long night... that summer of 1965 but as Shakespeare said: "When it rains... make sure you duck."

Television Toughman

In 1979, at age 43 and in the twilight of his storied career, Michigan Marty fought in Al Dore's first "Tough Man" contest at the Silverdo-

Michigan Marty vs. Swinehart "Toughman" Contest 9/21/79

Michigan Marty 1979

me in Pontiac, Michigan. There were eighty "tough men" in the program – all younger than "Michigan Marty." Marty put down the Black Label Scotch whiskey the day before the main event, and worked out on the body bag for ten minutes. He finished the Scotch, put on his boxing shorts, taped his hands, got "Ducky" Deitz, his 1952 opponent for the City of Detroit Boxing Championship, as his cornerman, got me, my 9-year-old son, Valentine, and my 63-year-old father in the audience as his cheer leaders, and finished fifth among eighty contestants.

Basking in the glow of that success, and now a 43-year-old Lion in Winter, Michigan Marty landed an interview on Phil Donohue's television show where he wore white silk boxing trunks, white silk tails and a white (comic-looking) top hat. That Michigan Marty was something to behold – by now 6′ 1″ tall and 275 lbs. of "Let's Rip This Joint Up." Donohue loved "Michigan Marty." Marty was good copy – good looks and a ferocious "I'll eat you up" attitude lurking ever so delicately beneath a sincere veneer of old world charm.

Regaining Sobriety

After going Hollywood, Michigan Marty got off the booze for good at the well-seasoned age of 45. The turning point? Michigan Marty and Johnnie "The Flake" Hill had taken a lot of action (bets) on NFL football games. Michigan Marty and Flake and others gathered in a rented motel room on Woodward Ave. in Highland Park and installed three TV sets so they could follow their money on each game. As that football Sunday in the Fall of 1981 wore on, and, as the booze flowed freely, and, as the air filled with a distinctive order of burnt hemp, Michigan Marty watched in awe as a quarterback for the New York Giants in television set number one threw a forward pass to a wide receiver for the San Francisco Forty Niners in television set number two who then, unbelievably, lateraled the ball to a Chicago Bears tight end in television set number three... touchdown! Wow! thought Marty. What a psychedelic play. When Michigan Marty could not confirm this "Ripley's Believe It or Not" touchdown with his friends in the motel room, and when he could not confirm this extraordinary play in newspaper accounts the next day, and, when I finally convinced him that only two teams play each other at a time, Marty decided it was time to get off the booze, and regain that sobriety that he lost twenty-five long, hard years ago. At age 45, Marty got off the booze cold turkey (a wonder he didn't die from a seizure), and got a legitimate job with the Iron Workers, setting him up for a future pension.

As a final encore, Michigan Marty, while working with the Iron Workers at Cobo Hall setting up the Detroit Auto Show in 1999, squared off with a young, sadistic, 34-year-old, 6′5″, 260 lb., bad actor, Local 98 electrician bully who made the mistake of calling Michigan Marty "old man." At age 63, Michigan Marty stopped that giant bully in his tracks – a one punch victory. The bully didn't answer the bell. Michigan Marty then retired from a long and lustrous career as "Detroit's Legendary Tough Man." That should have been the denouement of Michigan Marty's illustrious, tough man career… but it wasn't.

The "Joint"… "The Big Fight"

Even in retirement, Michigan Marty was not allowed to slip off quietly. In 2004, at age 68, Michigan Marty's colorful past resurfaced when he was confronted with David Hannigan's book, *The Big Fight*, which referred to one of Michigan Marty's two short-term stays at the Michigan State Prison on Cooper Street in Jackson, Michigan.

It comes as no surprise that Michigan Marty's great career as legendary tough guy had a few occupational hazards such as jail time. Baseball Hall of Famer Ted Williams lost five years of his major league career to World War II and the Korean War. Likewise, Michigan Marty's fifty-plus year career as a legendary "tough man" was also interrupted in the prime of his career by a tough guy's occupational hazard – "jail time."

Although Michigan Marty studiously avoided the police (a lesson he learned as a 3-year-old from our mother Jean), Marty's day-to-day exploits were eventually picked up on law enforcement's radar. Because Michigan Marty had only one direction, "straight ahead," he had a few go-rounds with the cops during traffic stops and at blind pigs, and even in his own rented house. The cops, in unsportsman-like manner, refused to accept their defeat and go on with their lives. Instead, harkening back to his early family days, Marty, like his mother Jean before him, was finally subdued and led off in handcuffs for fighting with the cops – an Irish misdemeanor. The non-Irish cops, however, saw the stand-up, knock-down brawls with them as a challenge to their authority – something more egregious and sinister than the Irish misdemeanors and technical fouls that our family saw them as. As a result, Marty, right in the peak of his legendary career, had to take two short vacations behind the walls on Cooper Street in Jackson, Michigan – full scholarship… thanks to the taxpayers in the great State of Michigan. What a great country!

During the first of Marty's vacations at Jackson Prison, he stayed sharp by fighting through the elimination rounds for the heavyweight championship of "The Joint." True to form, Michigan Marty landed in the finals to fight a convict named Alvin "Blue" Lewis for the undisputed heavyweight championship of Jackson Prison. Marty hurt Blue in the first round, and almost took him out. As Marty says, he let Blue "get away," and later lost the fight to Blue. Marty had to swallow that defeat and wear the crown of the second toughest man in Jackson prison. Marty wanted to avenge that defeat the next year with a rematch, but when the Parole Board came knocking, and offered Michigan Marty an option he couldn't refuse, "freedom via parole," Marty was gone… back on the free wheeling streets of Detroit with a promise of "good behavior."

Blue Lewis, serving time for a homicide in a stickup gone wrong when he was a 17-year-old, got an early release for helping quell prison riots during the same year as the 1967 Detroit riots. Blue Lewis went on to a professional boxing career, and fought a South American fighter, Corletti, at Detroit's Olympia in the 1960s. Corletti was then the number two ranked heavyweight in the world. I was at Olympia with Brother Marty when Blue Lewis knocked Corletti out of the ring, on to the apron and down onto the floor in the second round. Corletti could not answer the bell for the third round, and the world took notice of Alvin "Blue" Lewis from the Detroit Hood.

Blue was out of the joint. He was a world ranked fighter and "the real deal," and, maybe, with a tinge of regret, Michigan Marty wondered what might have been… but, on the other hand, Michigan Marty still had his wits. Later, on July 11, 1972, Blue Lewis fought Heavyweight Champion Muhammad Ali (whose great grandfather was an Irishman) in Dublin, Ireland at Croke Park for the heavyweight championship of the world. Blue lost to Ali in twelve rounds – a real slug fest. Blue Lewis later retired, and Blue and Marty have remained friends over the years.

In 2004, my St. Scholastica classmate and ex-cop, Neil Flynn, asked Michigan Marty to review *The Big Fight* by Dave Hannigan –

a good read which details Blue Lewis' fight with Muhammad Ali in Dublin, Ireland in July 1972, the month of Michigan Marty's 36th birthday. Hannigan's book details how Blue Lewis ended up in Jackson Prison – "I robbed a white guy and he died in the hospital later." Blue was convicted of murder as a 17-year-old, and was sentenced to twenty to thirty years. In Hannigan's book, Blue Lewis mentions how dangerous it was in Jackson

Officer Neil Flynn

Prison with prisoners negotiating their way between the Mafia, the KKK, Arabs, Whites, Blacks, Hispanic, etc. mentioning, ironically, that the only time he really felt safe in prison was when he was in the ring fighting.

Since Blue Lewis was doing a long stretch, he fought many times for the prison boxing title and, as a 6'4" 220 pounder, he won the title year in and year out. The only prison fight Blue Lewis mentions in Hannigan's book, *The Big Fight*, however, is the fight he had with my brother, Marty Lahti, whom Blue mistakenly refers to as "Marty Lardy." That's not the only erroneous description, however. Blue Lewis refers to Marty as a "mafia dude," a weight lifter who weighed 270 lbs., and a guy who had never fought anybody before. As Michigan Marty says – "you're wrong on all counts Blue."

Marty was way too independent and way too Irish to be a "mafia dude," and Marty had fought many, many fights – not during robberies Blue – but just for the sport of it Blue, "mano a mano." Marty weighed 230 lbs. when he fought you Blue, not 270 lbs. Additionally, Blue, you refuse to give Michigan Marty his propers. Marty almost took you out in the first round Blue. You were one punch away from going down for good. So Blue, my man, another day, another fight, and you could have been going down for the count.

Blue, if you are out there and reading the story of the Hood, here's the deal. First, Michigan Marty's lawyer needs you to do a written retraction. Second Blue, you gotta contact that Hannigan guy, and get all his books recalled, and all new editions must be corrected with the proper spelling of Marty's last name. It's "Lahti" not Lardi – got it? Third, all new editions gotta knock Marty's weight down from 270 lbs. to Marty's old weight when he fought you Blue – a svelte 230 lbs. Fourth Blue, you can keep the mafia description, but only if you preface mafia with "Irish" (as in "Irish Mafia"), and, finally Blue, you gotta account for all royalties you earned from Hannigan's book, and, if you got more than fifty bucks, you gotta take Michigan Marty's kid brother Fred and his St. Scholastica Grade School buddy, Officer Neil Flynn, out to dinner. No soul food Blue. We ain't got no appetite for soul food, Blue. They never served soul food at Richard's Drive-In or at Geiger's Drive-In or at the Dyna Inn, the Saratoga Farms or at the Checker Barbeque in our Hood. So, Blue, its got to be Mario's fine Detroit Italian restaurant on Second Ave. in the Boulevard Center area – the same Mario's Restaurant where Marty and John "Flake" use to "promote their game" during the blind pig days. Ask for "Nabil," Detroit's finest waiter. And, Blue, if you didn't get any royalties from Hannigan, then call Muhammad Ali and tell him to take us all to dinner because, if Michigan Marty didn't take some steam out of you in the Jackson Prison Heavyweight Championship fight, you might have beaten Ali – so Ali owes. Got it Blue? **LONG LIVE MICHIGAN MARTY.**

Staying Strong

And so did Michigan Marty live long… or, at least, relatively long, dying of lung cancer from second hand smoke on July 25, 2007 shortly after his 71st birthday. When I got the news Marty had terminal lung cancer with no options, I was in a tough two week trial in Wayne County Circuit Court. Instinctively, I knew I had to send Marty a short note that he could put under his hospice pillow to be his farewell reference for his last moments – something that pointedly captured his colorful life. I had an undeniable urge to give Marty a written symbol of his extraordinary life – a symbol that could put the impending death of Marty's Final Chapter into the overall context of his charismatic, grandiose life:

"Dear Brother Marty:
I am so sad to hear of your condition. You have always (always) been my hero. The big brother that I looked up to with such pride. The Legendary Marty Lahti that the whole Detroit Hood looked up. Now everybody's world is crashing down as the calls come in to my house, one after another. Despite your warrior reputation, you have always been a peaceful man. That peacefulness will serve you well now as you reflect on the great life you had in this rough and tumble world – a life that

in many ways was colorful beyond description, and a life ten times richer than what most of us have.

I am in a full fledged battle against the State Police and the Prosecutor's Office in *People vs. Michael Wade* – a full week of trial last week and another full week this week. If I could see you Saturday, I would love to do so. I'll call and see whether that's possible. Whether I see you or not, please know that I love you and respect you. There is no other like you."

**Fred and Val Lauck
and Brother Marty
2000**

**Brother Marty and
Sister Jeannie Valentine
2005**

**Sister Katie, Fred, Marty
and Debra Sandoval
2004**

**Marty, Frank Sandoval
and Fred
2002**

Marty died on July 25, 2007 his heart filled with courage, his will filled with character and his head held high – "bloodied but unbowed" – a living symbol of Native American beliefs.

> "When it comes your time to die, be not like those whose hearts are filled with the fear of death. So that when their time comes they weep and pray for a little more time to live their lives over again in a different way. Sing your death song and die like a hero going home."

And, so it ends, Brother Marty. The unrelenting march from the trauma of birth in the heat wave of 1936 to the trauma of death in 2007 is over, and, in between… **a few laughs and a few stories along the way.**

As you always told me Brother Marty: **"STAY STRONG."** We no longer have you to light our darkness, but we are clinging fast to your radiant memory. There's no other like you.

CHAPTER 13

Kronk Gym...
Busted Up Champions

Some from the Hood went to Kronk U., obtained a masters in pugilism, got busted up and went to the "joint"... like **WILLIAM "CAVEMAN" LEE**.

The world renown Kronk Boxing Gym was located at Warren and McGraw in the City of Detroit. Like much of Detroit, it is no more. In 2006, the Kronk Gym was closed. It's now a lifeless ghost of days gone by... a memory of what use to be. Marauders and modern day grave robbers, known as "metal thieves," stripped out the boiler and pipes, putting the last nail into Kronk's once glorious presence. But, in its heyday in the 1970s and 1980s, Kronk and its founder, Emanuel Steward, were synonymous with world boxing championships.

Kronk Warriors

There were other gyms across the country where world champions trained: Marvin Hagler's gym, Petronelli Brothers Boxing Gym, the 5th Street Gym in South Miami where, in 1963, I saw

Muhammad Ali, then Cassius Clay, train for his first heavyweight championship fight against the "Bear," Sonny Liston, and the Main Street Gym in Los Angeles where I saw the great welterweight from Panama, Roberto "Hands of Stone" Duran, train for his big fight against Pepino Cuevas. There were also a ton of YMCA boxing gyms strewn about America's decaying, urban landscapes where aspiring young fighters with big dreams worked out, including the YMCA on Woodward Ave. in Highland Park, Michigan, where I used to watch my brother, Michigan "K.O." Marty, work out after his parole from Jackson Prison where he fought Alvin "Blue" Lewis for the heavy weight championship of "the joint" in 1965 – with "Blue" later going on to fight Muhammad Ali in Dublin, Ireland on July 11, 1972 in a slugfest for the heavyweight championship of the world.

But, in Detroit, it was the Kronk Gym – the home of Thomas Hearns, Motown's own "Hit Man." Hearns acquitted himself with honor on the world stage even while losing two of the most sensational fights ever fought – thrillers against "Marvelous" Marvin Hagler and "Sugar Ray" Leonard. Tommy had both of them, literally, on the ropes before he let them get away. Tommy Hearns was an eight time world champion before they cut the gloves off of him and tied him down to the training table. But, watch out... knowing Tommy, he's likely to announce another comeback any day now, especially where he owes the IRS several hundred thousands of dollars. There is no fighter who epitomizes Kronk's glory days more than Tommy "Hit Man" Hearns.

Emanuel Steward was Kronk's legendary leader. First and foremost, Emanuel Steward was a visionary with a keen eye for boxing talent. His secondary role was trainer, promoter, TV color analyst and all around boxing guru. Steward trained all the big time Kronk champions, including Tommy Hearns, Hilmer Kinty, Milt McCrory, his little brother, Stevie McCrory, an Olympic champ who ended up as a "runner" for my dear friend, client and great trial lawyer, Albert

Lopatin (may he rest), and including Mickey "Sneaky Pea" Goodwin (may he rest) – a white, gifted, good looking, all-around athlete from

Melvindale… a hard-scrabble, gritty, smoke stack suburb of the City of Detroit.

Emanuel Steward also trained the undersized, but super energized, Leon Spinks. Leon and his brother Michael both won gold medals in the 1976 Olympics with Leon later defeating Muhammad Ali for the heavyweight championship of the world. But, poor Leon's career was derailed by wine, women and song as well as the loss of his false teeth to a "hooker" on Eight Mile

Mickey Goodwin
a.k.a. "Sneaky Pea"

Road in Detroit. You can't blame the girl; she was just looking for a souvenir from the "Champ." But, oh man, what an embarrassing headline for Leon. Kronk and Emanuel Steward also trained many other "main eventers" including Aaron "The Hawk" Pryor, Farris "Killer" Purify, Frank Tate, David Braxton, Nathaniel "Gator" Akbar, Leslie "Lemonade" Gardner, Darius "Doll Baby" Wilson, William "Caveman" Lee and nameless others – big on dreams, but short on the lightning reflexes and explosive punching power needed to make a name in the fight game.

Many notable fighters, born and raised far from the Detroit Hood, also left their homes just to train at the Kronk Gym under the watchful eye of Emanuel Steward, including tenacious warriors like Julio Cesar Chavez, a world champion in three different weight divisions, Oscar DeLaHoya, a gifted athlete and matinee idol, Evander Holyfield, a four time heavyweight champ, Lennox Lewis, heavyweight champion from Great Britain, present heavyweight champ, Wladimir Klitschko, and many others on their way up to the top of the boxing world.

My favorites of the Kronk stable of fighters were Mickey Goodwin, Tommy Hearns, Leon Spinks and William "Caveman" Lee – charismatic characters, one and all. In those "glory days" at the Kronk Gym, it was one amazing fight after another, one amazing caper after another, and numerous side shows and soap operas in between – like the Caveman Lee stick-up fiasco I'm about to tell.

The "Caveman"

The first time I heard of William "Caveman" Lee was 1981, just after his downside-upside fight with John LoCicero. After having his

William "Caveman" Lee
A Big Heart

head caved in (no pun intended) early in the fifth round, amazingly, the Caveman turned the tide of certain defeat into victory in the same round, winning with a knock out. Ring announcer, Al Bernstein, picked that round as one of the best fight rounds in boxing history. Later when his Kronk stable-mate, Mickey Goodwin, came up lame and cancelled his middleweight championship fight with "Marvelous" Marvin Hagler, Caveman Lee jumped into the ring as a last minute, unprepared substitute. Predictably, the Caveman took it on the chin when he ran into "Marvelous" Marvin's usual devastating buzz-saw. The Caveman was knocked down and... out for the count.

Things began to go downhill for the Caveman right after that spur of the moment, disastrous fight with Marvin Haggler. Caveman's career was over, but he hung on at the Kronk Gym as a sparring partner for Tommy Hearns whose own career was taking off like a rocket. Every day the Caveman sparred with Tommy Hearns, an already fragile Caveman took more shots to the head. Every night the Caveman took drugs to control the pain – trading the fog of the head shots for the fog of the drugs. One day, sitting around in his usual fog, Caveman thought of how he could make some fast money. After all, everyone around him seemed to be getting rich, and the Caveman certainly needed some money to "style" in the same fashion as the "main eventers" did. The accumulated punches were taking their toll, and nothing in Caveman's head was tracking clearly. But, hey, Caveman was a man with a plan – albeit not a well thought out one.

The Caper

Caveman left the Kronk Gym in Detroit one day, and drove northbound up the interstate into affluent Oakland County, Michigan. The Caveman got off the freeway at a small suburban town in North Oakland County. Just about a mile off the freeway, Caveman went into a professional office building and directly into a savings and loan telling everyone there present, "This is a stuck up." With the benefit of hindsight, Caveman could have more aptly said: "This is a fuck up." The teller calmly handed over the money in a canvas bank bag – the one with the telltale red dye surreptitiously planted in with the loot. Caveman split with the loot, and was trying to find his way back to the interstate when the red dye pellets in the bank bag exploded, staining the Caveman's skin and filling his getaway car with red smoke. The police, alerted by the bank alarm, were parked in the corner gas station near the interstate waiting for their culprit to surface – all the while the Caveman was driving toward the interstate with his head outside the car window, trying to breathe as the smoke from the telltale red dye billowed out his driver's side window.

What a sight! So many 911 calls came in about the car with the telltale red smoke and the driver with his head out the window gasping for breath, the dispatcher was able to easily trace Caveman's escape route just as if the cops had a "bear in the air":

"All cars, be on the lookout for a black male subject wanted for the stick up of the savings and loan. Armed and dangerous, he was last seen in a billowing red cloud of smoke heading toward the interstate, with his head stuck out the window, gasping for air."

Busted... Up, Down and Sideways

Seeing the dire plight of Caveman's hopeless escape, one cop with a sense of understatement questioned: "Do you think we have the right guy?" Cheech and Chong could not have improved on this comic caper. Caveman, whose life had already been descending to "hell in a hand basket," had just caught a tsunami heading in the same direction, and the poor, beat up Caveman couldn't outrun it physically, mentally or emotionally. The Caveman was arrested without a struggle, and taken to a holding cell. He was locked up with many other hapless characters trying to out run their own tsunamis – all awaiting a court date and a rendezvous with "justice." Caveman would be arraigned on armed robbery charges the next morning.

While waiting in the crowded holding cell, Caveman noticed the familiar face of Aram "Rocky" Alkazoff, one of the regulars at Kronk who used to work out and spar with the headliners. In moments of resignation and despair, comfort comes in small unexpected ways. With their chance meeting, Rocky and Caveman drew upon the familiar to console one another. Rocky, biding his time until his transfer to a federal prison, launched into a soulful lament about jail conditions as the wide-eyed Caveman listened:

"Caveman this place is as filthy, overcrowded, noisy, and as unfeeling a place as is in this United States of America. First of all you wear a pajama type outfit of green that is full of old sweat and smell, and all you have for your feet is these broken up slippers. The food is not fit for a human being, and there is so little that people fight for it. You get no fresh air ever. The place is either too cold or too hot, and always noisy. There is nothing to read. The phones rarely work, and, maybe, if you're lucky, you might get a shower. The mail hardly works. The sheriffs hardly do anything for you no matter how polite you ask, and you could go weeks without seeing a pencil, a scrap of paper or soap. You might get to watch an old television, which hardly comes in because they don't allow antennas, and you might get a torn up piece of an old newspaper to read… if you're lucky. All you can do is sit on a steel bench and just stare forward like a fool for hours at a time. There is no water, no food that's edible, and, if you want to go to the bathroom, you have to do it in front of everybody. Never in your life will you feel so ashamed, hopeless and less than a human being than in one of these. But, you know me Caveman, I don't complain."

Other than Rocky, the inmates were all black men ranging in age from eighteen to over seventy. They were all skinny and underfed. Most of them looked like "moon-for-the-misbegotten" characters. With their telltale signs of methamphetamine and crack cocaine habits, the hollow-eyed inmates looked like they just stepped off the streets of "desolation row" into "cold turkey" incarceration. Most of them were novices just starting out on their wayward path. In this desperate crowd, their faces said it all. It was obvious that before incarceration these lost souls were out there in the "free world" living on a steady, non-protein diet of mind altering, illicit drugs. For them, there was very little food on the outside and not much more to speak of on the inside. These poor, misfit souls had sores, scars and open abscesses from shooting bad drugs. They smelled. The whole place smelled. Caveman didn't feel good being there, but he was comforted by spending the afternoon in his new home with an old familiar face and acquaintance – even if Rocky was the only white guy in the joint.

In Court

Time and mental hardship crawled slowly forward until, finally, the Caveman was taken from the holding cell for his preliminary examination, and delivered to a courtroom packed with media and curiosity junkies. When the assistant prosecutor finally arrived, the courtroom was so crowded that he had to squeeze into a small space at the prosecutor's table with the officer in charge of Caveman's case almost sitting on his lap. Emanuel Steward and his brother James, a Kronk original, were sitting in the first row behind the defense table. The preliminary exam was a forgone conclusion. A few witnesses were called to testify to the minimum facts necessary to establish the elements of an armed robbery and "probable cause" to believe that the Caveman (still stained with the telltale red dye as he sat in the courtroom) was the armed robber of the savings and loan. Caveman's guilt was undeniable. It was an open and shut case. Caveman got caught red handed, or "red dye handed," as the case may be. The judge bound Caveman's case over to the Oakland County Circuit Court for trial.

Trusting Judge

The last order of business for the day was to address Caveman's bond. The prosecutor had the right to ask the judge to increase Caveman's bond, especially where facts indicated the likelihood of conviction was great – as it surely was for the still red-dye stained Caveman. But, the constitution requires a judge to set a "reasonable" bond in all cases, except in a murder one case. But "reasonable" is a subjective concept on which reasonable minds can reasonably differ so there's always a debate. Caveman's bond was set at $500,000 cash when he was first arraigned on the armed robbery charges. The prosecutor knew the $500,000 cash bond was high enough to keep Caveman locked up, and, therefore, he did not ask to the judge to increase the bond. Hey, if Caveman could afford a $500,000 cash bond, he would not have gone into the stick up business in the first place.

Just as the proceedings were closing for the day, the judge stood up in his flowing black robe, and was about to leave the bench when a hand went up in the first row of the spectator section. In a rather unorthodox move, Emanuel Steward raised his hand, and said he would like to be heard by the court. The judge, a confident person who was not overly influenced by his own position or power, was comfortable with questions from visitors seated in the courtroom – especially where family members or friends wanted to be heard on behalf of their loved ones, or wanted to inform the court of special circumstances that might affect the amount of the bond.

The judge asked Emanuel Steward to stand and place his name on the record. The judge recognized Emanuel Steward from his appearances on televised boxing matches, but, for the cold, written record of justice, Emanuel was just another name... albiet an Old Testament, Hebrew name translating to "God is with us". And, in retrospect, God was , indeed, sitting on Emanuel Steward's shoulder as he addressed the judge: "Your Honor, as to the question of bond of Mr. Lee, I know this is a serious matter, but I would like to ask the court if Your Honor would consider placing Mr. Lee on a temporary personal bond in my custody." Most lawyers would not be bold enough to even make that request. But, here was Emanuel Steward, a layman, pleading Caveman's case from the gallery and asking for custody of a man charged with a felony carrying possible life imprisonment... a highly unusual move. But then again, Emanuel Steward and his Kronk "universe" were all highly unusual characters living in the world of flat-out destruction – "mano a mano," a world that pits one man against another, and "may the best man win," and may the second best survive permanent brain damage.

"Your Honor," Emanual Steward continued, studiously avoiding the "Caveman" moniker: "I need Mr. Lee. Tommy Hearns has a major fight in Las Vegas in two weeks, and I need Mr. Lee to go with us to Las Vegas to continue Tommy's training and sparring. I will bring him right back after the fight and give him back to you." No one is ever allowed to leave the State while awaiting trial on such a serious charge. But, the judge, in another unusual move, did just the opposite. Still standing at the bench in his black robes, the judge granted Caveman a get-out-of-jail bond, and turned him over to Emanuel Steward:

> "Here we have a boxer whose brains have been scrambled from being hit in the head too many times. Where is he going to go? He could use a caretaker at no expense to the taxpayers. At least we know where Mr. Lee will be for the next couple of weeks or so. Mr. Steward, he's all yours. But, you will have to promise me you will bring him right back after the Hearns' fight."

The deputies from the jail who provided security for the court had smiles on their faces as they witnessed and later recounted this most unusual event. It seems that this particular judge in the staid halls of justice might be just as unusual as those Kronk characters, or could it be that the strange, unprecedented bond was a product of the judge's own personal experience of growing up in the whacked-out City of Detroit. Two and a half weeks later, the fight was over, and

Tommy Hearns won another championship, but the Caveman fell from grace again as he was returned to custody in the Oakland County jail. As Cavemen's favorite author, Shakespeare, use to say: "all's well that ends well" – well, at least for the moment. But, Caveman's plight was more like the impending doom of the man who fell off the ledge of a thirty floor skyscraper, and, as he plummeted head first past the eighth floor, was heard to say: "so far – so good." Caveman was now back in the county jail awaiting his rendezvous with justice and an upcoming trial.

Brain Damage and the Law

In courtrooms, words are used to describe and recreate past events. Words are carefully chosen by competing lawyers to, on the one hand, sharpen the emotional impact of past events by creating outrage, or, on the other hand, soften the emotional impact by creating compassion and understanding. Lawyers paint the very same past events into diametrically opposed characterizations for the jury to choose between – the prosecutor's version versus the defendant's version. In short, a trial is a war of words where the inarticulate are doomed to defeat. Caveman's compromised brain understood that undeniable proposition. He knew he needed a good trial lawyer. Caveman also knew that the court would appoint a lawyer to represent him at public expense. But, Emanuel Steward came to the rescue again, and hired a trial lawyer to represent the Caveman. Emanuel Steward was there for Caveman when Caveman needed him, as the Caveman was there for Emanuel when Emanuel needed him.

With Caveman back in custody, everyone knew he would be present in court at each and every stage of his criminal prosecution. Even though he was an inmate, Caveman had a personal chauffeur giving him room service. The sheriff would pick the Caveman up and deliver him to the courtroom at the appointed hour, and take him back to jail when the court hearing was concluded for the day. But, despite all the amenities of jail life, Caveman was far from worry free. Caveman had often boxed in public arenas before tens of thousands of raving, lunatic boxing fans, but, as he awaited trial, Caveman blanched to think that his trial would be open to public display with all the witnesses telling the story of his botched stick-up. How embarrassing, he thought. Caveman didn't have much left, but he still had his pride.

Caveman's attorney knew that Caveman had a right to raise an insanity defense at trial. Given the brain damage Caveman suffered as a prize fighter, it would be attorney malpractice and ineffective assistance of counsel if Caveman's lawyer didn't, at least... explore an insanity defense. Caveman's lawyer, therefore, filed a notice of a possible insanity defense. Based on that notice, the circuit judge ordered Caveman to be taken to the Center for Forensic Psychiatry in Ypsilanti, Michigan to undergo a mental examination for criminal responsibility. Just to cover all bases, Caveman's lawyer also ordered an independent psychiatric exam for a second opinion.

Consideration of the insanity defense was based solely on Caveman's professional career in the boxing ring where he suffered numerous punishing blows to the head – blows that could have easily killed other human beings. The issue... with the repetitive blows to the head and the ensuing, cumulative, traumatic brain damage Caveman suffered, did the Caveman know the stickup was wrong, or, if he did, was Caveman's impulse to stick up the savings and loan an impulse that he had no control over – "irresistible impulse." In short, the law's "right/wrong" test and "irresistible impulse" test would be a question for the jury to decide... if Caveman actually pursued an insanity defense.

Oh yeah! Scoff as you will at the insanity defense, or, as they said in the old neighborhoods in Detroit: "Insanity? – Ah… the defense of last resort" when you are caught red handed, or, as my man Flip Wilson would say: "The Devil made me do it!" But, the legitimacy of the insanity defense is well grounded in both the nature of our humanness and in the philosophy of the law.

A human being is held criminally responsible under our American system of justice because (unlike the rest of the animal kingdom) a human being has the "cognitive," mental power to know what they're doing and to know it's wrong, and because a human being has the "volitional" power of free will to control their actions by making a choice not to violate the law. But, when there has been a significant breakdown in the human mind so that the cognitive, mental power of a human being is so impaired that a person doesn't know what they're doing or doesn't know that what they are doing… is wrong, then law excuses their criminal act because they've lost the cognitive power of their human nature. Likewise, when there has been a significant breakdown in the human mind so that the volitional power of a human being has short circuited, and a person does not have the volitional power of free will to control their actions, "irresistible impulse," the law again excuses their criminal act because they've lost the volitional power of their human nature. In short, when a defect of the human mind deprives a human being of their cognitive power to know the difference between right and wrong, or when a defect of the human mind deprives a human being of their volitional power of free will to control their choices and resist criminal actions, then a human being is not criminally responsible for their actions. But, if you are acquitted by reason of insanity, you don't get a free pass. You don't go to jail, but you don't walk either. Not guilty by reason of insanity automatically incarcerates you in a mental institution – just another "lock up" where you supposedly get help (from a financially bankrupt state that can't afford to give you any help) until you are no longer insane (if ever), at which point you are then released with an affirmation of: "Good-bye, good luck, have a nice life, and don't go getting insane again."

Any lawyer representing the Caveman might have a difficult time explaining the theory of the insanity defense to Caveman because the Caveman led with his chin and his heart, not with his challenged and batter intellect. But, I suspect, it would be easier explaining the intricacies of the insanity law to the Caveman then it would be to talk show hosts and resident intellectual notables such as Rush Limbaugh, Bill O'Reilly or Glenn Beck of Fox News whose preconceived, self professed "hard on crime" views would reject an insanity defense out of hand without any considered thought – unless, of course, it was them or one of their family members who had run afoul of the law. It's always interesting to see Rush Limbaugh turn into a "bleeding heart liberal" on Constitutional law and Searches and Seizures when the subject of his own transgressions of the law arises.

But, for the Caveman, the insanity defense was not to be. Each of the two psychological examiners prepared a forensic, psychiatric report and sent it to the prosecutor and Caveman's attorney. Under law, the Caveman or any defendant is presumed to be sane, and, therefore, the Defendant has the burden to initially overcome that presumption with expert psychiatric or psychological testimony indicating legal insanity. If, and when that happens, the burden of proof then shifts back to the prosecutor to prove the Defendant's sanity at trial. But, in Caveman's case, neither psychiatric examination overcame the law's presumption that Caveman was legally sane when he stuck up the savings and loan. So, the insanity defense never got off the ground for Caveman. No doubt, the Caveman was suffering traumatic brain injury from a series of concussions and accumulated, concussive blows to the head, but the Caveman still had enough cognitive ability to know that robbing the savings and loan was wrong, and he still had enough volitional ability to resist the impulse to rob the savings and loan because he could have said "no" to the stick up temptation: "Lead us not into temptation and deliver us from evil." An insanity defense just wasn't in the cards for the Caveman.

Emanuel Steward told the lawyer who was defending Caveman that he would be pleased to come to court again and testify to Caveman's good character, and to testify that Caveman was a good man who was always on time for work, and that Caveman never stole anything before and was very loyal and helpful. Caveman's lawyer explained to Emanuel Steward that evidence of Caveman's good character was not admissible at trial to prove the Caveman did or did not stick up the savings and loan as he most assuredly did. Whether or not Caveman robbed banks before was simply not relevant to Caveman's guilt or innocence. Likewise, the prosecutor would be prohibited from introducing evidence that the Caveman was a bad character, and, therefore, more likely to rob the savings and loan. Manny was just trying to help in any way he could.

The Plea

Caveman had been in the Oakland County jail waiting for trial for about six months, and the inhumane conditions at the jail were starting to overwhelm him. Caveman needed to get out of the county jail and get a fresh start, even if it meant a change of scenery with incarceration in a penitentiary. Caveman told his lawyer, if he was going to go to prison after the trial, he might as well get the best deal he could get before trial and get on with it. Caveman knew the penitentiary had to be better than the county jail.

It was a plea bargain for the Caveman. Plea bargains are worked out in the greater majority of criminal cases, and thank heaven for plea bargains... because our courts do not have the available time or staff to try even half of the criminal cases assigned to their dockets. Caveman's deal – he would plead straight up to the "facts" of the armed robbery. But, the judge would accept his plea to a lesser offense of "unarmed robbery," and sentence Caveman to eight to twenty years in the state penitentiary. That was a fairly good deal on the one hand, but to my thinking four to twenty would have also served the ends of justice. But, Caveman was facing life, or any number of years up to life in prison on the armed robbery charge, and, with an eight to twenty year sentence and then available good behavior, Caveman would be eligible for parole after serving five years.

The plea deal was accepted by the court, and William "Caveman" Lee became a convicted felon, lost everything he had at the Kronk Gym, and was incarcerated in the state prison system for a minimum of five years. And, when Caveman gets out with his brain still

AP/Getty Images
Emanuel Steward
Kronk Star Maker

scrambled or even more scrambled... what then for the once promising Caveman? Who knows? Hope springs eternal, but, often times, reality trumps hope. Oh the wonderful world of pugs, pugilism, boxing promoters and discarded lives. But, you have to give it up for Emanuel Steward. He still lives in Detroit, stays loyal to his fighters and carries himself with a quiet dignity. Emanuel Steward has claimed his spot in boxing history, but William "Caveman" Lee slid into obscurity, a forgotten man, his upside, downside career and his overall record of twenty-three wins (twenty-two by knockout), and four losses (not counting his robbery conviction) preserved only in these pages... which I gladly write for the child-like man known as the "Caveman."

Hooray for the Hood

And, you have to give it up for my St. Scholastica grade school class-mate, Judge Jimmy "the Irishman" Sheehy, who, in an unorthodox judicial move, took a chance on the

Judge Jimmy Sheehy and Fred Lauck

Caveman, and bonded him out to Emanuel Steward so the "Caveman" could help the "Hit Man" win another world championship for Kronk.

And so it goes... with Detroit's children of the Greatest Generation running the gamut from boxing rings where prize fighters destroy each other with nature's law of "survival of the fittest" to civilized arenas like courtrooms where gentlemen and gentlewomen destroy each other with "civility" and "due process of law."

CHAPTER 14

Judge Connie Marie Kelley...
A Girl From The Hood

Some from the Hood were girls who became successful mothers and professionals... like **"CONNIE MARIE KELLEY"**– a woman for all seasons.

Bubbling up from the revolutionary decades of the 1950s and the 1960s, and riding the wave of opportunity that their Greatest Generation mothers and fathers secured for them, the daughters of the Greatest Generation decided that life had more to offer than the endless nurturing of children and husbands. In the 1950s and 1960s, some of the girls from the Hood opened the front door of their homes and peered longingly at the larger world outside. They silently acknowledged the pull of their maternal instinct, but they also heard a distant voice of new possibilities whispering in their ear: "Why not you?" Then, in a Shakespearean moment of "to be or not to be," or just "what to be," some of the girls in the Hood summoned up their courage, overcame their self doubt, took a deep breath and jumped into the fast moving current of life outside their homes and struggled to stay afloat as they vigorously swam toward the brass ring of higher education and economic independence. One such girl was Connie Marie Skinner – a girl with a vision, a dream, and the courage and work ethic to pull it off by making that long, arduous, upstream swim toward the elusive brass ring. This is the story of the "Honorable" (in the truest sense of the word) Connie Marie Skinner Kelley.

Jump on board the Connie Marie Skinner Kelley "All Night Express," and listen as I conduct Connie Marie's symphony: "A Woman for All Seasons." As we pull out of the station, know that we're going to cover a lot of ground, and we're going to range "far and wide." Why? Because Connie Marie was a very successful woman, mother, wife and "trial lawyer" long before she ascended to her position as Wayne County Circuit Court Judge in 2009. And, like any other successful woman, Connie Marie had a strong "supporting cast" whose background music and up-front examples left enduring imprints on her sweet and friendly soul. It would be fitting, therefore, to acknowledge the contribution of the Greatest Generation and others to the success story of Connie Marie. You might even want to reflect on how the lives of her supporting cast nurtured Connie Marie's spirit and soul and paved the way for her "life well lived" as a "Woman for All Seasons."

The Supporting Cast

First, there was Connie Marie's father-in-law, "Black" Jack Kelley (may he rest). Black Jack was a "landmark" in the City of Detroit... and not just on St. Patrick's day but 365 days a year. He was a legend and a mountain of a man who had more charisma in his devilish smile than most people have in their whole body. When you saw Black Jack Kelley, you saw an "Irish vision" and one heck-of-a-charismatic character. Black Jack was a carpenter by trade. He rose to the position of Secretary/Treasurer of the Carpenters' Union. He was also a public official serving twenty years on the Detroit Common

Kevin Kelley and
"Black Jack" Kelley

Council. He was appointed Deputy Director of Building and Safety Engineering for the City of Detroit by two different mayors – Mayor Jerry Cavanagh and Mayor Roman Gribbs.

By sheer good fortune, I got to meet the legendary Jack Kelley on just a single occasion during his colorful lifetime. I met my brother Marty Lahti (may he rest) and Jack Kelley for breakfast one day. My brother Marty and Black Jack were both legendary figures, and I knew I was in the midst of "greatness" that morning.

At the end of breakfast, Jack Kelley turned to me, locked me into his gaze, and asked if I knew about the "wee people," – "the fairies, the leprechauns?" Before I could answer Black Jack said: "Lauck... you know there's no wee people, no leprechauns, no fairies and I know there's no wee people, no leprechauns and no fairies." After a moment of silence, Black Jack leaned further into my quizzical eyes, and with a quiet and rather disconcerting voice said: "But that doesn't mean they're not out there!"

Well, I have to admit that Jack Kelley caught me by surprise. But, I didn't want to appear oppositional and risk getting knocked on "me backside" by a crashious right hand from Black Jack, so I let discretion take the better part of valor, and I simply leaned forward into Jack Kelley's fixed gaze and replied: "Mr. Kelley, you've got a point there." Jack Kelley, you fine charismatic Irishman, may you and your big heart rest in peace, and may we always honor your "larger than life," Greatest Generation memory.

Jack Kelley's wife, Connie Marie's mother-in-law, Mary Ellen Kelley, is the epitome of strength and grace that defines the Greatest

Generation. Mary Ellen Kelley's mother died when she was but 11 years old. Mary Ellen was left to raise her three younger siblings. Then Mary Ellen's father died when she was but 18 years old, and she was left as the "head of household" for her three younger siblings. As a teenager, Mary Ellen was already a hardened-in-the-fire, certified expert at holding families together. And, Mary Ellen Kelley held her own rather raucous Kelley family together with grace, strength, courage, commitment, loyalty, style and large doses of love.

Connie Marie's Greatest Generation father, Chuck Skinner, was a legendary football and wresting coach at Hazel Park High School

Legendary Coach Skinner leads Seaholm to another Championship

and at Birmingham Seaholm High School. I was there in late 1950s and the early 1960s playing for the Catholic Central Shamrocks, and competing against Chuck Skinner's superbly coached teams. He was the best. In 1984, Chuck Skinner was inducted into the Michigan High School Coaches Hall of Fame. A 2008 publication, *Football Rivalries,* details decades of football rivalries in the greater metropolitan Detroit area. *Football Rivalries* describes Connie Marie's father, Chuck Skinner, as the "toughest screw" (I guess that means someone who puts immense pressure on you) – the "toughest screw" to ever walk the sideline of a Michigan high school football game. Coach Skinner had six children. Supporting everyone on a coach's and teacher's salary was no easy task so Mr. Skinner became an entrepreneur on the side. He owned and operated Dairy Queens, Putt Putt Golf Courses and resorts in Northern Michigan. Chuck Skinner left the imprint of strength, commitment and entrepreneurship on the soul of his daughter Connie Marie.

Connie Marie's mother, Anna Petroff Skinner, was the daughter of Joseph Petroff – Connie Marie's grandfather. Grandfather Petroff had a prized ticket on the maiden voyage of the "Titanic," but he missed his railway connection in Bulgaria, and, luckily, missed the Titanic's ill fated voyage. Without that fortuitous good luck, Connie Marie's story would never have been lived or told.

Connie Marie's mother, Anna, told me that when she was just 14 years old she fell in love with Chuck Skinner. As Anna says, she pursued Chuck Skinner until he gave up and married her. Anna Skinner had six children – two daughters including Connie Marie and four sons. Anna Skinner spent her early child-rearing years taking her children on excursions to libraries and book mobiles, and parading through book fairs. As Anna confided in me, the toughest part of her parenting duties was "keeping the kids in books." All of Anna's six children were voracious readers by the time they were in the fourth grade. Connie Marie's mother left the love of the written word imprinted on Connie Marie's young soul, and Connie Marie ran with that gift, and parlayed the love of books into higher education and professional success. Connie Marie's only sister, Nancy Skinner, ran for a United States Senate seat out of the State of Illinois a few years back, but sister Nancy lost to that upstart Barack… Barack… What's his name… Barack Obama.

Connie Marie has two sons plus a niece she raised. Connie Marie's oldest son is Andrew McNeely. Her youngest son is Kyle. Both Andrew and Kyle were members of the Cranbrook High School State Championship Hockey Team – two rough and tumble hombres challenging their grandfather, Chuck Skinner, for the "toughest screw" of the family award. Connie Marie also raised her niece Angela from the time Angela was a year old.

Another great influence in Connie Marie's life is her friend and longtime mentor Bob Milia. Bob is a contemporary of mine. He is the most impassioned trial lawyer I have every known. Bob gave Connie her first job in the practice of law. In 1978, when Connie started law school at Wayne State University, Bob hired Connie as his law clerk. Connie worked as a law clerk for Bob Milia throughout law school, and with him thereafter as a lawyer. Bob has been Connie Marie's mentor and friend now for over thirty years. Connie "lucked out" when her path serendipitously crossed the path of Bob Milia, and Bob gave Connie Marie her head start as a "trial lawyer."

Last, but never least among Connie Marie's support group, is Kevin Kelley – Connie's husband, confidant, political advisor, best friend, soul mate and lover. Kevin Kelley graduated from my high school, Catholic Central, in 1976. Kevin then obtained a masters degree in Public Administration from Western Michigan, and is now working on his doctorate. Kevin has held elective office – both as a Redford Township Supervisor and as a Wayne County Commissioner for eight years. Kevin has all the charisma of his father, "Black Jack" Kelley, but I dare say, if I ever had a dispute with Kevin Kelley, I would be a lot less likely to end up on "me backside." There was a popular song from the early 1960s that captures Kevin Kelley's soul and spirit… "To Know Him is To Love Him."

That's Connie Marie's supporting cast, the ones who sang her background music and the ones who led with quiet, but up-front example, the ones so very close to her heart, and the ones who left enduring imprints on her soul and spirit and paved the way for her "life will-lived." But, just how did those imprints from Connie Marie's "Supporting Cast" influence her life? Well, stay in your seat, keep those seatbelts fastened, and, as the Connie Marie Kelley "All Night Express" takes a gentle sweeping turn, look out of the right side of your window, and you will see silhouettes of those imprints playing out before you as distinct influences on the evolving "life and times" of Connie Marie Skinner Kelley.

A Child in a Hurry

Look back in time with me to yesteryear. See that blur of white energy just outside the window! That's Chuck Skinner's mad dash to Mt. Carmel Hospital on April 6, 1956. Connie Marie Skinner was born that day… just two minutes after her father dropped her mother Anna off at the emergency room door of Mt. Carmel Hospital (on Outer Drive at Schaefer in Detroit). I remember that early April 1956 arrival well. I was in Sister Gertrude Mary's Seventh Grade English class at St. Scholastica just down the road a piece on Outer Drive and Southfield Road when I heard Connie Marie land in the Northwest Detroit Hood. She landed ceremoniously with a loud splash followed by a quickly disappearing stork lopping southbound down Schaefer towards Frank Collin's Irish bar, Federals and the Mercury Theatre.

Connie Marie must have been bored with gestation. It was a photo finish drop-off followed by a two minute delivery. No sooner had her father parked the car when he had to circle back to the parking lot, get the car and head back home with his precious cargo – the brand spanking new life of Connie Marie Skinner. In honor of Connie Marie's serendipitous arrival, Sister Gertrude Mary declared the rest of the day off at St. Scholastica, and my classmates and I followed the brightest star in the sky eastbound down Outer Drive to Mt. Carmel Hospital. But, by the time we arrived at the hospital, Connie Marie was already signed, sealed, delivered and heading home in her 1956 style… invisible car seat.

Kid with a Dream

Time passed quickly. Fourteen short years later in 1970, just like her mother before her, 14-year-old Connie Marie fell in love. But, she did not fall in love with a man. She fell in love with an "ideal." At age

14, Connie Marie stood on her porch, full of youthful exuberance and free of self doubt, and... she had a dream. No... not a dream. Make that an epiphany. Connie Marie had an epiphany of grandiose proportion. She was going to be a lawyer. But... but... so what? There are thousands of lawyers in Michigan alone. But... wait... not just a lawyer. She was going to be a lawyer so... so... she could **"help others."** That's the so what!

Young 14-year-old Connie Marie's dream was not diminished or inhibited by reality. Ah, "reality" – that fear that the adult kingdom rationalizes to road-block the path that leads to good deeds and "helping others." But, 14-year-old Connie Marie was fearless. She was full of youthful exuberance and free of self doubt, and she knew what the future held for her. But... another 14-year-old, one more in touch with reality or with a better understanding of the history of the woman's rights movement in America, would have had good reason for self doubt, good reason for inhibition, fear and... hesitation.

In 1920, just thirty-six short years before Connie Marie's birth, the 19th Amendment to the United States Constitution was finally passed, and women were, after a long, arduous struggle including arrests, imprisonment and hunger strikes, finally guaranteed the right to vote. But, even after passage of the 19th Amendment, women in the State of Michigan were still not accorded the full rights of citizenship, and still not allowed to participate as jurors in the search for justice. In fact, I could take our "All Night Express" over to the Michigan Central Depot in downtown Detroit right now, dock it and then hop a short cab ride to the Wayne County Circuit Court, and show you an inscription in a modern day, Wayne County courtroom that still stands as a reminder of past discrimination against women. Let me explain.

Fair Jury... No Women Need Apply

In 1925, Dr. Ossian Sweet left Florida, moved to Detroit and bought a home in an all white neighborhood at 2905 Garland Ave. Soon after, white rioters gathered outside Dr. Sweet's home. The spark was lit and the "mob mentality" kicked in. The righteous, riotous mob threw bricks and rocks through the windows of Dr. Sweet's home as Dr. Sweet's family huddled in fear, and as Dr. Sweet flashed back to the smell of burning flesh from the earlier burning-at-the-stake attacks on blacks he had witnessed as a child in his home state of Florida. Suddenly, a shot rang out from inside Dr. Sweet's darkened home, and a white man, Leon Breiner, fell dead in the street. The mob abruptly dispersed and an eerie calm fell over the scene. Dr. Sweet was arrested and charged with Murder in the First Degree.

The NAACP decided that a white lawyer was needed to represent Dr. Sweet in what was sure to be a racially charged all white jury

Clarence Darrow

trial. For America, in the twentieth century, was still struggling 150 years later to fulfill Thomas Jefferson's eloquent, self evident promise in the Declaration of Independence that "all men are created equal." The NAACP chose famed "trial lawyer," Clarence Darrow, who had just concluded his defense in the Scopes Monkey trial in which he depicted his adversary, the great orator William Jennings Bryan, as a close minded, bible thumping caricature. After finishing the Scopes Monkey trial, Clarence Darrow, at age 69, decided he had just enough energy left to take on yet another demanding social cause.

The trial judge in Dr. Sweet's murder case was 35-year-old Frank Murphy, a former prosecutor, who would later become Michigan's favorite son – Mayor of the City of Detroit, Governor of the State of Michigan, Governor-General to the Philippines, United States Attorney General under President Franklin Roosevelt and United States Supreme Court Justice.

Frank Murphy

During the jury selection, Clarence Darrow "voir dired" (French for "speak truly") the all white-male jury. Darrow confronted the prospective jurors head on telling them that they were all prejudiced because they all had preexisting ideas, judgments and notions on how life is, or how life ought to be. Darrow simply acknowledged life's preexisting prejudice, his own, the jurors, and even ours at this very moment as we ride the Connie Marie Skinner Kelley "All Night Express." Prejudice or preexisting belief is simply part of the human condition, especially as we grow and mature from opinionless, know-nothing kids to sophisticated adults who freely and happily share our opinions with the world just to prove our own self worth. After acknowledging the permeating prejudice of society, Darrow simply asked the jurors if they could set aside their prejudice for that one glorious moment that they would sit in judgment of another human being, Dr. Ossian Sweet, and judge Dr. Sweet just like the jurors would judge a white man. Darrow confronted the jury's prejudice head on and exacted a promise from them, and held the jury to their promise.

During closing argument, Darrow turned the jury's attention to the plight of Dr. Sweet telling the jury that he "has never seen **twelve good men** who, if you could get them to understand a human cause, were not tried and true." Clarence Darrow's phrase is now inscribed in a courtroom in the Wayne County Circuit Court. And, the point… "twelve good men" – because, in 1925… five years after the passage of the 19th Amendment guaranteeing women the right to vote, and just thirty-one short years before the birth of Connie Marie Kelley, women were still being denied the right to participate as jurors in the pursuit of justice in the City of Detroit.

Pursuit of the Dream

But, as I said… in 1970, 14-year-old Connie Marie, fearless, uninhibited by reality and free from self doubt was blessed that she didn't know then what she does know now about the social and legal barriers that have been erected by society to block the paths that women have set out to travel in pursuit of their dreams. As a 14-year-old, Connie Marie didn't know that women from her mother's generation, by and large, if they even had the opportunity for higher education, went to college to study home economics or secretarial skills, or perhaps just to find a husband. She didn't know that women who went to law school and passed the bar exam were, at best, destined for a job in a law firm as a "legal secretary." As I say, 14-year-old Connie Marie, fearless, uninhibited by reality and free of self doubt, knew she **could** become a lawyer. No – make that she knew she **would** become a lawyer. No – make that she knew she **must** become a lawyer. And Connie Marie would need every bit of that resolve and determination to fulfill her dream to become a lawyer on her mission to "help others."

Connie Marie graduated from Bishop Foley Catholic High School in 1974. She then attended the University of Michigan and, in 1978, after four years of intense study, after four years of waitressing tables in Ann Arbor and at Peabody's in Birmingham, Michigan, and, after four years of begging and borrowing student loans for tuition (truly a confident investment in herself), Connie Marie graduated with a degree in "Philosophy" from the University of Michigan. Connie Marie must have intuitively known that the law itself is the philosophy of human nature – a mix of obligations, duties and rights. Obligations, duties and rights that are set, balanced and defined and then reset, rebalanced and redefined over the decades and millenniums, ebbing and flowing from "freedom from control" to "control of freedom." But, during all the ebbing and flowing and the tides of change, there is that one constant that always remains – a never ending effort by those in charge, the establishment, to control and drown out the voice of the "have-nots." Connie Marie's strong background in philosophy would serve her well in supplementing her dream to "help others," and to be the voice of strength for those who have no voice in our society so dominated, as it is, by money and power.

Finally, in the fall of 1978 at age 22, Connie Marie was prepared to take a giant step forward toward realizing her dream to "help others." Connie Marie was accepted into law school at Wayne State University. She was now in the philosophy of law – head over heels. Connie Marie rented a hotel room at Palmer and Woodward in the Cass Corridor area of Detroit. Connie told me that… it was in that rented hotel room that she came face-to-face with her first cockroach. As Connie Marie says: "he was a cute little guy" that she nick-named "Cucaracha." "Cucaracha" and his bug buddies hung around Connie Marie's rented hotel room for three years of law school bugging her and keeping her company as she studied Contracts, Torts, Constitutional Law, Criminal Law, Civil Procedure, Criminal Procedure, Uniform Commercial Code, Wills, Trusts, Taxation and the overlay of Aristotelean logic, Res Ipsa Loquiter, the rule in Shelly's case, the Rule Against Perpetuities, habeous rippus and horpus capias and… God save us all from "the law" that is supposed to save us all from one another.

But, that finely furnished hotel room in the cold, hard-scrabble corridors of Detroit's Cass Corridor was not going to pay for itself.

So, in her first year of law school, Connie Marie saw a help-wanted ad on the bulletin board of the law school. The law firm of Milia and Kern was looking for a law clerk. Connie Marie interviewed and the job was hers. Thus began a thirty plus year relationship with trial lawyer Bob Milia who became Connie Marie's mentor and friend. What a serendipitous moment for Connie Marie. She met Bob Milia,

Mentor Bob Milia, Fred Lauck, Judge Jim Sheehy, and Al Meyers 2006

a man much like her own father – a non manipulative man, truly interested in Connie Marie's welfare. Connie Marie law-clerked for the Milia and Kern law firm for all three years of law school. Finally, after three years of rigorous academic accomplishment in law school, and a crash bar review course, and the harrowing coming-of-age experience of writing a bar exam for three days, Connie Marie passed the bar exam and became Connie Marie "J.D." – "Juris Doctor" – a doctor of laws. Now in 1981, eleven long, demanding years after the epiphany of a 14-year-old girl on her front porch, one half of Connie's dream came true. She was now a lawyer. Connie would then spend the next twenty-seven years of her life as a trial lawyer making the other half of the dream, "helping others," come true.

A Novice Trial Lawyer

Within days of passing the bar exam, Connie Marie's mentor, Bob Milia, gave Connie Marie fifteen client files with fifteen different motions for her to argue in Wayne County Circuit Court on Friday – motion day. With a fair amount of trepidation, Connie Marie went forward knowing she had to overcome the fear of being responsible for the welfare of others if she was to realize her dream of "helping others." "Fear of failure" just comes with the territory when you live the dream of helping others. "Fear of failure" is the constant companion of all trial lawyers. It's that fear of failure that becomes trial lawyers' driving force as they swim upstream, trying to help others less fortunate negotiate fair treatment from a cold and ruthless establishment, and as they try to give a voice to the cause of others, as well as giving some semblance of hope and quality of life to those who have very little.

After several years with Milia and Kern, Connie Marie left to join Brian Smith in the practice of law. Brian (may he rest) was a fine lawyer from the University of Detroit Jesuit Law School. Brian was developing a law practice in new areas – employment law and sport's agent law. Working with Brian Smith, Connie Marie represented Detroit Red Wing stars Ted Lindsay, Johnny Wilson and Mickey Redmond. Connie Marie grew up with star athlete and coach, Chuck Skinner, as her father. She certainly wasn't intimidated by the Red Wings stars. In fact, Brian Smith intuitively knew that he was better off with Connie Marie as his point man (or, in Connie Marie's case, his "point woman") with the NHL hockey players because Connie Marie's natural winning personality and her sound legal ability would generate immense "good will" for Brian's law firm.

While working with Brian Smith, Connie Marie started her family. Son Andrew was born in 1985. Son Kyle was born fifteen months later in 1986. And, during the same period of time, Connie Marie took in her niece, Angela Skinner, when Angela was a year old. Connie Marie had three children all under the age of 15 months. But, no more invisible car seats like Connie had in 1956. It was now 1986, and, everywhere Connie went, she took along three car seats.

Think of it. In my years as a trial lawyer, I have constantly felt overwhelmed and overworked, but I wasn't raising children. Connie

Marie was arranging day care services at home, day care services outside the home, and, at the same time, working full time as a trial lawyer. I asked Connie how in the world she was able to do it. Connie said she just put one foot in front of the other which I guess means, "be careful and **don't think** too much about your plight or you'll despair." Although I cannot imagine how Connie Marie was able to survive those years, I suspect women are emotionally stronger than men. Perhaps, women just intuitively go on automatic pilot so they can keep their head above water without lamenting their condition. Maybe it's like Woody Allen said: "ninety percent of life is just showing up." At times, however, when the family's needs were threatened, Connie Marie backed off for the best interests of her family and worked part time. But, whatever it took, Connie Marie had that very same resolve she had as a 14-year-old girl (long before the present day Nike commercial), and she was able to **"just do it."**

Trial Lawyer Entrepreneur

Finally, Connie Marie, supported by her own father's spirit of entrepreneurship, headed out on her own, starting her own law firm, "Mallon and McNeely." It was then that I ran into Connie Marie again after years of not seeing her. I was walking through the Oakland County Circuit Court on motion day about 1990 when I saw Connie Marie. She had just won a large jury verdict in a case representing a woman who sued her employer for discrimination. On motion day, the employer was in the Oakland County Circuit Court asking the judge to set aside the jury verdict Connie had just won and dismiss the case. Great theory! The employer wants the judge to trump the jury's voice so that the last five years of turmoil and heart break in a client's life, and the last five years of litigation, time, effort, and emotional anguish in a trial lawyer's life, not to mention the jury's time, effort and sacrifice – all to be wiped out by the stroke of the judicial pen ala "We the People of the Jury" have spoken followed by a judge who says: "Your voice is cancelled" and the establishment chalks up another victory over life's "have-nots."

As Connie explained her case to me that morning in Oakland County Circuit Court, I couldn't help noticing how engaging, buoyant and impassioned she was – taking on her client's cases and taking on life in general with an idealistic passion. As I was caught up in her charismatic rapture, I didn't say: "one day this Connie Marie is going to be a good trial lawyer." What I did say, silently to myself: "today, this very moment, '30-something' Connie Marie is already a great trial lawyer" – "helping others."

In 1996, as luck would have it, Connie and Bob Milia hooked up again. Bob was a partner at the law firm of Powers, Chapman, DeAgosting, Meyers & Milia. Knowing how well his past mentorship of Connie Marie worked out, Bob Milia suggested that Connie Marie join Bob's firm, Powers Chapman. Connie joined the firm in 1996, and, eventually, became a partner – the second female partner in the eighty year existence of the Powers Chapman law firm.

Then, in 2009, in a brilliant campaign spearheaded by her husband and political confidant, Kevin Kelley, Connie Marie was elected Wayne County Circuit Court judge. But, as I said in the beginning, Connie Marie was a very successful trial lawyer for twenty-seven years before she became a judge. As a trial lawyer, Connie Marie fulfilled the epiphany... that dream she had as a 14-year-old girl... the dream to "help others" and fight against the power of the establishment for those who had no voice. For what is the mission of a trial lawyer, if not to "help others"? For what is a trial lawyer, if not a lawyer who represents the common man and the forgotten woman against the rich and powerful of the establishment to make sure the rich and powerful play by the rules, that the government and all of its agencies play by the rules, that corporate America plays by the rules, that the police play by the rules, and that the American insurance industry plays by the rules? And, for twenty-seven years, day in and day out, Connie Marie realized her dream. She was an outstanding trial lawyer who helped the underdog – the "common man" and the "forgotten woman," and she did it with compassion, grace, elegance, courage and skill that she inherited from the rich environment and nurture provided by her supporting cast's background music and upfront example.

Tragedy... Act of God or Man?

Let me share with you a single example of Connie Marie's tenacious work as a trial lawyer. On a dark, rainy night, an excessive amount of rain water had accumulated in a freeway underpass in the greater Detroit area. Two unsuspecting motorists plunged into that watery underpass and had a minor collision. They pulled over to the side of the underpass to exchange drivers' and insurance information. As they stood by, helplessly, at the side of the roadway, another unsuspecting motorist plunged into the watery underpass, lost control of his vehicle, and plowed head long into them. The man was critically injured, and the woman lived long enough to have her legs surgically amputated before she died.

Connie Marie took the case. But, like all trial lawyers, she questioned herself. What is the case? No one is responsible for rainfall. Rainfall is an act of God. But, Connie Marie rolled up her sleeves and went to work, determined to find that "needle-in-the-haystack" that had caused that dangerous accumulation of water on the roadbed of the underpass. Connie Marie looked at thousands of documents in the State of Michigan's archives. She filed a lawsuit against the construction companies that built the freeway, the overpass and the underpass. With eight lawyers opposing her, Connie Marie finally got to the truth. During the construction of the freeway, the contractors failed to remove the leftover concrete debris from the site – instead burying the debris under the road bed, and, in the process, blocking the storm sewer drains. Bingo! It wasn't an act of God. It was (as it usually is) an act of man… a negligent, careless and wholly avoidable act that set the stage for future human tragedy, heartache, suffering and loss of life and limb. Connie Marie, with eight lawyers opposing her, obtained a $2.5 million dollar recovery. It doesn't bring life or limbs back, but $2.5 million is, hopefully, expensive enough to keep the freeway contractors from playing Russian roulette with someone else's life and limbs the next time around.

Isn't it ironic that… of all the strong and committed football players her father, Coach Skinner, coached over his brilliant Hall of Fame career, his daughter Connie Marie turned out stronger and more committed than the best her father coached and mentored. And, isn't it ironic that… of all the great endurance that Coach Skinner's wrestling champions had, his daughter, Connie Marie, had more endurance and stamina than any of them as she tirelessly pursued the cause of justice to "help others."

It's been a long train ride into the surrounding landscape of the "Life and Times" of Connie Marie Skinner Kelley as well as an expansive, swelling symphony of "a life well lived" for "A Woman for All Seasons." We have ranged far and wide, and we covered a lot of ground, but we were rewarded with a unique glimpse of the "goodness" that comes from "knowledge" and "discipline" directed toward "helping others." Or, as the Basilian priests taught Connie Marie's husband, Kevin Kelley, and me at Catholic Central High School: "Teach me goodness, discipline and knowledge."

Petition of Requests

That Connie Marie Skinner Kelley certainly lived up to her billing. She was proof positive that some from the Hood were, in fact, girls who became successful mothers and professionals. But, if I could be so bold, I would, based on my own forty plus years of experience as a trial lawyer, present a petition of requests from the citizens of the realm to the Honorable Connie Marie Kelley.

Request Number One

Your Honor, may you always use compassion in judging the cases that come before you – not sympathy or prejudice and not bias, but compassion… for compassion partakes of wisdom, which plays the highest role in the search for justice. Although the Goddess of Justice, Lady Justice, is blindfolded, and cannot see the color of the skin or the race of the supplicants before the bar of justice, she is still a woman, and, even when blindfolded, she is permitted to feel a woman's compassion, and use her compassion as wisdom to resolve the real life disputes and the human tragedies entrusted to her judgment.

Never forget the moral lesson of justice and wisdom so elegantly and artistically depicted in the large Austrian etching by Ivo Saliger. The entire background of the etching shows a subtle silhouette of an imposing, yet barely visible, Lady Justice. The blindfolded Lady Justice holds the scales of justice in one hand and a large sword in the other. She is depicted subtly, almost hidden, yet powerfully lurking behind the central figure of the painting – a judge in a rich black robe, with pitch black hair and vibrant complexion who stands looking down at a kneeling supplicant of much less visible power, in light clothing, with light hair and a worrisome, beseeching look, glancing up into the strong face of the powerful judge who has ultimate control over his fate. The painting then explodes into a moral lesson of justice and wisdom as you realize that the face of the powerful judge figure that dominates the etching and the face of the powerless supplicant before him are **one and the same face**. Honorable Connie Marie Kelley, when you see yourself in the faces of the supplicants before you, justice will be served.

Request Number Two

Your Honor, please remember that "textualism," as a rule of interpretation of laws, is not the God of Justice. "Textualism" is but one semantic theory, among many competing theories, used in the interpretation of legislative enactments. Legislators, many times influenced by the money and the power of lobbyists, special interest groups and other influence peddlers, pass a law that later applies to numerous situations and to a myriad of fact patterns that the legislature could not have foreseen – even if they had a crystal ball. So, in divining the intention of the Legislature when they pass a law, remember justice is not necessarily served by deferring to the literal reading of a "text" of a written law to cover a situation the Legislature never had in mind, or even foresaw when they passed the law.

Request Number Three

Your Honor, be not afraid of being derisively labeled by your political enemies as a "judicial activist," for all judges are constantly required to fill in the blanks and connect the dots to decide what law applies, and just how that law fits each new and unique human cause that finds its way into your courtroom. Your Honor cannot use a "one size fits all" legal philosophy for each unique human cause that comes before you. To do so, would adopt a formula of certainty, but a certainty of injustice. As we learned in law school, most rules of law are better known by their exceptions. Grasp the unique facts of each case that comes before you and master those unique facts – for, as they also said in law school, "out of the facts, the law will arise." As United States Supreme Court Justice (and Ronald Reagan appointee), Anthony Kennedy, said in May of 2010 in dismissing often repeated Republican criticism of "activist judges": "An activist court is a court that makes a decision you don't like." As I said, Your Honor, be not afraid to be labeled a "judicial activist" by your political enemies for history will judge you mostly by who your enemies are.

And, even if you are derisively labeled a "judicial activist" by your enemies, just remember that you will stand side by side and shoulder to shoulder with such great past jurists as Earl Warren – United States Supreme Court Chief Justice who wrote the Court's opinion in *Brown vs. The Board of Education*, a unanimous opinion that outlawed segregation in public school systems, paving the way for blacks to attend public high schools where they lived and State Universities of their choice. And, if your enemies derisively label you as "judicial activist," you can also stand side by side and shoulder to shoulder with United States Supreme Court Justice William Brennan, a diminutive man with the big heart, who was proudly known as the "Great Liberal." You can also stand side by side and shoulder to shoulder with Frank Murphy – Michigan's favorite son, who was not only the Recorder's Court trial judge in Dr. Ossian Sweet's case, but who was also Mayor of the City of Detroit, Governor of the State of Michigan (who refused to deploy the national guard to break up the auto worker's sit-down strike), Governor-General of the Philippines, United States Attorney General under President Franklin Roosevelt, and the United States Supreme Court Justice who wrote the dissenting opinion in *Korematsu vs. The United States* giving us a treasured lesson in human rights by opposing and dissenting against the forced relocation of Japanese American citizens during World War II. Frank Murphy was truly a "new dealer" before the "New Deal."

Although Justice Frank Murphy's political enemies would label him a "judicial activist," history has vindicated Frank Murphy on all counts just as history will vindicate Your Honor if your political enemies label you as "judicial activist." Your own special brand of true justice will expose your enemies as political demagogues who would "cry wolf." Be not afraid of your enemies derisively labeling you as a "judicial activist" for, as the Irish say, Your Honor: "the character of a man or a woman is measured by who their enemies are."

Request Number Four

Your Honor, simply stated, give "hope" to those who have none. In doing so, Your Honor, you will be the Father Solanus Casey and the Father Clement Kern of the legal profession – two larger than life, renowned Detroit priests who lived the message of Jesus in the mean streets of Detroit as they ministered to the poor and downtrodden at the Capuchin Soup Kitchen on Mt. Elliot and at Holy Trinity Parish in Corktown.

Request Number Five

Your Honor, give "voice" to those who have none. Give voice to the down trodden and oppressed. Give voice to the "common man" and the "forgotten woman." And never... Your Honor, never allow the rich, the powerful, the peddlers of influence, the intellectuals, or any other elitist group to silence the voices of the "unwashed masses" or of the dwindling "middle class" – for they, more than all the others, are the backbone of our nation. It is those "unwashed masses" and those from the ranks of the "middle class" that toil in our hard-scrabble economic landscape just to make ends meet and just to keep their families fed and protected with shelter. And, it is they who in-variably do the dying and suffering in our wars and police actions across the globe. Theirs is a voice that needs to be heard. Protect their voice from the elite and from the ruling class of America – even if it is a voice of opposition or dissent, and even if it is a voice spoken in anger or frustration and lacking in social grace or diplomacy.

Request Number Six

Last, Your Honor, always remember your biggest asset is your "judicial independence." Guard it jealously. For this is an era where judges have stood by in subservient fashion and allowed the legislature to dictate formulas for the sentencing of defendants, allowed the legislature to cap the amount of jury verdicts, and allowed the legislature to dictate statutory ground rules for expert witness qualification. Your Honor, you are independent. "Independence" is your biggest asset. You are not subservient to the legislative branch of the government. You are not subservient to the executive branch of the government. You are a separate and co-equal branch of our government.

Your Honor, you are not part of the government team. You are not a teammate of the legislature. You are not a teammate of the executive branch of government. You, and the jurors that sit in your courtroom, must remain independent and free from political influence. You, and the jurors that sit in your courtroom, must be independent and free from the influence of lobbyists, special interest groups and moneyed, influence peddlers. Those traders of political favors don't whisper in your ear or pay for your vote, and those influence peddlers don't whisper in the jurors' ears or pay for the jurors' vote – like they do with the executive and legislature branches of the government. True, the influence peddlers, special interest groups and lobbyists like the

Chamber of Commerce mount self serving advertising campaigns ("frivolous lawsuits," "trial lawyers," etc.) to brain wash or influence would-be jurors before they are even called to jury duty. But, you and the trial lawyers in your courtroom, can and must use the "voir dire," jury selection process, just like Clarence Darrow did in the Ossian Sweet case to expose any pre-existing prejudice that the special interest, influence peddlers have purposely injected into the American psyche.

"We the People" look to Your Honor to protect us from the excesses, the tyranny and the unconstitutional actions of the legislative and executive branches of government – all through the exercise of your "judicial independence." And, we look to you to jealously guard the right of "We the People" to decide our disputes through the right to "trial by jury." For, in a democracy, the right to trial by jury is the single greatest check and balance against oligarchies, totalitarian influences and the wealth and power of the American "ruling class." If not a jury, who is going to hold the rich, the powerful and the ruling class of America accountable for wrong doing and misdeeds? The executive and legislative branches of government, while "under the influence" of the "I owe you," "one hand washes the other," blackmail mentality of lobbyists and special interest groups will be tempted to shy away from judging their rich and powerful friends and benefactors, and might not hold them accountable to the "rule of law."

And, if not a jury, who is going to protect the "little guy," the "common man," and the "forgotten woman" from political charges or charges based on insufficient evidence, or from the unlawful actions which are visited upon them by the rich, powerful "ruling class" of America. As I say Your Honor, your judicial independence is your biggest asset, and you must use it to protect yourself and the jurors in your courtroom from the political influences of the rich and the powerful and the ruling class of America and their influence peddling friends who, day in and day out, contribute millions of dollars to ruling class politicians to promote hidden agendas behind closed doors – hidden agendas that have nothing to do with the common good.

The Page Turns

On January 1, 2009, the Honorable Connie Marie Kelley embraced a new calling as Wayne County Circuit Court judge. One door has closed for Connie Marie and another one has opened. Congratulations to our own Connie Marie on her first life – a life well lived as a very successful woman, mother, wife and "trial lawyer"... "helping others." And God speed to Connie Marie on her second life as a Wayne County Circuit Court judge... still in the pursuit of her now almost forty year old dream to "help others."

May God hold Connie Marie in the palm of His hand and grant her the wisdom of Solomon and the patience of Job. Connie Marie from the Hood is truly our **"WOMAN FOR ALL SEASONS."**

The Honorable Connie Marie Kelley
Father Chuck Skinner
Mother Anna Petroff Skinner
2009

CHAPTER 15

Taking On General Motors, Insanity... And Broken Hearted Melodies

Off and Running

After graduating from the venerable University of Detroit Jesuit Law School on May 3, 1969 at age 26, I undertook the rite of passage and passed the Michigan Bar Exam. I then spent six months in private practice working for Bill McCririe in Brighton, Michigan. Although I was learning something new every day, I knew I was not where I had to be. I always wanted to be a "trial lawyer," but there was not enough action in Brighton. I had no choice. I had to follow my own star. So, I quit, and ended up right where I should have been in the first place.

In 1970, just eight months past the Bar Exam, I landed a job as an assistant prosecuting attorney working for that great Irishman and Wayne County Prosecutor, William Cahalan. A prosecutor? Kind of ironic for a kid whose father made his living outside the law as a "bookie," and whose brother Marty beat up cops for recreation, eventually fighting his way into Jackson Prison where he fought highly ranked heavy weight, Alvin "Blue" Lewis, for the Heavy Weight

Championship of Jackson Prison in 1965. As I say... "ironic." But, I intuitively knew that one fair-minded prosecutor could do more good for those poor souls caught up in the unrelenting harshness of the criminal justice system than ten good defense attorneys. Besides, it also gave me a chance to go no-holds-barred against the violent criminal element of cowardly bullies who assault others who are no physical match for them. I was bound and determined to be a match for those violent bullies, and, in the courtroom, I enjoyed staring, without blinking, straight into their intimidating and manipulative faces.

At the Prosecutor's office, I was in trial every week learning how to be a trial lawyer. From the very first week I started in the summer of 1970, until I left fifteen months later, I prosecuted murder cases, drug cases, assault cases, rape cases and even some white collar crimes – including a successful prosecution against attorney Edward May of Livonia, Michigan who bilked money out of various bankers and athletes, including Detroit Tigers Hall of Famer Al Kaline and Tiger strong arm pitcher Joe Sparma (a former quarterback at Ohio State under the legendary Woody Hayes). Forty years later, in 2010, I read with more than passing interest that Edward May is at it again as he stands charged in another fraudulent investment scheme, victimizing a host of innocent investors, including my lawn care man and my plumber.

Although it was forty years ago, I will never forget my first trial. I started out as an assistant prosecuting attorney in the summer of 1970. I spent my first day with Art Koschinski signing criminal warrants, and talking sports. The second day I was thrown into the lion's den as I was assigned to a Recorder's Court jury trial against a defendant charged with several counts of obtaining money under false pretenses. I never tried a jury trial in my life, but I knew that everything in life had to start somewhere so this is where the reality of my dream would begin. With only a half hour notice, I read through the Detroit

Police Department's investigation report. The report indicated that the Defendant, who claimed to be an investigator for various Detroit personal injury law firms, had defrauded his middle aged, "lonely hearts club" girl friend out of her four bank accounts. After I read the investigation report, the Detroit Police officer in charge of the case was walking me through the victim's bank books, explaining various fraudulent withdrawals by the Defendant. I was 27 years old, and never had a bank account (I don't even remember a piggy bank), so I was struggling to understand what the bank book entries meant. Suddenly, and without warning, Judge John Kadella, a visiting judge from Dearborn, Michigan, and his clerk Marg Long appeared. The case was called: *The People of the State of Michigan vs. blah, blah, blah,*" and off I went on my maiden voyage – an uncertain journey toward the elusive quest for justice.

The jury was picked in short order. Why not? I had no idea how to conduct an in depth "voir dire" (French – meaning "to speak truly") to uncover prejudice, pre-existing bias and the preconceived notions of prospective jurors. At that time, I had no idea how a person's neighborhood, family influences, economic status, health, education, employment background, age, sex, race, ethnic background, interests, hobbies, lifelong opinions, pre-existing ways of viewing the world, or their opinions of lawyers and the judicial system created predisposed ways of interpreting the facts that would be presented at trial. But, as I later learned, the reality is that two different people, viewing the same set of facts, often see and report dramatically different versions of what happened based upon their own past influences. No doubt, jurors subconsciously use their past influences and their pre-existing beliefs and opinions as a reference point or as a pair of glasses to look through as they see their own particular, subjective version of what the objective facts show. For example, the objective facts may show an arrest of a black man by a white cop, but a juror with a law enforcement background sees something much different than what a juror who belongs to the NAACP sees. They both could pass a polygraph on what they claim to have seen, even though they subjectively see and honestly report diametrically opposed versions of the objective facts. Maybe a predisposed way of seeing things (subconscious prejudice or prejudgment) was just what the great German author and philosopher Goethe noticed when he commented: "We usually find what we're looking for."

As I say, the jury was picked in short order, and I then stood face to face with a real, live jury for the very first time in my real, live life, making a real, less-than-lively opening statement trying to communicate to the jury some sense out of the charges and the victim's four different bank accounts. When I finally saw that the jury and I were both hopelessly lost in my opening statement, I decided to fess up: "I'm sorry for the confusion. Let me start over. Again, I apologize, but this is the first trial I ever had." My vulnerability and honesty must have hit a noticeable chord with the jury at that moment because Defense Attorney, Ron Gold, stood up and irrelevantly blurted out: "Well, Your Honor, this is only my second trial." One of the jurors, a large black man with arms folded across his chest and a cynical look of experience on his face, then blurted out: "Well this is going to be a real battle of the lightweights!" And so it was. After two days of trial by confusion, the jury could not come to a verdict. The jury was hung, eleven siding with me for conviction and the large black, cynical looking foreman voting for acquittal. Judge Cadella declared a mistrial, and I declared a moral victory. I survived jury trial 101, but never in my four decades as a trial lawyer have I ever seen the jury foreperson as the lone holdout. In retrospect, I suspect my vulnerability must have resonated well with all the jurors except the foreman whose own pre-existing belief probably echoed a silent parting shot to the prosecution: "Good-bye and good riddance to the white cops and their lightweight assistant prosecutor, Lauck."

After a year and three months with the prosecutor's office, I made a backward move, and became the first law clerk for newly appointed Federal Judge and super ego, the Honorable Robert E. DeMascio – all at the suggestion of my father's own criminal lawyer, little ("throw yourself on the mercy of the court") Frankie McLain (old time actor Barry Fitzgerald look-alike). I lasted six long, depressing months as law clerk for Federal Judge DeMascio, and, in March of 1972, I gladly parted company with His Honor. Then I spent the last $1,500 I had taking my beloved father to St. Petersburg Beach, Florida, hanging around Woody's Deck Bar in Madeira Beach and listening to "Summer Wind" by Frank Sinatra. We both returned to Michigan broke, a condition I learned to live with growing up. I had no job offers and no prospects, but, hey, I had a law degree, and I knew I would land on my feet.

I had already maxed out my experience at the prosecutor's office, and I knew that I needed experience in civil trial work if I was going to fulfill my dream to be a "trial lawyer for all seasons." In the spring of 1972, I was lucky enough to land a job with Plunkett, Cooney, Rutt & Peacock, a personal injury defense firm – then affectionately known as the Irish Catholic Mafia for civil trial lawyers where raises and bonuses were computed on the basis of the number of children you had. At my hiring interview, senior partner William Patrick Cooney (who actually pursued me for the job) personally vouched for me telling his partners: "Lauck is a diamond in the rough and I'm going to smooth him over." Cooney's partners Bob Rutt, John Peacock and Bill Stanczyk looked at each other in confusion and amazement until Bob Rutt asked Cooney: "Bill, who the hell is going to smooth you over?" The point was well taken, but William Patrick Cooney (may he rest) was one hell of a trial lawyer – fearless and courageous, he took 'em all on.

In the spring of 1972, I started at Plunkett, Cooney for $11,500 a year thanks to Wayne County Circuit Court Judge Joe Rashid. Judge Joe Rashid was a beautiful man who had seen me in action in his law school classroom, and later as a prosecutor in his courtroom. Judge Rashid had recommended me to the mega law firm Dykema Gossett. But I turned down an $11,000 a year job with Dykema Gosset because I knew I wasn't cut out for their corporate structure. But, I used Dykema's $11,000 offer as leverage to get $11,500 a year from Plunkett Cooney with the mandate from Bob Rutt: "Okay, but there will be no raises for three years, no matter how many children you have."

So... off I went, with a chance to get experience in personal injury civil cases, and an opportunity to meet a diverse, free-spirited

**Susan Spalding Brochert and Frank Brochert...
A Good Man and a Great Trial Lawyer**

cast of characters that I still love to this day: Bill Cooney (may you rest)... thank you for your belief in me; Frank Brochert (may you rest)... a contemporary of mine and the pride of St. Charles High School on the lower east side of Detroit, the best of the best (and it figures he would get one of the best girls from my own Northwest Detroit Hood as a wife – the lovely, dynamic and gorgeous Sue Spalding), Charlie McGorisk (may you rest), Joe Lujan, Leonard Nagi, Larry Donaldson, Bob Martin, Jim Cole, Jan Paskin, J. P. O'Leary, Tom Ryan and one of the brightest, most colorful characters I ever met, "Johnnie Boy" Jacobs.

The Wandering Years

After four years at Plunkett Cooney, a restlessness set in – a restlessness that grew out of thirty-two straight years of dedication to academics, college athletics, bar exams and trial lawyer apprenticeship. Man – it was time to go on sabbatical, or, as they say in Australia, time to go for "a walk-about." I never got to hang out on the street corners when I was growing up. I never got to lay back. I never got to hang out and just have a childhood. Like all my contemporaries, I had no financial safety net. So, I was driven. But, I had been going to school since I was 5, and working since I was 9. I needed a break.

Influenced by Jack Kerouac's *On the Road* and it's invitation to an extemporaneous life style, it was finally my turn to give in to rest-

**The Wandering Years
1974-1976**

lessness of youth. In 1974, I was off to see America. I bought Kesey's Magic Bus, a "hippie" van, and Christine Golting (her father a lawyer) and I set out to see "what's happening" – to see the East Coast (Gettysburg to honor the 57,000 silent dead, the Amish country of Pennsylvania to honor the silent living, New York City, Boston and Cape Cod), and to see the Wild West (Denver, Colorado Springs, Aspen, Basalt, Eagle, Rifle, Steamboat Springs, Glenwood Springs, Colorado for the hot spring baths, and on into the Canadian Rockies, Medicine Hat, Moose Jaw and Saskatoon – "Runnin' Back to Saskatoon" by Burton Cummings of the "Guess Who" – back down to Big Sky Montana, Jackson Hole Wyoming where I would later try a major "wrongful birth" case in *Horn vs. Dr. Roux* in 1989, Idaho, Grand Canyon, Carefree Arizona, San Francisco, living in the Marina District for a short time, Carmel California, etc.). Then back home to the Hood in Northwest Detroit… but, only for a moment.

In December 1975, almost 33 years old, I headed out alone for California. I settled in Los Angeles for a while, moving into a studio apartment in West L.A. (just south of the Overton exit of the Santa Monica Freeway) to study for and take the California Bar Exam. It was the disco era, and, on the weekends, I hung out with my St.

Scholastica grade school classmate, Fred Saxe (who grew up seven houses from me in Detroit), and with L.A. District Attorney, Joey Civitate, socializing in Marina Del Rey, hanging out with the Beautiful People at Pip's (Dustin Hoffman, Bill Murray, Playboy's Hugh Hefner and his consorts) and at Carroll O'Conner's bar, "The Gingerman," in Beverly Hills, going to boxing matches at the "Olympia" in downtown L.A., breakfast in Brentwood (UCLA)... Oh the joy of youth when coupled with... some time on our hands and, of course, some walking around money.

But, for the most part in L.A., I studied, studied, studied and studied some more for the California Bar Exam – from 7:00 a.m. to 1:00 p.m. Monday through Friday, and then three bowls of Raisin Bran cereal (my first food of the day), and then back to the books from 2:00 p.m. to 5:00 p.m., and then off to the Bar Review course from 6:30 p.m. to 9:30 p.m., followed by two Big Macs and two large orders of fries, fall asleep, get up the next morning and do it all over again – finally becoming a member of the California Bar in the summer of 1976. After my money ran out in September 1976, I decided to return home to the Detroit Hood and raise my then 6-year-old son, Frederick Valentine, rather than practice in California... a good decision by any measure.

Therefore, in late September of 1976, I jumped into my Jaguar convertible, and, as a solitary sojourner, I set out to take the infamous "Route 66" from Los Angeles to Chicago and then I-94 into Detroit. When I reached San Bernardino, California on the first day of the epic journey, the L.A. smog and my own mild depression finally lifted. Then, it was on to Barstow in the California desert (120 degrees), Kingman, Arizona for the night, then a stop in Winslow, Arizona only because "Take it Easy" by the Eagles left me no choice:

"Well, I'm standing on a corner in Winslow, Arizona, it's such a fine sight to see. It's a girl, my Lord, in a flatbed Ford slowin' down to take a look at me. Come on, baby, don't say maybe. I gotta know if your sweet love is gonna save me."

I didn't see a romantic savior in Winslow. All I saw were poor American Indians hanging outside the small restaurant that I was

"Cochise"
Standing on a Corner
Winslow, Arizona
1976... on Route 66

bold enough to walk into. The Indians were peering through the restaurant window at me because, at age 34, with a sun tanned face and a bandana and a great grandfather who was full blood American Indian, I looked like one of them, and they couldn't figure out why one of their own was bold enough to walk into a white man's restaurant – "Didn't I know my place?" Or, maybe they thought I was an emissary from the Indian Nations checking on treaty violations. To this very day, that encounter with those ("who the hell does he think he is") white men in that Winslow, Arizona café allows me to personally identify with Detroiter Bob Seger's song, "Turn the Page":

"Well you walk into a restaurant, strung out from the road, and you feel the eyes upon you as you're shaking off the cold. You pretend it doesn't bother you but, you just want to explode."

That encounter also reminds me of the original European colonists who left Europe and reestablished their lives in America. When the Europeans arrived, they had the Bible and the Native

Americans had the land. In short order, the Europeans had the land and the Indians had the Bible. I left Winslow, Arizona on that beautiful, sun-filled September 1976 day, and got into my Jaguar, but the faces of the Native Americans standing on the outside of the restaurant are still etched in my memory today, thirty-five years later. And, I still hear them silently questioning: "Who is this guy and how bad is he?" To this day, they still don't know that I was just some nondescript, wayfaring kid from Detroit, a child of the Greatest Generation, broke again, just trying to find my way home. I left Winslow, heading eastbound on "Route 66": Albuquerque, Gallup, New Mexico, Amarillo, Texas, Oklahoma City and on to Chicago. After three days drive, I finally re-entered the center of civilization – the Hood of Northwest Detroit.

Striking Out on My Own... Running with the Bulls

I arrived back home in the Detroit Hood at the end of September 1976 at age 33. I subleased an office from my former prosecutor buddies, Bernie Friedman, now a Federal Judge, and Bob Harrison, still a great trial lawyer. I hung out my shingle: "Lawyer in need of clients" – "Will work for food or money." I was on my own, and it felt great. It felt exhilarating. But, I was broke again. I had no clients and no prospects, but I had a law degree, and, therefore, unlike my own beloved Greatest Generation father and mother with their eighth and ninth grade educations, I had an "opportunity" to change my present financial fortune, or, more aptly put, change my present financial misfortune.

After all, my present financial misfortune was of my own making. During my life on the road, I had squandered my own $30,000 fortune that I had saved over the prior four-year period – a ton of money in the 1970s. When I arrived back in the Detroit Hood, I wiped out what was left of my savings by buying some great, lawyer suits at Chelsea in Wyandotte (thanks to Christine and my father for the color coordination and art direction). It was the right thing to do because: "you don't get a second chance to make a first impression." I knew I could count on the fact that when the world saw me in my gorgeous, new, well-fitting, lawyer-looking suits, it would leave the right impression: "This guy must be somebody."

Most people mistake impression for substance… at least for a while. As my St. Scholastica and California connection friend, Fred Saxe, said: "Lauck, you just create an impression of yourself, and hold on to it until it becomes a reality." – kind of like you can literally create, invent or reinvent yourself according to your needs. But, as Fred Saxe's plunge into obscurity and an early death proved, there is only short term gain with impression. Long term gain requires substance. Impression without substance and commitment is soon unmasked and uncovered as meaningless and hollow. But, impression with substance, commitment and opportunity is a guarantee of success.

Now that I looked like a lawyer, I went back down to renew old acquaintances in the Detroit Recorder's court and in Wayne County Circuit Court where I was an assistant prosecuting attorney. Hopefully, I could score some criminal assignments representing indigent defendants so that I could reestablish myself in my hometown. I wasn't going to get rich representing life's poor and downtrodden in criminal courtrooms, but at least I could earn some journeyman wages and pay some overhead. And, a special "thank you" to my law school classmate, the lovely Judge Susan Borman, for giving me my first criminal assignments.

In the next eighteen months, I tried well over thirty jury trials to conclusion. Life was like running with the bulls in Pamplona Spain –

lots of pitfalls, but, if you can stay on your feet and keep running even through exhaustion and fatigue, you'll reach a "vision quest" where the exhilaration of life will outweigh the depression of exhaustion – provided you don't die first. Two of the cases I tried during that eighteen month, trial marathon were insanity defense cases: the Bruce Ramsey "Devil Murder case," and, the most memorable, the Robert Smith plant shooting at the General Motors Forge Plant in Detroit.

"Smitty" Lands in Detroit

The Robert Smith case, like many of the criminal cases in the Detroit Recorders Court in the 1960s and 1970s, started off in rural America, south of the Mason Dixon Line. Robert Smith was born in Alabama, quit school in the third grade, and immediately went to work full time picking cotton alongside his mother and grandmother. What a stark difference from my upbringing where education and abundant opportunity opened so many doors for me, and where the focus of my whole life was to fully and exhaustively prepare to dance with life so that when the door of "opportunity" opened I could hit the ground running. Robert Smith's life, on the other hand, at least his early life, was to follow the tradition of slavery even though he was officially designated as a "free" man living in the land of the free and the home of the brave, eating apple pie and later working for "Generous Motors" – as it was known in those "it-will-never-fail" days.

Robert Smith's mother sold her only cow (you could not make this up), and used the proceeds to send her son Robert north on a Greyhound bus to the "industrial revolution" where Robert could find a real job. In a latter day version of *Jack and the Beanstalk*, Robert Smith landed in Dayton, Ohio and easily got a factory job – as you could in those days. Shortly thereafter, Robert Smith, now known as "Smitty," climbed up another branch of the beanstalk, landed in

Detroit and found a job operating an overhead crane at the General Motors Forge Plant in Detroit near the border of Hamtramck – where I once taught math at Hamtramck High School in 1965.

Robert was eventually assigned to foreman Jimmy Gaston – an ominous and foreboding combination. Bad blood marked their relationship from the beginning – bad blood that soon would spill real blood. Foreman Jimmy Gaston saw Robert Smith for the unsophisticated, country bumpkin Robert was, and the two immediately clashed. I think it's fair to say that Jimmy Gaston played with Robert Smith's mind much the same way that the Caine Mutiny crew played with the mind of Humphrey Bogart's character, Captain Queeg, in the movie *The Caine Mutiny*. Time cards were hidden, pay was docked, reprimands were issued, time off suspensions were given, and, all the while, Robert Smith was clinging to his job and trying to hold on and weather each new storm that Jimmy Gaston threw at him. Robert Smith, in a state of confusion (some natural and a lot created by Jimmy Gaston), desperately tried to hang on to his GM job so he could provide for his three young children in the "now-you-see-your-time-card, now-you-don't," dream-like, "hide and seek" world created by his foreman, Jimmy Gaston. I'm sure the whole on-going Robert Smith escapade provided many a raucous laugh for Jimmy Gaston and his cohorts at the expense of their country bumpkin target, Robert Smith. Eventually, as usually happens when we deny another person's humanity, Robert Smith became depressed and then demoralized. He saw no way out from the house of cards that Jimmy Gaston created from all kings and a lone jack. Finally, Robert Smith's spirit was broken as he found himself hopelessly falling further and further down the "Alice in Wonderland" well that his controlling and manipulative foreman, Jimmy Gaston, created for unsophisticated bumpkins like Robert Smith.

—

The Genie of Destruction Gets Loose

Depressed, dispirited, demoralized, and without coping mechanism, Robert Smith fought the demons of suicide. He intuitively knew that he couldn't abandon his children like his father before him had abandoned him. Finally, on October 12, 1977, Robert Smith, on automatic pilot, armed himself with a shotgun, loaded it with birdshot, drove to the plant gate and shocked the unarmed GM Guards as he walked right through the plant gate, with the shotgun at "port-arms" telling the guards he had "come to get Jimmy Gaston." The guards scrambled, called the Detroit Police, called the Hamtramck Police, and desperately tried to locate and warn Jimmy Gaston – which they were unable to do because, ironically, Jimmy Gaston was not at his usual work station. Jimmy Gaston was in a meeting with the Labor Relations Management Team, again trying to sabotage Robert Smith's employment with General Motors.

Six hundred yards later, still marching at "port-arms," Robert Smith caught up with Jimmy Gaston at the Labor Relations meeting, and Robert Smith's long pent up depression, rage and fury blew the lid off his self control. The genie of violence and destruction broke loose. It was out of the box and beyond recall. Robert Smith broke into the meeting shouting: "Come out Jimmy Gaston, come out!" Jimmy Gaston dove under a desk for cover, and Robert Smith discharged the shotgun, seriously injuring Jimmy Gaston, and, in the process, superficially wounding Labor Relations employee, Christine Gerstenberg – whose father, Richard Gerstenberg, was CEO of General Motors. Robert then turned on his heel, retraced his steps, and marched 600 yards back to where he started. Once he exited the plant gate, Robert was surrounded by Hamtramck Police with drawn guns trained on him. After a short, tense moment of suicidal thought, Robert finally threw the shotgun down and sobbed like a child. Robert Smith was arrested, lodged in the Wayne County jail and charged with two counts of assault with intent to murder. He knew his life was over.

"Smitty" and Lauck... Fortuitous Connection

Days later, I was appointed by a Recorder's Court judge to represent Robert Smith in a case eerily similar to a prior plant shooting at Chrysler in Detroit... defended by local attorney, Kenny Cockrel, father of Kenny Cockrel, Jr. who took over as mayor of the City of Detroit when disgraced mayor, Kwame Kilpatrick, was convicted of perjury and jailed in 2009. In my first court appearance, I asked the court to order both a mental status exam for competency to stand trial (did Robert Smith understand the nature of the charges against him and could he assist me in his defense?) and a mental exam for criminal responsibility to determine if Robert Smith was legally insane at the time of the shooting – did he "cognitively" know the difference between right and wrong, and, if he did, did he have the "volitional" free will to control his actions (or, stated differently, was Robert Smith, at the time of the shooting, under the not-to-be-denied influence of "irresistible impulse?").

Insanity... ???

The court referred Robert to the State of Michigan's Forensic Center in Ypsilanti for evaluation. Veteran psychologist, Newton "Bud" Jackson Ph.D., was chosen to perform the two mental status exams, and evaluate Robert Smith. Dr. Jackson found Robert Smith competent to stand trial, but also found Robert legally insane at the time of the shooting because, as Dr. Jackson indicated, Robert Smith's free will was overcome by an "irresistible impulse" – something all my friends and I in the Northwest Detroit Hood would have absolutely laughed out of the neighborhood in the old days: "Sure I was caught red-handed, but I didn't mean to shoot anybody because I was insane, so how about some probation and a little night school. I'll get a GED and we'll all kiss and make up, sing songs around the campfire, and be friends forever (or at least until the next 'irresistible impulse' takes over)."

But, through my Jesuit education at the University of Detroit Law School, I had made a break with my past, knee jerk philosophy of the Hood in Northwest Detroit, and I came to fully accept the insanity defense as fundamentally sound, both philosophically and legally. An animal has no volitional power and, therefore, no free will. Put food in front of a hungry animal, and it has no choice; it will eat the food or, if there is no food, the animal will eat you. Put food in front of the human animal, a man or a woman, and they may or may not eat to survive. A human being, even though hungry, may exercise the volitional power of their free will by choosing not to eat, but rather to fast for a higher good, just like the Catholics fast during Lent, just like Mahatma Gandhi, Martin Luther King, or Dick Gregory, though hungry, turned down food and fasted for the higher good of "political freedom" or "racial equality," just like Bobby Sands and other Irish zealots in the late 1970s and early 1980s went on hunger strikes and starved to death for their vision of a free Ireland, or just like the so-called "terrorist" prisoners at Guantanamo Bay, Cuba went on hunger strikes during the year 2007. Only the human animal has free will, and only the human animal can use that free will to overcome the primal instinct of survival and "just say no" to food or to the temptation to commit a crime.

But, if the human animal loses the volitional power of free will, they are no longer a man or a woman, no longer a human animal, but rather they are, volitionally speaking, just another animal in the animal kingdom, and, as such, they are not responsible under our laws for acts which would otherwise be criminal – such as shooting Jimmy Gaston. So insanity and its "irresistible impulse" prong have a logical and legitimate basis arising out of the nature of man and the philosophy of the law. Legal insanity provides a defendant with a complete defense to criminal responsibility. Dr. Newton "Bud" Jackson specifically found that Robert Smith was legally insane at the time of the shooting, and, therefore, not criminally responsible for intentionally shooting his foreman Jimmy Gaston and unintentionally shooting Christine Gerstenberg in the process. But, the remaining question to be vigorously debated at trial... was Dr. Jackson's assessment of Robert Smith's "irresistible impulse" psychologically sound and legally correct? The open question for the jury at the upcoming trial... was Dr. Jackson's opinion that Robert Smith was legally insane due to "irresistible impulse" when he shot his foreman Jimmy Gaston and Christine Gerstenberg, a valid psychiatric/forensic opinion or not?

The Wayne County Prosecutor's office appointed veteran trial lawyer Robert Butler to prosecute Robert Smith. I had tried other high profile cases against Bob Butler in the 1970s and 1980s, and I knew he was one of the best – bright, articulate, well liked by jurors and doggedly determined in a detective "Colombo," Peter Falk-like fashion. But, Prosecutor Butler had a problem. The State of Michigan's Forensic Center which was staffed with well qualified mental health experts,

Prosecutor Bob Butler, Governor Jim Blanchard and Wayne County Prosecutor and former Judge... John D. O'Hair.

and which rendered objective mental health opinions for the Court itself, untainted by the stigma of expert witness "opinions-for-sale," had clearly found that Robert Smith was legally insane, and, now, the only option for Prosecutor Butler was to obtain a "for-hire" opinion from another psychologist or psychiatrist.

Getting Ready for Trial

While I was waiting to see what Prosecutor Butler's next move would be, I had numerous jailhouse visits with Robert Smith preparing for the inevitable trial. I intuitively knew that when you take on the security and the staff of a General Motors plant, and when General Motors CEO Richard Gerstenberg's daughter also gets shot, there weren't going to be any apologies accepted, no making up and no plea bargains. It was going to be a knock down, drag out affair with one of the most powerful corporate presences in the world, or, as the Greatest Generation said in those days: "As General Motors goes, so goes the fate of America."

Besides General Motors' involvement and its overarching influence, I had to deal with Robert Butler. Prosecutor Butler was one of only a handful of opposing lawyers that I ever had a good relationship with over forty years as a trial lawyer. Perhaps it was one of my weaknesses, but I didn't see the point in being friends with, or even socially polite to, someone who was trying to destroy my case and my client and, many times, my reputation. So, it made sense to me to keep my adversaries at arm's length on the other side of the table so that I could always see what they were up to, and so that, when I went after them full bore, they could never accuse me of blindsiding them. Establishing my opponent's respect for my ability and integrity is crucial. Being friends or being polite to them was a distant second.

But, it was almost impossible not to like Bob Butler. He was kind and compassionate, and he had a winning personality. It was just who he was. But, make no mistake about it, and don't get lulled into a false sense of security, Prosecutor Bob Butler was a tough guy. He wasn't going to roll over or allow any advantage. So, the handwriting was on the wall. Get ready for trial because this is going to be a major undertaking against adversaries with unlimited resources and staying power and an unswayable motive to bury Robert Smith and his court-appointed attorney. General Motors, after all, is America, baseball and apple pie, and Robert Smith and his court appointed lawyer Lauck are merely two questionable no-counts trying to win the day for Robert Smith by claiming: "Well, Robert Smith didn't really mean it or, alternatively, the devil made him do it."

But, the first order of business for me was to get to know Robert Smith – to really know him. So, I visited Robert in the old Wayne County jail numerous times. Although it's hard to imagine a more dreary place than the old Wayne County Jail, I thoroughly enjoyed my visits with Robert. I quickly developed a great relationship with him. He was kind and gentle. He was a sweetheart. He took no drugs, and he drank no alcohol. He was a man of disarming simplicity – much like an uneducated version of the Benedictine and Basilian priests who guided the early lives of my classmates and me in Northwest Detroit at St. Scholastica Grade School and Catholic Central High School.

Robert Smith didn't have a racial bone in his body. He was fascinated with white people. They seemed like another species to him. Robert told fond stories of the plantation where he picked cotton with his mother and grandmother, and how the owner's son, Colley Wilkinson, and Robert grew up and played together, and how Colley later "took to drink," and would come home after a night of partying and fire his gun into the air and "whoop it up." Robert told me of shotgun houses in the South, and about the challenges of relocating in the industrial north, and of the oppressive heat rising from the floor of the GM Foundry into the cab of his overhead crane, and of the electrical arcing that terrified him when exposed wires in his crane came in contact with one another, and how, in unadorned simplicity, he would use a stick to "beat out the fire" (not even knowing of the phenomenon of electrical arcing, and even thinking he was really beating out fire with a stick when, in reality, the impact of the stick eventually separated the contact of the exposed wires and stopped the electrical arcing). Robert told me of growing up without a father, and how, later in life, he found his father, sick and dying, and how he took his father in and loved him and nursed him through his final days, and how important it was for him to be the father to his own children that he never had.

Robert Smith never said it, but, after all the hours in the Wayne County jail with him, it finally dawned on me. The overhead crane  job at the GM Forge Plant was the most prized possession Robert had in life because it was this job, and only this job, that allowed Robert to fulfill his role as father and provider, and to support and nurture his children, and to be the father to his own children that he never had. It was almost as if Robert Smith's job at General Motors was the symbol of his own manhood or fatherhood or the life raft that

Robert Smith   kept him from drowning. That General Motors job, that symbol of manhood and fatherhood, that life raft, was his most important possession in this world. With it, he mattered, his life mattered, and he could support his children, but, without that job, nothing mattered. Without the GM overhead crane job, Robert was still just the fatherless, dead-end kid from Alabama who suffered in silence alongside his mother and grandmother as they picked cotton in the economically segregated South.

All I ever saw from Robert Smith in the Wayne County jail was joyfulness and kindness, as if being in jail was a tranquil respite from his daily battle of survival with Jimmy Gaston and the hierarchy at General Motors. But, after organizing the bits and pieces, the details and circumstances of his life story, and, most importantly, after sorting out the irrelevant cacophony of discordant words, sounds, emotions and contradictions, I was able to piece together the compelling story of a sweet, naïve, fatherless kid who grew up in poverty in the rural South, a half a degree removed from slavery, who took the proceeds from the sale of his mother's only cow to purchase a one-way ticket on a Greyhound bus to the industrial North – a man who finally caught up with his own father just in time to walk the last mile with him, nurse him through his last illness and bury him, a man who married and was raising three children and staying out of trouble, but who now, through life's uncontrollable circumstances, coincidences and vagaries, was a 36-year-old, black, man-child, looking at the bleak future of life in a Michigan penitentiary without a family. That story, Robert Smith's story, was the human event that I painstakingly found, and that I portrayed in my opening statement to the jury. After my opening statement, I returned to the defense table to find Robert Smith staring at the floor, silently weeping. Robert Smith told his life's story to me joyously, but when I told it back to him, I suspect he, like the jury, really heard his life story for the first time. But, let's not get ahead of ourselves.

Prosecutor Bob Butler

On the other side of town, Prosecutor Robert Butler knew that there had to be the "other side of this story" of "irresistible impulse," the "other side of the story" that Bob Butler would portray in the courtroom – after all, life and law are always open to interpretation. Which shades of gray are more white and which are more black? And, I'm sure General Motors' subjective view of the Robert Smith/Jimmy

Gaston story was much less favorable for Robert than the opening statement I pieced together. Although I don't know for a fact, I'll give you strong odds that, since GM's plant security was at stake, and, since GM's CEO Richard Gerstenberg's daughter Christine was also shot, GM was bringing a lot of political power and influence to bear on the Wayne County Prosecutor's Office not to let Robert Smith get away with his absolutely, violent and lawless act – regardless of Robert Smith's life story.

GM's political power and influence was probably behind Prosecutor Robert Butler's hiring of prominent "Forensic Psychiatrist," Ames Robey M.D., who prosecutor Butler was going to use to counter my psychologist from the Forensic Center, Bud Jackson. Dr. Ames Robey was a well known psychiatrist who had recently scored a knockout victory over celebrity defense attorney, F. Lee Bailey, and his notorious client, Albert DeSalvo, "The Boston Strangler." Attorney F. Lee Bailey wrote an account of the DeSalvo trial in his best-seller, *The Defense Never Rests*. In his book, Bailey prominently featured the Albert De Salvo trial and the prosecutor's key witness, Psychiatrist, Dr. Ames Robey's role in that trial.

I had previously tried an insanity case in 1977 in *People vs. Bruce Ramsey*, the Devil Murderer. Bruce Ramsey stabbed his wife numerous times in front of his two young children. Kneeling astraddle over his supine wife, Bruce Ramsey alternately held back the knife with his left hand around the wrist of his right arm, and then, apparently losing the emotional battle over the knife, Bruce Ramsey would take his left hand away releasing his right hand to plunge the knife into his wife as he shouted with each stab wound: "Let the Devil out, let the demons free." After the stabbing, Bruce took his dead wife to bed and fell sound asleep with her in his arms, convinced that she would awake in the morning, "free of the demons."

Based on my experience in the Ramsey case, I was fully aware that the insanity defense law in Michigan had been tightened considerably by the Michigan Legislature and Michigan juries were now being misled and enticed to render a brand new verdict of "Guilty but mentally ill" – a verdict that deluded the jury into thinking they were helping the Defendant out and approving mental health treatment in prison. But, the reality was that incarceration for "guilty-but-mentally-ill" defendants was no different than incarceration for any other Defendant who was found just plain "guilty." As a result, I knew the jury in the Robert Smith case could be easily deluded into believing a "guilty-but-mentally-ill" verdict was a kind, helpful middle ground that balanced the right of society to security with the right of a mentally ill defendant to psychiatric care – as I say, a lie. Therefore, I knew I had my work cut out for me in the Robert Smith case.

Doing My Homework on Dr. Ames Robey

F. Lee Bailey was an interesting character. I had been interested in his trial-lawyer career since I was in law school. Bailey had a resume of challenging trials: Dr. Coppolino's acquittal of murdering his wife on retrial, Albert De Salvo, the "Boston Strangler," Patty Hearst, the Symbionese Liberation Army (SLA) murder trial arising out of Patty Hearst's kidnapping, brainwashing, followed by her criminal career as a foot soldier for the terrorist SLA group, and later his work with National Football League great, O.J. Simpson's, legal "dream team." My interest in Bailey was, obviously, not reciprocal. When I ran into Bailey and some blond bombshell at a private club, "Pips," in Los Angeles in the 1980s and introduced myself, he blew me off in a heart beat: "Nice not to know you kid." "But, Lee… can I have a dance with the blond?"

Importantly, however, I knew F. Lee Bailey had previously taken on prosecutor Butler's expert psychiatrist, Dr. Ames Robey, in the Albert De Salvo, "Boston Strangler" case so Bailey could give me an insightful read on Dr. Robey's modus operandi. Therefore, I started my preparation to cross examine Dr. Robey by reading F. Lee Bailey's chapter on the DeSalvo, "Boston Strangler" case, in Bailey's book: *The Defense Never Rests*. Bailey clearly pointed out that psychiatrist Ames Robey would use every question I asked at trial as a "soap-box" opportunity to drive home the guilt of Robert Smith in an impenetrable thicket of psychiatric jargon. An example of the impenetrable, psychiatric jargon that Dr. Robey used in the DeSalvo, "Boston Strangler" case was captured in Bailey's book:

> "'Over the last, oh, year and a half,' said Robey, 'I have seen him [Albert DeSalvo] vacillate back and forth in terms of his chronic illness – at some times appearing almost like an acute anxiety hysteric, a neurotic, at times appearing much more obsessive and compulsive, again at other times appearing much more overtly paranoid and appearing very close to wild overt psychosis... the term we tend to apply particularly with this mixed alternating pattern... is schizophrenic reaction, chronic undifferentiated type... sociopathic features, obsessive features, hysterical features. At one time, depressive features, paranoid signs.'"

After overcoming my initial reaction of self doubt, and the need to flee and leave the defense of Robert Smith to someone much smarter than me, I settled down and dug in, knowing my key was (as it always has been) commitment and hard work. Dr. Robey's strategy convinced me to spend hours memorizing the definitions in the Glossary of Psychiatric Terms so that I could both follow Dr. Robey's circumlocution of psychiatric jargon, and be prepared to challenge his testimony point for point, in an instant, just to show the jury that

Dr. Robey was not going to leave me behind in his psychiatric fog. In addition, I sought a consultation with prominent, local psychiatrist, Emmanuel Tanay M.D., author of *The Murders...* a book which dissects the common, psychiatric cause of murders – a "**Dissociative Reaction.**"

Dr. Tanay Consultation... "The Murders"

Dr. Tanay. Now there's another interesting character. In his book *The Murders*, Dr. Tanay indicates that the source of all human

behavior is divided into three basic components. The "**id**" (or the "**child**") houses the basic, primal "**instinct**" of human nature that we are all born with like the instinct to survive and the suckling instinct. As you can imagine, the "id," with its instinct of survival, has the potential to jump into action in a heart beat with verbal resistance or aggression, and even strike out with violence

Dr. Emmanuel Tanay and take a life. The "**super ego**" (or the "**parent**"), on the other hand, houses the **learned behavior of restraint** – the moderation of our impulsive, instinctual behavior which we learn as we grow and mature (akin to problem solving in a mature, adult manner). The "**ego**" (or the "executive **decision maker**") houses that part of the personality that decides, at any given moment, whether the "id" is going to dominate the human response with the primal instinct of aggression or even violence or, alternatively, whether the "super ego" is going to stifle the basic instinct of aggression and violence, and respond with adult maturity, moderation and non-violence.

As Dr. Tanay indicates, those with **overly developed parental control** – those who respond with the "super ego's" adult maturity, moderation and non-aggression, time after time, day after day and year after year, those who deny and shut down, again and again, the primal response of the "id's" instinctual aggressiveness, those who never even verbally resist or challenge others, are prime candidates to eventually explode out of control. Invariably, the explosion occurs because (according to Dr. Tanay), the aggressive, pent-up "id" causes the "ego" to short circuit and lose its ability to control and choose whether the "id" should respond with aggression or violence or whether, on the other hand, the "super ego" should respond with non aggression and moderation. With the executive "decision maker", "ego," short circuited and inoperable on the sidelines, the aggression of the pent-up "id" jumps into overdrive, runs wild and out of control, and headlong into the unthinkable... a murderous act with the murderer unaware of what's going on, and without any conscious intent to kill – because, as Dr. Tanay indicates, the out of control murderer is driven only by the overwhelming impulsiveness of an "id" that jumps out of the box, and marches to a long pent-up beat that will no longer be denied. For a musical explanation, listen to Kenny Roger's song about Tommy: "The Coward of the County."

Feathering in Psychiatry with... The "Human Event"

Theoretical? You bet. But, we are at the forensic juncture where law and psychiatry meet, and Robert Smith's state of mind (legally, "mens rea") was going to be put under a microscope before a lay jury in a court of law. And, the good trial lawyer is the one that will help the jury feel comfortable with the psychiatric terms the jurors have never (or seldom) encountered in their lives. But, at the same time, the good trial lawyer will not allow the jury to get so absorbed in the psychiatric dynamics and terminology that they lose sight of the "human event" that is being played out in the courtroom. Both law and psychiatry and other professional disciplines are not ends in and of themselves. Rather, they are schools of thought that are supposed to serve mankind: part philosophy, part science, and part wishful thinking that, in the last analysis, have but one purpose – to serve human beings. As I say, therefore, a good trial lawyer will never let the field of psychiatry, psychology, medicine, economics, accounting, meteorology or any other so-called field of expertise dominate or overshadow the "human event" that is being played out in the courtroom. Expert testimony to compliment the "human event" – yes. But, expert testimony that consumes, dominates, or overshadows the "human event" – never.

So back at the ranch, I was doing my home work, reading extensively, lugging around a load of books on psychology and psychiatry, and trying to figure out how the vast array of those arcane and esoteric terms and concepts would fit into the upcoming trial, and how I could use those terms and concepts to explain the psychological dynamic of the "human event" that I saw in the case – Robert Smith's overhead crane job at the GM Forge Plant was the most important possession that Robert had, and that Robert had to keep that job at all costs… if he was to be the father to his children that he himself never had. Was that overhead crane job at GM somehow Robert Smith's enduring, irreplaceable, psychological symbol of manhood or of fatherhood or survival itself? Was the GM job the psychological symbol of the father Robert never had until he found his father sick and dying, just in time to walk the last mile with him? And, did foreman Jimmy Gaston's personality conflict with Robert Smith, and his attempt to drive Robert from the GM Forge Plant with his game of "hide-and-seek" with Robert's time card and the reprimands and suspensions fuel the subsequent human events that led to Robert Smith's murderous rage?

I knew the limitations of psychiatric theory, and I knew that the upcoming trial would provide no definitive answer to the question of why Robert Smith did what he did. But, I knew that, if I were to shape the psychological and psychiatric jargon and nomenclature around the "human event" of Robert Smith's life, I had to be able to fight the battle of psychiatry and psychology head-on at trial, word for word, term for term, definition for definition and concept for concept – just to make sure the jury didn't get led down a blind alley by the overwhelming psychological expertise, and thereby miss out on the "human event" that I had to put on display at trial. I also knew that nothing good would happen if the jury suspected Robert Smith's lawyer was being intimidated or pushed around by the psychiatric presentations. Therefore, I needed to remain in charge of the psychiatric testimony to keep the jury's confidence so I could be persuasive later on in closing argument when I would feather in the esoteric, psychiatric terms into the vernacular of the "human event." In short, I had to make sure the "human event" of Robert Smith's life story became and remained the center piece of the trial. The "human event" of Robert Smith's life story had to have stand-alone significance, and, thereafter, the psychological expert testimony could be used to merely confirm, in psychological terms, what the jury already comfortably understood from their own, lay perspective – the "human event" of Robert Smith's life story.

Self Doubt Creeps in… Again

Such was my overwhelmed state of mind on that wintry, blustery night in February 1978 when I had a consultation appointment with prominent, forensic psychiatrist Dr. Emmanuel Tanay, *The Murders* author, at his Fisher Building office to obtain his advice on what I should be doing. I really liked and respected Dr. Tanay – a good man with a great mind. Before the meeting with Dr. Tanay, I stopped by my father's office, "Lauck Art Studios," on the south side of the

Boulevard across from Detroit's landmark Fisher Building (from illegitimate bookie to legitimate commercial art studio owner). I had my psychiatric research in a briefcase, and I stopped by for a short visit with my father to pick up additional psychiatric research materials my father had obtained for me. My father had a ninth grade education, but he later picked up forty-nine hours of college credit at the University of Detroit in "General Studies" with a 3.7 grade point average, and, if there was a greater student of human nature or human emotion than my own semi-educated father, I never met 'em. I knew my father could provide great insight for my on-going pursuit of the Robert Smith case. What I didn't know at that moment was… that I would need him for yet another shot of confidence when my age old companion, "self doubt," came creeping back into my life again.

The time to meet with Dr. Tanay arrived, and, for what I was paying Dr. Tanay for his consultation, I certainly wasn't going to keep him waiting. Down the elevator and outside I went, and on into the cold, blustery winter snow and traffic. I sprinted northbound across West Grand Boulevard at mid-block, dodging snow and cars as I headed toward Detroit's landmark, the Golden Towers of the Fisher Building. At 35 years of age, I was still quick on my feet with the same uncanny balance I had as an athlete in my youth. But, ironically, as I headed across West Grand Boulevard, I crossed over the very same plot of ground where my 77-year-old great-uncle, Lafayette Montroy, was killed by a car during a blinding snowstorm on St. Patrick's Day in 1934. As I hustled across the Boulevard heading straight for the Fisher Building, crossing over the very same piece of ground that uncle Lafayette took his last breath on more than fifty years before, I thought to myself: "Not a good omen."

Dr. Tanay escaped the Holocaust and made it to the United States leaving many of his family members to a cruel fate – which, I think, created a great sense of guilt in Dr. Tanay, and something,

I suspect, Dr. Tanay struggled with for a lifetime. I also suspect Dr. Tanay's experience with the Nazis gave him a deep resentment for governmental authority which may account for the fact that he was the go-to psychiatrist for the Defense when the State of Michigan charged someone with murder. Some have indicated Dr. Tanay's ego lessened his impact with a jury, but, I for one, disagree. Anyway, in the Robert Smith case, my courtroom psychiatric expert was not Dr. Tanay. Dr. Tanay was merely my expert consultant in the Robert Smith case because I had the luxury of having a non-paid, expert psychologist from the State of Michigan's Forensic Center, Newton "Bud" Jackson, Ph.D., as my expert. Since the court itself sent Robert Smith to the Forensic Center for evaluation, I had the distinct advantage of not having solicited, nor paid for, an expert witness' opinion. Challenge Dr. Jackson's credentials if you want. Challenge Dr. Jackson's opinion if you want. Tell the jury he is only a psychologist and Dr. Robey is a preeminent Doctor of Psychiatry, if you want. But, Dr. Jackson was no hired gun. Advantage Robert Smith. Lauck – one up. Prosecutor Butler – one down.

Dr. Tanay greeted me warmly, and, after a few minutes he asked: "Who is going to testify for the Prosecution?" When I replied: "Dr. Ames Robey," Dr. Tanay's tone became somber and he volunteered: "Dr. Robey is brilliant!" Over the next hour with Dr. Tanay, all I heard was the echoing replay of a recording in my own mind, over and over again: "Dr. Robey is brilliant, Dr. Robey is brilliant, Dr. Robey is brilliant"… and you, Lauck, as you found out from your I.Q. test results at Catholic Central in 1960, are dull normal. "Dr. Robey Brilliant" – Fred Lauck dull normal. "Poor Robert Smith," I thought: "he's dead." There's an old saying in criminal law: "innocent until proven broke." "Well," I thought to myself, "in the Robert Smith case, it should be 'innocent until appointed a retarded lawyer'." Advantage the Prosecution. Prosecutor Butler – 10 up. Lauck – 10 down. But, if I work really hard, maybe I can reduce Butler's advantage. Prosecutor Butler – 7 up. Lauck – tepid H^{2}O.

After our consultation, I paid Dr. Tanay his $75.00 per hour fee, picked up my psychiatric homework which by now had lost its energy, and, as I took my dejected, intellectually defective self back across the Boulevard in the continuing snowstorm, I knew I must have picked up bad karma right where my great uncle Lafayette Montroy took his last breath. Self doubt crept in again, and undermined my confidence again, or, as they say: "If you think you will, you might, but, if you think you won't, you can't." One part of me wanted to throw my psychiatric Cliff Notes and Psychiatry 101 lesson plans on uncle Lafayette's death spot and run away. But, my crestfallen self retraced my steps to my father's office. Back up in the elevator to the second floor, and into my father's office I returned. I slumped into the chair across from my father's desk wearing an invisible sign that only I could read: "inadequate once again."

For the past thirty-five years of my life, my father had always been able to restore my confidence and raise up my low self image. But, now, I was beyond hope and beyond help from my father. I knew we were both out of our league, and hopelessly done in by the "brilliance" of real professionals. "So what happened?," asked my father. After a short, indecisive moment of silence, I just gave it up: "Dr. Tanay said that 'Dr. Robey is brilliant'." My father quizzically stared at me in silence for a good thirty seconds, and nothing was said. The he burst out: "Brilliant? – What the hell does that mean? Light shines out of his eyes?" I looked at him quizzically as I considered his strange response. And, then I got it. Thanks again, Pa. Yes, I got it again for the umpteenth time. Nobody can defeat us. We both grew up hard and tough, and we fear no living soul. I'll see you in the courtroom

Ames Robey M.D., and I will bring the inheritance of my strength and determination, and I will match wits with your "brilliant" self until hell freezes over, and I will defeat you. It was another defining moment in my life of many defining moments from a father who had supreme (repeat for emphasis "supreme") confidence in me. What could he have possibly seen in me? I didn't see it, and I'll bet most others didn't see it either, but, because he was one of the few people in life I trusted, I just accepted that something must be there. May you rest in peace, great man. And may you feel my love for eternity.

Battle Lines are Drawn

The battle was shaping up for the upcoming trial. I not only had Ames Robey M.D. and General Motors to contend with, but I also had career prosecutor Robert Butler on my horizon of obstacles. Robert Butler graduated from Highland Park High School in 1960. He had many kids and spent his trial-lawyer career working as an assistant prosecutor in Wayne County, prosecuting cases out of Recorder's Court in the Frank Murphy Hall of Justice (named after Michigan's favorite Irish son, the Honorable Frank Murphy – Recorder's Court Judge in the 1920s, Mayor of the City of Detroit, Governor of the State of Michigan, Ambassador to the Philippines, United States Attorney General under President Roosevelt, and Justice of the United States Supreme Court). I tried three major cases against Bob Butler in the 1970s. He was the Wayne County Prosecutor's best trial lawyer. Bob Butler's low key, unassuming style and his sincerity, along with his great communication skills, made him very appealing to the jury. Whenever you drew Bob Butler as the prosecutor on any given criminal trial, you knew you had your hands full. I truly liked Bob Butler and, as I say, he was one of only a handful of opposing lawyers that I ever got along with on a personal basis.

I'm not big on the superficial "civility" of social etiquette in general, especially in a courtroom. The opposing lawyer wants to destroy my client and me, and the feeling is mutual. Trial work is hard work and hard ball. There's always a lot at stake. In a courtroom, I am trying to get my client's message heard, loud and clear, and I will not let "civility" or any other form of social etiquette get in the way of my need to clearly and truthfully state my client's message in no uncertain terms. I just don't have the time or inclination to be "pals" with adversaries or give off a facade of feigned, social etiquette. Just keep adversaries in front of you and at arms' length, and, if they show you that they're worthy of your respect, like Bob Butler, then you can change the rules of engagement, somewhat, so long as your client's rights are never jeopardized.

The weeks passed by and spring arrived, heralded, as usual, by Detroit Tigers baseball announcer, Ernie Harwell, from the Song of Solomon:

> "For, lo, the winter is past,
> The rain is over and gone,
> The flowers appear on the earth:
> The time of the singing of birds is come,
> And the voice of the turtle is heard in our land."

"Rock and Rollin'"... In the Trenches of Justice

Now, it was not only the time for the "Voice of the Turtle;" now, it was the time to give voice to the "human event" in the case of *People of the State of Michigan vs. Robert Smith* and the two counts of assault with intent to murder that were about to play out in the adversarial ritual of justice in an American court of law.

Outside the Frank Murphy Hall of Justice, there was a spectacle featuring historical antagonists as old as mankind itself – the haves versus the have-nots, Labor versus Capitalists. Every day, outside the Recorder's Court, Frank Murphy Hall of Justice, a group of the

United Auto Workers (UAW), union employees carried signs: "Free Robert Smith," "Unfair working conditions," "GM Exploits its Labor." Obviously, Robert Smith was useful to their larger cause.

Picket lines...
Frank Murphy Hall of Justice
1978

The first day of trial presented a most humorous and larger than life symbol of the clash between Labor and Capitalists. Mrs. Gerstenberg, the wife of General Motors CEO Richard Gerstenberg, and the mother of victim two, Christine Gerstenberg, arrived at the courthouse in style in her chauffeur driven, extended-body limousine – a diminutive, downsized passenger of one arriving in an upscale, upsized limo for many... which, for some, reflected her temporal importance. After her grand exit, Mrs. Gerstenberg confidently strode through the gauntlet of union picketers with her silver-blue hair held high. That stark and ridiculously comical contrast between the white collar "haves" and the blue collar, UAW "have-nots" picketing in front of Recorder's Court was not lost on GM, and Mrs. Gerstenberg's larger-than-life ride was put in mothballs for the rest of the trial. But, like clockwork, every morning General Motors vehicles emblazoned "GM Courtesy Cars" would pull up to the Frank Murphy Hall of Justice, and drop off that day's witnesses (mostly management types), guide them through the throng of UAW picketers, and safely deposit them in the court room of Judge Joseph Maher – run by his tough court clerk, Walter Abick... who by this time in my career had grown tired of fighting me, and decided he would try to befriend me thereby avoiding the road to constant confrontation.

There was even the gorgeous black woman (and I mean "gorgeous") who did her best to entice me and befriend me during courtroom breaks over a three day period at the beginning of the trial. She was stunning, and, at another place and time, even tempting. But, I was disciplined and determined, if nothing else, and I had just enough good old paranoia and distrust to know that GM would love to be privy to my trial strategy or to my personal peccadilloes – the Irish misdemeanors in my background. So, I followed my Irish mother's lifetime advice: "Trust no one and walk softly past graveyards" (with my mother explaining to me a month before her death in 1989, that distrust and graveyards are connected because: "how do you know they're really dead?"). Okay! But, after three days, this gorgeous woman disappeared for good never to be seen again in my lifetime. As my bookie father would say: "Five will get you ten she's a spy." As my Irish mother, with her everlasting need to keep me humble, would say: "Don't flatter yourself."

Well, on to the trial… rockin' and rollin' in the gritty trenches of life, where words are weapons and the semi-literate, unarmed as they are for the battle, are destined to defeat. Assistant prosecutor, Robert Butler, was supported by all the wealth, power and staff of both the State of Michigan and General Motors (but he'd be a great trial lawyer anyway), and he was prepared, willing, ready, able and looking for a chance to bury both Robert Smith and me. The General Motors/Robert Smith incident was a highly visible case with the expected abundance of media publicity. Therefore, sorting out the pre-existing thinking of prospective jurors took some time, but jury selection eventually gave way to opening statements. In his opening statement, Prosecutor Butler put Robert Smith's dastardly deed all together for the jury and the world to see. I responded with the human event of Robert Smith's life story, including the sale of his mother's only cow to buy Robert a bus ticket to the industrial North. After hearing my portrayal of his life story in my opening statement, Robert Smith wept silently, and away we went, both sides out to devour one another – not by the law of the jungle, but by "due process of law."

The days turned into weeks. The Masters Golf Tournament was played at Augusta. The Tigers had their annual rite of Spring: "Opening Day." The weather was moderating, and, all the while, Prosecutor Butler and I were still swinging at one another with General Motors and Robert Smith sitting on the sidelines as spectators watching the spectacle of justice in an American courtroom.

Defending the Indefensible

One of my highlights at trial involved the cross examination of victim number two, Christine Gerstenberg (her married name "Gay"). Christine's mother, with her blue-gray hair always catching my attention, sat in the court room visibly supporting the Prosecution, her body language visibly urging her daughter Christine to crush me during my cross examination. Christine Gerstenberg Gay was an attractive, but timid, young lady, probably about 30 years old, but certainly close to me in age. Obviously, her father Richard Gerstenberg, as CEO of General Motors, drove home the point to his daughter Christine that, since she was employed by GM's Labor Relations Department and involved in the discipline of Robert Smith, she had better be well versed in GM's union contract with the United Auto Workers of America (UAW) – especially where an important side issue on Robert Smith's pattern of discipline involved "mandatory overtime" under the UAW contract.

On direct examination by Prosecutor Butler, Christine spoke in generalizations about the overtime subject as her mother smiled on, and occasionally shot me one of those triumphant, haughty "take that!" looks. On cross examination, it was a different story. When confronted with the specific language of the union contract, it was obvious that Christine, even though the General Motors authority on mandatorily-required overtime, could not begin to interpret the dense language of the UAW's contract with General Motors. Toward the end of her cross examination, Christine stubbornly clung to the fact that she had no problem understanding the UAW contract on mandatory overtime (What else could she do?).

Finally, I set up a question which walked her right through the dense thicket of the UAW contract language. First, I set out the facts regarding Robert Smith's past overtime during the year of the shooting. Then I asked her whether Robert Smith, who could barely read a newspaper, would have any problem reading and understanding various provisions of the UAW contract to determine whether he would be mandatorily required to work further overtime during the year of the shooting. Christine emphatically replied that Robert Smith would have no trouble reading the UAW contract himself and figuring out for himself the answer to the question on "mandatory overtime." Now I had her.

I followed up by asking her college-educated, Labor Relations self to walk me and the jury through the specific, overtime language of the UAW contract so the jury and I could figure out for ourselves, and verify that Robert Smith would have no problem understanding the UAW contract language on "mandatory" overtime. The contract immediately started out with an unintelligible hypothetical:

> ...unless as otherwise required by Section 42A, Subsection d" [OK put a paper clip there, Christine... and off we go to Section 42A, Subsection d]. Section 42A, Subsection d starts out "provided this subsection has been implemented by the procedures set forth in ratification documents [another paper clip, please, so we can check on the ratification documents] and, except as otherwise required by the implementing

sections of 905 B regarding mandatory overtime accumulated over a three year period [another paper clip, please], and off we go to Section 905 B [and somebody please provide me with Robert Smith's prior three year overtime history so we can match it against, and incorporate it into, the UAW's easy to understand contract].

After running out of paper clips, I continued my cross examination: "Ms. Gerstenberg, is it still your position that Robert Smith would have no problem understanding the language in the UAW contract to determine whether he was mandatorily required to work overtime on the day of the shooting?" Answer, "Yes," but a lot less emphatic. Next: "Ms. Gerstenberg, you have already told us that, under the UAW contract, Robert Smith was required to work overtime on the day of the shooting so would you please walk me and the jury through all of the applicable sections and subsections we have just paper clipped, and show us how those sections and subsections support your position?" Christine was dead in the water. She was dead and the jury knew it. She was dead and she knew it. She was dead but her mother didn't know it… yet. Silence! A pregnant, deafening, thirty seconds of silence. No answer even attempted. Point made.

My instincts told me: "Point made; move on." Therefore, next question: "Ms. Gerstenberg, isn't it true that it would take a brilliant (there's that word again) Philadelphia lawyer to walk us through all of the applicable sections and subsections and 'provided that's' and 'unless required bys' just to figure out the answer to my question on 'mandatory overtime'?" Silence! No answer for another thirty seconds. I looked at the jury. They got it. I heard the competitive side of my nature say, "Bury her!" But, I also heard the practical side of my nature say: "Pick on her and you lose your advantage. It's over Lauck. Let her off the hook," and don't worry about the misguided jury instruction that says only a witness' answer is evidence. In this case, a non-answer was the best evidence to prove my point. I stepped back with Christine's deafening silence still palpable, and I saw a hint of tears start to flow. "I'll withdraw the question, Your Honor; no further questions." I let her off the hook with her dignity still somewhat intact. The point was proven without an answer. Neither Robert Smith, nor Christine Gerstenberg Gay, nor the jury, nor I could reliably figure out Robert Smith's obligation to work mandatory overtime under the UAW contract… despite GM's haughty protestations to the contrary.

Prosecutor Butler knew when discretion was the better part of valor. He purposely let it go. "No follow up questions, Your Honor." As I turned and walked back to counsel table with a sense of subdued triumph, Christine's mother, Mrs. Gerstenberg, her eyes desperately searching for my eyes, shot me another one of her patented, haughty "Take that!" looks, smugly believing that her daughter Christine put me in my place. As Goethe, the great German philosopher, said: "We tend to find what we're looking for." And, I'm sure that when Christine and her mother met up with Christine's CEO father, Richard Gerstenberg, the report was good; Christine put both Robert Smith and his obstructionist, sleight of hand lawyer in their places. I never saw either one of those two fine ladies again. But, I would love to have a cup of coffee with the now sixty something-year-old Christine Gerstenberg Gay to see how her life played out. Something tells me that her life, although most likely financially and emotionally secure… was probably uneventful. But, I'd still like to have a cup of coffee with her just the same.

Psychiatric Main Event

After three weeks of dodging picket signs, after three weeks of trying to figure out what influences General Motors' witness-employees were being subjected to during GM "courtesy car" rides to the Frank Murphy Hall of Justice, after three weeks of tracing foreman Jimmy Gaston's "hide-and-seek" shell game conspiracy to drive Robert Smith out of the GM Forge Plant, after three weeks of saying "Good Night" to a fatigued Robert Smith as the Wayne County Sheriff's deputies led him back to his "Trial Central Headquarters" in the Wayne County Jail, after three weeks of alternating exhilaration and tedium that ebbed and flowed in Judge Maher's courtroom, after three weeks of a grinding trial... the psychiatric, main event was finally scheduled to begin, and the jury was anxiously awaiting the anticipated, guided tour around the chambers of Robert Smith's mind to view the root cause of Robert Smith's murderous rage that struck such a stark contrast to his natural, gentle simplicity.

To some extent, however, the jury was to be disappointed... because the forensic issue in an insanity case is generally limited to whether the Defendant was legally insane – did the defendant know right from wrong, or, alternatively, if the defendant knew right from wrong, were the defendant's actions compelled by an "irresistible impulse?" The forensic, psychological testimony would not necessarily provide the root cause of any such insanity. When psychologists and psychiatrists freeze the frame on the Defendant's state of mind at the time of a murderous rage, they are already juggling unavoidable ambiguity, and opening themselves up to the legitimate discrediting that: "they can't read minds." Therefore, most psychologists and psychiatrists are hesitant to dive down into even murkier waters, and start discussing the actual root cause of the legal insanity of the murderous rage, especially where those root causes could be seen by the jury as an attempt to shift the blame to others (my father's expectations, my mother's withdrawn love, the harsh environment of my childhood, etc.).

Nonetheless, whether I received psychiatric support or not, I was sticking with my causation theme of the "human event" – Robert

Smith's job at General Motors was the sole possession he had in life that would allow him to be what, at all costs, he must be... the emotionally and financially supportive father to his children that he himself never had. And, the studied attempt by Jimmy Gaston or anyone else to take Robert's GM job away from him was a threat to Robert's very existence and his crucial role in life – a threat that triggered Robert Smith's most basic evolutionary, primal instinct to survive. That's why, in my opinion, Robert was about to kill himself in those moments after the shooting as Robert stared-down with the Hamtramck police, everybody armed to the hilt. After the shooting, Robert knew the GM job was gone, and, therefore, he was already dead. Based on my hours of jail conversations with Robert Smith and my experience with life, I was convinced that my causation theme of the "human event" was accurate, and I certainly wasn't about to waffle or to let it go. As they say: "You gotta stay with the one that brought you to the dance."

Newton "Bud" Jackson Ph.D. – Front and Center

My psychiatric witness from the Michigan Forensic Center, Newton "Bud" Jackson Ph.D. was called first. Dr. Jackson didn't look

Newton "Bud" Jackson
Dean of Enlightenment

like a doctorate of anything. He didn't present himself in a Ph.D. light. He was a homespun guy who could disarm you with his charm, humility and humor, but, make no mistake, Dr. Jackson was an expert in building confidence with the jury, and in sharing his thorough understanding of human nature. During my direct examination, the jury took in every word of Dr. Jackson's testimony on Robert Smith's non-culpability based on legal insanity – "irresistible impulse."

Now it was time for prosecutor, Robert Butler, to try and elicit the "other side of the story"… if he could.

My method of cross examination is to prepare, prepare, and prepare and master the roadmap for the trip I want to take the witness on, and then demonstrate to the jury and the witness that the trip I'm taking them on is pre-ordained, and that they have little or no chance but to follow my bouncing ball which I use to drive home the "human event" that is evolving at trial. Prosecutor Butler was different. His approach was reserved, even soft in tone and "Detective Colombo"-like, humbly asking generic questions that only challenged witnesses in small, unnoticeable increments – with the witnesses (like the proverbial frog in water that is incrementally heated up) failing to notice that they just got cooked. But, Dr. Jackson was no novice. He had worked at the Forensic Center for years. He had great command of the language. He was a skillful communicator. Dr. Jackson knew his field of psychology thoroughly, and he could explain the dynamics of human psychology to the jury in such a way that the jury would not lose sight of the "human event" that was evolving before them. Prosecutor Butler would not lull Dr. Jackson into a false sense of security, and knock him out of the box. But, with the advantage of 20-20 hindsight, I must confess, Robert Butler was more of a "Wiley Coyote" than either Dr. Jackson or I suspected.

Prosecutor Butler started his cross examination by addressing the details of Dr. Jackson's background, education and work experience, and pointing out at every chance he could that Dr. Jackson was a psychologist and not a psychiatric, medical doctor like the magnificent forensic psychiatrist, Dr. Ames Robey. Prosecutor Butler then introduced his theme, "psychotherapy," asking Dr. Jackson whether Dr. Jackson had ever been a psychotherapist working with patients, to which Dr. Jackson replied: "Yes, for a number of years," and whether, "as part of his background and training, Dr. Jackson had ever been on the other side of the psychotherapy couch as a patient," to which Dr. Jackson replied that: "as part of his background and training, he himself was a therapy patient for five years." "Great! Great!," I thought: "Dr. Jackson has a scope of experience that is far broader than I realized, and that broad scope of experience is certainly going to elevate his credibility and resonate well with the jury."

Prosecutor Butler... Sets the Trap

Prosecutor Butler then asked Dr. Jackson to tell the jury what psychotherapy was, and to describe the ultimate purpose of psychotherapy. Dr. Jackson rose to the occasion, and gave an explanation that, like the precision of a fine mirror, reflected the jury's own experience in life. Dr. Jackson began by focusing his answer on what kind of patients generally seek out psychotherapy. Admitting to somewhat of an "oversimplification," Dr. Jackson testified that generally two categories of patients seek out the benefit of psychotherapy. "First," Dr. Jackson indicated: "there is a group of patients who have suffered a traumatic episode, perhaps witnessing the death or grievous injury of another... Post Traumatic Stress Syndrome as it is known. Those patients need help in overcoming the psychological impact of that trauma on their emotional psyche. Those patients are the easier cases to deal with," Dr. Jackson continued: "because those patients are usually aware of both the emotional pain and the traumatic incident that is the source of their pain. Those are the easier cases because, generally, everything is up front in the conscious mind of the patient – both the emotional pain and the cause of the pain."

"Next," Dr. Jackson continued: "there is a second group of patients that are the more difficult cases – cases where the patient has lived a life of denial for years and decades, and the key word is 'denial' because all the patient knows is that there is just emotional pain without any apparent cause." "For example," Dr. Jackson continued: "many patients come to psychotherapy and report psychological pain which is just a general malaise of discontent including such descriptions as 'unhappy,' 'depressed,' 'anxious,' 'uncertain,' 'lack of direction,' 'lack of motivation,' 'loss of spark,' 'lack of interest' 'vague feeling of discontent,' 'colorless days,' 'sense of failure,' 'exhaustion', and, in more serious cases, an 'impending sense of doom' or 'hopelessness' – all without any cause the patient is aware of in their conscious mind, or with possible causes the patient alludes to, but which the psychotherapist knows just doesn't add up to the emotional pain the patients report they are suffering. These patients also generally report that they are having trouble with acting out in social settings, employment settings or, in public, with inappropriate, exaggerated or dysfunctional responses that go well beyond the normal responses to life stresses." Dr. Jackson continued: "As a psychologist, this second group of patients presents a very challenging paradigm or enigma because their present symptoms of unhappiness and discontent are usually caused by past emotional trauma from years or even decades ago with the patients still running away from or distracting themselves from that past emotional trauma by pushing the past trauma out of their conscious, aware, mind. As a result, the past trauma invariably ends up in the **subconscious, unaware, mind**. In a word, the psychological process of pushing trauma out of the conscious, aware, mind into the subconscious, unaware, mind in order to buy temporary, short term emotional relief is called **'denial'** – a historically documented bugaboo of human nature."

This testimony about therapy had nothing to do with Robert Smith. When Robert Smith was picking cotton in the South as a 5-year-old, while the white kids were going to school, he wasn't spending any of his hard earned pittance on weekly therapy visits to discuss how the hopeless gloom of his family's post-slavery life was affecting him. I thought about objecting, but withheld my objection because Dr. Jackson's testimony ostensibly related to his background and qualifications, and his mastery of the subject matter. Besides, Dr. Jackson was a shining star of information on human nature, and the jury was engrossed in Dr. Jackson's testimony. So, there could be no harm... or so I thought.

Prosecutor Butler followed up by putting Dr. Jackson's answer into a summary, stating that what he heard Dr. Jackson say was that: "the most challenging of therapy patients are the 'unaware' ones who don't know what's on their mind because the past trauma that is causing their present symptoms of unhappiness and discontent is buried in their subconscious mind through the well recognized psychological phenomena of 'denial.'" Dr. Jackson admitted the correctness of prosecutor Butler's paraphrase of his answer. Dr. Jackson then volunteered an example of how the old bugaboo of "denial," in an attempt to secure short term relief from emotional pain, actually sets us up to suffer long term pain, indefinitely. "For example," Dr. Jackson continued: "if a child sees his mother frequently sipping on a bottle of Jack Daniels, drinking herself into a stupor, the child will feel the pain of rejection and the loss of the mother to the stupor of alcohol. Most times, a child is unable to confront the mother's drinking. Most times, a child is also unable to even recognize or confront the feeling of rejection and loss of his mother's love and attention caused by the mother's drinking. The child has not yet developed the ability to confront the mother, nor has the child yet developed any coping mechanism to protect the child from the mother's alcoholic stupors. So, the child will resort to denial by mentally putting the mother's drinking out of sight and out of mind, 'This isn't really happening,' and the child will distance and distract himself from the pain of the loss of his mother to alcoholic stupors by focusing on other events."

"But," Dr. Jackson continued: "denial is an 'intellectual' exercise only, and it does not remove the 'emotional' pain of rejection and loss from the human psyche. The emotional pain of the child's rejection and loss of his mother's love and attention is simply pushed out of the conscious mind through 'denial,' and it ends up below the surface of the conscious, aware, mind by drifting down into the subconscious, unaware, mind where it will, unknown to the child, fester like an open wound just waiting for the stress of life to throw salt on that open, yet denied, emotional wound. At the moment the stress of life throws salt on that subconscious wound of rejection and loss of love, the child, or the adult that the child has grown up to become, will suffer strong emotional symptoms of sadness, anger, helplessness, hopelessness, betrayal, rejection and even rage, often accompanied by anti-social, dysfunctional behavior – all the while the adult, the child has now become, has little or no memory of the mother's drinking episodes because those hurtful episodes were 'denied' years or decades ago."

"For example," Dr. Jackson continued: "long after the child of the alcoholic mother becomes an adult, an unaware glance at a Jack Daniels bottle or a similar-looking bottle, or the mere mention of the name 'Jack' or the name 'Daniel' could defeat years of attempted 'denial' as the now adult, without being aware of what's going on or why, is right back in touch with yesteryear's emotions and the decades-old, negative feelings of rejection and loss of love which, despite denial, have continued to fester like an open wound in the subconscious, unaware, mind. The net effect is that the adult, the child has now become, feels the old pain of 'unhappiness,' 'sadness,' 'isolation,' 'discontent,' 'depression,' 'despondency,' 'anxiousness,' 'hopelessness,' 'uncertainty,' 'impending sense of doom,' 'anger' and even 'rage' without knowing why or what's going on, or worse yet, by putting the blame on some pseudo non-cause."

The jury was absorbed. Dr. Jackson touched the jury's experience of their own lives, and was taking their experience on a sight-seeing tour of new phenomena, new possibilities, and perhaps new solutions to old problems. As Dr. Jackson took a breath, Prosecutor Butler took back control, and asked Dr. Jackson: "Do the people you are describing ever have a chance to reverse 'denial,' and bring their suppressed bad memories out from their unaware, subconscious minds and into their conscious, aware minds, and thereby see that 'denial' of past memories is responsible for the present emotional pain they suffer?" "In other words," continued Prosecutor Butler: "can a person in 'denial' ever find out what's really on their mind by delving into and discovering what's in their subconscious mind?" I wasn't sure, but I thought perhaps Prosecutor Butler, with this question and his previous questions, was developing some kind of a theme about people not knowing what's on their minds. I was beginning to get a drift of something, but I was a step or two behind Prosecutor Butler. Dr. Jackson, however, seemed to hit a chord with the jury, and appeared extremely knowledgeable, so I didn't object.

Dr. Jackson and I continued to bounce along on Prosecutor Butler's circuitous cross examination with Dr. Jackson testifying that: "Yes, people can eventually gain 'insight' and discover what repressed memories unknowingly reside in their subconscious, unaware, minds – repressed memories that are causing their present emotional pain, and that's where psychotherapy comes in." Dr. Jackson explained that when a patient comes to him asking for help because of a general, unexplained malaise of discontentment or with strong feelings of unhappiness, sadness, discontent, etc. or when a patient comes to him with a history of dysfunctional or excessively strong responses to life's normal stresses, Dr. Jackson recommends psychotherapy.

Dr. Jackson, after having described the underlying variables of general emotional discontent, dysfunction, exaggerated acting out, the role of "denial" and the role of the "subconscious, unaware, mind" in that emotional discontent, dysfunction and acting out, was now, finally, in a position to answer Prosecutor Butler's original question of what psychotherapy was and the purpose of psychotherapy as well as Prosecutor Butler's last question of whether a person in "denial" can ever find out what's in their subconscious, unaware, mind.

The jurors tightened their seat belts as Dr. Jackson continued his clinic on human nature. "Psychotherapy is the prescription for undoing the long term negative, emotional effects of 'denial.' A therapist, like myself (and others) use psychotherapy to assist our patients to gain 'insight' into their subconscious minds. Psychotherapy generally uses the strategy of a question and answer session, usually one hour at a time, over months or years, to guide the patient as the patient goes backward in time to undo 'denial' thus allowing the patient to **find and confront** the old, emotional demons of long ago. The undoing of 'denial' is, as you might expect, based on allowing and guiding the patient to go back in time and rediscover the old, painful traumas of the past, reopen the emotional scars that those past, painful traumas caused, relive those past painful traumas, re-feel the past painful emotions caused by those past traumas, and then throw out the past inadequate coping mechanism of 'denial,' and take a long, hard look or re-look at those old, painful traumas, and confront them again, this time head-on without any 'denial.' Now that the patient has revisited, reconnected to and gained insight into the past traumas and overcome 'denial,' the patient is in a position to resolve those past emotional traumas with new coping mechanisms which ultimately include: First, an admission by the patient that the past traumas could have been somewhat exaggerated by the patient as most children are overly sensitive to the slights and stresses of life; Second, an emotional venting by the patient that allows the patient to fully express anger and rage at those who brought those past traumas to the patient's life, after which the patient has usually expended the emotional energy of anger or rage from past traumas; and, Finally, an acceptance of the pain, rejection and loss the patient suffered long ago – mixed with a realization that life is not perfect, not always fair, and it's just a part of life to be let down, at times, by those we love or those we need the most."

Continuing, Dr. Jackson noted: "Now that the pent-up energy of the past trauma has been relived, confronted and dissipated through acceptance, and now that the festering wound in the subconscious has seen the fresh light of a new day, forgiveness and emotional well-being can set in buttressed by the recognition that those who were responsible for the past traumas didn't know any better. It is that **'acceptance and forgiveness'** that ultimately heals the festering wound of the past trauma. 'Forgiveness' is the key, almost magical, element. Since children hold themselves personally responsible for a problem with an adult, the (now adult) child, by forgiving the adult who brought the past traumas to them, in essence forgive themselves – because the (now adult) child finally realizes that the past trauma that gave rise to 'denial' was the adult's problem, not the child's doing or responsibility. That bears repeating," continued Dr. Jackson. "Since children generally fault themselves when there is criticism by or friction with an adult, forgiving the adult automatically puts the blame where it belongs... on the adult. As a result, forgiving the adult automatically absolves the child of any perceived blame as the (now adult) child finally sees **'it wasn't my fault.'** Now that the patient has made the psychotherapy journey over months or years, and rid themselves of 'denial,' and reassessed the past through adult eyes and with adult coping mechanism, the (now adult) patient has, in many important ways, overcome denial by neutralizing and dissipating the negative energy of those past traumatic events on the patient's present emotional well being."

Just as Prosecutor Butler was about to ask another question, Dr. Jackson courteously begged Prosecutor Butler's indulgence to let him finalize the most important part of his answer. Dr. Jackson continued testifying: "that it is crucial, in understanding the role of psychotherapy, that no one should talk in terms of a 'completely different person' being forged out of psychotherapy nor should anyone speak in terms of a person being 'cured' by psychotherapy." Dr. Jackson continued: "Expectations should not be set with those parameters in mind. First, psychotherapy does not create a different person. We are all a product of our past including the good, the bad, the ugly, the happy moments and the traumatic moments. So, who would really want to be a completely different person? In fact, the strength of our character was forged from surviving past traumas. Surviving our past tells us, no matter what, when called upon, we will survive life's future traumas."

"So," continued Dr. Jackson: "we are not a different person when we finish therapy. We are the same person. But, we have a new-found insight into the weakness of our psyche. Now, when we are confronted with the same old general, negative feelings of 'unhappiness' or 'discontent,' we have the 'insight', repeating for emphasis, we now have the **'insight'** to know where those negative feelings are coming from, and we can, therefore, neutralize those negative feelings based on the 'insight' acquired in psychotherapy. 'Insight and knowledge' of **'why'** we are feeling 'unhappy or discontent' is the key psychotherapy offers us to understand and overcome emotionally negative feelings." "Secondly," Dr Jackson continued: "we should not speak in terms of cures. After psychotherapy, we are still the product of our background and the influences in our background which have shaped our personality and our character just as the blacksmith with fire and an anvil shapes a horseshoe." "No," Dr. Jackson continued: "we are not cured, but we have been freed from 'denial' by the truth of our lives, and our negative feelings have been validated because they were caused by actual events and traumas in our lives. Therefore, every time the old feeling of emotional malaise comes back to haunt us through 'unhappiness,' 'sadness,' 'isolation,' 'discontent,' 'depression,' 'despondency,' 'anxiousness,' 'hopelessness,' 'uncertainty,' 'impending sense of doom,' 'anger' and even 'rage,' we at least now have 'insight,' and we are able to recognize those demons for what they are, and recognize what past traumas have given birth to those demons, and we have already accepted those past traumas as part of our lives, of who we are. And, most importantly, we have forgiven those who have visited those past traumas on us, and, in the process, we have forgiven ourselves, since the adult who caused the past trauma in our lives has now been uncovered as the actual fault of the problem, not us – the vulnerable child."

"One last point," implored the crusading mental health guru Dr. Jackson as the jurors' eyes approvingly said, "Yes." "When the old malaise of ill feelings comes back as 'demons on the haunt,' I always tell my patients to use the **'fifteen minute rule.'** Don't avoid. Don't deny. Focus directly on the demons and their emotional impact, and focus directly on the past trauma that caused those ill feelings, and lament your loss and your emotional distress with a sadness that you allow to enter the very core of your being. Purposely allow those ill feelings, and the past traumas that bring on those ill feelings, into the core of your soul, and mourn your plight, and mourn your plight, and mourn your plight, again and again... **but for no more than fifteen minutes.** Most patients report back to me that, once they allow themselves the fifteen minute time period to lament, mourn and grieve their emotional ill feelings and their past traumas, they can't get through the whole fifteen minutes. But, by giving themselves a green light to grieve, the **opposite of denial** occurs. The patients report that they are reinvigorated emotionally, and they are ready to go on with their lives leaving the old demons and emotional malaise behind them once again until those ill feelings resurface at some later interval… for another 'fifteen minute go round'." Dr. Jackson finished by telling the jury that the fifteen minute rule is the exact opposite of the "don't-think-about-an-elephant" rule. "If I told my patients to concentrate on not thinking about elephants, elephants are all they would think about. If I told my patients not to think about the malaise of bad feelings that beset them or not to think about the past emotional traumas that gave birth to those bad feelings, I would be advocating another form of 'denial' which wouldn't work any better than the patient's denial from yesteryear – which is what ultimately brought them to me for therapy in the first place."

Dr. Jackson's psychological theories about "denial," unresolved conflict, the subconscious, unaware, mind, and the benefit of psychological therapy hit an emotional chord with the jurors' own lives. The jurors seemed to like Dr. Jackson, and seemed to enjoy his straight forward discussion on emotional suffering and the psychological theory underlying therapeutic treatment for such emotional suffering. But, what did this have to do with Robert Smith, and whether he was legally insane at the time he shot his foreman Jimmy Gaston and Labor Rep Christine Gerstenberg? Nothing that I could discern, but what was I missing?

Prosecutor Butler suddenly shifted gears again, took control of Dr. Jackson's testimony, and pressed on: "Dr. Jackson let me take you away from the general concept of psychotherapy, its use and benefit, and ask you some specific questions about your involvement in psychotherapy. Dr. Jackson, you have previously told the jury that you, as part of your training, have been in psychotherapy as a patient," to which Dr. Jackson replied, "That's correct, as part of my training." "How long were you in psychotherapy as a patient, Dr. Jackson?," continued Prosecutor Butler. "As I previously testified, Mr. Butler, five years," – an excellent answer, I thought, again demonstrating the extensive scope of Dr. Jackson's training and experience. Finally, Prosecutor Butler wrapped up that area of the questioning by asking Dr. Jackson whether that five years of psychotherapy as a patient gave him, Dr. Jackson, a full insight into his own mind, conscious or subconscious, to which Dr. Jackson humbly responded: "No, there's always more to learn" – another great answer not only endearing Dr. Jackson to the jury for his humility, but also showing that Dr. Jackson was not a know-it-all (an image I suspected Dr. Ames Robey might later cast in the courtroom and into the jury box).

Prosecutor Butler finished up the area of psychotherapy with one last question by restating his prior question in a slightly different way. Reminding Dr. Jackson of the five years he spent as a patient in psychotherapy, Prosecutor Butler asked Dr. Jackson whether, if the opportunity ever presented itself again, Dr. Jackson would engage in more psychotherapy as a patient in the future to learn more about his own mind and his own motives, to which Dr. Jackson again responded, "Yes" – again, another display of humility, sincerity and vulnerability, sure to endear Dr. Jackson to the jury. Prosecutor Butler then went on to other areas while I sat back, elated at Dr. Jackson's performance – blissfully unaware of the fact that Prosecutor Butler had set the trap.

Prosecutor Butler then cross examined Dr. Jackson on his findings and analysis concerning Dr. Jackson's evaluation of Robert Smith's state of mind at the time of the shooting of his foreman Jimmy Gaston and the accidental wounding of Labor Relations Rep Christine Gerstenberg. After finishing up, Prosecutor Butler asked Dr. Jackson how long he had spent with Robert Smith to determine Robert Smith's state of mind at the time of the shooting, to which Dr. Jackson replied: "Eighteen hours over a four-day period" – certainly no perfunctory or cursory examination, I noted gleefully. Then, as Prosecutor Butler was about to pull the string on the trap he set,

Judge Maher rose from his seat, indicating: "Time to take a break, jurors – no wonder psychotherapy sessions are limited to one hour." An energized jury filed into the jury room for a break. As I walked out into the courtroom hallway, my mood was elevated. I had no idea then, that fifteen years later in my life, I would file into Dr. Newton "Bud" Jackson's office, and sit down on his psychotherapy couch to search out my own demons of "denial" that were dismantling my own peace of mind later in my life, as a 50-year-old lawyer.

When involved in a trial, trial lawyers regularly work through the court breaks, including the lunch break and the nighttime, home-to-relax-and-sleep break. I had already finished Dr. Jackson's direct examination which supported Robert Smith's insanity defense so I could let my guard down a little. But, Prosecutor Butler was in the middle of cross examination, and his entire prosecution depended on whether he could dismantle Dr. Jackson's opinion that Robert Smith was legally insane due to "irresistible impulse." Prosecutor Butler's courtroom respite during the break was, therefore, filled with the pressure of last minute details and reorganization of his thoughts for the continuation of his cross examination of Dr. Jackson when Judge Maher again took the bench.

Prosecutor Butler... Springs the Trap

"All rise – court is back in session and Dr. Jackson, you are reminded that you are still under oath," intoned Judge Maher. Prosecutor Butler arose from the prosecutor's table, walked past the Detroit Police detective in charge of the case, and with a more pronounced purpose in his step, almost a "pounce," Prosecutor Butler went for Dr. Jackson's jugular. "Dr. Jackson, how much time did you say you spent interviewing Robert Smith?" – to which Dr. Jackson replied: "As I said, eighteen hours over four days." Prosecutor

Butler continued: "Dr. Jackson, didn't you tell us before the recess that the purpose of psychotherapy is to allow the patient to discover what's really on their mind?" – "Yes." And, that you spent five years in psychotherapy as a patient?" – "Yes, as part of my training." "And, that, if the opportunity ever presented itself, you would go back for more psychotherapy to get further needed insight into what's going on in your own mind?" "Yes:" answered Dr. Jackson. "And, again, you've just told us you spent eighteen hours interviewing Robert Smith" – "Yes, over four days," answered Dr. Jackson. "Well, Dr. Jackson, if after five years of psychotherapy, you still don't have full insight into what's going on in your own mind, how is it that you can tell this jury what was going on in Robert Smith's mind at the time he pulled the trigger when, in fact, you only spent eighteen short hours with Robert Smith – a minute fraction of the five year period you spent trying to figure out what was going on in your own mind?" "Okay," I said to myself silently: "That's where all this testimony about psychotherapy was going." I got it, albeit a little late, as I once again thought to myself: "done in again, Lauck, by your dull normal I.Q."

All the while, Dr. Jackson readied himself to answer Prosecutor Butler's unanswerable, trap question. But, Prosecutor Butler wasn't going to allow his highlight moment to be missed, rushed or under-played. It was as if Prosecutor Butler had snuck out of the courtroom and into a pay phone booth in the court hallway, dumped the ever humble, non-assuming, "Detective Colombo" persona, called the planet Kryptonite, and emerged from the phone booth as a relent-lessly-pursuing masked, crusader of justice and "Superman" of cross examination. Prosecutor Butler, for emphasis only, withdrew his last question, and went right back for Dr. Jackson's jugular. It was Prose-cutor Butler's moment, and he wasn't going to let anyone miss it: "Dr. Jackson, let me restate the question. Dr. Jackson, if you can't figure out what's going on in your own mind in five years of psychotherapy, and if you would gladly spend more time in psychotherapy in the future to try and figure out what's going on in your own mind, as you now admit, how were you able to figure out, in just eighteen hours with Robert Smith, what was going on in his mind at the time he pulled the trigger and blasted away at his foreman, Jimmy Gaston?" Dr. Jackson turned to the jury with whom he already had a great rapport, and looking straight into their eyes, deftly responded: "I'm a much harder case to crack. Robert Smith is a man of unadorned simplicity, a man without guile, without strategy, without duplicity – a man of transparency that anyone could see through in an hour. I just spent the remaining seventeen hours crossing all the t's and dotting all the i's so I could ensure no mistakes were made." To tell you the truth, at that precise moment, I'm not sure who got whom, but I know both of them got me. Prosecutor Butler sat down. He did what he could with Dr. Jackson, which I thought was great cross examination, perhaps the best I had ever seen.

Ames Robey M.D. – Front and Center

Now, it was time for Prosecutor Butler to unveil the shining light of psychiatric expertise – none other than world-renown forensic psychiatrist, Dr. Ames Robey. "Your Honor," said Prosecutor Butler: "The Prosecution calls Dr. Ames Robey to the witness stand." I whispered to myself: "Let's give it up for Dr. Robey!" The only thing missing was the "boast of heraldry, the pomp of power" and a drum roll. Ames Robey M.D. entered the court room – a tall, thin figure of erudition with a balding pate, large prominent forehead housing a large frontal cortex and large temporal lobes portending a "brilliant" presence. Dr. Robey, light on his feet, carried himself as a visiting dignitary. Perhaps, I thought to myself, Dr. Robey's purposeful presence was a visit from the Gods to us mere mortals living in the Detroit Hood.

Prosecutor Butler began his direct examination going to great lengths to establish and lay out for the jury the thoroughbred pedigree of Dr. Robey, stressing again and again Dr. Robey's formal education, his professional experience, his numerous scholarly writings, his worldwide lectures, his abundance of professional organizations as well as Dr. Robey's hundreds of court appearances as a forensic psychiatrist. At that moment, I'm sure the jury felt they were in the presence of greatness and "brilliance." It was then that I first thought about changing my strategy. Perhaps, I would not attack Dr. Robey right out of the box. Perhaps, I would show true deference to Dr. Robey's position as the courtroom's alpha male of erudition – at least for the initial cross examination, after which I was sure I would probably change tactics by resorting to my true nature, start swinging and see who was still standing when the final bell rang.

Prosecutor Butler brought out all the salient features on his direct examination – Dr. Robey's initial contact with the Wayne County Prosecutor's office, his initial review of a factual summary of the case, his in-depth review of the entire police file, his in-depth review of the preliminary exam transcript, his interviews and psychological testing of Robert Smith, his review of Dr. Jackson's testing, his dissecting, fault-finding of Dr. Jackson's opinion, and, finally, Dr. Robey's ultimate opinion that Robert Smith didn't qualify for the defence of insanity because he didn't meet the initial, legal prerequisite of "mental illness," and, even if for the sake of argument Robert Smith was mentally ill, Robert Smith shot his foreman, Jimmy Gaston, because of a deep-seated resentment for Jimmy Gaston's position of authority, and certainly not because of any "irresistible impulse" or because of any inability to tell the difference between right and wrong. Case closed. Robert Smith was fully and legally responsible for the shooting of Jimmy Gaston and the wounding of his Labor Relations Rep, Christine Gerstenberg. So sayeth Dr. Robey.

Dr. Robey and Prosecutor Butler had fully and effectively shut the door on any insanity defense and Prosecutor Butler triumphantly announced: "No further questions, Your Honor." As Prosecutor Butler returned to the prosecutor's table, Judge Maher intoned: "Your witness, Mr. Lauck."

Showdown with Dr. Ames Robey

I arose with a great sense of anticipation like I was about to fight for the heavyweight championship of the world, or about to bat cleanup in the seventh game of the World Series. We were in the fourth quarter of this long-winded, four week pursuit of justice, but I had plenty of time left on the clock to pick apart the deficiencies in Dr. Robey and his presentation. Under the glare of the lights, and in front of a packed courtroom, I purposely checked my 35-year-old aggressive nature, and slowed my approach to the podium. Suspiciously eyeing Dr. Robey, I heard the echo of my own thoughts: "this cross examination is what I was born to do. Without it, I wither and die on the vine. With it, win, lose or draw, I have a life with meaning. It's my journey... my destiny. It's what I longed to do. It's what I had to do. Let's slug it out, Ames Robey! It's me and you, mano a mano, and neither one of us has a place to hide. The universe of justice is watching, so, as they say in the Hood in Detroit: "Let's throw down and get it on."

As I approached the podium with my notes and cross examination materials, I caught a glimpse of my father sitting forward on a bench in the back of the courtroom, and I thought of him and his father as I said to myself: "Here I am, a lawyer, standing in an American courtroom." And, I thought to myself... this is certainly a long way from my grandfather, Frederick William Lauck's fourth grade education, his move from St. Louis Missouri in 1917 to Detroit,

Michigan to find work at Ford Motor's Highland Park Plant, and his part in the "Battle of Miller Road" with Walter Reuther's union boys squaring off against old man Henry Ford's designated hit man, Harry Bennett, and his army of ex-cons at the overpass on Miller Road in Dearborn, Michigan and his early death at age 48. And, this is certainly a long way from my own father's ninth grade education and his pangs of hunger on the "mean streets" of Detroit during the Great Depression of the 1930s and his struggle through life with limited opportunity. And, this is certainly a long way from the logging camps and mining towns of my mother Jean McKelvy Montroy's Minnesota childhood with its brutal winters in such forlorn places as Duluth, Hibbing, Tower and Eli, and a long way from the early and tragic death of her 17-year-old brother Sherwood Montroy in a logging accident in 1918 with Sherwood's battered body laid out in the family parlor, with pennies on his eyes to hold them shut, and his burial on the snow swept plains of desolation-row, Minnesota. And, it's certainly a long way from the ravages of the flu pandemics of 1918 and 1919, and the Dust Bowl of the 1930s that the Greatest Generation endured, and certainly a long way from the ravages of alcoholism that beset my family, and a long way from their destitution in "soup lines" during the financial ruin of the Great Depression. But, through it all, through the hardships of hard-scrabble life, those survivors carried on, living lives of quiet desperation, and, eventually, at their last hour, succumbing to graves with nameless markers, forever remaining faceless and nameless on life's social registry.

But, then, I thought… every once in a while, even in the bleakest of family histories, good fortune smiles on one of the survivors' descendants, and graces that lucky descendant with "opportunity." That unearned, serendipitous, good fortune of "opportunity" somehow fell from the Greatest Generation to me. Now, generations of desperation later, I was the lucky one, the one chosen to stand up as a lawyer in an American courtroom as the judge called out my name: "Mr. Lauck, your witness," putting me squarely in charge of the fight for justice for another no-count, another one of life's desperate survivors, Robert Smith. Two no-counts – randomly, or, perhaps, fatefully and inexorably locked together in the battle for fleeting justice and for Robert Smith's life.

When I reached the podium, I noticed how relaxed, confident and self-possessed Dr. Robey looked in the witness chair. Unflappable! He'd been there before. Almost a "catch-me-if-you-can" look of smugness. Dr. Robey was playing in his own psychiatric ballpark, and he knew it… even though he lived in the Boston area, a stone's throw from Harvard, just across the Charles River. Dr. Robey was an out-of-town, forensic expert, and, yet, he confidently claimed "home field advantage." As I reflected on his long-winded circumlocution of psychiatric jargon and nomenclature that F. Lee Bailey wrote about in the Albert DeSalvo, Boston Strangler case, I thought to myself, it is probably in large part his ballpark because, by and large, we're going to have to play by the definitional ground rules of forensic psychiatry. Dr. Robey's ground rule number one: keep hammering his ultimate conclusion to the jury – "not mentally ill" and "not insane." Dr. Robey's ground rule number two: resist my effort to shed any light on how he got to that "not mentally ill" and "not insane" conclusion – with Dr. Robey's effort concentrated toward obscuring the basis of his ultimate conclusions behind the dense, impenetrable fog of psychiatric verbiage projected out into the courtroom in Dr. Robey's usual confident and smug manner. As I was about to confront and cross examine Dr. Robey, that inner voice that usually tells me: "Jump him," was telling me not to commit myself, and to proceed slowly so that both the jury and I would have a chance to see if Dr. Robey would unwittingly undress himself in front of the jury, and show us who he truly was.

"Good morning, Dr. Robey," I started. "Dr. Robey, you are a very well spoken and experienced forensic psychiatrist who has testified numerous times across the country, so I would greatly appreciate it if you would be patient with us as the jury and I try to understand what you told Prosecutor Butler on direct examination." In the world of my Northwest Detroit upbringing, that statement alone would have been a signal that someone was trying to con someone, but Dr. Robey graciously accepted my praise and smiled, telling me he would do the best he could to help both the jury and me understand how Robert Smith was not legally insane. An instinct of charm and praise that was not really who I was, was somehow guiding me now, and I threw more adulation on Dr. Robey's ego fire. "Dr. Robey, you have been cross examined by some of the finest lawyers in the United States of America, haven't you?" My question was more about the "finest lawyers in the United States" than it was about Dr. Robey, so he hesitated: "to whom do you refer, Mr. Lauck?" In my Northwest Detroit Hood it was: "Who the hell you talkin' about?," and I was sure that Dr. Robey's "to whom do you refer?" response was our Detroit jury's first signal that, perhaps, Dr. Robey was not one of them, while, perhaps, Robert Smith was.

I followed up: "Well, Dr. Robey, when I say you have been cross examined by some of the finest lawyers in the United States, I was referring to the fact that you have been cross examined by the great Texas lawyer, Percy Foreman, who never lost a client to the electric chair. I was also referring to the fact that you have been cross examined by the great San Francisco personal injury lawyer, Melvin Belli, who represented Jack Ruby in Texas after Ruby shot President Kennedy's alleged assassin, Lee Harvey Oswald, on national television in November of 1963. I was also referring to the fact that you have been cross examined by the great Boston criminal lawyer, F. Lee Bailey, who represented Dr. Coppolino and the Boston Strangler, Albert

DeSalvo, among others. So, when I say you have been cross examined by 'some of the finest lawyers in the United States of America' that's to whom I refer."

I was doing Dr. Robey's "name dropping" for him while he reveled in self adulation via cross examination. Dr. Robey, proud to have his name vicariously associated with such celebrity trial lawyers, smiled broadly, and then answered coyly: "Well Mr. Lauck, if that's your name (I assured him it was), I can only agree that I have been cross examined by some lawyers who thought they were the 'finest lawyers in the United States of America'" – an apropos, but not too subtle distinction that certainly wasn't lost on the jury, and yet, perhaps, another signal to the jury that Dr. Robey wasn't one of them while, perhaps, Robert Smith was. To be honest, my approach was totally foreign to me. I was somewhat like a fish out of water, but I was elated to be standing out of the way, allowing Dr. Robey to undress himself so willingly, and show the jury who he really was. For a stark contrast, I then grabbed for the rung of humility, and told Dr. Robey that I certainly was not the same caliber lawyer as Percy Foreman, Melvin Belli or F. Lee Bailey, so, again, the jury and I would need all the patience he could give us as we tried to work our way through and understand his testimony.

I then proceeded to the substance of Dr. Robey's testimony. I noticed the jury sitting on the front seat of their chairs in the jury box, looking intently at Dr. Robey, silently suggesting that they were most eager to hear from him despite, perhaps, some misgivings about the lofty esteem he held for himself. I asked Dr. Robey what **date** he first saw Robert Smith and, true to the description of Dr. Robey in F. Lee Bailey's book, *The Defense Never Rests*, Dr. Robey shot out of the starting blocks verbally with the jury at rapt attention. Dr. Robey never came up for air as he threw out every psychiatric description known to man...

...melancholia, affective disorders, manic depressive vacil-
lation, vacillating at times between depression and mania
marked by hyperactivity, though, in reality, many manic de-
pressives never reach the manic stage of hyperactivity, manic
depressive now known as bi-polar, mood disorder, unresolved
conflict, Freudian neurosis, personality disorder, maladop-
tion, malediction, a dichotomy marked by functional deficits
and organic deficits or even neurological deficits

and, on and on, and on and on... reminding me of my father's assessment that an expert is someone who concentrates his efforts on an ever
diminishing, limited area – "learning more and more about less and
less, until, eventually, the expert knows everything about nothing."

And, on and on, went with Dr. Robey lost in his own minutia.
After several minutes, the jury could no longer hold on to their attentive
posture, and, noticeable to everyone in the courtroom except Dr.
Robey, the jury's posture of attention silently relaxed as they slid back
in their seats. As Dr. Robey continued, the jurors began to look around
at each other with quizzical glances seeking some visual clue whether
other jurors were following Dr. Robey's circumlocution, round and
around journey, through the landscape of psychiatric nomenclature
and jargon or, alternatively, whether Dr. Robey's testimony more
closely resembled Shakespeare's description of a tale told with "sound
and fury but signifying nothing." In contrast to the jury's silent slide
out of, and away from, the incomprehensible psychiatric testimony
of Dr. Robey, Dr. Robey himself was surfing along at full sail on a
tsunami of mental illness and legal insanity discussing:

...psychosis, thought disorders, schizophrenia not to be confused with schizoid features and personalities, hallucinations,
visual, verbal, tactile, and olfactory delusions, including delusions of grandeur, obsessive compulsive behavior and the
impact of those terms on the historical legal rule of insanity

emanating from the old English common law case of Daniel McNaughton, the seminal case for legal insanity, and the later common law definitions of the volitional, psychological deficits of "irresistible impulse."

Another glance at the jury. They were through. They were done. "Take me out of the game, coach." They sat all the way back in their seats, noticing everything in the courtroom but Dr. Robey's incomprehensible lecture on mental illness and insanity. The jury gave up the impossible task of trying to follow what the "brilliant" Dr. Ames Robey was saying. Dr. Robey, oblivious to it all, finished with a flurry discussing the impact of:

> ...his heretofore previously described psychiatric terminology on Michigan's new definition of "Guilty but Mentally ill," referring to substantial disorders of thought or mood, significantly impairing judgment, behavior, capacity to recognize reality and the ability to cope with the ordinary demands of life, with the legal definition of mentally ill encompassing the psychiatric definition of psychosis, either the thought disorder of schizophrenia or the mood disorder of manic, depressive disorder, now bipolar, mood disorder, but not necessarily a major depressive disorder.

Finally, Dr. Robey fell into a triumphant silence. After the expected bombast of his long winded circumlocution of an answer, I just sat on that peaceful bubble of silence like I was levitating in the courtroom. I must have looked (as I felt)... bemused. I said nothing. I simply stood motionless, allowing the ensuing, dramatic, change-of-pace silence to punctuate and magnify the ridiculousness of Dr. Robey's non-ending answer to my question of what date he first saw Robert Smith. The silence woke the jury up. As the verbal assault on the jurors' psyches ceased, the jurors looked up from their hopelessly, lost reverie just in time to hear Dr. Robey eventually punctuate his answer and the ensuing silence with his own question: "Mr. Lauck, I hope that adequately answers your question?," to which I replied: "Dr. Robey, your answer was so 'brilliant' I forgot the question." The jury picked up immediately. They were relieved that they weren't the only ones left in the wake of Dr. Robey's galactic fog of circumlocution – perhaps the final convincing signal to the jury that Dr. Robey was not one of them, but that Robert Smith and his less than "brilliant" lawyer Lauck… were one of them.

I exploited that difference one more time by asking Dr. Robey: "if the cultural background of his 'brilliant' academic career and his larger than life presence in the hallowed halls and ivy trimmed buildings of Harvard made it somewhat difficult for him to understand and evaluate what was going on in the mind of a simple, naïve, humble, man-child like Robert Smith who started off picking cotton in Alabama at age five, and then ended up on a Greyhound bus to the industrial North with the bus ticket financed by his mother's sale of her only cow?" Dr. Robey's answer didn't matter. Again, it was the question that mattered because it was the question that said it all, a question that once again signaled the jury that Dr. Ames Robey really wasn't one of them, but certainly Robert Smith and Robert's mother were one of them, a mother and a son who walked in step with the jurors' own lives – jurors who were just trying to support their families and get through life, and, perhaps, like Robert Smith… just trying desperately to hold on to a job, and be the parent to their own children that some of the jurors didn't have.

After the above fifteen to twenty minutes of cross examination, if you could even call it cross examination, I sensed the jury was siding with psychologist Newton "Bud" Jackson Ph.D. rather than psychiatrist Ames Robey M.D. Now that Dr. Robey had unwittingly disclosed to the jury who he was, I took up my usual and comfortable role as an adversarial hit man. I took on Dr. Robey directly. Now that the jury was sliding toward our corner, I was in the enviable position of being able to cross examine Dr. Robey head-on, on his own psychiatric terms and labels. No more Mr. Nice Guy. No more deference. Just Dr. Robey and I going toe to toe on his opinions to show that his opinions were flawed, unreliable and pretentious, and, most importantly, to show the jury that when Robert Smith's attorney later stands before them in "closing argument" and weaves the psychiatric concepts and terms into the "human event" involved in the case, the jury will know that Robert Smith's lawyer knows what he's talking about, and the jury will fully consider my views because I have already won their confidence by showing them during my actual cross examination of Dr. Robey that Dr. Robey's "brilliance" did not blind anyone to the truth or reality of the case – all accomplished with a footnote of appreciation for the broad scope of my Greatest Generation father, Frederick Valentine Lauck's, ninth grade education and his "Streets of Detroit" Ph.D. in human nature. Ironically, all the while I worried about Dr. Robey's "brilliance" doing me in, little did I know that his "brilliance" would actually do him in. As they say, the race doesn't always go to the swiftest. But, in retrospect, it was Dr. Robey's so-called "brilliance" and my own self doubt that drove my extensive preparation for Robert Smith's defense.

The testimony of Dr. Robey concluded, and Judge Maher ordered an afternoon recess. I walked out into the hallway of the courtroom feeling a great sense of relief. Finally, I could let go of the exhaustive preparation for Dr. Robey's cross examination. My father, always humbly standing in the background, was the first to greet me. I had no sooner reached him when Dr. Ames Robey came out into the hallway, sought me out, gave me his card and said: "Maybe we could do some business together someday." Interesting! I'm living and dying on this court appointed case, making a $3,000 total fee for more than a month's pressure-packed trial, barely enough money to pay my secretary and rent for the month I was in trial, and, yet for Dr. Robey, the case was just another business venture. Maybe, Basilian priest, Father Stoba, was correct, after all, when he told me after my junior year at Catholic Central in 1960, that my aptitude testing clearly showed I wasn't cut out to be a lawyer because I was too confrontational and too emotionally involved to be a lawyer. But, Father... "If you ain't confrontational, you'll get run out of the Hood, and if you aren't emotional, you've got no reason to get out of bed in the morning," and, "if you are not comfortable confronting the State of Michigan, the Wayne County Prosecutor's office and General Motors, you better not aspire to become a trial lawyer anyway."

We Await the Verdict...

Prosecutor Butler and I presented closing arguments to the jury. Judge Maher instructed the jury on the law. The jury went off to deliberate. At that point I felt the same way I do after any case I ever tried. Relief, relief and more relief. The endless preparation, the second guessing, the long work days and waking up at 3:00 or 4:00 in the morning with the case running through my mind was over. Whatever the verdict, I did what I had to do without compromise. No stone was left unturned. I could look at the reflection in my mirror and say: "Good job, Lauck; you and Robert Smith took the risk of trying the case, and you made every sacrifice necessary to show Robert Smith's case in its best possible light to the jury, and, now that your participation in the case is over, there is nothing further you can do to help the case or hurt the case. It's out of your hands and in the hands of the jury. Thy will be done." I shook hands with Prosecutor Butler: "Great job, as usual Bob, especially your cross examination of Dr. Jackson." Most of the time I would not have even talked to my opponent, but Bob Butler was different. He was a class act and a gifted trial lawyer. No verdict was returned, and homeward bound I went and slept like a baby in the bosom of the Lord.

The next day the jury was still deliberating while I was at work in another courtroom: "No rest for the wicked," or at least for aspiring trial lawyers. Then, the call came in from Judge Maher's court: "The jury has a verdict." I was a good mile away over at the Lafayette building. I walked that mile to the Frank Murphy Hall of Justice on a cold, raw April day through downtown Detroit. I could have taken a cab, but why… when I could walk an exhilarating mile in the beauty of the cold and the silence – my own peaceful eye of the hurricane even though right in the midst of the "mean streets" of downtown Detroit. And, besides, I spent a month in trial, and nothing was going to happen, and no verdict would be returned until I got to Judge Maher's court. For a brief moment, I would be the indispensable link that lay between Robert Smith and his rendezvous with justice. Nothing would happen until I got to court. What a beautiful, relaxing walk I took that cold April day as I headed toward Robert Smith's destiny.

I went through the same front doors of the Frank Murphy Hall of Justice that the GM security employees had gone through with their witnesses over the last thirty days, negotiating those witnesses past the UAW hourly workers protesting GM's working conditions. No hint of that confrontation was left on the courtroom steps this day; those two historical antagonists of capitalists and labor were off to new ventures and new battles. It felt anti-climactic. Up the elevators alone, and into the court room ready to receive the verdict. As usual, Judge Maher's clerk, Walter Abick, was in his rush, rush, agitated mood: "Where the hell have you been? We were waiting for you." "So what?" I thought. "You called me. You know where I was, and now I'm here." But, I didn't have the energy to play with Judge Joseph Maher's always anxious court clerk. I was exhausted.

Robert Smith, was brought out from lockup, and took his seat next to me while the jury shuffled in – too somber looking for my liking. When the jury reached their seats, Walter Abick called the case and Judge Maher asked the obvious: "Have you reached a verdict, and if so, who will speak for you?" The foreman rose and answered: "Yes, Your Honor." Judge Maher asked Robert Smith and me to stand and face the jury. Robert Smith and I rose, faced the jury, and stood there unflinchingly looking the Fate of Justice straight in the eye. For a moment, my mind wandered as I wondered if this is what Jesus felt just before he was condemned. Judge Maher asked the foreman to read the jury's verdict. The foreman looked down at the verdict form, while Robert Smith and I stared straight ahead at the jury – are we condemned or are we free? The jury foreman strained to read the jury form, and then just blurted out: "Not guilty by reason of insanity."

That's it. It was over. Despite the concentrated, committed effort by Prosecutor Butler, the People of the State of Michigan and General Motors, despite their wealth of resources and personnel, the jury found Robert Smith "not guilty by reason of insanity." Robert Smith wept silently, again, as he had done during my opening statement. I don't remember my emotional reaction, but it was probably tied up in the same thought process I always have when a jury returns with a verdict. Win, lose or draw: "how wonderful it was that a no-count kid from Northwest Detroit was allowed to stand up in a Court of Law and speak to the judge and jury on behalf of another no-count kid from the deep South who had really got himself into a tight squeeze. And, how wonderful it is that the jury had to listen to the no-count kid from Northwest Detroit speak on behalf of the no-count kid from the South. You gotta love America." But, I suspect, for every Robert Smith, there are ten others who fall to their fate through the trap door of uneven justice.

Under law, the State of Michigan had the right to hold Robert Smith for sixty days to determine whether he was still legally insane,

and hold him indefinitely thereafter until (if ever) he was no longer insane. After twenty-nine days, the State of Michigan released Robert Smith as no longer insane and returned him to his family... to again be the father to his children – a father that he never knew. As far as I know, Robert Smith was never in trouble again.

And, the last chapter of the Robert Smith saga?... a UAW fringe group, in support of the rights of the "working class," published a

Smitty, his wife JoeAnn, and their three children

pamphlet, *It's Right to Rebel! Lessons in the Struggle to Free Robert Smith, a Detroit Auto Worker*, claiming victory, as well as full credit, for Robert Smith's acquittal:

> "It's right to rebel if you gotta work in hell." This chant, coming from the lips of workers from Detroit's Chevy Forge plant and other Detroit auto plants... sums up the feelings of the many people who worked to build a mass movement to free Robert "Smitty" Smith. The chant was echoed by pickets outside Detroit's Frank Murphy Hall of Justice, and its fighting spirit was brought inside the courtroom by the Forge workers and supporters who lined the benches everyday during the three-week trial.
>
> Robert Smith was charged with assault with intent to commit murder for shooting his foreman, James Gaston, on the morning of October 12, 1977.
>
> He had run up against a wall of harassment – paychecks withheld, time card missing, arbitrary suspensions and disciplines and everyday intolerable work conditions as a crane operator. Smitty had been working a seven-day week over

2000° furnace temperatures, when Gaston sent him home again that morning. Smitty just couldn't take it anymore.

 From GM's point of view, it was an 'open and shut case.' The Detroit papers had branded Smitty as a 'gunman.' The government worked with GM to put together a top-notch prosecution team to make an example of Smitty, to put him behind bars for a long time.

But, today Smitty is free. The struggle to free him holds important lessons for all those fighting against the injustices and brutalities of this capitalist system – whether in the plants, schools or communities. This pamphlet, *It's Right to Rebel*, sums up some of these lessons."

Opportunity Stays on My Shoulder

The Robert Smith saga in my life was over. That was the last time I tried a case against Robert Butler, and the last time I saw him speak in a court room. Realizing that "civil" trial work better enables a lawyer to support a family, I switched gears, and went on to represent many clients in civil cases, including Jeff Rupersberg, a journeyman electrician out of Local 58 IBEW, who was walking on the ground floor of a hotel construction site when he was struck by a plummeting 24 lb. guard rail post that was knocked off the ninth floor by a wind-blown crane load, permanently taking away Jeff's quality of life ($8.1 million jury verdict); Eric Spaggins, a 20-year-old homeless kid, who snuck into the Renaissance Hotel in downtown Detroit on a cold, blue January night seeking shelter to escape frostbite, and hoping to find some half eaten food left outside a hotel room, when a Detroit cop found him, chased him through the hotel fountain and struck him in the head several times with his service revolver, causing schizophrenia – a difficult causation argument ($2.4 million jury verdict with a $3.9

million recovery); Margaret Felix, the 35-year-old daughter of two judges who was killed in a horrible intersection collision by a (runaway-acceleration) pickup truck ($2.35 million recovery); Jim Nelson, a Hubble, Roth & Clark engineer, who was checking a Consumer Power gas leak in downtown Rochester, Michigan, when the building he was standing next to blew sky high, killing him ($1.8 million recovery); Martens Ice, a law firm client that was sued by their two senior, founding partners ($1.2 million jury verdict on a counterclaim).

I also represented well-to-do divorcing spouses where the issues were the value of the husband's on-going business enterprise with the wife claiming she was entitled to one half of the 10 million value of the business while the husband claimed the wife was entitled to one half of the $236,000 value of the business (high stakes for someone – especially if the husband has to pay half of 10 million dollars to keep a company worth $236,000, or if the wife only gets half of $236,000 for her share of a 10 million dollar business). I also litigated many commercial and law firm split-up cases, representing great trial lawyers like Albert Lopatin and Saul Bluestone of Detroit, Bill Kritselis and Fred Abood of Lansing, Michigan, John Conlon of Kalamazoo, Michigan, Brian Lavan of Brighton, Michigan, Doug Shermeta, the bankruptcy guru, from Troy, Michigan, George Smrtka, Bob Horn of Jackson Hole, Wyoming (one trial in Jackson Hole, Wyoming and one trial in Riverton, Wyoming), John Charters of Troy, Michigan, Les Martens, Duane Ice, Stuart Israel, Chris Legghio, Paul Geary and Renate Klass of Royal Oak, Michigan, Brian Legghio, an outstanding criminal lawyer out of Mt. Clemens, Michigan, my St. Scholastica buddy, Jerry Surowiec, of Farmington Hills, Michigan whose calling card said: "Reasonable Doubt for a Reasonable Price" and "Confession is Good for the Soul, but Not the Case so Take the Fifth!," "No-nonsense" Tom Vincent of Gesu Parish in Detroit who justifiably left a Lansing police officer, process server on the floor of his law office for the EMS to scoop up (which led me into the macabre world of Ingham County Circuit Judge Judge Tom Brown), and, perhaps, the best of all... a great trial lawyer and great friend, Bill Wertheimer, out of Bingham Farms, Michigan.

Albert Lopatin **Bill Kritselis** **John Charters**
Detroit's "King of Torts" Lansing's "King of Torts"

Fred Lauck and George Smrtka **Bill Wertheimer**

Though I became a civil trial lawyer, I still continued to try some criminal cases and obtained numerous "not guilty" verdicts including Chicago truck driver, Adam Narowcki, who crashed his rig, without braking, into a stopped line of traffic on I-94 in St. Joseph, Michigan at 60 m.p.h. killing four people in a fiery crash; and Canadian truck driver, Leonard Martin, who was involved in a fiery crash on M-59 in White Lake, Michigan that took the life of Kristin McLain, daughter of Detroit Tiger pitching star, Denny McLain, the last major league pitcher to win thirty games in one season (1968); and John Stetz who was accused of blasting a high powered cigarette boat into a cabin cruiser killing three people on Belleville Lake in Belleville Michigan; and Tony Sandoval, my half Irish, half Mexican 21-year-old carpenter client, from Holy Redeemer High School in Detroit who was framed for the shooting death of his 19-year-old girl friend and her assailant, Johnny Waugh, both of whom were killed in a shoot out with Mexican gang members of the "Cash Flow Posse" in a "blind pig" in southwest Detroit – what a cast of characters to cross examine... utterly ruthless, and how I escaped with my life I'll never know as a

Fred and Frannie

year later, in 2003, I turned the corner and was suddenly surrounded by the same gang members in the parking lot of the Ranchero Restaurant in southwest Detroit as I was carrying my 1-year-old daughter Frances to our car. Frances probably saved my life. I also remember the helplessness I initially felt as I was emotionally surrounded by law enforcement in Melvindale when I represented ironworker, Andrew Jackson Payne, who was accused of murdering the Melvindale High School football coach, Albert Ligetti, in a barroom brawl as the coach and his friends were on the way to a Melvindale police officer's retirement party. But I don't think any client will ever be more memorable than my half man-half child client, Robert Smith, who, but for a fair trial in a court of law before Judge Joseph Maher and a jury of his peers, would have lost his family... forever.

Broken Hearted Melodies

Bob Butler spent a full and rewarding career in the Wayne County Prosecutor's office until his retirement in 2005. The next time I saw Bob Butler after his retirement was on November 16, 2006 at the Wujek-Calcaterra funeral home for the funeral of his beloved (almost) 3-year-old granddaughter, Jenna Elizabeth Butler (November 26, 2003 – November 11, 2006). Jenna embraced eternity as she lay sleeping peacefully in a small white casket while her twin brother Brady, her older siblings, her parents, grandparents, and a roomful of mourners looked on. First the mother Michelle spoke: "Jenna was my angel born with broken wings." Then Jenna's grandfather, Bob Butler, my broken-hearted, old warhorse of a trial lawyer friend spoke, and I was transported back thirty years as I saw Bob Butler at his finest, courageous hour deliver a eulogy fit for angel Jenna, reminding everyone of the positive side of Jenna's short existence – all of our lives touched by the broken-winged angel Jenna.

Last, I saw Bob Butler's son Eric speak about the role of a father – a man who protects, provides and problem solves for his children, and I was transported back to my father Frederick Valentine Lauck's words: "At age 40, every man realizes he is a failure." It took a lifetime for me to realize what my father said, and how profound it was. I buried my father when I was 39 years old, just four years after the Robert Smith case, and it was then I realized that all sons are raised to protect, provide for, and problem solve, but that, inevitably, we fail when the stakes are the highest. Our dedicated best effort falls short as we utterly fail to protect our loved ones when they slip from our arms into the unrelenting grip of disease and death. We give our loved ones the best medicine money can buy, but the unstoppable march of death overtakes them. We throw our best problem solving efforts at death, but we fail again and again. Bob Butler, his son Eric, Robert Smith and I are all living testaments that a man's protective role in life is ultimately destined to fail. Momentary victories of protection like the Robert Smith case are fleeting and long forgotten, merely a transient upbeat in the syncopated rhythm of life and death, always followed by the inexorable downbeats, and eventually, flat lines on an EKG. But, through it all, life is an exhilarating adventure, sometimes protected in the eye of the hurricane while other times tempest tossed in the winds of destiny.

As I shuffled past angel Jenna's last earthly remains on that rainy, wind-swept day in November of 2006, I couldn't help but notice the

The Butler Family

floral rainbow – a rainbow made up of carnations of vibrant red, soft pink, sky blue and lavender, and I knew that angel Jenna's life, short and tragic as it was, would still find its place in the great subconscious of mankind, and that, one day, in the not too distant future, "somewhere over the rainbow," the entire cast of the Robert Smith case would meet again, and I would personally tell angel Jenna the story I have just recounted here about the courage and skill of her grandfather, Prosecutor Robert Butler, Esquire. Until then, little Jenna, rest in peace with the angels, sweetheart.

—◦◦◦—

So you want to be a trial lawyer? Well then focus on life's heartache and on life's downtrodden souls. Never, never stop learning about life, and never, never stop learning how to tell the story of life, and, maybe, just maybe, one day you'll be as lucky as Bob Butler and me, and, maybe, just maybe, you will live long enough to fulfill your dream. As the venerable singer "Sassy" Sarah Vaughn sang, life is a "Broken Hearted Melody." "Broken Hearted" because we are all destined to lose our lives, but, nonetheless… a "Melody." So sing the song of life, all its notes, all its chords, all its melodies, all its harmonies and all its emotions, and cry all your tears and laugh all your laughter before it comes your time to go.

Epilogue

God bless the children of the Greatest Generation! They took
the courage, strength, commitment, ideals and compassion of
the Greatest Generation, embraced the opportunity of education,
and "came of age" in America's great eras – the steady paced "Age of
Innocence" of the 1950s, and the faster and sometimes frantic paced
1960s "Age of Social Revolution."

And, on and on, the children of the Greatest Generation went…
into adulthood where they never missed a meal, drove new cars, had
health care, pensions, a roof over their heads, and money to spend
on entertainment, travel and fashion. But, without the sacrifice,
commitment and the role models of the Greatest Generation shining
their glorious light on the darkness in their world, none of it would
have happened. Thank you Greatest Generation! May we always,
always honor your memory.

BOOK III

Winding Down... Losing Our World

WINDING DOWN ... LOSING OUR WORLD???

What does it mean??? You ask? If you are a child of Greatest Generation parents, you don't ask because you know. But ... for those not "Children of the Greatest Generation"...

WINDING DOWN... LOSING OUR WORLD

OUR LANDMARKS ... "GOING, GOING ... GONE"

We "Children of the Greatest Generation" have lost our neighborhood landmarks that we depended on to tell us... when we were home. As the "Old Announcer," Van Patrick, use to say after a Tiger home run disappeared over the outfield wall in the 1950s: "Going, Going... Gone." So also... the landmarks of the "Children of the Greatest Generation": "Going, Going... Gone." After a hundred years, no more Tiger baseball at the "Corner" of Trumbull and Michigan Avenue: "Going, Going... Gone." After 80 years, no more "Holy Corners" at Southfield and Outer Drive: "Going, Going... Gone." Little Sisters of the Poor, Sarah Fisher Home for the Aged... Gone. Mercy College... Gone. Benedictine High School... Gone. Benedictine priests... Gone. St. Scholastica Grade School... "Going, Going... (soon to be)...

Gone." And, the culturally divergent and emotionally rich Detroit neighborhoods that "once upon a time" nurtured the souls of the "Children of the Greatest Generation," that once guided them socially and spiritually and that always protected and secured their physical and emotional well-being: "Going, Going... (irretrievably)... Gone."

OUR IDEALS... "GOING, GOING... GONE"

We "Children of the Greatest Generation" have lived long enough to see the Ideals of our Greatest Generation parents challenged, abandoned and at times outright rejected: "Going, Going... Gone." In our youth, we followed behind in the footsteps of the Greatest Generation, constantly learning from them and embracing their philosophy of life... until, in the later stages of their lives, the Greatest Generation invited us to **"step up"** and walk side-by-side with them. It was then... as the Greatest Generation walked toward the sunset of their lives, that they asked us to hold fast to their philosophy of life and share it, when the time came, with those impatient generations who now "dance with life" as the Greatest Generation once did. The Greatest Generation now whispers from the grave:

"Center your lives around the ideals of **justice** for all of God's children, **freedom** for the oppressed, **fairness** to the downtrodden and **equality** for all races. Resist the temptation of runaway materialism and greed. Don't be a universe unto yourself. Rather, be of service to others.

"First, be a **child of God** and then a staunch member of some religious organization. First be a **citizen of the world** and then a patriot of some parcel of land. That way... you will see yourself in others and others in you, and it will be easier to 'love your enemies', or... at least, be at Peace with them, and live by the Golden Rule of 'doing unto others as you would have them do unto you.'"

CHAPTER 16

Detroit Judge…
Slays Lady Justice

A Fighting Chance for "Smitty"

In 1978, Robert Smith received a fair trial before Judge Joseph Maher – a judge who stayed out of the case, and let the lawyers slug it out. After all, trials are "adversarial proceedings" where dueling lawyers engage in a "war of words" to create competing verbal and emotional versions of the past events being litigated. A jury, based on their common sense and background, are left to choose which one of the competing versions (or how much of one version or the other) is the truth of the matter… after which the jury then arrives at a verdict by applying the law of the land that the judge gives them. This "adversarial system" works amazingly well in America as, by and large, jurors from all walks of life with generally little in common come to a common understanding of the truth of the case as expressed in their verdict. The "adversarial system" worked well in 1978 in the case of *People vs. Robert Smith*. No one claimed they did not receive a fair trial. In the Robert Smith case, the system worked as it was supposed to work. The lawyers slugged it out; the judge refereed the slugfest, and the jury decided the case… the essence of "due process" of law.

No Chance For Wade

But, 30 years later in 2007, a trial lawyer's worst nightmare… representing an innocent man charged with First Degree Murder. A man who, despite his innocence, has no chance for an acquittal because the judge's committed agenda was to take away the jury's vote and guaranty a conviction by telling the jury they must (repeat for emphasis must) convict the Defendant… a deplorable situation where the trial judge administered the "death penalty" to justice and "due process" of law and condemned an innocent man to prison.

In 2007, Michael Wade, a long time security guard at the Detroit Police auto impound yard, stood trial for First Degree Murder for the

**Tom Burczynski
World Renowned
Ballistics Expert**

death of Edward Browder, a 51-year-old fugitive, drug addict and professional thief. Despite being innocent and despite a vigorous defense supplemented by impeccable expert testimony from New York ballistics expert, Tom Burczynski, and world renowned pathologist, Werner Spitz M.D., Michael Wade had no chance (repeat no chance)… because a Wayne County Circuit Court judge, living in the shadowland of injustice, cast her shadowy agenda across the jury box, telling the jury they had no choice… but to convict.

When a judge is bound and determined to see a Defendant convicted, the best defense, the best experts, the best lawyering and even the Defendant's innocence are no match. Michael Wade's story of injustice and his years of false imprisonment are captured in both the sentencing remarks made on Michael Wade's behalf and in Her Honor's sentencing comments.

———⁕———

Expanded Sentencing Remarks... July 30, 2007

The Location

As Your Honor is aware, my client, Michael Wade, is a 48-year-old security guard, husband, father and grandfather who, until this case, had never been arrested, let alone convicted of a crime. For the last 13 years, Michael Wade has worked as a security guard at the Detroit Police auto impound yard, an isolated six acre tract of land located at East-bound I-96 and Schaefer Road in Northwest Detroit – a great neighborhood when I grew up in that area, but now... a drug infested, battle ground filled with violent criminals and numerous other poor, innocent, law abiding souls who have no choice but to live in the war zone created by an unrelenting, lawless and violent criminal element. As Your Honor is also aware, when you are inside the six acre impound yard, you find yourself isolated and cut off from the surrounding neighborhood as you stand alone among a sea of impounded vehicles that provide hundreds of hiding places where wrongdoers can lurk and wreak havoc against any security guard who dares to secure the police impound yard from the criminal element that haunts that surrounding Northwest Detroit neighborhood.

Putting Life On The Line

During his 13-year tenure as a security guard for the Detroit Police auto impound yard, Michael Wade made numerous arrests of drug addicts, thieves and violent felons... a dangerous job by anyone's description. Your Honor heard the trial testimony that fugitive Byron Osby pulled a 15-inch long knife on Michael Wade and Michael's boss, Greg Errigo, as they caught him stealing parts from vehicles in the impound yard. Michael Wade and his boss arrested Byron Osby at gunpoint. Thank heaven Byron Osby wasn't the only one who was armed. Osby is presently a fugitive on his knife wielding charges. Now fearful, law abiding citizens anxiously wait for the police to find Byron Osby so that he can be taken off the streets and held criminally responsible for his felonious assault… before he wreaks further havoc on future innocent victims.

Your Honor also heard the testimony that, just two weeks before the incident involved in this case, Michael Wade was standing in the impound yard when a shot rang out and a bullet "whizzed" past his head and struck a nearby van. At trial, Your Honor saw the picture of the van with the fresh (un-rusted) bullet hole. Thank heaven the neighborhood sniper's aim was an inch or two off target. Defending himself against knives and firearms are but two of the many dangerous incidents that my client, Michael Wade, faced over the 13 years he provided security at the Detroit Police auto impound yard. As I say, a dangerous job by anyone's description, and that dangerous job of securing the Detroit Police impound yard in a crime infested Northwest Detroit neighborhood, fell to Michael Wade for the princely sum of $50.00 a night.

Even testimony from State Police officers confirmed what we all know… that the neighborhood surrounding the Detroit Police auto impound yard at Eastbound I-96 and Schaefer is a very dangerous area, rife with drugs and violence. State Police Trooper Setla testified that he would purposely avoid this particular neighborhood after dark. State Police Sgt. Cindy Fellner testified that when the State Police interviewed witnesses in the neighborhood, the witnesses refused to be seen talking to the police because it would cost them their lives.

It comes as no surprise then that Michael Wade, as an arm of law enforcement, has been attacked by the knife wielding Byron Osby and shot at by an unknown neighborhood sniper when he was doing nothing other than patrolling the impound yard and securing the vehicles in the yard – vehicles that belong to our citizens, vehicles which were involved in accidents and towed from accident scenes or vehicles that were stolen and later recovered... vehicles that were awaiting pickup by the citizens that owned them.

In this very dangerous, drug addicted, violent neighborhood, Michael Wade is the one that the police and citizens alike (and their auto insurance carriers) count on to protect the citizens' impounded vehicles so that the army of neighborhood drug addicts and larcenous piranhas don't strip those vehicles to the bone. In short, Michael Wade is the one who protects the "expectations" of our citizens (and their auto insurance carriers) to retrieve their vehicles from the Detroit Police auto impound yard in the same condition their vehicles were in when they were brought into the impound yard.

Suddenly... A Fugitive Intruder

On the evening August 10, 2006, Edward Browder (a professional thief, a fugitive from justice and a 51-year-old drug addict who was high on crack cocaine, with an extra supply of crack cocaine in his tennis shoes) broke into the Detroit Police auto impound yard carrying a duffel bag full of burglar tools. Later that evening, while Mr. Browder was plying his trade as a professional thief, and stripping a Buick LaSabre owned by 24-year-old Tony Hann, Michael Wade discovered Mr. Browder, put his shotgun on him, and attempted to arrest him: **"Freeze!"**

But, fugitive Browder had other plans. He was not going to be arrested. As the State Police admit, Mr. Browder threw a tire iron at

Michael Wade, narrowly missing him. Michael Wade responded by firing a non-fatal, bean bag round that missed. Then, as Mr. Browder tore off through the impound yard (to do what?, to hide where?, to join whom?, and to wreak what further havoc?), Michael Wade fired a warning shot into the ground using the thundering, echoing sound of a Brenneke shotgun slug to clear the area and keep the assaultive Mr. Browder running out of the impound yard… a legitimate response that would, hopefully, insure that Mr. Browder, the dangerous fugitive and intruder of the night, would not hide and "lie in wait" in any one of the hundreds of hiding places in the six acre impound yard, and wreak further havoc or present further danger to Michael Wade.

Michael Wade was 40 to 50 yards away from Mr. Browder when he fired that warning shot into the ground. That warning shot, like the proverbial "one-chance-in-a-million," "shot in the dark" ricocheted (as the Michigan State Police ballistic expert, Sgt. Rayers confirmed at trial) and struck Mr. Browder, accidentally killing him. The **bottom line**. Mr. Browder's assaultive, unlawful actions and his ongoing, unlawful life style and his continuing "criminal enterprise" triggered the incident that resulted in his accidental death. As they say in the Detroit neighborhood where I grew up: "Mr. Browder, 'high as a kite' and engaged in an ongoing criminal enterprise, brought it to Michael Wade's doorstep, so it's on him… no 20-20 hindsight or Monday morning quarterbacking needed."

Bias and Star Chamber Agendas

Unbelievably, Michael Wade was charged with first degree murder – a charge reserved for the most heinous of violent offenders like "hit men," contract killers, those who with "aforethought" poison others intending to kill them or those who "lie in wait"… waiting for the right opportunity to murder. And, now, at the time of sentencing, for the very first time, I may have gotten a glimpse of why Michael Wade was charged with first degree murder... for simply doing his job as a security guard and protecting police-impounded vehicles. Today, for the first time... today, at the time of sentencing, I found out that Mr. Browder's cousin, a Mr. Johnson, is a policeman. Although Your Honor let Mr. Johnson speak as a witness against Michael Wade today at sentencing, Your Honor refused my request to have Mr. Johnson identify himself by giving his full name as well as the name of his police department. Why? "Due process" of law and the 6th Amendment's "confrontation clause" compel open disclosure of all witnesses who provide information to the court. Secretive, "Star Chamber" courts which hid the horrors of secret inquisitions from the eye of public accountability were abolished in England 366 years ago in 1641. There is no legal justification for this court's "Star Chamber" secrecy in this case. This is not a case involving national security or national intelligence or a case involving the sensibilities of a young victim of tender years. Yet, this court has fully and actively participated in concealing the full name of a witness as well as the name of the police department the witness works for. Why??? The answer... because Your Honor's judgment in this case is influenced by, and clouded with, bias against security guards in general, and security guard, Michael Wade, in particular, "security guards"... a profession you previously labeled, in knee jerk fashion, as "tin gods" and "liars."

Before trial, in an unguarded moment, Your Honor willingly volunteered and shared with me your broad sweeping, generalized indictment of security guards: "Put a badge on a security guard and they think they're god," and (paraphrasing Your Honor): "Security guards beat people, and then lie about it, denying they did it." In an unguarded moment, Your Honor boasted about your past career... prosecuting "security guards" for the Michigan Attorney General's office. Six months before trial, while you stood at the bench in a black robe, in an empty courtroom, you were so absorbed in sharing your past career with me that you forgot you were talking to a lawyer representing a "security guard" charged with first degree murder in your courtroom. Your Honor's admitted, pre-existing bias against security guards stacked the deck against Michael Wade at trial. Now, at sentencing, Your Honor continues to stack the deck against Michael Wade with your unconstitutional agenda that promotes a secretive process, purposely blocking my request to find out who a witness is, and the name of the police department the witness works for. It would be of great interest to find out what "influence" this police-witness relative of Mr. Browder brought to bear on a case in which a security guard was charged with first degree murder... for aiming and firing a shot into the ground which ricocheted, accidentally killing an assaultive fugitive, "intruder of the night." There must be some explanation for the outrageous "murder one" charges brought to bear against Michael Wade, and Your Honor's defensive blocking of my legitimate request to have a witness fully identify himself tells me that Mr. Browder's police officer cousin probably holds the answer to the question of why Michael Wade was outrageously charged with first degree murder.

Jury... You Must Convict

There is no doubt (repeat for emphasis, **no doubt**) that Mr. Browder was killed by a single ricochet shot. After a two-week trial, the evidence conclusively showed that the Brenneke slug that killed Mr. Browder was indeed a ricochet shot. So says State Police ballistics expert, Sgt. Rayer. So says Brenneke's United States ballistics representative and world renowned ballistics expert, Tom Burczynski, who confirmed ricochet with unassailable ballistics testing he did for Brenneke. So says world renowned pathologist, Werner Spitz, M.D., who writes and lectures on pathology issues in three different languages,  who lectures Your Honor and other Wayne County Judges on pathology issues and who, 44 years ago, in 1963, was appointed to President John F. Kennedy's "cause of death" team when President Kennedy was assassinated in Dallas, Texas. Yet, despite the agreement by these three experts that a "ricochet" shot killed Mr. Browder, the jury convicted

Werner Spitz, M.D.
World Renowned
Pathologist

Michael Wade of Involuntary Manslaughter for **"pointing and aiming" a firearm at Mr. Browder** when the gun discharged... a verdict that is contradicted 180 degrees by the evidence at trial which showed beyond all doubt that Michael Wade's shotgun was "pointed and aimed" at the ground when it discharged, not at Mr. Browder. Simply stated, Your Honor, it is a logical and legal oxymoron to convict anyone of "pointing, aiming and discharging" a firearm at another person when the firearm was pointed, aimed and fired into the ground and ricocheted. But, Your Honor was not going to let that small detail of Michael Wade's innocence derail your committed agenda to make sure he was convicted.

Nor was Your Honor going to let the jury's **verbal** "Not Guilty" To Homicide verdict stand in the way of your committed agenda to convict Michael Wade:

"THE COURT: All right, ladies and gentlemen, welcome back. You've reached a verdict. Would the foreperson please stand. Madam Clerk.
COURT CLERK: Members of the jury have you agreed upon a verdict? If so who shall speak for you? State your name for the record, please.
JUROR ELEVEN: I will...
COURT CLERK: How do you find the defendant - -

THE COURT: He has to take the verdict form out of the envelope, please. Thank you.
COURT CLERK: **How do you find the defendant, Michael Wade, as to Count 1?**
FOREPERSON: **Not guilty.**
COURT CLERK: As to Count 2, Felony Firearm?
FOREPERSON: I'm sorry. We've got portions of.
THE COURT: Go ahead.
FOREPERSON: Okay. Count 1, Homicide Murder First Degree, Not Guilty to - -
THE COURT: **Which box did you check, sir? [on the Jury Verdict, written form]**
FOREPERSON: **The bottom box, "Guilty of the Lesser Offense of Involuntary Manslaughter"**
THE COURT: Okay. So that's the box that all the members of the jury checked?
FOREPERSON: Yes." (Jury Verdict of 6/29/07, p 22, 23)

There it is. It couldn't be clearer. The jury found Michael Wade Not Guilty of Count One… the Homicide charge. The jury clearly said so. But, Your Honor nullified the jury's **verbal** "Not Guilty" verdict by purposely preparing your own **written** jury verdict form that compelled the jury to find Michael Wade guilty of Manslaughter… even if the jury wanted to acquit Michael Wade.

Despite the 200 plus year old constitutional guaranty of the right to trial by jury, Your Honor took away Michael Wade's right to trial by jury. Your Honor nullified the jury's voice of "Not Guilty" by insisting that the jury check the "Guilty of Manslaughter" box on the jury's written verdict form – a form that you wrote up and forced on the jury… all over my strenuous objection that you were legally required to use the unbiased, neutral jury verdict form that the Michigan Supreme Court directs all trial judges to use in all homicide cases.

Your Honor's agenda was to insure that the jury would convict Michael Wade. That's why you rejected the Michigan Supreme Court's approved verdict form and drafted your own, flawed verdict form. Let me repeat so that there's no doubt about what happened with the jury. Consistent with Your Honor's admitted bias against security guards like Michael Wade (tin gods and liars), Your Honor rejected the Supreme Court's approved written jury verdict form for homicide cases. Instead, Your Honor hand crafted your own unapproved, flawed jury verdict form that left the jury no choice but to find Michael Wade guilty of Manslaughter (no matter how the jury felt).

Under Your Honor's hand crafted, unapproved and flawed jury verdict form, once the jury found Michael Wade "not Guilty" of Murder I, the jury was left with only two other options... either guilty of Murder II **OR** guilty of Involuntary Manslaughter. Your flawed jury verdict form put the jury in a loop where "all roads led" to Guilty:

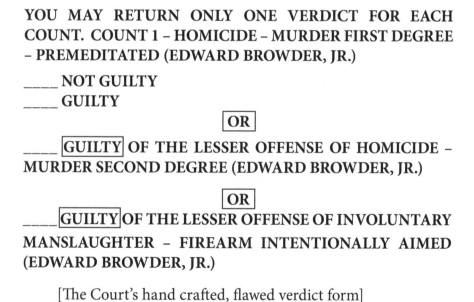

POSSIBLE VERDICTS

YOU MAY RETURN ONLY ONE VERDICT FOR EACH COUNT. COUNT 1 – HOMICIDE – MURDER FIRST DEGREE – PREMEDITATED (EDWARD BROWDER, JR.)

_____ **NOT GUILTY**
_____ **GUILTY**

OR

_____ **GUILTY** **OF THE LESSER OFFENSE OF HOMICIDE – MURDER SECOND DEGREE (EDWARD BROWDER, JR.)**

OR

_____ **GUILTY** **OF THE LESSER OFFENSE OF INVOLUNTARY MANSLAUGHTER – FIREARM INTENTIONALLY AIMED (EDWARD BROWDER, JR.)**

[The Court's hand crafted, flawed verdict form]

As anyone can plainly see, Your Honor's hand crafted, unapproved and flawed jury verdict form guaranteed Michael Wade would be convicted of Manslaughter.

In addition to directing the jury to find the Defendant, Michael Wade, "Guilty" on Your Honor's own flawed, written verdict form, Your Honor also told the jury **verbally** that they did not have the option to acquit the Defendant:

> "THE COURT: All right. Ladies and gentlemen, I'm going to **walk through**, right now, **the verdict form** with you and if you don't understand, let me know...
> Count 1, Homicide Murder in the First Degree, Premeditated, as it relates to Edward Browder, Jr., it's either Not Guilty, Guilty, OR Guilty of the lesser offense of Homicide **Murder Second Degree,** OR Guilty of the lesser offense of **Involuntary Manslaughter...**
> So, that's Count I, and **those are the choices that you may consider.** Okay" (Jury Instruction discussion of 6/28/07, p 113, 114).

The prosecutor also encouraged you to tell the jury they must find the Defendant Guilty of at least Manslaughter:

> "**[PROSECUTOR]**... **I'm in agreement with this Court.** It's either – the verdict can either be Not Guilty or Guilty of Murder One **or Guilty of Murder Two or Guilty of Involuntary Manslaughter.**" (Jury instruction discussion of 6/28/07, p 126, 127).

While you and the prosecutor were both telling the jury they had to convict the Defendant of something, I was telling both of you, to no avail, that you were horribly wrong in taking away Michael Wade's right to a trial by jury by directing the jury to finding him Guilty:

"MR. LAUCK: Or Not Guilty. What happened to Not Guilty?... **You're directing a verdict of Guilty.**" (Jury Instruction discussion of 6/28/07, p 127, 128)

* * * * * * *

MR. LAUCK: You left out the Not Guilty option, Judge.

THE COURT: The Not Guilty is right there, Mr. Lauck, right there. That's the first choice they have.

MR. LAUCK: **That's under Murder One, only.** They should be told they've got a choice of Not Guilty as to the other two [Murder Two and Manslaughter]. That's all I'm saying.

THE COURT: Okay. And **that is not an accurate statement of the law**.

MR. LAUCK: **They don't have a choice of Not Guilty as to the other two?**

THE COURT: **No, [in the presence of the jury]** because see, those are the lesser offenses. Do you all understand what the Court is saying?

Have a seat, Mr. Lauck, because I don't want you to confuse this jury." (Jury Instruction discussion of 6/28/07, p 120)

The bottom line, Your Honor. The jury found Michael Wade Not Guilty. But, you created and forced the jury to use your unapproved, flawed, written verdict form that was purposely rigged by you so that the bouncing ball would land on "Guilty" every time... all day, every day. On the verdict form you devised, all roads led to Guilty no matter how the jury saw the case. To say that you purposely engineered Michael Wade's guilty conviction by taking away his constitutional right to trial by jury, would be a most civil way of describing your absolute lawlessness as well as the legal injustice that you brought crashing down on Michael Wade. To say that you have abused the power of your office to support your own personal vendetta against security guards in general and against Michael Wade in particular would be a more apt description.

The Value Of Life

But, let me leave the area of Michael Wade's unlawful conviction that Your Honor purposely rigged, and let me turn my attention to sentencing matters. As I watched your performance throughout the Michael Wade trial and on numerous other unrelated matters that came before Your Honor during the breaks in the Wade trial, it became very apparent that you are compelled, even driven, to share your strong opinions with the very captive audience in your courtroom, including your "Right to Life" opinions. Obviously, therefore, in representing Michael Wade in a case where a life was lost, I must address your strong "Right to Life" opinions head on. So, let me share with you my view of **the value of life**.

Even though Mr. Browder was a drug addict, a fugitive and even though he had a ten year history of theft at the Detroit Police auto impound yard, Mr. Browder's life had value, and, when his life ended, all of us suffered a loss. As the poet John Donne said: "Ask not for whom the bell tolls," it tolls for all of us when life is lost.

During Michael Wade's trial, I was poignantly aware of the value of life and the loss of life. Since I started this trial on June 18, 2007, I have lost four loved ones to the unrelenting grip of death. I buried my brother Marty. I buried a sister-in-law, Anne O'Kane. I buried a 36-year-old friend of the family, Billy Wertheimer, a kid who grew up with my son. I buried Benedictine Priest, Father Livius Paoli, my first football and baseball coach at St. Scholastica in Northwest Detroit where I grew up. For two weeks, I literally tried this case by day and attended wakes by night. I recognize the value of life and the tragedy of loss of life. And, even though Mr. Browder was a drug addict, long time professional thief and fugitive who triggered the entire incident in which he lost his life, I still valued his life... as diminished as it was. I personally believe in "Right to Life." I also believe in the right to "quality of life" after birth. That's why I have spent much of my 38-year legal career as a trial lawyer representing physically and emotionally injured persons who are hopelessly locked in a battle for justice against government, against corporate America and against insurance companies. As I say, I strongly believe in the value of life.

Value Of Life... Two-Sided Coin

But, the value of life is a two-sided coin. On the other side of the "value of life" coin, is the duty we all have to value our own life, to keep our own life safe and to keep our own life out of harm's way. First and foremost, each of us must value our own life by keeping it drug free. I'm not talking about the nickel and dime marijuana cases I see come before you with your ever-present lectures you give to young men and women who were using marijuana recreationally. Every day, for two weeks in your courtroom, I've heard you lecture the young men and women who appear before you, telling them they are a burden to their parents while the parents are always the saintly angels who have done no wrong. Despite your lectures, I think the law of averages alone tells us that the problem with some of the young men and women who appear before you is precisely the parents... their lack of skill in raising or in loving children or in providing their children with a safe, stable home environment, free from chaotic, unpredictable and mercurial mood swings. Yet, with only a limited idea of what's going on in their home lives, you rush to judgment and jump on the young offenders time and time again... once again bashing their already low self esteem – a modus operandi that is sure to drive the youthful minor offenders further away from the main-stream values and morals Your Honor claims to represent.

Your standard lectures could just as easily be given to the parents and to the older generation whose drugs of choice are alcohol and the highly addictive nicotine in cigarettes that are marketed freely to each new generation of children with the blessing of our government... even though in the 21st century we all know that highly addictive nicotine cigarettes wreak havoc on physical health, and lead to crippling lung disease, heart disease and death. Wouldn't it be nice if you had the ambition to target your same lectures to cigarette manufacturers who, with the blessing of our government, sell highly addictive nicotine across the counter to young men and women of each new generation who just don't appreciate the dangers of nicotine addiction... that same nicotine that, in "second-hand" fashion, took my brother Marty's life just days ago. As I say, on the other side of the "value of life" coin, there is an obligation for all of us, including the deceased Mr. Browder, to protect ourselves and not risk our lives with drugs. I'm talking about nicotine and alcohol abuse, and I'm talking about cocaine, heroin, ecstasy, LSD, and I'm talking about crack cocaine that the 51-year-old deceased Mr. Browder was addicted to and that he was high on the night he died.

Also, on the other side of the "value of life" coin, there is the obligation to protect our lives by staying out of harm's way... physically. There is the obligation that we not put our lives at risk by breaking into people's homes, that we not put our lives at risk by breaking into businesses, and that we not put our lives at risk by stealing the goods or possessions of others. I value Mr. Browder's life. Your Honor values Mr. Browder's life. But, the reality is that Mr. Browder didn't value his own life. Mr. Browder had an obligation to value and protect his own life, but he didn't. Mr. Browder was 51 years old. He wasn't a kid. He was a crack cocaine addict, and the testimony showed that Mr. Browder had been breaking into and stealing from the Detroit Police auto impound yard for ten years. No one disputes this. Both Your

Honor and I valued Mr. Browder's life but, sadly, Mr. Browder didn't value his own life, and that's precisely why we're here today.

In fact, the City of Detroit, my hometown, is filled with thousands of people like Mr. Browder who just don't live up to the obligation to value or protect their own lives. It may not be popular to say that. It may be politically incorrect to say that. But, it's the truth and I stand by it, and so do the hard-working people who live in the City of Detroit and who have to endure endless frustration, imposition and suffering caused by a number of their own reckless, fellow citizens who have no value for life... theirs or anyone else's. Let me share some examples with Your Honor:

First, there is Waltar Marihugh... a 24-year-old who didn't value his own life. He climbed a light pole to steal copper, was electrocuted, fell to the ground and burned to death... just one month after Michael Wade tried to arrest Mr. Browder. As the September 21, 2006 *Detroit Free Press* reports, Mr. Marihugh's mother indicated her son was a drug addict. Waltar's mother valued his life. Your Honor and I valued Waltar Marihugh's life, but he didn't value his own life. Sadly, like Mr. Browder in the case before you, Waltar Marihugh is responsible for his own death, not the electric company whose copper Waltar Marihugh was stealing.

A week after Waltar Marihugh's death, another story appeared in the September 27, 2006 *Detroit Free Press*... a story of thieves who removed all the bricks from St. Cyprian's church. St. Cyprian's pastor, Rev. Donald Lutas, was quoted in the *Detroit Free Press*: "Whoever the receivers of the goods are should be bold enough to admit there is a problem." And, Your Honor, so should you and I and the rest of us in this city be bold enough to admit the two-fold problem in the City of Detroit... out of control theft and thieves and drug addicts who put their lives and ours at risk every day because they have no value for their lives or ours.

Next there is the October 16, 2006 *Detroit News* story that reports that, just two months after Michael Wade tried to arrest Mr. Browder, a Habitat for Humanity organization built a home for a poor family, but, before the family could move in, thieves stole $40,000 worth of plumbing, sinks, toilets and faucets. Could there be a greater example of lack of respect for life or for the needs of others? The question answers itself.

The same October 16, 2006 *Detroit News* article also reported how the internationally acclaimed Kronk Boxing Gym (headed by legendary fight trainer, Emanuel Steward, and world champions, Thomas "Hit Man" Hearns, Hilmer Kinty, Mickey Goodwin and others), met a cruel fate from thieves and drug addicts who put the last nail in the Kronk Gym's coffin by stripping out the boiler and pipes. There will be no more young kids who dare to become "Kronk Champions" thanks to the lawless element of the City of Detroit who have no value of life... their own or the lives of others.

As a kid, I used to swim at Brennan Pools on Plymouth Road in Northwest Detroit... Olympic length pools and Olympic diving boards. But, again, just two months after Michael Wade tried to arrest Mr. Browder, the October 16, 2006 *Detroit News* reports that the lawless element who have no value for life and no respect for the needs of others were at it again. They stole $400,000 worth of copper out of the Brennan Pools. No more next generations to swim and dive at Brennan Pools as I did as a kid during the long, hot, endless, joyful days of Detroit summers. No place left for youthful respites. Now, kids in Detroit just "stay on guard" physically, mentally and emotionally until the endless adrenaline surge of "fight or flight" destroys the quality of their lives, jangles their nerves and, eventually... shortens their lives.

Next there is the Arnold Home for the Aged located at Avon and 7 Mile in the City of Detroit, just three blocks from where I grew up while attending St. Scholastica and Catholic Central. During our June 2007 trial, reporter Scott Lewis used his popular "Problem Solvers" program and his media presence for a successful law enforcement operation. As reported during Michael Wade's trial, Channel 2 News caught the thieves on camera stripping the Arnold Home. Scott Lewis and Channel 2 News spurred the Detroit Police into action and arrests were made. As the owners of the Arnold Home told Channel 2 News, the unrelenting problem of theft occurred because the **owners could no longer afford to pay for security**.

When my St. Scholastica grade school classmate, Father Mike, took over as pastor of our St. Scholastica Parish from Father Livius on January 7, 2007, Bishop Quinn officiated. After mass, Bishop Quinn went out to the parking lot and found his car sitting on the ground, all four wheels and tires taken by thieves who now control my old neighborhood... reminding me of an incident a couple years before when the thieves stole my vehicle out of the same St. Scholastica parking lot, in broad daylight, while I attended a reunion mass. No media coverage for either of these two brazen daylight thefts. Bishop Quinn and I just joined the quiet "masses of victimization" who live in quiet rage, silent desperation and a pervasive hopelessness because... in the City of Detroit the value of life and the needs of others are in short supply.

Even during this trial, my cell phone was stolen from the washroom ledge on the fourth floor of this courthouse while I was throwing some cool water on my face during a morning break. Look down to cool off. Look up... no phone. Adios. Also during the closing arguments of this trial, there was a brawl in the fourth floor hallway. Your courtroom sheriffs and even the State Police officer in charge of this case, Detective Bundsuh, jumped the court railing and bolted out of the courtroom during closing arguments to quell a donnybrook from another case. What would the legendary Frank

Murphy (Recorder's Court judge for the City of Detroit in the 1920s, Mayor of the City of Detroit, later Governor of the State of Michigan, U.S. Ambassador to the Philippines, United States Attorney General, United States Supreme Court Justice and great Irish statesman) think... if he knew there was very little security in the City of Detroit – even in his namesake, the Frank Murphy Hall of Justice, where we are now discussing the fate of Michael Wade?

Let me give you an **overview**, Your Honor. In the first nine months of 2006, the October 16, 2006 *Detroit News* reported that: "the City's Lighting Department alone has lost 7.5 million dollars worth of materials this year to scavengers"... repeat, **7.5 million, one city department and not even a year**. Also, according to the *Detroit Free Press*, AT&T's problem with scavengers stealing cables has resulted in "hundreds of customers... without phone service at varying times." A spokesman for Mayor Kilpatrick's office quoted in the September 27, 2006 *Free Press*, indicates: "It's a horrendous problem." The mayor's office wants to go after the scrap dealers. Yet, the scrap dealers like Joel Silverstein of Silvers Metal Co. was quoted in the September 26, 2006 *Free Press* saying that the City "needs to bring in more police and monitor the streets of Detroit"... a classic case of finger-pointing. The City blames the scrap dealers for receiving stolen goods, and the scrap dealers blame the City for lack of police protection. And, all the while, "Rome is burning," and our law abiding citizens take it on the chin, again and again, until we are all reeling on the ropes trying to stay on our feet while those who don't share our "value of life" pummel society's life and values into unconsciousness.

Your Honor, I have just given you the tip of the iceberg. Multiply the above by ten thousand, and you'll start to see the true picture of the City of Detroit, 40 years after the 1967 riots – a city in full decay, a city filled with drug addicts, thieves and violent characters who don't give a damn about your life, your children's lives, my life or even their own lives... a city full of walking dangerous confrontations looking for unsuspecting victims to explode on. And, yet, we endlessly ask the same naïve, sophomoric question: "What's wrong with Detroit?" "Why can't we attract new business?" "Why do we have such a budget deficit?" "Why do the lawns in our parks go uncut?" "Why do eyesore-criminal-haven, abandoned homes wait to eventually crumble?" "Why do broken water pipes rupture and remain unrepaired for days and weeks as water spills through the streets?" "Why are Emergency 911 services and Emergency Fire Department services so woefully inadequate?" Why... ? Why... ? Why... ?

Police Won't Solve The Problem

So the question becomes: "How do we solve the problem of marauding lawlessness?" Your Honor, you're an elected official. "What's your solution?" You're a self-proclaimed "tough judge." "What are you going to do to solve the problem?" And the answer? Apparently, your answer is I'm doing the best I can. But, Your Honor, what you do is nowhere near enough to solve the problem. During the course of the Michael Wade trial, you told me you were elected by the citizens of Wayne County to "protect" them. And, as I'm sure you will recall, I evoked your anger when I replied that you were not a law enforcement official, and that your judicial role was to protect Michael Wade's right to a fair trial. But, let's put our difference of opinion aside for a moment, and assume, for the sake of argument, that your judicial role is, as you claim, to protect the citizens of Wayne County. Your Honor, quite frankly, you are not protecting Wayne County citizens on any consistent or systemic basis. You and the rest of the judges are, at best, merely putting out fires. I started in the practice of law as a prosecutor in 1970, and I've been practicing law for 38 years since, and I know the courts aren't going to solve the problems I have detailed for you.

Strange as it may seem, I also know the Detroit Police are not going to solve the problem. In July 2006, three weeks before Mr. Browder's death (repeat... **three weeks before**), Michael Wade arrested Mr. Browder for breaking into another car in the Detroit Police auto impound yard. At that time, Mr. Browder was a fugitive on an outstanding drug warrant. After Michael Wade arrested Mr. Browder, he waited for hours for the police to show up. Michael Wade then handed Mr. Browder over to the Detroit Police, but the police released Mr. Browder without arresting or arraigning him on that outstanding fugitive warrant (see Wayne County Circuit Court file #04-001611). Mr. Browder was a fugitive for months, and when the Detroit Police finally got their hands on him three weeks before his death, thanks to Michael Wade, the police let him go again. The Detroit Police aren't going to solve the problem.

The Michigan State Police aren't any better. They're not going to solve the problem. As Your Honor is aware, another one of the neighborhood's career criminals is Byron Osby. He was a friend of the deceased, Edward Browder, and a co-conspirator in their on-going, joint criminal enterprise that, for the last ten years, targeted the Detroit Police Auto Impound Yard that Michael Wade was trying to protect and secure. On September 5, 2005, a year before Mr. Browder's death, Byron Osby was arrested by Michael Wade and turned over to the Detroit Police. Byron Osby was charged with feloniously assaulting Michael Wade with a 15-inch long knife, and with breaking into a vehicle in the Detroit Police auto impound yard. Mr. Osby obtained a bond and skipped out on his bond, and, like Mr. Browder, became a fugitive.

One year later, during the investigation in the Michael Wade case, the State Police found Byron Osby and spent a significant amount of time questioning him, and found out directly from him (as the State Police detail in their written report) that Osby had been stealing from the Detroit Police auto impound yard for "approximately eight years," and that the Deceased Edward Browder had been stealing from the impound yard "for a lot longer." Despite Byron Osby's admission to the State Police of "eight years" of criminal activity in the Detroit Police Impound Yard, the State Police never ran a computer LEIN check on Byron Osby while they were questioning him to find out whether he was wanted on any outstanding warrants. Repeat, the State Police, with pre-existing knowledge that Byron Osby had been stealing from the Detroit Police auto impound yard for "eight years," never ran a LEIN check on Byron Osby while they were questioning him to see if he was wanted. A simple LEIN check would have revealed within a minute or less that Osby was a fugitive wanted on an outstanding warrant for assault with a 15-inch knife against Michael Wade and Michael's boss, Greg Errigo, and for theft at the Detroit Police Auto Impound Yard. Although they could have and should have arrested Byron Osby, the State Police just let the dangerous fugitive Osby walk away... again. This ludicrous scenario sounds like a scene out of *Keystone Cops*.

Courts Won't Solve The Problem

And, the courts aren't any better, Your Honor. When Byron Osby was finally arrested... months after the State Police let him go, and after being a fugitive for well over a year, he was bound over for trial on Felonious Assault of Michael Wade with a 15-inch knife and for Felonious Breaking and Entering into a Vehicle at the Detroit Police

Auto Impound Yard. Thereafter, the judge in that case set another bond, and Mr. Osby put up $500.00, and was set free again by the Wayne County Circuit Court, and, to no one's surprise, Byron Osby took off again becoming a fugitive for the second time (see Wayne County Circuit Court file #05-9326) – prompting the question… do the Police or the Courts have any real interest in pursuing the dangerous career criminal, Byron Osby?

Let me share another story with you that again shows the futility of relying on the courts in Detroit to solve the never ending problem of theft by a lawless element that have no value of life… theirs or anyone else's. As Your Honor recalls, Mr. Browder's cousin, Johnny Turner, dropped Mr. Browder off at the Detroit Police Auto Impound Yard on the night of Mr. Browder's death, and saw Mr. Browder disappear into the impound yard with a black duffel bag full of burglar tools. In January of this year, six months before our trial started, Mr. Browder's cousin, Johnny Turner, broke into a Detroit school, and was caught stealing copper from the school. The prosecutor filed an habitual (three time loser) charge against Johnny Turner, and then cut a deal for three time loser Johnny Turner to serve seven months (**repeat, seven months**) after which Johnny Turner served two weeks (**repeat two weeks**), and was released because of prison over-crowding (see Wayne County Circuit Court file # 07-04527). Obviously, Johnny Turner has no value for his own life or the lives of our kids who are entitled to be educated in a school not stripped to the bone by a marauding, plundering Johnny Turner. Just as obvious, it is painfully apparent that neither the police nor the courts have the ability or the will to solve the never-ending theft problem in the City of Detroit, or the multitude of other problems caused by the thousands of criminal mentalities that have no value for life, theirs or anyone else's, and no consideration for the rights or the needs of others.

And the media can't be expected to solve the problem. Channel 2 TV's "Problem Solvers" used their power and visibility to solve the problem of the looting of the Arnold Home for the Aged, but the media, although helpful on occasion to solve a single, isolated problem, are not a law enforcement presence in the City of Detroit, and cannot be counted on to solve the theft problem on any systemic, long term basis.

Michael Wade... The Solution

So who's going to solve the problem of pervasive, unrelenting theft and violence in the City of Detroit and other cities by drug addicts who have no value of life... theirs or anyone else's? The answer... private enterprise, enlisting security guards like Michael Wade. Until the social scientists can establish an effective and reliable program for drug addiction, theft, low self image, fatherless homes, poverty, etc. (if they ever can), the only viable alternative for protection from marauders and intruders who have no value for life is private enterprise... private enterprise which will hire security to protect society's interest in reducing crime. That's it! Michael Wade is that security who was hired by private enterprise, the Michigan Auto Recovery Yard, to protect the vehicles owned by citizens that have been towed to the Detroit Police auto impound yard and are awaiting recovery by their owners. So, Your Honor, as you see, private enterprise and Michael Wade are the only viable answer to the problem.

Michael Wade is the **solution**. Fifty-one year old Edward Browder, who had no value for life (his own or others), is the problem that society asks Michael Wade to solve... a problem that the Detroit Police Department can't or won't solve; a problem that the Michigan State Police can't or won't solve; and a problem that the Courts can't or won't solve. And, solving that problem is exactly what Michael Wade was doing when he first arrested fugitive Edward Browder and turned him over to the Detroit Police Department in July of 2006, three weeks before Edward Browder's death. And, solving that problem a second time is exactly what Michael Wade was doing in August 2006 when he attempted to again arrest Mr. Browder on the night of his death: "Freeze!" But, Mr. Browder, in an attempt to resist arrest and escape his lawful arrest, resorted to violence by throwing a tire iron at Michael Wade. And, Michael Wade's response... ? After ducking a tire iron thrown by Mr. Browder, Michael Wade fired a warning shot from 40 to 50 yards away, firing that warning shot into the ground in an effort to use that loud, echoing, reverberating sound to clear the area and keep Mr. Browder running off the premises of the Detroit Police auto impound yard so Mr. Browder wouldn't hide in one of the hundreds of hiding places in the impound yard and wreak further havoc or present further danger to Michael Wade. But, as a result of the consequences triggered by Mr. Browder (**repeat for emphasis...** as a result of the consequences **triggered by Mr. Browder**), that warning shot, like a one-in-a-million, "shot in the dark," ricocheted and struck Mr. Browder, accidentally killing him.

No Second Guessing with 20-20 Hindsight

And, how does the law view the actions of security personnel that our society asks to solve the problem of non-ending theft and violence? How does the law view the security responses of security personnel like Michael Wade who must make instant decisions in the dangerous, dark corners of life? Quite clearly, the law cautions Your Honor not to use the "calm of contemplation" within the cozy confines of your courtroom to "second guess" the security response of the Defendant Michael Wade. The law correctly recognizes that Michael

Wade was simply working his job when he was, without warning, faced with a confrontation, not of his making, a confrontation with a dangerous drug addict and violent intruder of the night, a confrontation requiring Michael Wade to make instant decisions for his own safety... without any time to reflect or deliberate.

Therefore, the law cautions Your Honor to recognize that Michael Wade was alone and isolated from outside view in the Detroit Police auto impound yard, and was facing unknown danger under the cover of night... certainly a harrowing experience for any of us. In short, the law cautions, as I advised Your Honor in writing before trial, not to use your 20-20 hindsight to "second guess" the security response of Michael Wade who was simply doing his job:

> "It is far easier for a jury and court long after the fact in the quiet contemplation of a jury room or in the ivory tower of a law library to determine what more prudent and practical action could have been taken, **but a police officer often has but a short time to make decisions and make them he must**." *J.C. Ealey Jr. vs. City of Detroit*, 144 MICH APP 324, 332 (1985 – reversing a civil jury verdict against the Defendant police officer **as a matter of law** in a police shooting case)."

✳✳✳✳✳✳✳✳✳✳✳✳✳

> "**Our society is more and more critical of courts** because it feels the judicial system too often supports the person committing crimes and dramatically **fails to support the victims of crime and the police** in their attempts to slow the growing tide of criminal activity." *J.C. Ealey vs. City of Detroit*, 144 MICH APP 324, 330-331 (1985).

✳✳✳✳✳✳✳✳✳✳✳✳✳

> " ...it is incongruous to expect a defendant [**security guard**] to retire to safety when his job commands that he remain. It is illogical to demand that he flee when by so doing he, as well as his employer and the theater owner, may arguably be held civilly accountable for the havoc wreaked in his

absence. It is unrealistic for this Court, **safely isolated in its appellate aerie** [bird sanctuary], to enforce a rule whose practical application in the instant setting denies common sense." *People vs. Johnson*, 75 MICH APP 337, 342 (1977 – reversing a **security guard's** conviction for his killing of an unruly theatre patron because the security guard had no duty to retreat)."

****

"Despite the fact that some jurisdictions have cut back on the justifiable use of deadly force, many others have maintained the common law rule, and **there is good reason for doing so. The fact remains that the police cannot be everywhere they are needed at once.** The occasion may arise where the private citizen is confronted with **the choice** of attempting a citizen's arrest, or letting the felon escape. In order to **make the citizen's arrest**, it is regrettable, but sometimes necessary, to **make use of deadly force.**" *People vs. Whitty*, 96 MICH APP 403, 416 (1980). FN #7

****

"See also Perkins & Boyce Criminal Law (3d ed), p 1099: '**Firmly established in the common law** of England was **the privilege to kill a fleeing** felon if he could not otherwise be taken, **a privilege extended to the private person** as well as to the officer....'
"'If a felony be committed and the felon fly from justice,... **it is the duty of every man to use his best endeavors for preventing an escape; and if in the pursuit the felon be killed** where he cannot otherwise be overtaken, **the homicide is justifiable**', 1 East, Pleas of the Crown, p 298 (1803)." *People vs. Couch*, 436 MICH 414, 421 (1990)

So, as I advised Your Honor in writing before trial, Michigan law would have allowed the Defendant Michael Wade to intentionally shoot Mr. Browder, a fleeing felon, directly in the back if necessary to stop Mr. Browder's flight. Certainly, therefore, Michael Wade's much less drastic action of firing a warning shot into the ground (which ricocheted and struck Mr. Browder) should lead to no criminal liability whatsoever.

And, to make matters worse, Your Honor even refused to instruct the jury on the right of a citizen like Michael Wade to use fatal force to stop a fleeing felon's (Mr. Browder's) flight... even though six months before trial, on January 26, 2007, while ruling on my motion to dismiss, you stated that the fleeing felon defense was "a question of fact for the jury to decide." In January 2007, as you say, it's a question for the jury to decide, but then six months later, just before the jury begins to deliberate, you refused to instruct the jury on the law concerning the right to use fatal force to stop a fleeing felon. Kind of like a shell game. Now you see it, now you don't. Based on your words, Your Honor, I tried Michael Wade's case on the right of a citizen to use fatal force to stop the flight of a fleeing felon. But, then, Your Honor reneged and pulled the rug out from underneath the Defendant's defense, and refused to instruct the jury on the lawful right and "duty" of the Defendant Michael Wade, or any citizen, to use fatal force, if necessary, to stop a fleeing felon's flight... just part of Your Honor's on-going campaign to make sure a "tin god" security guard (as you refer to Michael Wade) gets convicted. Your Honor correctly saw a "Not Guilty" verdict on the jury's horizon, and you did every thing in your power to head that "Not Guilty" verdict off at the pass.

It's On Mr. Browder

Let me finish by telling Your Honor how Mr. Browder's August 10, 2006 death could have been avoided. First, if private enterprise had not hired a security guard, Mr. Browder could have had full reign and a license to steal whatever he wanted to from the Detroit Police auto impound yard. That's one way Mr. Browder's death could have been avoided. Society could have just caved in and given Mr. Browder and others like him full reign to do whatever they wanted. So, if the Detroit Police Department and private enterprise had merely given up and turned over the Detroit Police auto impound yard to Edward Browder, Byron Osby, Johnny Turner and the rest of the neighborhood drug addicts and criminals, then Mr. Browder wouldn't have been killed… or would he? Maybe, if one of the drug addict criminals decided to be kingpin and declare the yard as his, and his alone, Mr. Browder might have been killed anyway for infringing on the kingpin's territory.

But, in the last analysis, the legal and moral responsibility for Mr. Browder's death lies with Mr. Browder because **IF…**

…**IF** Mr. Browder valued his life

…**IF** Mr. Browder valued the life and rights of others

…**IF** Mr. Browder was not a drug addict

…**IF** Mr. Browder had not been stealing from the Detroit Police auto impound yard for ten years

…**IF** Mr. Browder was not high on crack cocaine on the night of August 10, 2006

…**IF** Mr. Browder did not break into the Detroit Police auto impound yard on the night of August 10, 2006

…**IF** Mr. Browder had submitted to the lawful arrest that Michael Wade was attempting on August 10, 2006,

…**THEN** Mr. Browder would not have been accidentally killed.

So… who is to blame for the accidental loss of Mr. Browder's life? The security guard hired by private enterprise to secure the Detroit Police auto impound yard or Mr. Browder himself? The question answers itself. Although that answer had no impact on you at trial, perhaps that answer will now guide you in sentencing Michael Wade. Let the punishment fit his non-existent crime.

The Sentence

And what did the self-proclaimed "tough judge" do at sentencing? The short answer... she stayed true to her past form and let her pre-existing bias against security guards rule the day.

When confronted before trial with her voluntary statements of general bias against security guards (tin gods and liars), and when asked, therefore, to step aside and disqualify herself from hearing the trial, Her Honor insisted she could be fair despite her admitted biased comments. But, Her Honor was anything but fair. At trial, Her Honor was the prosecutor in black robes – objecting to Michael Wade's presentation where the prosecutor raised no objection, refusing to follow the law or the rules of evidence no matter how clear and unambiguous, currying favor with the jury by baking and delivering brownies to the jury the very day after she provoked a confrontation with the Michael Wade's attorney by telling him (for the second time) in the presence of the jury that he was "confusing the jury" and... the final coup de grace, insuring Michael Wade's conviction, first with her own flawed, non-standard jury verdict form that directed the jury to find the Defendant guilty of at least manslaughter, and, second, with her verbal instruction to the jury telling the jurors that they did not have the option of finding Michael Wade "Not Guilty."

At sentencing, consistent with her pre-existing bias, Her Honor lamented that Michael Wade was not found guilty of murder, and lamented that the sentencing guidelines (which she re-engineered in over-ruling the Probation Department's recommendation of proba-tion) limited the Defendant's sentence to only a 5 to 17 year period:

> "The thing that **troubles** the court, and frankly, if I heard the case and I were the trier of fact, I would have convicted you of Second Degree Murder because I think the evidence

supports that. But that's my opinion and I'm not the jury and **I'm not going to change the verdict** because of that" (7/30/07 Sentencing Transcript p 50, 51)

* * * * * * *

"There is no question, if I had my way, **I would send you away for a long time.**" (7/30/07 Sentencing Transcript p 53).

Could there be any clearer evidence of Her Honor's biased agenda to get Michael Wade for a non existent crime? Thereafter, Her Honor went from bias to vindictiveness, suggesting that the prison population would give Michael Wade his comeuppance when the prisoners discovered that he was a security guard:

> "THE COURT: But I think prison isn't going to treat you so well, regardless of what the sentence of this court is.
> "DEFENDANT: Yes, Ma'am.
> "THE COURT: Because they're going to find out that you were a security guard and that you thought you knew what you were doing. And, you know what? **Even among the criminals there's some code.**" (7/30/07 Sentencing Transcript p 52, 53)

What code was her Honor talking about? The "code" among criminals that says: "Let's beat or kill law enforcement personnel?" How dare an elected official hang Michael Wade (or anyone) out as bait for the prison population by condoning or inciting prisoner abuse?

Finally, not content with her verbalized threats to Michael Wade's safety in prison, her Honor went from her own temporal punishment of **5 to 17 years** to the anticipation of a harsher punishment by a vengeful God when Michael Wade meets his maker:

> "But you see, there's simply nothing, Mr. Prosecutor or Mr. Johnson or the members of the family of both sides, that this

court can do, Mr. Wade, to you **that a higher authority isn't going to do**. This is just a step in time." (7/30/07 Sentencing Transcript p 52 – a rather incoherent juxtaposing of words, but the message of greater punishment by a "higher authority" is clear.)

And all of this – directing the jury to find Michael Wade guilty, unlawfully securing Michael Wade's conviction, hanging Michael Wade out as bait for the prison population and hoping for harsher punishment and condemnation by God... all of this because of the admitted pre-existing bias against security guards as "tin gods" and "liars."

Michael Wade was society's answer to the endless problem of the lawlessness by those who have no value for life or the rights of others. Her Honor's bias against Michael Wade and her blindness in failing to see the true picture of the Michael Wade case reminds me of the old expression... "Judge, if you are not going to provide the solution to the problem, at least get out of the way so you don't become the problem."

Help Wanted

After Michael Wade was convicted, imprisoned and morally condemned, the Detroit Police auto impound yard should have put out a **"Help Wanted"** sign on the front gate:

"**Help Wanted**. Security guard needed to secure Police impound yard in a dangerous, high crime area. $50.00 a night for risking your life. No benefits, but a potential for lifetime room and board if you are convicted of doing your job."

A Wrong... Belatedly Righted

Such is the upside down, "Alice in Wonderland" world in a Wayne County Circuit Courtroom in Detroit, Michigan in the first decade of the 21st century... Judge Annette Jurkiewicz Berry presiding and abusing her power to nullify the Bill of Rights and Michael Wade's constitutional right to a trial by a jury, or, as a very conservative, Republican Court of Appeals panel said in reversing Michael Wade's conviction:

> "...[T]he jury was not given the opportunity to find Defendant either generally Not Guilty or Not Guilty of the Lesser-Included Offenses **in violation of his constitutional right to trial by jury**" *People vs. Wade*, 283 MICH APP 462 (2009)

What else could the Court of Appeals do? It was either throw out the right to jury trial or reverse Michael Wade's unconstitutional conviction.

Sleight of Hand... Injustice

Thereafter, the Wayne County Prosecutor, Kim Worthy's, appellate division was bold enough to ask the Michigan Supreme Court to overrule the Court of Appeals and reinstate Michael Wade's conviction on the false premise that (even though the jury verdict form was flawed and deprived Michael Wade of his constitutional right to trial by jury), still Judge Berry properly instructed the jury of their "Not Guilty" options with her **verbal** jury instruction... an absolute false claim. Based on the prosecutor's false claim, the Michigan Supreme Court reinstated Michael Wade's Manslaughter conviction on December 2, 2009:

"The jury verdict form was not dispositive because the trial court properly instructed the jury.... In light of the jury instruction, the trial court's error in using the improper verdict form was harmless."

More grave injustice. The Wayne County prosecutor misled the Supreme Court into believing that Judge Berry properly instructed the Jury **verbally**. The truth! Judge Berry verbally told the jury that they did not have the option of acquitting Michael Wade:

"MR. LAUCK: Or Not Guilty. What happened to Not Guilty?... **You're directing a verdict of Guilty.**" (Jury Instructions of 6/28/07, p 127, 128)

* * * * * * *

MR. LAUCK: You left out the Not Guilty option, Judge.
THE COURT: The Not Guilty is right there, Mr. Lauck, right there. That's the first choice they have.
MR. LAUCK: **That's under Murder One, only.** They should be told they've got a choice of Not Guilty as to the other two [Murder II and Manslaughter]. That's all I'm saying.
THE COURT: Okay. And **that is not an accurate statement of the law.**
MR. LAUCK: **They don't have a choice of Not Guilty as to the other two?**
THE COURT: **No, [in the presence of the jury]** because see, those are the lesser offenses. Do you all understand what the Court is saying?
Have a seat, Mr. Lauck, because I don't want you to confuse this jury." (Jury Instructions of 6/28/07, p 120)

A Wrong... Righted Again

Thereafter, a Motion for Reconsideration was filed on behalf of Michael Wade to inform the Michigan Supreme Court that the

Wayne County Prosecutor's Office misled them. Finally, therefore, on April 30, 2010, three plus years of imprisonment later, the Supreme Court reversed themselves **seven to zero** and reinstated the Court of Appeals opinion setting aside Michael Wade's conviction for Manslaughter, and ordering a new trial (what else could they do?).

But... how do you explain to Michael Wade that we finally won after he spent three plus years of his life locked up like a caged animal? How do you explain to free-world America that a judge's personality and bias trumps the rule of law and our constitutional protections? And, what happens to those poor, wrongfully accused souls whose lawyers do not fight the endless battle to free them?

Despite the laudatory goals of the "Bill of Rights" and despite its centuries' old guaranty of trial by jury, one misguided judge, living in the shadowland of injustice can bring justice, "due process" of law and fair play to its knees by abusing her power and trumping the United States Constitution, Thomas Jefferson and the almost 250 years old American system of justice.

Facing Judge Annette Jurkiewicz Berry on a daily basis makes you wonder whether the American Revolutionary War was fought in vain. As the Children of the Greatest Generation wind down, more and more, we seem to live in a world that is no longer ours. The fair trial for Robert Smith in 1978 was the world that belonged to the Children of the Greatest Generation. The legal bludgeoning of Michael Wade in 2007 by Judge Annette Jurkiewicz Berry was a world more akin to what we Children of the Greatest Generation would have inherited if the Greatest Generation had lost World War II... a scary thought.

Finally... It's Over For Michael Wade

On July 20, 2010 and on August 26, 2010, a plea bargain agreement was reached with the Wayne County Prosecutor's Office and

Michael Wade walked free with credit for time served... three plus years of his life irretrievably lost. Visibly upset that Michael Wade had finally broken her reign over his life, the Honorable Annette Jurkiewicz Berry, in her customary fashion, did a slow burn, and then misdirected her visible anger at the prosecutor who, she claimed, filled out the time-served, plea form improperly... the last touch of irony from a judge whose own flawed (jury verdict) form cost the taxpayers of Wayne County and Michael Wade dearly.

But... Deja Vu All Over Again... For Ron Ragan

Does the victimization of the "good guys"
ever end... in Detroit, Michigan?

At midnight, on April 19, 2011, my 70-year-old, Irish-Serbian friend, Ron Ragan, was "homebound" in his Northwest Detroit home... recovering from the surgical removal of a large section of his colon. As the twilight of restorative sleep descended on him and soothed his discomfort, suddenly, in the dark of night, he was painfully jolted back to consciousness by the terrifying sound of a loud boom. As he awoke, he heard "intruders of the night" breaking though his dining room window. What led these bold, ruthless "intruders of the night" to believe that Ron was not at home? Or, worse yet, maybe they didn't care. And, if they didn't... woe is 70-year-old, debilitated Ron Ragan at the hands of these, "do-whatever-they-want-to-do" marauders of the darkness.

In fear and acting justifiably on the human instinct of survival, Ron Ragan retrieved his loaded .38 calibre, registered handgun (thank heaven he had a firearm in his home!), and fired a warning shot from the edge of his broken window toward the ground below. The next day Ron found out from neighbors that the 25-year-old home invader was found on a lawn four doors down the street, lifeless... dead on arrival at Sinai Grace Hospital.

But, just as in the Michael Wade case, the death of the 25-year-old home invader is not the moral nor the legal responsibility of Ron Ragan... who was merely the target of ruthless, middle-of-night, home invaders. Michigan law clearly justifies and supports homeowners who use firearms to ward off criminals who would invade or attempt to invade their home. Statutory law in Michigan protects homeowners by cloaking them with a (rebuttable) presumption that the innocent homeowner... is about to be killed or seriously injured during a home invasion (or an attempted home invasion). Therefore, Michigan law presumes that a homeowner's response in using fatal force, without warning, and directly against a home invader is a justifiable, lawful response of "self defense" (Public Act 311 of 2006, MCL 780.951).

This statutory protection that presumes it is legitimate and justifiable self defense for homeowners to use fatal force against lawless, home invaders is nothing new in Michigan. It is merely a statutory codification of the age-old, common sense doctrine that "a man's home is his castle." Under that doctrine, home invaders who break into (or who attempt to break into) another man's castle do so at the risk of their own death... a doctrine previously established with dramatic flair by famed trial lawyer, Clarence Darrow, in Detroit, Michigan in 1925 during his defense of a black doctor, Dr. Ossian Sweet, who killed a white man who was part of an angry mob that gathered outside of Dr. Sweet's home. Michigan's favorite son, the Honorable Frank Murphy, was the presiding judge in the Ossian Sweet case, and, today, on the first floor of his namesake, Frank Murphy Hall of Justice in Detroit, there is a plaque commemorating the long-established principle of law that "a man's home is his castle." Therefore, end of the Ron Ragan story... right? Wrong!... at least not the end of the story in Detroit where the victimization of crime victims by both criminals and the government never ends.

Within 15 hours of the breaking out of Ron Ragan's glass, dining room window (and the attempt to enter Ron's home), the Detroit Police Department submitted an "affidavit for a search warrant" (for Ron Ragan's home) to a judge in the 36th District Court in Detroit pointing out (as the deceased's accomplices admit) that the deceased:

> "was attempting to break and enter a residence... and was shot when he stuck his head into the window" (search warrant affidavit 11000825 of 4/19/11 by Detroit Police Officer Derrick Maye).

Unbelievably, based on a Detroit Police affidavit that clearly shows that Ron Ragan's home was being vandalized and broken into (and despite a statutory, legal presumption that Ron Ragan was, therefore, acting in self defense), the Detroit Police obtained a search warrant for Ron Ragan's home, broke his front door off the hinges while he was away, searched and ransacked his home and garage, arrested him when he returned home, took him into custody, left his front door wide open for other neighborhood marauders to again invade his "castle" and help themselves to whatever the police didn't take. The police then jailed Ron Ragan overnight... where he shivered, uncontrollably, in pain, throughout the long, cold night sitting on a concrete floor until the police released him to my custody the following morning. And, all this irrational, unlawful and misguided abuse from the heavy hand of our government because Ron Ragan had the misfortune of being a crime victim in the great City of Detroit, where victimization by marauding criminals and a lawless government never stops. And, when Ron Ragan asked for return of his registered .38 firearm (for which he has a CCW permit)... to protect himself from any possible future retaliation (and for return of other personal property taken during the ransack search of his home), the Detroit Police response: "**No!**"… "investigation continuing."

Ron Ragan now waits word from the Wayne County Prosecutor  on whether he will be charged. Facetiously, or maybe not, you can only hope that Ron Ragan will be fortunate enough to follow in Michael Wade's footsteps so that someday down the road of life (maybe years from now), he will be able to escape from the long, domineering shadow of thugs, criminals, oppressive law enforcement and the court system in Detroit… if he can emotionally and financially stay the course in the "Alice in Wonderland" world known as "Detroit," Michigan.

Ron Ragan

The Children of the Greatest Generation are winding down and truly losing their world… a world where common sense and rational thinking once prevailed and where "good" was rewarded and "evil" punished.

The "Great Depression of 2008" America's "Ruling Class" And Trial Lawyers

*T*he role of a trial lawyer in America is... ? Hold that thought for a moment.

When I was 14 years old, my eighth grade educated, Irish mother gave me a very practical lesson in life: "Money rules the world." Since we had none, I saw her comment as unsettling then... in 1957, as

Mother Jean Lauck

well as a self defeating prediction for my future. Instantly, I knew that, in order to have some control over my destiny, I would have to prove her wrong. So, I replied that "truth, justice and hard work" ruled the world. Nine years later in 1966, I started the University of Detroit Law School to prove my point. Now 21 years after my mother's death and 42 years after I graduated from law school, I hang my head as I lament... my mother was right.

American Ruling Class

Make no mistake about it. There is a "ruling class" in America. It's comprised of two powerful groups who have a monopoly on power and wealth... **American capitalists** and **elected politicians**. Absent an occasional uprising of courage (think women suffragettes, Rosa Parks, "freedom riders," Vietnam War protestors, etc.), the rest of us are merely hostages whose lives and financial security hang in the balance the "ruling class" creates. "We the People" are usually helpless to challenge the concentration of power in the "ruling class." Even our right to vote seems illusory as we vote in a new group of politicians with different faces and different promises, but with the "same-o, same-o," "ruling class" mentality... "don't take a courageous stand, and do the right thing, or you may not get reelected." As the great writer, Leon Uris, noted in his prologue to *Trinity*: "There is no past; there is no future; there is only history repeating itself over and over, now." And, so it seems... as I reflect on America's ruling class and their defining role in the Great Depression of 2008.

The American capitalist segment of the "ruling class" (think insurance industry, corporate America, investment bankers, money managers and Wall Street – not small businesses) have but a single focus... the financial bottom line. Their purpose is to take in and keep as much of other peoples' money as the law will (or will not) allow. "Greed" is in their DNA. In fact, all of us bear the evolutionary imprint of greed in our DNA. Before the use of currency, the evolutionary instinct of survival created "hoarding" (the more food and goods accumulated, the better the chance of survival), and "gluttony" (the more food stuffed in excess of actual need, the better the chance to survive the uncertain period until the next meal). The evolutionary remnants of caveman "hoarding," "gluttony" and "greed" live within us today as vestiges of our survival instinct.

Make no mistake about it. The evolutionary imprint of instinctual greed drives the American capitalist segment of the ruling class. They are in it for their own excessive need for financial profit... gross profit, adjusted gross profit, net profit, profit, profit and more profit. And, even if they have enough money for five or ten lifetimes, their own sense of importance, self image and uncontrolled "ego" compels them to strive for still more and more as they repeat their mantra: "money is power and power is money." For the American Capitalists, the goal is money, money and more money, and the power money brings. The American capitalists have no interest in the "common good"... although, coincidentally, during good times capitalistic ventures do provide (as the economists in the Reagan administration would say) "trickle down" benefits which, in 2011, appear to be nothing more than "minimum wage" trickle down (without benefits) for those lucky enough to find a job, any job.

On the other hand, the focus of the elected politicians segment of the American "ruling class" is (or should be) squarely on the "common good." Yet, the American capitalist segment of the "ruling class," violating the prohibition "lead us not into temptation," exploit the weakness of human nature by plying our elected politicians with money, power, favors and, most importantly, with the "tacit" understanding that, if you play ball with us and our "special interests" agenda, we won't target you for defeat in the next election by contributing millions to your opponent's campaign. As Tom Udall, Democratic Senator from New Mexico, told *New Yorker* magazine reporter, Larry Doyle, in 2010:

> "People know in their hearts – they know this place is dominated by special interests. The overall bills are not nearly as bold because of the influence of money."

The power and influence of special interest money is so big that many of our elected politicians have left political office to become lobbyists, and get richer by funneling special interest money to their elected, politician friends and compatriots they left behind in the halls of government.

The obvious problem. The corruptive influence of money and favors from the "ruling class" capitalists passed on to our "ruling class" politicians bought "ruling class" capitalists what they paid for... a steady green light of **"unregulated"** capitalism – all contrary to the common good and the voice of "We the People." And, how do the "ruling class" elected politicians respond? They rationalize their compromised integrity by telling "We the People" that "markets know best" and "what's good for capitalism is good for America"... reminiscent of the "Greatest Generation's" anecdote that: "what's good for General Motors is good for America" (while, today, General Motors exits from bankruptcy hoping to survive and repay the billions the American taxpayers floated them in bailout funds).

The end result? During the first decade of the 21st century, the "ruling class" of America, with its corruptive and reckless brand of unregulated capitalism, destroyed our economy by creating a "housing bubble" of horribly inflated home values... the precursor to the Great Depression of 2008. The American "ruling class" also brought us "credit default swaps," non-transparent insurance policies, that banks and mortgage companies used as a hedge against their own reckless, subprime loans that helped fuel America's devastating "housing bubble"... the same "credit default swaps" that brought super insurer AIG (American International Group) to its knees along with the rest of us non-ruling class members of America.

Bet... The American Economy To Fail

Some of the smarter Wall Street money managers even devised a plan to win billions (not millions) by betting on the collapse of the American economy. These smarter-than-the-rest, handful of money managers developed computer models that enabled them to see the "housing bubble" on the horizon as well as its imminent collapse. They then purchased insurance policies known as "credit default swaps" for a relative pittance, and just waited for the collapse of the American economy. And, when the American economy collapsed a year or two later (as they predicted), these handful of money managers parlayed their bet against the American economy into billions (not millions) for each of them, and they rose to the ultimate position of power in a world where "money rules the world" while the rest of us non-ruling class Americans were left with the wreckage... the loss of our biggest assets: our homes and our future financial security.

Where is the criticism from the American "ruling class" for those few, opportunist Wall Streeters who used opaque and unregulated "credit default swaps" and made billions by correctly betting on the collapse of the American economy? Where is the criticism of our American Congress that stood by passively with their head in the sand doing nothing while their fellow "ruling class" members, the American capitalists, ran our economy (not theirs) into the ground? Where is the criticism for our Congress' dismissive treatment and marginalizing of warning voices like President Clinton appointee Brooksley Born? While former Vice President Cheney's daughter brands trial lawyers who dare to represent those "accused" (for emphasis, **"accused"**) of terrorism as un-American, where is her outrage (or her father Dick Cheney's outrage) for those homegrown, economic terrorists who saw the meltdown of the American economy on the horizon, and then made billions betting on the American economy to fail when the "housing bubble" burst? The Answer: There is no outrage because the Wall Street brethren are the Cheney family's comrades-in-arms in America's "ruling class."

Runaway Capitalism... Subverting Common Good

Thanks to the "green light" of unregulated capitalism that our "ruling class" capitalists bought (and paid for) from our "ruling class" politicians, and thanks to the "housing bubble" that our "ruling class" capitalists drove through that unregulated green light, the rest of us non ruling class Americans plunged into the "Great Depression" of 2008... the harshest of downturns which included: the eroding of the property tax base which virtually bankrupted state and local governments (as well as our children's educational institutions), which included the insolvency of institutional pension plans that were supposed to protect retiring Americans, which included the substantial diminishing of our IRA accounts and savings accounts that were earmarked to sustain us in our later years of life, and which included the accumulation of toxic assets on the balance sheets of the banking and mortgage capitalists... who then shut down our credit markets, the very life blood of capitalism – despite the 750 billion dollars President George W. Bush set aside in TARP funds (Troubled Asset Relief Program) to bail out the "too big to fail" banking and Wall Street financial institutions.

The "Great Depression of 2008" also brought us bankruptcies of everything from "Mom and Pop" operations to General Motors, Chrysler, their suppliers and numerous other "trickle down" insolvencies, as well as double digit unemployment. Now, middle-class, American kitchen tables are filled with anger, anxiety, depression and heartache where there used to be happiness, joy, story telling and expressions of love and compassion. Now, us non-ruling class Americans sadly salute the final benediction and death knell of our American working class – America's strength... its beloved middle class. Hyperbole? Poetic license? I wish it were so.

Ironically, the total losses to the American economy from bank robbers (such as Jessie James, John Dillinger, a working man's hero of the last Great Depression, "Pretty Boy" Floyd "the outlaw," "Baby Face" Nelson, Willie Sutton... "Your Honor, I rob 'banks' because that's where the money is," and the rest)... never put a dent in our economic engine of capitalism, but the American "ruling class" capitalists, riding our politicians' wave of unregulated - "laissez-faire" capitalism and greed, brought our economic engine of capitalism to its knees, crashing right down on top of the lives of our suffering masses. And, all that unbridled theft of American resources and all that financial ruin without accountability. The financial guru of unregulated capitalism, Alan Greenspan, apologized to a complicit American Congress because his ideological model of unregulated capitalism, "Markets Know Best" (even unregulated, "fraudulent" markets), was recklessly wrong. But, there was no accountability... no accountability, but lots of rewards for the misdeeds of the "ruling class" as we non-ruling class Americans were forced to bail out the American capitalists with billions of dollars in taxpayer money just to save our economy because, after all, the American capitalists were "too big to fail." And, now, we non-ruling class Americans face the distinct possibility of future financial failure as we try to figure out how to bail out... the "bail out" of crescendoing debt.

Isn't it ironic and isn't it self serving. The "ruling class" are "dyed-in-the-wool" capitalists when it comes to putting their ungodly profits in their own pockets, but, after they crashed the American economy, those same capitalists hypocritically became socialists asking the government to bail them out. As Public Television's well respected Bill Moyers repeated: "They capitalized their profits and socialized their losses." And, when the question of "Why"??? the economy crashed with the "Great Depression of 2008" is asked and that question shines the light of inquiry directly on the misdeeds of the "ruling class"… the "ruling class" tries to divert the hurt, anger and betrayal of the American psyche by directing the raw emotions of us non-ruling class members toward one of their own "ruling class" comrades… scapegoat and "super thief" Bernie Madoff.

Rivaling the Wall Street gang's subversion of the common good, we have the capitalists of the American health insurance industry who double our health insurance premiums every three to four years while skimming ungodly bonuses off the top of our health insurance premium dollars. Then, without a hint of shame, the health insurance industry justifies their theft of our insurance premium dollars by pointing to the Dow Jones increase in value of their insurance company stock… an increase in stock value they deviously contrived by bragging to Wall Street how little they spent of our insurance premium dollars on our health care needs. Oh, okay, I feel much better now that I know the handsome bonuses for the insurance executives are generated from not spending our insurance premium dollars on our health care needs. And, I guess, I am also comforted by the fact that when it comes to choosing between health care benefits for policy holders or their own bonuses… the insurance executives will do the right thing.

For a glaring example of how the power of special interest money subdues the common good, we need go no further than the State of Michigan where restaurant and bar industry lobbyists thwarted "smoke-free," safe environments for Michigan residents for years on the Republican's specious "all or nothing argument," even though the citizens of New York, California and numerous other states had smoke-free environments for years and decades. And, on a related issue, the American "ruling class" continues to keep the commercial stream of cigarettes and highly addictive nicotine (and slow suffocating death and heart disease) flowing to the next generation of shortened lives while, at the same time, they level the full power criminal justice against anyone who dares violate "ruling class" America's fundamental morality against smoking a non-addictive, marijuana cigarette. Let's all have Martinis with our lobbyist friends after work and celebrate the triumph of special interest money over the common good, but God save the poor sucker who lights one up for his Martini equivalent or for relief from pain because law enforcement is dedicated to chase down that "public enemy number 1."

Given the greed and the need for power encrypted on our DNA, given the weakness of human nature in the face of the corruptive influence of money and power, given the ever present lobbyist influence shifting the focus of our politicians away from the common good to special interests, given the coziness of the "one hand washes the other" mentality and the "IOU" relationships between American capitalists and the legislative and executive branches of government, and given what author, Ambrose Bierce, calls the "conducting of public affairs for private gain"… it is unrealistic to expect the executive or legislative branches of our government to keep their eye on the "common good."

The end result? Monumental decisions and broad policy pronouncements affecting the financial security of non-ruling class Americans are made by a handful of self-perpetuating politicians while "under the influence of money" from lobbyists, special interest groups and power brokers who are totally detached from the common good… a recipe for disaster that brought us the repeal of The Glass-Steagall Act (that since the Great Depression of 1929 legally protected us non-ruling class bank depositors and our bank accounts from reckless investment banks); a recipe for disaster that brought us bundling of mortgages that were exempt from the protective regulation and scrutiny of the Security and Exchange Commission and the Commodity Futures Trading Commission; a recipe for disaster that hid the danger of an unregulated capitalism on the common good; a recipe for disaster that gave a green light to financial managers to skim multimillion dollar bonuses off the top of Americans' hard-earned retirement accounts even though no value was added to those accounts and very little, if any, performance given; a recipe for disaster that gave the green light to insurance CEOs to skim multi-million dollar bonuses off the top of our health insurance premiums while, at the same time, those insurance companies fought tooth and nail to pay out as little of our insurance premium dollars as possible on our medical care; and a recipe for disaster that gave us the "Great Depression of 2008" which brought our economic engine of capitalism to its knees as our "ruling class" politicians, over and over, breached their fiduciary duty to tend to the common good of "We the People." And, all this unregulated attack on the American economy and on America's "non-ruling class" financial security while the investment bankers, brokerage houses, Wall Street, insurance industry and their lobbyists were making millions and millions of dollars in campaign contributions to our elected politicians to keep the green light of un-regulated capitalism in the "on" position, and all this while the executive and legislative branch of the government turned their backs on warning signs and voices arguing for transparency in the complex, financial maneuverings of Wall Street, investment houses, bankers and the insurance industry.

"Ruling Class" Demagogues... and the Art of Distraction

And how does the American "ruling class" respond to the overwhelming and (still) ongoing financial ruin that they have wrought on America???... They simply try to cover their tracks and hide while deceptively pointing the finger of blame at innocent non-ruling class members. Now, three years after the Great Depression of 2008, the American "ruling class" cover their tracks by engaging in the centuries-old tactic of "distraction by demagoguery"... seeking to distract America's attention away from Wall Street and the "ruling class" corruption that gave birth to the Great Depression of 2008. As we enter the year 2011, and, as our American city and State governments struggle with the loss of tax revenues and operating capital (brought on by the Great Depression of 2008 with its collapse of the economic twin towers of real estate values and employment), we are once again being distracted and manipulated by an American "ruling class" that shifts the focus of the "Great American Debate" away from themselves... through "distraction by demagoguery."

"Distraction by demagoguery" is a Machiavellian, red herring tactic that the American "ruling class" has repetitively used throughout our history in order to control the content and the message of the "Great American Debate," and shift the focus of the debate away from their own actions... like their role in causing the Great Depression of 2008. The strategy behind "distraction by demagoguery" is to create a sacrificial target, a pseudo-enemy target, out of Americans' anger, fear and anxiety, and then invite non-ruling class Americans to expend all their physical stamina, their intellectual energy and their emotional angst railing against those strategically created, pseudo-enemy targets. Think of yesterday's Hollywood "Communists" that "ruling class" Senator Joseph McCarthy so piously and so self-righteously targeted for destruction in the 1950s.

"Distraction by demagoguery" generally works because "ruling class" America is able to exploit and take advantage of the wounds they inflicted on the American psyche, like the psychological wounds they inflicted on America with the Great Depression of 2008 – wounds that run the gamut from Post Traumatic Stress Disorder on one end of the spectrum to anger, fear and anxiety in the middle of the spectrum to a general (can't quite put your finger on it) malaise of discontent and ambivalence on the other end of the spectrum... **a mood disorder** that follows us non-ruling class Americans around like a black cloud, inhibiting our joy, interfering with our family lives, our relationships and our sleep. The American "ruling class" plays that American mood disorder (they created) like a finely tuned fiddle, and capitalize on the emotional disharmony that they imprinted on the American psyche by giving us non-ruling class Americans a sacrificial, pseudo-enemy target that we can all vent our anger, fear, anxiety and hurt feelings (of betrayal) on as we distract ourselves from the real issues... the actions of the American "ruling class."

"Distraction by demagoguery" has a definite psychological allure to us non-ruling class Americans because it psychologically **justifies** our preexisting, wounded psyche (oh, that's why I'm so upset), and because it **alleviates** our black cloud, mood disorder by giving us someone to proactively go after, someone to sink our teeth into as the "Great American Debate" continues. Then, the final demagogue to urge Americans over the top of the ramparts to chase down the pseudo-enemy target, sacrificial lamb thrown up by the "ruling class"???... their "talking heads" media trumpeting "mob-mentality," emotion and easy to digest, broad sweeping sound bites... specifically designed to overshadow reason, deliberation, subtlety, nuance and the need to balance America's diverse interests.

Concrete, historical examples of past, pseudo-enemy targets created by the "ruling class" strategy of "distraction by demagoguery" include: Trial Lawyers (whose only goal is to... "rip off the system"), Juries (who always seem to make "outrageous financial awards"), Scientists (like Galileo the "Heretic" who challenged the Bible by pronouncing the sun to be the center of our universe), Teachers (who challenged God's word by promoting the heresy of "evolution" in the classroom), Catholic mackerel snappers (like John F. Kennedy who wanted to impose Papal Rule on America), Muslim hordes (who justified the Crusaders' march to the Holy Land to kill innocents in the name of "Christianity"), Jews (like the "Shylocks" who were single handedly responsible for the failure of the German economy in the 1930s), the Hollywood film industry (like the "Communists" of the 1950s that the great visionary, Senator Joseph McCarthy, exposed), Black Ns (like F.B.I. target and adherent of civil disobedience... the "uppity" Martin Luther King Jr. who needed to be taught his place), Mexican Wetbacks, Irish Micks, Italian Wops, Immigrants in general, Medicaid, Medicare, Welfare, Labor (closet Marxists who dare to attack the sacred tenets of "Capitalism"... through their ruse of "fair wages" and "safe working conditions") and a host of other so-called "trouble makers" that "ruling class" demagogues have targeted and distracted us with over the course of history.

Now, the 2011 "new kid on the block"???... today's poster boy, pseudo-enemy target brought to the "Great American Debate" by the good offices of the American "ruling class"... to purposely distract us by demagoguery???... the new, pseudo-enemy target???... **Labor** and Unions in general and "Government Employees" in particular. And, once again, the distraction by the American "ruling class" demagogues is working as intended. "Ruling class" America has now reshaped the "Great American Debate" by "sleight of hand" to purposely shift the debate away from themselves... away from their Wall Street brethren, away from the greed of Investment Bankers, away from AIG, away from the Madoffs of the world and away from other "ruling class" profiteers who brought us the Great Depression of 2008 – while, right this very moment (but removed from the scrutiny of the "Great American Debate" by "ruling class" sleight of hand)… the "same-o, same-o," insatiable Wall-Street greed continues unabated and unseen, as "ruling class" greed is again on target to set us up for the next Great Depression five to ten years down the road (if the bailout deficit doesn't get us before then).

While we non-ruling class Americans bite into the great distraction of the "ruling class" demagogues, and fill the "Great American Debate" with the so-called "abuses" of Labor, Unions and "Government Employees," the "ruling class" demagogues are (if you can believe it) voting in their "ruling class" Legislatures (with the urging of their "ruling class" governors) to launch a two front attack against "Government Employees" to: (1) eliminate the employees' right to "collective bargaining" (the inalienable, God-given right of human beings in the working class to band together in an attempt to "negotiate" and improve their lot in life, improve their hourly wages, their benefits or the safety of their working conditions) and (2) to give State appointed fiscal managers the unilateral power to nullify existing, enforceable contracts that "Government Employees" have already negotiated, signed, sealed and delivered – while, ironically, at the very same time, the States are reducing taxes on business, hoping that the new-found profits the States now hand to business with the stroke of the legislative pen will be used to create jobs, as opposed to lining the pockets of business' executives with additional, high end bonuses… not a good bet based on history.

The message the American "ruling class" sends to America???… neither the inalienable right of "collective bargaining" for workers nor the "Rule of Law" on contractual agreements restricts them from doing what they want. If the "ruling class" demagogues are able to de-stroy the "collective bargaining" rights of Labor, or, if they are able to unilaterally nullify preexisting labor agreements… **goodbye** middle class (including our soldiers who fight our country's wars, including our police and firefighters, including our teachers and including our auto workers), and... **hello** entrenched "ruling class" Monarchies and demagogues who will "lord it over" the financial security of the rest of us non-ruling class Americans. And, even if you favor today's result against government employees, because it doesn't involve you this time around, you can say **goodbye** to any protection by the "Rule of Law," and you can say **hello** to the "Rule of Men" as the American "ruling class" now "lies in wait" with firm precedent to undermine the financial well being and contract rights of all other non-ruling class Americans... the next time around. While Americans are distracted by "ruling class" demagogues who manipulate the content of the "Great American Debate" for their own self serving agenda, America's non-ruling class is being economically bludgeoned while under the influence of "distraction by demagoguery."

I am not unmindful of the financial deficits our cities and states have inherited as a result of the Great Depression of 2008 (brought to us by "ruling class" America), but what now gives that reckless, plane-wreck "ruling class" the right to force Labor to forfeit both their inalienable right to bargain collectively and their contractual rights secured by preexisting, enforceable labor agreements... just so that the "ruling class" can cover the "gambling losses" that they inflicted on the rest of us by refusing to regulate their "ruling class," Wall Street, Big Bank brethren.

I also know that abuses in any group or social program are always open for debate, criticism and correction. There are abuses in all groups, professions and social programs, but we don't lay waste to the entire group, profession or social program because there are abuses. Lobbyist corruption and special interest abuse exists this very moment in the halls of our Democracy, but we don't throw out the democratic form of government because of ongoing abuses and corruption. As the great University of Detroit Law School professor, Alan Sultan, once yelled out to his bewildered freshman class in the fall of 1966: "You don't throw the baby out with the bath water." Now, 45 years later, we are no longer bewildered. We see what's going on.

And, what's going on is that... the American "ruling class" demagogues are distracting the "Great American Debate" away from themselves and focusing it on Labor and Unions in general and "Government Employees" in particular, and throwing up those pseudo-enemy targets as distractions for angry and betrayed, non-ruling class Americans to chase down. The chase the "ruling class" strategically sets in motion works. While we non-ruling class Americans reflexively attack one another under the auspices of the "Great American Debate," we fail to notice "ruling class" America laughing all the way to the bank. While America is being distracted and seduced by the American "ruling class" with their "sleight of hand" version of the "Great American Debate," on such topics as "collective bargaining" (the only weapon middle class Labor has to fight against runaway, unregulated capitalism) and on Labor agreements (negotiated and signed as arms-length transactions), the "Rule of Law" is being systematically and unilaterally destroyed by the American "ruling class"... who will then have the absolute power of "lawlessness" to "lord it over" the financial security of the rest of us non-ruling class Americans.

America's "ruling class" is expanding the gap between the rich and the poor at an alarming rate while they coin a phrase to tell us that the loss of wages and benefits, and the ever increasing work load of the American worker is just... the "**New Reality.**" But, while America struggles with the insolvency of our national and local governments, mega corporation General Electric is reported to have earned 14.2 billion in profits in 2010, and paid no U.S. taxes (repeat, no U.S. taxes period). That's over three billion in taxes the U.S. treasury won't get... a three billion dollar short fall that we non-ruling class Americans will have to make up so that G.E. can spread that three billion around in executive bonuses… subsidized by us non-ruling class tax payers. You have to give it up for the "ruling class" of America. They certainly know how to use "socialism for the rich" while targeting American "labor" as the pseudo enemy in the "Great American Debate." As my eighth grade educated mother would tell me (stealing a line from the 1920s song: "Ain't We Got Fun")… the "New Reality" is nothing more than an Old Reality: "The rich get richer and the poor get laid off."

Last Hope… Trial Lawyers and Juries

But, we are not without hope. A sliver of hope arises out of the Bill of Rights and its constitutional ideal of "trial by jury." That hope is entrusted to the judicial branch of government and to "trial lawyers" who will challenge America's "ruling class" and demand their accountability before an American jury of "We the People"… trial lawyers like the ones in New York who are now seeking to impose equitable, constructive trusts on the ill-gotten billions that financial advisors skimmed off the top of investors' hard earned savings and retirement accounts before they (merely) sent the investors' hard earned money on down the line to the Bernie Madoffs of the American "ruling class." And, when a jury is impaneled in those gigantic financial conspiracies (or any other case in this country), that jury (or any other jury in this country) will hear all the facts and apply the law the judge gives them and render a fair and impartial verdict, uncorrupted by the money, the power or the influence of lobbyists or special interest groups because those purveyors of self-interest capitalism will not be allowed into the jury room to whisper in the ears of jurors or to ply the jurors with money or favors for the jury's vote… like they do with the executive and legislative branches of government. Nor will those purveyors of self-interest capitalism be able to "threaten jurors" (like they do to the legislative and executive branches of government) that the jurors better vote for the "ruling class" or they will not be able to sit as jurors in future cases. So, as a last resort, consistent with the American ideal of democracy, it is a "trial lawyer" working with a jury of "We the People" that is the ultimate "check and balance" to bring accountability to bear for the misdeeds of the rich, the powerful and the politically connected "ruling class" of America.

Ruling Class Attacks on Jury Trials

But, watch out and jealously guard the right to trial by jury for... if the rich, powerful and politically connected "ruling class" can do away with **or even limit** the right of trial by jury, they will be well on their way to avoiding accountability and perpetuating their position in the ranks of the "ruling class" of America forever – all to the detriment of the common good and the silent voice of the rest of us. The "ruling class" of America know they can't intimidate the trial lawyers or kill them off as a Shakespeare character suggested. The "ruling class" also know they can't directly do away with the constitutional right to trial by jury. But the "ruling class" of America is financially well positioned, and you can safely bet they will continue to do their very best to avoid accountability by jury. You can safely bet that... money is no object and the "ruling class" of America will do everything money can buy to artificially limit the voice of American juries that hold the "ruling class" accountable to "We the People."

In Michigan, the "ruling class" has waged war on the right to trial by jury, and has been very effective in doing away with, and limiting the right of juries to speak for "We the People." Think "governmental immunity"... a reprehensible legislative enactment that takes away all accountability when our Michigan citizens are killed, maimed or injured by negligently designed roadways (like intersections with four-way green lights inviting everyone to cruise through). Think Michigan's drug liability law which, unlike any other state in America, frees up drug companies from almost all accountability to Michigan citizens injured by dangerous side effects of drugs (e.g. Vioxx, Avandia, Fosamax, Celebrex, Crestor, Zyprexa – no recovery or accountability in Michigan despite their deadly effect). Think also of monetary caps in medical malpractice cases that limit accountability by limiting the amount of pain and suffering damages a patient can recover even though a jury (purposely kept in the dark about the cap) awards a higher amount that the jury thought was fair and reasonable (thanks, but no thanks, jurors, for your efforts). Think of legislative restrictions of expert witnesses to give testimony to the jury. To this day, I can't believe the Michigan Supreme Court, a co-equal branch of government, stood by impotently and allowed the legislature to invade the province of the Court's own rule making authority by telling the judicial branch of government which expert witnesses are (or are not) qualified to testify in a court of law... especially where the Michigan Supreme Court had already adopted their own qualification of expert witnesses in the "Rules of Evidence." Also, think "tort reform," in general, including the most recent effort by federal legislators to pass more tort reform as a trade off to health care reform... a great idea, at least, until it is you or your loved ones who are injured, maimed or killed by the avoidable negligence of others.

Judges On The Attack... Against Jury Trials

And, now, a further attack on the right of an American jury to hold the "ruling class" accountable to "We the People." Many judges are trading their "judicial independence" for a spot on the "ruling classes" political team. Developments over the last decade or two show that the centuries' old hallmark of the judicial branch of government, "judicial independence," is being compromised on a wholesale basis by some of our judges who, apparently, want to be in the power-broker loop of the "ruling class," or who, apparently, need the campaign contributions from special interest groups and their capitalist supporters to mount a successful run for judicial office. Think of the campaign contribution in *Caperton vs. Massey* where a CEO whose company was a defendant in a pending civil case contributed three million dollars to a judicial candidate for the West Virginia Supreme Court. With the help of his three million dollar benefactor, candidate Brent Benjamin was elected to the West Virginia Supreme Court and then (surprise of all surprises) newly elected Justice Benjamin cast the deciding, tie-breaking vote saving his (three million dollar) political benefactor from a judgment the jury had rendered against his benefactor... a practice condemned by the United States Supreme Court and by the Conference of Chief Justices representing the leadership of America's state Supreme Courts. As the Conference of Chief Justices wrote:

> "The Constitution may require the disqualification of a judge in a particular matter because of extraordinary out-of-line campaign support from a source that has a substantial stake in the proceedings."

Unbelievably, however, two "ruling class" members of the Michigan Supreme Court filed a brief with the United States Supreme Court claiming that some general "presumption of judicial integrity" should win the day, and allow Justice Benjamin to stay on the case, and save his three million dollar benefactor from a jury verdict... an opinion that fails to understand the reality of human nature (unless, of course, you look at life through the elitist prism of the "ruling class"). Thank heaven, the U.S. Supreme Court listened to the Conference of Chief Justices (rather than the Michigan Supreme Court Justices) and disqualified West Virginia Supreme Court Justice, Brent Benjamin, from saving his three million political benefactor from the jury verdict against his benefactor.

Make no mistake about it. It is glaringly obvious that the "ruling class" of America is at this very moment undermining the fundamental concept of "judicial independence" so they can further limit their own accountability under the American system of trial by jury. Think of the broadening judicial interpretations of "governmental immunity" by the Michigan Supreme Court which more and more do away with any accountability for governmental employees who carelessly and negligently kill, maim or injure our non-ruling class Americans. Think of seriously injured auto accident victims whose cases for the last six years in Michigan were taken from the jury and forever dismissed under the rule in the Kreiner case because, in the subjective opinion of the judge, the victim's admitted serious injuries that permanently impact the victim's lifestyle did not destroy enough of the victim's quality of life (now, finally, overruled by *McCormick vs. Carrier*). Think of the "open and obvious" doctrine (today's surreptitious "contributory negligence") where, again, there is no accountability because the injured victim's case is taken from the jury and forever dismissed because the easily correctable danger which injured the victim was, in the subjective opinion of a judge, "**there to be seen.**" This "there to be seen," "open and obvious" doctrine was miraculously and maliciously applied by the Michigan Supreme Court majority to a blind man (*Sidorowicz vs. Chicken Shack*, 469 Mich 912 – 2003, read and weep)... leading to the inescapable conclusion that the only thing that was "open and obvious" in the blind man's case was a complete lack of judicial vision and common sense which was trumped only by our Supreme Court's callous disregard for the welfare of our disabled citizens. The former Michigan Supreme Court Justice who authored that malicious opinion, Cliff Taylor, was quoted in *Michigan Lawyers Weekly's* March 1, 2010 edition: "I believe this court will be honored in Michigan history. It's already a significant and important court in American Jurisprudence." Really? Also, think of judges taking away civil cases (and even defenses in criminal cases) from the jury on the grounds that "no reasonable juror would find _____" (**fill in the blank**)... where judges look into a crystal ball, and, as the great German philosopher Goethe says, find what they were looking for to begin with, telling us what a jury that was never impaneled would have done with a case the jury never heard.

Finally, in an attempt to limit their own accountability, the "ruling class" of America is attempting to brainwash and poison the mind of prospective jurors long before jurors are even called to jury duty. Think of anti-trial lawyer advertising campaigns brought to you by your local Chamber of Commerce and their deceitful half true horror stories and their effective propaganda and brain washing phrase: "frivolous lawsuit"... invariably everyone else's lawsuit but yours. Obviously, all trial lawyers and all trial judges must confront this kind of pre-existing bias in jury selection by a thorough (and I repeat for emphasis, "**thorough**") "voir dire" of the jury. Any trial judge who is truly "independent" and not part of the "ruling class" of America will have the foresight and courage to allow the trial lawyers themselves to "voir dire" the jury, and gain insight into any such juror bias and pre-existing beliefs purposely injected by such special interest advertising campaigns for the purpose of biasing future jurors and limiting accountability. Trials are adversarial proceedings between competing trial lawyers, and the most adversarial aspect of any trial is to address and ferret out preconceived notions and beliefs of jurors which would interfere with an unbiased, open minded deliberation by an impartial jury.

As Clarence Darrow said in the 1925 Ossian Sweet case, tried before Judge Frank Murphy in the Recorder's Court for the City of Detroit: "I have never seen twelve jurors, who, if you could get them to understand a **human cause**, were not tried and true." But, the "ruling class" of America, in their self perpetuating attempts to increase their power and limit their own accountability, are doing everything money can buy to make sure the jury never hears the human cause or, if the jury does, they hear it with a predisposed bias in favor of the "ruling class" and against trial lawyers and their clients.

Role Of The American Trial Lawyer

We end where we began. The role of a trial lawyer in America is... ?

The answer: The role of a trial lawyer in America is to bring the "ruling class" of America before a jury of "We the People," and hold them accountable for their misdeeds. And, if you think I'm wrong, just ask yourself who would still be the Mayor of the City of Detroit, today... if it were not for trial lawyer, Michael Stefani, who exposed Mayor Kwame Kilpatrick and his City of Detroit "ruling class," "pay to play" junta. When trial lawyer, Michael Stefani, exposed the corruption in Mayor Kwame Kilpatrick's administration, he woke up the Michigan Attorney General, the State Police, the Detroit Police, the Wayne County Prosecutor's office and the Detroit newspapers... who then smelled blood and took up the chase way late in the game, finally indicting Kwame. Afterwards, Wayne County Prosecutor, Kim Worthy, called a news conference so she could pretend that she was the top-dog, J. Edgar Hoover, law enforcement officer who nailed Kwame... far from the truth. It was trial lawyer, Michael Stefani, of

DeLaSalle High School, who exposed Kwame... with the rest of the "ruling class" politicians just jumping on the publicity-for-reelection bandwagon.

As my mother said, "money rules the world." As I would say 54 years later: "a jury of 'We the People' trumps the money... unless, of course, the money and power of the 'ruling class' prevent the jury from speaking."

**Michael Stefani...
He Succeeded While
Others Slept**

AP/Getty Images

**Kwame Kilpatrick
"I told you... I didn't
have no lap dance with
that woman."**

AP/Getty Images

**"On further reflection..."
"Maybe I had just one lap dance."**

CHAPTER 18

A Kid's Improbable Journey Jesuit Guidance... And Vignettes Of Trial Lawyers

Alumnus of the Year Award
September 16, 2006

Dean Mark Gordon, Fred Lauck, President, Fr. Gerard Stockhausen SJ

Who's Here From The Hood

Father Gerard Stockhausen, S.J., President of the University of Detroit Mercy, Mark Gordon, Dean of the Law School, and Michael Costello, President of the Law School Alumni Board, thank you very much for this wonderful "Alumnus of the Year Award" from the University of Detroit Mercy Law School. There are certainly more deserving alumni, but there is no one more appreciative. This award reminds me of what my St. Scholastica Grade School classmate, Fred Saxe, once told me: "**Create an impression** and stay with that impression until the impression eventually becomes a reality."

Speaking of St. Scholastica grade school, let's do a roll call and see who's here from the first grade class of 1949.

FRANCIS "HIT MAN" DEMERS of Local 58 International Brotherhood of Electrical Workers – present and accounted for.

Frank Demers and Fred Lauck
Grade School Classmates

Frank's mother, Eileen, was a Clancy. Frank's grandmother on his father's side was an O'Reilly. Frank's uncle, Jack O'Reilly, was Chief of Police in Dearborn under Mayor Orville Hubbard, and, later, mayor of the City of Dearborn after Hubbard. Frank's cousin, John O'Reilly, is presently the mayor of the City of Dearborn. Frank's father, Frank Demers Sr., was a Detroit Police Sergeant who arrested the 1950s heartthrob crooner, Johnny Ray ("Walkin' my Baby Back Home" and "The Little White Cloud That Cried"), on a morals charge in Detroit ending the singer's career. Interestingly, my dear friend Frank married Nancy Ray, no relation... but great symmetry. God bless you Nancy for taking care of our neighborhood "humorist" for 40 years of marriage. As Frank tells me, when he arrives home each night, his greeting from Nancy is consistent: "Welcome home, Baby," or, at times: "Frank, we need to do an intervention on your raggedy ass self."

NEIL FLYNN – present and accounted for. Neil's father, Cornelius Flynn, a Detroit cop, was born in Ireland, and was a court officer for Judge Joseph Gillis of Recorder's Court... the original Judge Gillis, a 300 lb. football player for the University of Detroit in the 1920s. Like his father before him, Neil was also a Detroit cop for many years. Neil's mother, Julia Dunleavy, was born in Bohola, County Mayo, Ireland. She took no prisoners. Her family emigrated from Ireland, came to Detroit and started a long line of illustrious "Dunleavy's" Irish taverns. Neil's older brother, Jim Flynn, may he rest, was a tough trial lawyer and his younger brother, Ernie Michael... a long time U. S. Customs officer.

CHARLES UZELAC – present and accounted for. Charlie's father, Bill Uzelac, was the long-time golf pro at Plum Hollow Coun-

try Club in Southfield, Michigan where he also owned and operated the pro shop and golf cart and driving range concessions. Talk about an entrepreneur. Charlie's father moonlighted on three separate money making businesses at Plum Hollow while ostensibly working as Plum Hollow's "golf pro." Charlie's father lived into his nineties and died in December 2006. Son Charlie, my St. Scholastica classmate, spent many years in Hollywood earning a living as a "working" actor.

Charlie Uzelac
"I Ain't No Stunt Man"

Imagine that, one of the kids from the Hood had an acting career. In one of Charlie Uzelac's western movies, the director told Charlie to "drive" his horse... **WHAT?** "Okay, Charlie, 'ride,' not 'drive.' I get the distinction." Hey, I grew up at Six Mile and Southfield Road in Northwest Detroit, and I never even saw a rabbit until I was 23 years old, and I know less about horses than I do about rabbits. Anyway, the director told Charlie to stage his death by "riding" his horse up to a moving buckboard and dive headfirst into the buckboard just as the "bad guy" shot Charlie. Much to the director's chagrin, Charlie refused, telling the director to "get a stunt man for the job." An angry director shut down the shoot while whispering unflattering remarks about my man Charlie's courage and lack of daring. The next day the stunt man showed up, got his game plan from the director, responded "piece of cake," got shot, catapulted off the horse headlong into the buckboard, promptly broke his ankle and collarbone, and was taken off the shoot on a stretcher. My man Charlie was not just another pretty face. Charlie knew his limitations... even if the stunt man didn't.

PATRICK SHANKIE – present and accounted for. Patrick's mother was a Canham. His uncle, James Canham, was the former Chief

Patrick Shankie
A Dear Irishman

Judge of the Wayne County Circuit Court... a judge I prosecuted a couple of high profile criminal cases in front of in 1971. Pat Shankie was one of three Irish brothers (Jerry, the hotelier in Alpena, and Tom, the "Friendly Ford" dealer in Monroe) who attended St. Scholastica. The Shankie boys created such a ruckus in the neighborhood west of Southfield Road that the family, wanting to stay in the parish, but also wanting to avoid the dilemma of future problems with their non-understanding, non-Irish neighbors moved just east of Southfield Road, staying in the parish and, eventually, graduating from St. Scholastica. To the Shankie family's credit, none of the Shankie boys did hard time. In fact, they all ended up as success stories and generous, kind Irish souls, each journeying through life with a great sense of humor and a willingness to help out whoever is in need.

JUDGE JIMMY SHEEHY – present and accounted for. Jimmy Sheehy was known around our St. Scholastica Hood as "Cash & Carry." While the rest of us were at 9:15 a.m. Sunday mass at St. Scholastica, Jimmy was selling the "Jewish News" door to door. Jimmy Sheehy was later elected District Court Judge in Rochester, Michigan doing the impossible... unseating an entrenched incumbent judge, Mildred Vlaich. Who would have guessed that "Cash & Carry" Sheehy would have graduated from law school and become a judge? But, "Cash & Carry" you were one of the most gracious judges I ever had the honor to appear before. Thank you for the great latitude you gave me in your courtroom, especially in Skip Bunk's arson case when I asked a humorless, dour Rochester Fire Chief the Edgar Allen Poe question from the 1845 poem, *The Raven*... whether: "every separate dying ember wrought it's **ghost** upon the floor," to which the poker faced Fire Chief replied: "The house was not haunted as far as I know, Mr. Lauck."

HELEN RUTH IVORY – present and accounted for. Helen's father, John F. Ivory, a fine Irishman and a helluva an athlete, went to Catholic Central with my father in 1929. Mr. Ivory confessed to me in the early 1980s while buying me lunch at the Hunt Club in Bloomfield Hills (as he indulged a few cocktails and drew a map of his old neighborhood on a white tablecloth with a black ballpoint pen while dodging the furtive, disapproving gestures of the wait staff) that he had a crush on my mother in high school. Good taste! Jean was gorgeous. Just think, Helen, my mother willing, I could have been your brother. But, then... we never would have been holding hands on the way home from St. Scholastica in the fifth grade as we were wont to do. Helen's uncle, Bob Ivory, another Catholic Central athlete and an All American football player at the University of Detroit, played for the Detroit Lions.

MARY LEPINE – present and accounted for. Mary lived next door to Helen Ivory. Mary is my cousin from the Irish side of my fami-

ly – the McKelvys and the Monaghans from Fermanagh County, Ireland. Mary's grandmother, Kitty McKelvy, and my grandmother, Mary McKelvy, were sisters. Mary's father, John Lepine, was an outstanding musician... piano and horns. Mary's son Fred inherited the music gene. He writes music for Kid Rock and Uncle Kracker. He also performs on stage with Kid Rock at every

Fred Beauregard and
Mary Lepine Beauregard

mega concert across the United States and internationally. Mary's husband, Fred Beauregard, was a left-handed pitcher for the University of Detroit during the 1960s... their most successful baseball era.

MARY BROZEK – present and accounted for. Mary almost got me expelled from St. Scholastica in the fourth grade. I had a crush on

her, but my limited command of the language didn't allow me to verbally express my ardent feelings for her. Therefore, as a fallback to communication, I resorted to symbolism and purloined her bicycle from the playground... to get some attention, and to show that my feelings were deep and true. But, her father didn't understand. He

Mary Brozek and
Sr. Colleen Hickey

mistook the symbolism of amorous intention for "common thievery," and almost got me expelled from St. Scholastica. Or, with the benefit of hindsight from raising my two beautiful daughters, Jessie and Frances, maybe Mr. Brozek understood much more than I thought he did. But, I don't think Mary knew what the symbolic theft of her bicycle was supposed to convey.

SUSIE SPALDING – present and accounted for. Susie married Frank Brochert from St. Charles High School (on the lower east side

of Detroit). Frank died six months ago on March 8, 2006 at age sixty-three, after a long, hard and courageous battle. He was a great man, a great trial lawyer and a dear friend. I agreed to accept the "Alumnus of the Year" honor only if Frank Brochert would be a posthumous co-recipient. Frank, you were the best,

Susan Spalding Brochert and Frank Brochert

and it's only fair that you got one of the best from our Detroit Hood, Susie Spalding, as your mate.

L. BROOKS PATTERSON, Oakland County Chief Executive Officer. L. Brooks Patterson? Going once, Going twice. No response.

Absent without excuse. L. Brooks Patterson was two years ahead of my class at St. Scholastica. He was last year's "Alumnus of the Year" recipient. Hearing no response, I assume L. Brooks is missing in action despite his RSVP. No surprise there. His car probably got stuck... (again) on the railroad tracks somewhere, and he's probably in an incognito mode, surreptitiously walking back home and staying under the media radar. Don't send out any SOS. L. Brooks has survived these

L. Brooks Patterson The CEO "Walking Back Home Under the Radar"

(shall we say, missing in action, to avoid public scrutiny) moments many times in the past. He'll eventually surface.

379

ROBERT ARGENTA – present and accounted for. Bob was the youngest of three sons born to Giovanni Argenta and Amalia Marche-

The Argentas: John, Dr. Lou and Dr. Bob

sotti who came from the small village of Zebadessi in the Province of Piemonte, Italy. Eventually the Argenta family settled in St. Scholastica Parish, and raised three sons who attended St. Scholastica Grade School and Catholic Central High School with me. The oldest, John, an architect, graduated from Catholic Central High School in 1958 (three years before me) and then from the University of Detroit Architectural School in 1964 – two hundred and five architect hopefuls started and John and five others graduated six years later. The middle brother, Louis, graduated with me in 1957 from St. Scholastica and in 1961 from Catholic Central High School, and went on to become one of the world's foremost cranial-plastic surgeons, operating on infants and young children born with serious cranial and facial deformities. Doctor Lou artistically restores symmetry to the deformed faces of those unfortunate newborns. Bob Argenta, the youngest of the three Argenta brothers, graduated from the University of Detroit Dental School, and has practiced dentistry in the greater metropolitan Detroit area for decades. What success stories for first generation sons of Greatest Generation, Italian immigrant parents.

I represented the youngest son, Bob Argenta D.D.S., in the early 1980s for injuries he received in an auto accident. Bob was rear-ended and suffered an acceleration-deceleration neck injury which, although not visible or verifiable on standard x-rays, interfered with his ability to work a full forty hour week in the practice of dentistry.

We demanded the $20,000 insurance limits to settle the case. The defendants offered $5,000. So, in May, 1982... off we went to settle our $15,000 difference through "due process of law" and trial by jury with Irish-Catholic Judge, Harold Ryan, presiding.

During jury selection, one of the prospective jurors, a middle-aged woman, in civilian clothes, identified herself as a "Dominican nun" from the Adrian, Michigan order. Since the strength of Bob Argenta's case rested squarely on whether the jury believed Bob's (unverifiable) subjective complaints of pain, I wasn't going to miss a chance to tell the Dominican nun that she could trust both Bob Argenta and me because we spent eight years of education and moral mentoring under the tutelage of the Dominican nuns. My jury "voir dire" of the good nun got right to the point: "Sister... my client, Bob Argenta, and I are both products of Dominican education; we attended St. Scholastica Grade School together in the 1950s." Defense Attorney, Conrad Ceglowski, a Polish Catholic himself, immediately jumped to his feet: "I object, your honor. Mr. 'Luck' (he purposefully refused to pronounce my name correctly) is improperly currying favor with the jury." Well... so I was, but, as the great Federal Court of Appeals Judge, Learned Hand, said in a case involving a request for sexual favors: "It doesn't hurt to ask." Judge Ryan quickly jumped in to support defense attorney Ceglowski, inquisitively asking: "What's the relevance, Mr. Lauck?" The Holy Spirit hit me right between the eyes at that very moment, and I begged the very Catholic Judge Ryan's indulgence to ask one more follow-up question which I promised would show the relevance. Judge Ryan begrudgingly allowed me to follow up with: "Just one last question, Mr. Lauck, and you better tie it in."

I took advantage of that interruption to again bury my unadorned, "currying favor" stiletto into the heart of the insurance company lawyer, Conrad Ceglowski. Refocusing on the Dominican nun sitting in the jury box, I began again from the beginning: "Sister, as I was saying before I was interrupted by Mr. Ceglowski, my client Robert Argenta and I are both products of the Dominican education, having attended St. Scholastica together in the 1950s." Judge Harold Ryan and my adversary, Conrad Ceglowski, looked on with "so what?" written all over their faces. Then, I finally got to relevancy of that apparently irrelevant, "currying favor" question: "Sister, the Dominican nuns always taught Robert Argenta and me to 'offer up our pain and suffering for the poor souls in Purgatory,' who still await their heavenly reward." "But," I continued: "Judge Ryan will instruct you at the end of this case that, under our law, my St. Scholastica classmate (there it is again, Conrad), Robert Argenta, is entitled to receive **'money damages'** for his 'pain and suffering.'" "So," I continued: "the question is, Sister, can you make the transition from your world of spiritually, postponed gratification and purgatory to the law's world of present gratification of monetary damages for a couple of St. Scholastica kids… for Bob Argenta's pain and suffering?" The Irish Catholic Judge, Harold Ryan, tried to repress a smile while Conrad Ceglowski grimaced (what else could he do?).

And, off we went headlong into the "due process of law" battle for justice with the good Sister assuring me she would follow the law, but hastening to add that she "did not believe in big verdicts." For reasons unknown to me, Conrad Ceglowski didn't use a preemptory challenge to dismiss the good Sister from the jury, and the good Sister came through for us. She became the jury foreperson, and awarded Bob Argenta $340,000 in a case in which my dear insurance company adversary, Conrad Ceglowski (a rather penurious, strange looking guy to begin with), thought Bob Argenta and I should have "walked" with only $5,000. And, to think, this courtroom vignette of Robert Argenta occurred in an American courtroom 60 years after Robert Argenta's "Greatest Generation" father, Giovanni Argenta, left Zebadessi Italy in 1918... alone, a weak and hungry 12-year-old bound for Ellis Island, New York and the American Dream in the New World of unlimited possibilities.

We also have a couple of other luminaries with us tonight from the East Side Hood of Detroit. First we have St. Catherine High

Joe Henze
A Work of Art

School legend, **JOE HENZE**. Joe was an All State football player at St. Catherine's High School in 1959 and 1960. Joe and I played football at the University of Detroit in the early 1960s when our schedule included Boston College (with hot-shot quarterback and future National Football League star, Jack Concannon), University of Miami, Florida, Memphis State, Cincinnati (with future National Football League star, Brigg Owens, at quarterback), and the University of Kentucky (with future National Football League star Roger Byrd at running back, and future first round draft pick of the Cleveland Browns, Tom Hutchinson, at wide receiver). That University of Kentucky team was a national story on the cover of *Sport's Illustrated* in 1963. Kentucky's head coach, Charlie Bradshaw, a disciple of legendary Alabama coach, Paul "Bear" Bryant, believed in torturous football practices, including holding team scrimmages under a chicken wire obstacle course that hung four feet above the practice field. Coach Bradshaw systematically reduced his 80-plus scholarship football team at the University of Kentucky to 29 players, or, as *Sport's Illustrated* called the Kentucky "Wildcats" on the cover of their magazine in the fall of 1963... Kentucky's "Thin Thirty."

Joe Henze was "the man" at the University of Detroit in the early 1960s. He was a prototype of today's athlete... big, strong, agile, and he could run like the wind. Nobody we played could handle Joe. In fact, our own coaches couldn't handle Joe. He was a work of art, albeit an unbridled work of art that needed some "touch up" around the rough edges of the canvas. Joe finished his career in the Canadian Football League, then spent a career at Ford Motor as a plant foreman and superintendent, and, after retiring, became a very successful entrepreneur and developer.

We also have my court reporter, the gorgeous **BARBARA ESSIAN** and her brother, **JIMMY ESSIAN**, with us tonight. Barbara and Jimmy

Barbara Essian and Fred Lauck

are two kids out of a family of thirteen children. The Essians attended St. Martin's High School on the lower east side. Jimmy was a three-sport star athlete at St. Martin's. He turned down a football scholarship at the University of Michigan as a running back and signed with the Philadelphia Phillies baseball team. Jimmy Essian spent twelve years in the American League as a catcher for the Oakland A's and the Chicago White Sox. During a rather spirited game against the Yankees, Reggie "Muscleman" Jackson, known in baseball folklore as "Mr. October" and "the straw that stirs the drink," got hit by Jimmy Essian's pitcher. Reggie took umbrage and rushed the pitcher's mound to retaliate. Essian's job was to protect his pitcher from the always, hard charging Reggie, but Jimmy couldn't get out in front of Reggie quick enough to head him off at the pass, so Jimmy jumped on Reggie's back, and, as Jimmy says, "sixty feet, six inches later," he and Reggie arrived at the mound ("Thanks for the ride, Reggie"), and Reggie Jackson began pummeling Essian's pitcher with Jimmy Essian still on Reggie's back. Jimmy finished his career as the manager of the Chicago Cubs, but, even tonight, he looks like he is in good enough shape to catch a double header.

Another special guest we have with us this evening is **FATHER RICHARD ELMER**…Basilian priest and President of Catholic Central High School. Father Elmer came

Fr. Richard Elmer and Helen Ivory

back to Catholic Central High School in 1960… my senior year. Although he never used the actual words, Father Elmer sent me a message, loud and clear, that I had value and that I was worthwhile… one of the most emotionally helpful messages I ever received from a supportive "Greatest Generation" of parents, priests and other mentors. Father Elmer was the vision for, and the fund raising force behind, Catholic Central High School's new $30 million dollar campus in Novi… a sight to behold.

Finally we have **"MR. COOL," TONY "T" MOOTER**, my dear Catholic Central High School classmate and his gorgeous wife, Terri

Terri Mooter and Husband Tony
The "Godfather"

Tyler, from Tyler, Texas. Tony grew up in Epiphany Parish on the west side of Detroit. From those humble middle class roots, Tony became one of the most successful entrepreneurs of my generation… a corrugated box manufacturer. Who ever thought that "Mr. Cool" at the sock hops in the late 1950s and at the Gay Haven Night Club in the 1960s, commanding the dance floor with Detroit's own Motown sound, would later become such a rich, successful business man… a man whose accomplishments and success are second only to his generosity and his uncanny ability to always stay in touch with his middle class roots.

Impression Versus Reality

Again the phrase I began with: "If you create an impression over time and stick with it, that impression will eventually become a reality." You heard one impression in the introductory remarks of University of Detroit Mercy Law School Alumni President, Michael Costello: "smart," "very smart," "graduated number one in his law school class of 1969," "highest mark on the bar exam," etc. Now let me share with you the actual, not-so-charming "reality" that secretly lurks behind that created "impression." I had a very interesting, but lack-luster career for eight years at St. Scholastica with the Dominican nuns. Those nuns were as tough on me as I was on them. Although they won all the battles, I wasn't going to lay down for them. I held my ground. The nuns had to win their victories over me the old fashioned way: "they had to earn them." The nuns had to vanquish me to win… and they did. They needed to keep up with my rambunctious self or even a step ahead of me, and they did.

At St. Scholastica Grade School, education was a distant, distant second for me because I was destined for one thing only… athletics. As I once told my sixth grade math teacher: "Sister, the only math I need is 6 points for touchdown plus an extra point equals 7, plus a 3 point field goal equals 10, and throw in an occasional 2 point safety and now it's 12 points. So, Sister, my math career has ended, and I'm off to a career as a professional football player."

But, when I started the ninth grade at Catholic Central High School at Hubble and Outer Drive in Northwest Detroit in the fall of 1957, I knew I was on thin ice with new and overwhelming academic and athletic challenges. I knew if I didn't "study, study and study" some more, I would flunk out. So… after seven hours of classroom academics, I practiced football until 6:00 pm every day (or boxing, wrestling and baseball during their seasons). After practice, I was homeward bound to eat, then two to two and a half hours to study Math, Chemistry, Physics, English, Latin and Theology. And, just when everyone caught their breath before bedtime, I was off to deliver my night *Free Press* route... my mother's sports-eligibility prerequisite: "no paying job, no sports." Through the weeks, months and years, I was finally able to acquire study habits, nurtured by the Basilian priests who told me I was "okay"... a "different" version of "okay" to be sure, but a "variation" of normal... a little more supportive than the message I received from the good old Dominican nuns at St. Scholastica Grade School.

Finally, in 1960, in the spring of my junior year, all 200 of my junior-year Catholic Central classmates were told that we were going to meet with Father William Stoba, and get some "academic and aptitude test results." Since I was, academically, the number two student in my junior class, I was looking forward to sharing my academic success story with Father Stoba, and getting some compliments on my test results. As I entered Father Stoba's office, I received a kindly "Hello, Fred." Then, a moment of silence as Father Stoba peered over my academic charts and test results. Did I detect a slight look of bewilderment? Father Stoba was obviously, and, perhaps, incredulously impressed with my record of academic achievement. Father Stoba put down the test results, and glanced up with a quizzical expression: "Amazing!" I gave Father Stoba my best toothy smile for his ability to discern greatness even when camouflaged in the IQ charts and aptitude test results that lay shimmering in triumphant glory on the desk in front of him.

Father Stoba then launched in: "Fred, everyone in your Junior class of 200 young men have the academic potential to do better than they are doing if they would only apply themselves and live up to their potential, but you... you... ah... Fred, I don't know how to say this… you can't do as well as you're doing." What? What did he say? Sensing that I had just heard something negative, I asked: "What does that mean, Father?" to which Father Stoba replied: "Fred, you are the only student in your junior class of 200 students who can't do better than you're doing. In fact, Fred, I don't understand how you can do as well as you're doing." What? Sensing my evaluation was going down hill (not to mention my fragile self image that I had just spent the last three years building up from ground zero), I again pursued Father Stoba: "What's wrong with me now?"

Father Stoba reassured me that nothing was wrong with me "per se" (whatever that meant), but there was a slight hiccup with my IQ. Now, I was coming unraveled. A simple IQ Test that doesn't lie had uncovered the inadequacies that had always haunted me… inadequacies that I thought I had hidden from human view, buried and left behind long ago. Now, I was on the run again with my old companions, self doubt, humiliation and my constant shadow… "less than the rest." "What's wrong with my IQ Father?" Father Stoba replied: "Nothing is wrong with your IQ, Fred." "It's normal…… well…… it's **dull normal**." Well, that was it. It was out. It was over. I couldn't hide. I was forever intellectually defective: "dull normal." Father Stoba's words painfully echoed and reverberated in my head: "dull normal," "dull normal," "dull" and "dull." Father Stoba continued: "Fred, I just don't understand how you can do as well as you do academically with your 'dull normal' IQ." There's that word again, "dull, dull and dull."

As a kid, I would have run through a brick wall or fought a wild beast bare handed just to distance myself from the description "dull." At that moment, you could have put a stake through my heart, and ended it all right there in Father Stoba's office: "dull, dull and dull." Father Stoba summed it up: "Fred, you are a classic 'over-achiever'" – a phrase that I would spend the rest of my life coming to grips with emotionally… a phrase that carried the unmistakable message of "basically inadequate," and "certainly less than the rest." But, at that very moment, Father Stoba's message told me what I had to do in my life. I realized then, almost fifty years ago, in 1960, that I had to work twice as hard as everyone else so that I could be, perhaps, 5% better. Certainly not a good mathematical trade off, but one that I had to learn to live with if I didn't want my defective IQ to get discovered over and over again and hold me back from my dream "to be somebody." To say that Father Stoba's message bottomed me out emotionally would be a grave understatement. I felt hurt and rage for being defective, for being inadequate, and for being less than... again and again. But, at the same time, Father Stoba's message generated a lifetime (default) "game plan." If I was going to compete successfully at the highest levels, I had to make a full time commitment to overcome my defective, "dull normal" I.Q. which translated into only a single coping mechanism: "I must work twice as hard as everyone else."

Finally Father Stoba changed subjects. "Fred, what do you want to be?" "A courtroom lawyer," I replied. "Well, Fred perhaps you should rethink that idea"... a second recoiling blow driven into my psyche. My already fragile self image was in "free fall." "Why, Father?" "Because," Father Stoba replied: "your aptitude testing shows that's not such a good idea. You're really suited to be a farmer; you're not suited to be a lawyer." Here we go again, I thought. Another test that confirms I don't have the intellectual fire power or ability to fulfill my dream. Father Stoba assured me (if "assured" is the right word) that my aptitude testing was not a question of "my intellectual limitations" (thanks for reminding me, Father), but rather was a question of "my emotional limitations." "Come on," I thought to myself: "this is piling on." It's time to stand my ground and confront Father Stoba... way past time to confront him, especially because it sounds like Catholic Central is about to retroactively renege on my admission, and send me back to the nuns at St. Scholastica.

You know this story is true. I couldn't make this stuff up... and why would I even want to? "Okay, Father," I started: "How can a written test tell you I can't fulfill my dream to be a lawyer, and that I should be a farmer?" "Well, Fred," Father Stoba replied: "the aptitude testing shows that you are way too confrontational to be a lawyer." "Look, Fred," Father Stoba continued: "for example, the test asks you... 'If you see your avowed enemy across the street, do you, a. Ignore your enemy, b. Glance over and then ignore your enemy, c. Shout over at your enemy, or, d. Other and, if other, write in your response.'" "And, Fred, you checked, 'd. Other,' and wrote in that you would 'cross the street, and look your enemy right in the eye and tell him what you thought of him.'" "Well, Father," I replied, now starting to seriously confront Father Stoba: "isn't that the honest thing to do? I want my enemies to know exactly where they stand with me, or, as my Irish grandmother would say... 'You can tell the character of a man by who his enemies are'." Father Stoba replied: "Okay, Fred, I'm not saying your response is right, and I'm not saying it's wrong. I'm just saying it's too aggressive and confrontational for the studious, problem-solving, gentlemanly profession of law." "On the other hand," Father Stoba concluded: "if you were a farmer, you would be self-employed, working in the fields all by yourself so you would be in a... well, in a confrontational-free... ah... zone, and, for your sake and the sake of others, everyone would be better off." To me it sounded like I was going to be an axe murderer unless they could isolate me from society on some farm.

Be careful what you say to teenagers. My dream to become a trial lawyer could have ended right there, almost fifty years ago, in Father Stoba's office... but for the only God-given gift I ever had... "determination." In retrospect, with almost fifty additional years of life, I suspect that some milquetoast, American Bar Association, establishment lawyer in charge of "Civility in the Profession of

Law" contributed to the aptitude testing philosophy of the 1950s and 1960s. In retrospect, now with four decades experience as a trial lawyer, if push came to shove, I would put my money on some

Fred Lauck 1960
"Dull Normal
Confrontational Kid"

idealistic, confrontational kid. And, if I were in charge of setting the aptitude criteria for trial lawyers who have to take-on, and do battle with, the overwhelming power and wealth of the government, law enforcement, the insurance industry and corporate America on behalf of the downtrodden and the underdogs of society, I would check "confrontational" as a plus sign for a trial lawyer, and hope that some determined, "won't-take-no-for-an-answer," confrontational kid with great aptitude for lawyering doesn't get talked into the solitary life of farming or animal husbandry. In reality, that idealistic, confrontational kid already has the necessary potential to develop the courageous demeanor a trial lawyer needs. With work, you can always tone down a confrontational kid, and teach him the art of diplomacy, but you will never get the king's lackey to shout: "Give me liberty or give me death!" That's easy to see now with almost fifty years of hindsight. But, in 1960, in my junior year at Catholic Central, the only coping mechanism I had to battle against rejection, depression, isolation and rage was "determination" and a revolutionary refusal to accept my lot in life and a belief that I could "will myself to be what I wanted to be." If I were to fulfill my dreams, I had to use my God-given gift of "determination" to invent myself by creating the perception of a trial lawyer "for all seasons" and, hopefully, somewhere further down the pursuit of life, that "created" perception, that "willed perception" would become a reality. In the meantime, I shared my pain with no one.

Jesuit Education

University of Detroit Six Mile Campus 1964

Let's move forward to 1963. As I said, our football team at the University of Detroit was competing against Division I rivals, Miami of Florida, Boston College, Kentucky's "Thin Thirty," Memphis State, Xavier, Villanova, University of Dayton, Cincinnati, and others. There was also the academic side of life... Mathematics (my major), Chemistry and Philosophy (my minors), English, German, Aristotelian Logic, Fine Arts, Music Appreciation, and various electives vying for attention with a fall football schedule, winter workouts (boxing and wrestling the likes of Steve Stonebreaker when he was an "All Pro" linebacker for the Baltimore Colts... thank heaven I knew how to fight and he didn't), spring football practices and summer factory jobs at R.C. Mahon, Jervis B. Webb and Mavis Pop Co. for $2.00 an hour. It was overwhelming, but, with determination, I just kept plugging along, one day at a time, and kept doing what I was doing because I was supposed to, and because I intuitively knew that this rigorous path and training regimen had to lead to somewhere good that would somehow yield some future emotional reward. But, more than that, I was negotiating the obstacle course that my ninth grade educated father laid out for me – a path illuminated with only "blind trust" in my father's wisdom... a path out of the rather bleak emotional wilderness that, by chance, was my birthright.

But, things didn't always go smoothly. There was always some Father Stoba "sound alike" reminding me of what my limitations were... what I could do and what I couldn't do. Emotionally and socially, I was still struggling with my aptitude test results at Catholic Central... a flat out struggle of "determination" against "fear of failure," an exhausting struggle that whispered in my ear each day, every day: "Don't take 'no' for an answer," and "stand your ground or you will have nothing left, and they'll knock you off the edge of a flat world, and you will free fall into the vacuum of obscurity."

One day, I had a little confrontation... a "misunderstanding," shall we say, in the Student Union at the University of Detroit. The "powers that be" met... some for expulsion and some for a second chance. The "second chance" wisdom of Jesuit priests, Father Steiner (legendary University of Detroit football star of the 1920s) and Father Heutter (a gentle, Jesus-like man) prevailed... with one condition. The Student Union was "off limits." But, therein was another one of my self created dilemmas. I was a scholarship athlete, with meals provided at the Student Union which was now "off limits." And, I certainly (and literally) couldn't afford to provide my own meals, unless I quit school and went to work. Before I even knew what a "Catch 22" situation was, I was in one. Jesuit priest, Father Steiner, came to the rescue again. Twenty dollars-a-week cash in my pocket from the University of Detroit for my meals. Now, thanks to the Jesuits, I'm living large and eating like a king at "Temple's Finer Diner" on Livernois and Puritan... an endless supply of chili dogs, burgers, french fries and onion rings: "Put a little extra high fat chili on my high fat french fries, please." I was the envy of my teammates who were stuck with training table meals of tasteless nutrition, but, today, I often question whether my cholesterol problems began right then and there with my "Temple's Finer Diner" breakfast, lunch and dinner diet. As we sit here tonight, I just caught a glimpse of my old teammate, Joe Henze, with his lingering Pavlov reaction at the mere mention of the "Temple's Finer Diner" deep fried, dining experience. "Man... it don't get any better."

The point to remember, however. If it weren't for the support of those beautiful Jesuit priests, Father Steiner and Father Heutter, I wonder if I would be a lawyer today. Thank heaven I didn't live in the "zero tolerance" world of today. If I did, I wouldn't be here tonight. Thank heaven I was brought up in the living concept of forgiveness and redemption... in the Jesuit and Basilian tradition. The reality. Without forgiveness and redemption, I'm not even a lawyer... let alone, "Alumnus of the Year."

Levitating Column Of Law Books

Fast forward to 1965. In December 1965, 22 years old, I graduated from the University of Detroit with a 3.3 average with a major in Mathematics, and minors in Chemistry and Philosophy... not too bad considering the great expanse of time I devoted to NCAA football and playing hide-and-seek with the campus cops. But, that's another story of confrontational episodes for another time. After graduation, I spent six months working as a computer programmer for Ford Motor Company (rudimentary "AutoCoder" and "Cobol" with main frame computers the size of a small house... a laptop for the "Jolly Green Giant"). But, I didn't want to be a science guy. I wanted to be a lawyer... with due apologies to my aptitude test results. So, I took the LSAT (Law School Admission Test), scoring 485... a score that wouldn't even put me on the "waiting list" today for the University of Detroit Mercy Law School freshman class. Once again, the University of Detroit was there for me, gave me a shot and let me into their freshman law school class 40 years ago in 1966. I borrowed $600.00

to invest in myself... a student loan for the first semester's tuition, and I was off and running.

The Thursday before Law School started, I borrowed a car and drove over to the Law School, got my class schedule, my law books and first day assignments (homework before the first day of classes even started, what was that about?... I would soon find out I was swimming in a fast current – keep up or drown). After picking up my books and class schedule, I drove over to my father's office in the Stephenson Building in the New Center area of West Grand Boulevard and Cass Ave. I wanted to show my father the huge pile of law books I had just purchased. It was a struggle getting those law books out of the car, into the building and up to the 6th floor. The elevator was the biggest challenge. Into the elevator's closing doors I went with all my new law books piled high... **Crash!** The books ended up on the floor as the elevator started up to the 6th floor toward "Lauck Studios" – a small commercial art studio with two artists and my father as owner and a sales force of one... my "ex bookie" father now a courageous entrepreneur, a small ("legit") businessman.

My father was 50 years old at the time. His first love was the "bookie operation" he ran in the 40s and 50s, but the Federal Kefauver Committee cracked down on gambling in the mid-1950s and put him out of business... no more off track betting. I remember the lean times and anxiety that followed, but it could have been worse. He could have been in the movie industry, and he could have been blacklisted by the now thoroughly discredited fraud, Senator Joe McCarthy. Recently, I've heard a rumor that today's right wing might try to reinvent history and raise Senator McCarthy up from the scrap pile of history. A little harsh? McCarthy needlessly ruined the lives, reputations and financial well being of many until his fearless enemies were finally able to expose him for the maniacal fraud he was. And, you can bet some other yet unknown (or partially known) accusatorial demagogue is waiting in the wings as I speak tonight to take Joe McCarthy's place and grab fifteen minutes of fame.

The worst thing that happened to my father in the bookie business occurred when the Detroit cops "planted" on his operation (a small rental office with twelve phones in River Rouge, Michigan). The cops saw my father loading what they suspected were his bet slips in the front hubcap of his vehicle. Ever mindful of a possible bad "search and seizure," the cops loosened my father's hubcap, and then laid back in a surveillance mode until my father came out and drove off with the cops in quiet, undercover pursuit. The hubcap came off, and bet slips blew everywhere down Jefferson Ave. The cops pulled my father over for littering, but upped the ante to "bookmaking" after securing a few bet slips and confirming their authenticity. My father's worst nightmare… calling all his betting customers and asking them which horse they bet in which race. No surprise… most bet the winning Post, and my father's payouts to the bettors escalated. With large financial obligations to his betting customers mounting, my father could not afford to pay for legal representation by the Detroit bookies' go-to lawyer Frank ("throw yourself on the mercy of the court") McLain, a Barry Fitzgerald look-a-like (see the timeless classic movie, *The Quiet Man*, starring John Wayne, Maureen O'Hara and Barry Fitzgerald).

Without funds, without a lawyer, without an education, alone, depressed, uncertain, with financial ruin and incarceration in his future, and without any political influence (or so he thought), my father appeared before Judge Joseph Gillis, the very same 300 pounder who anchored the University of Detroit's offensive line in the 1920s, and teammate to the likes of Father Steiner (Jesuit priest who saved me and my meal ticket), Nate Goodenow Esq. (a former Alumnus of the Year), Federal Judge Thomas "Tiger" Thornton (another former

Alumnus of the Year) and Frank "Dutch" Bowler, my first football coach at St. Scholastica. In the courtroom, Judge Gillis, an imposing, menacing figure at best, took the bench with his usual greeting: "Let the perjury begin."

Court Officer Cornelius Flynn (father of my St. Scholastica classmate, Neil Flynn) called the case of *People of the State of Michigan vs. Frederick Valentine Lauck*. The cops told the very same story I have just recounted to you here, after which Judge Joseph Gillis asked my father for his side of the story. My father, humbled and intimidated by his lowly and lonely position in Judge Gillis' courtroom and without any attorney, simply told Judge Gillis that the police officer's account was true. There was dead silence in the courtroom... a dead silence that generally follows the unexpected. Then, the ever cantankerous, but fair-minded Judge Gillis, probably a betting man himself, and, apparently, moved by my father's lowly plight, asked: "Mr. Lauck, do you have a family?" to which my father responded, "Yes." Judge Gillis, looking for a hook to hang his hat on, followed up: "How many children do you have?" to which my father responded: "Three, Your Honor." Judge Gillis, still looking for that elusive hook to hang his hat on, followed up again: "Where do they go to school?" to which my Father replied: "I have a son at Catholic Central and two daughters at St. Scholastica." The good Catholic judge, Joe Gillis, in elated tone responded: "Now we've got something to work with." Judge Gillis then looked into the eye of the arresting officer, and, quietly, but, with the authority of his judicial office, pronounced: "Officer... the Defendant Mr. Lauck sounds like a working stiff to me, not a criminal... case dismissed." And, God's justice trumped man's sometimes short-sighted, temporal justice.

Back to the fall of 1966 and the visit my oversized law books and I paid to my father at his office. The Stephenson Building elevator continued upward to my father's sixth floor "Lauck Studios" office while I deftly balanced a four foot vertical column of law books (torts, property, contracts, civil procedure and criminal procedure). As the elevator stopped at the sixth floor, I made a cautious exit, and headed

toward "Lauck Studios." Unable to see because of the law books that protruded above my 6'2" frame, I used my peripheral vision to make my way along the hallway and into my father's office. As I entered, my father was confronted by a levitating column of detached law books. "It's me, Pa," I said as the law books tumbled helter-skelter onto the floor, and my father's humorous

"Lauck Studios"   smile magically appeared where the law books once floated. That moment is frozen in time. My father, with his ninth grade education, was staring at me in disbelief as he saw a year's worth of law books crashing about him, heralding the first year "baptism of fire" that lay ahead for me at the University of Detroit Law School.

That day, that moment in my father's office, is etched in my memory. That was the day. That was the moment… the moment when I fully realized that I was going to make it. That was the moment I understood that I was going to be a lawyer. That was the day that I fully realized that my dream of becoming a lawyer would come true, and that nothing was going to stop me. That was the day I knew that my future was not going to be measured or limited by some intellectual or emotional potential (or lack of it). That was the day that I fully realized that I was in the door of law school, and that, therefore, I was now in control, and my god-given gift of "determination" would see me through three years of law school… a determination that would not be denied, a determination that would be my constant companion through the three-year obstacle course of law school, and through an arduous, "coming-of-age," three-day bar exam that would, ultimately, usher me and all of my intellectual, emotional and social defects into the practice of law.

Jesuits... Honoring A Trial Lawyer... ???

Now 40 years later, who would have guessed that I would end up at this beautiful Grosse Pointe, lake-front estate of Dr. Golden with all of you. University of Detroit Mercy Law School Alumni President, Mike Costello, called me about four months ago to tell me that I had been chosen as "Alumnus of the Year." I listened to him on the telephone, and I figured it was a "setup" in progress with some kind of hoax brewing. The wheels of my mind were working overtime as I tried to rapidly figure out how to stay out front of the hoax and run with it. Finally, it started to sink in that Michael was serious, and that somehow the University of Detroit Mercy Law School had, through oversight, inadvertence or just plain bad judgment, made a colossal mistake... choosing not a judge, not a politician, not a Corporate Captain of America, but rather a "trial lawyer" as Alumnus of the Year. During our phone conversation and for days thereafter, I kept asking myself: "Why would the University of Detroit Mercy School of Law choose to honor a trial lawyer... ???"

Last year, our law school honored Oakland County Chief Executive and former Oakland County Prosecutor, L. Brooks Patterson, as Alumnus of the Year. L. Brooks, as Alumnus of the Year, made good sense. After all, L. Brooks Patterson was a well known figure, a consummate politician and a lightning rod who always seemed to find the center of the media storm that rages endlessly through the political profession. But, the only thing L. Brooks and I have in common is that we both went to St. Scholastica grade school... although he was two years ahead of me. There were also other obvious differences. Brooks lived in the Rosedale Park area of the parish. His father was a business owner, and he lived in a colonial home with the traditional three bedrooms upstairs. My father was a "bookie" with a ninth grade education, and we lived in a two bedroom bungalow with parents in one room and the kids stuffed into the other room or into the unfinished basement or the unfinished attic where you froze in the winter and sweated it out in the summer. Brooks' twin brother, Steve, became a dentist. My older brother, Marty, went to Jackson prison for fighting cops, and ended up fighting for the heavyweight championship of Jackson prison against Alvin "Blue" Lewis – who later fought Muhammad Ali in 1972 in Dublin, Ireland for the Heavyweight Championship of the World. Every time I hear the name, L. Brooks Patterson, my mind reflexively plays out an indelible image from 1952, and I see L. Brooks with an embarrassed smile on his face running through the playground at St. Scholastica in his white "fruit of the loom" underpants, chasing his older classmates who had "de-pantsed" him. I never got into that game, but L. Brooks sure seemed like he was having a grand time.

The year before last, the Alumnus of the Year Award went to Maura Corrigan, Michigan Supreme Court Justice, first appointed to the bench by the former anti-trial lawyer Governor of Michigan, John Engler. Justice Corrigan was rumored to be on President Bush's short list for a future appointment to the United States Supreme Court vacancy which gives you an insight into her judicial philosophy. The only thing that the Honorable Maura Corrigan and I have in common is that we both went to the same law school. Maura's father was a doctor. Maura's husband, former law school professor Joseph Grano (may he rest), was a good man and an excellent professor at our law school, but he spent his career railing against the wisdom of, and the lack of constitutional support for, the Miranda requirement that police warn suspects of their 5th Amendment constitutional right to remain silent. But, how did his "academic" protest serve mankind? As a fundamental issue of justice, constitutional law and human rights, I see no harm in the government advising anyone, suspects or otherwise, of their constitutional rights. For my money, an informed citizenry should be the ideal goal so why spend all your energy railing against such an innocuous rule as Miranda's requirement that citizens be informed of their constitutional rights. The memory that jumps to mind at the mention of Justice Corrigan's name is her wonderful address to the Irish Lawyers at the 2006 Dinner Dance: "As Irish, when you are troubled, we are troubled" – a supportive, generous and compassionate philosophy of wisdom that, quite frankly, I don't find in her decisions as, time after time, the government, the insurance industry and corporate America win at the expense of the little man and the forgotten woman... both of whom get bashed in the head by the Michigan Supreme Court majority appointed by anti-trial lawyer and ex-governor, John Engler.

As I say, the Alumnus of the Year Award made imminent sense when it was given to L. Brooks Patterson last year and to the Honorable Maura Corrigan the year before. But this year's choice... a trial lawyer as the University of Detroit Mercy Law School Alumnus of the Year... ? Why would the Law School choose to honor a trial lawyer? Why would this fine Jesuit Law School, soon to celebrate 100 years of continuous education of lawyers, do something so politically incorrect as to honor a trial lawyer? Don't the Jesuits know how politically incorrect it is to be a trial lawyer, let alone honor one? On the national front, our esteemed leader, George W. Bush, loathes trial lawyers, and has adopted a national agenda to rid us of trial lawyers or at least neutralize the impact of trial lawyers... although six years ago, when his election to the Presidency of the United States was in doubt in Florida, he hired a staff of trial lawyers to rescue his presidency.

But, again, why would an order of priests as sophisticated, as worldly wise and as bright as the "Jesuits" honor a trial lawyer as Alumnus of the Year? Aren't the Jesuits aware of the comments of Michigan U.S. Congressman, Dr. Joe Schwarz, in his campaign litera-ture mailed out before this year's August primary with the picture of a pig representing the image of trial lawyers:

> "Tired of greedy personal injury lawyers lined up at the court house trough feeding on outrageous settlements? Isn't it time to put these pigs on a diet? Joe Schwarz thinks so. Congressman Joe Schwarz is fighting in Washington to enact real tort reform… and make sure these personal injury lawyers stop exploiting the legal system. Call congressman Schwarz at 202-224-3121. Thank him for helping clean out the pig pen."

So there it is. Michigan citizens now have options. "Call Sam" for representation by a trial lawyer, or "Call Joe" to help him clean out a pig pen of trial lawyers. But, the point… even our Michigan politi-cians know trial lawyers don't get honored. They get put on a diet… although when the State of Michigan took on the Tobacco Industry seven or eight years ago for the billions of dollars the State was seeking from "Big Tobacco," the State didn't use their own, government-em-ployee lawyers at the Attorney General's office. They hired trial law-yers. Even then, the State of Michigan wouldn't commit State funds to pay those trial lawyers… opting instead for a one third contingency agreement. The decision was a good one for the citizens of Michigan as the trial lawyers got eight billion dollars for the State of Michigan coffers from Big Tobacco. Now Big Tobacco will have to make up their billions in losses by quickly addicting today's children to their highly addictive drug, "nicotine," guaranteed to continue the downward spi-ral of compromised lungs and hearts for the next generation, and their painful companion… a slow, suffocating death with emphysema.

As I say, after my call with Mike Costello ended, I spent days pondering why my Jesuit alma mater, the University of Detroit Law School, would do something so politically incorrect as honoring a trial lawyer. Finally the answer began to unfold. First, the Jesuits are a rather politically incorrect bunch themselves, and, perhaps, I was a politically incorrect "bird of a feather." Secondly, the more I thought about it, the more I was able to see that the philosophy and the values of the Jesuits and the trial lawyers are, indeed, "birds of a feather."

Combining a liberal arts degree in Mathematics, Chemistry and Philosophy in 1965 in undergrad school with my law school degree in 1969, I have had seven years of Jesuit education at the University of Detroit. The Jesuits that taught me and the Jesuits I came in contact with including, Father Norbert Heutter, Father Paul Harbretch and former University Presidents, Father Celestin Steiner, Father Malcolm Carron and Father Robert Mitchell stressed "love" as the basis of their theology. Same thing for the Basilian priests I had at Catholic Central High School and the Benedictine priests I had at St. Scholastica Grade School. The emphasis of these fine priests was not on the theological mysteries of the Immaculate Conception, the Holy Trinity or even the Divinity of Christ. Their emphasis was on "love," "peace" and "forgiveness"… treating others as you would have them treat you, the Sermon on the Mount, the Eight Beatitudes and "Judge Not." As former University of Detroit Mercy president Sister Maureen Faye said at the 1997 Red Mass: "We will walk first in another's shoes before we judge them."

Non Judgment…

I know that at certain times it is absolutely imperative to pass temporal judgment on others, such as jury duty or the duty of a parent to judge their children's friends. When my beautiful daughter, the dynamic Jessie Valentine, turns 16 years old, ten years from now, or when my other daughter, the captivating Frances Sandoval Lauck, turns 16 years old, twelve years from now, you can bet I'll try to make as many discriminating judgments as possible for all would-be suitors who appear at my door... even if it means being more interested in my daughters' virtue than I was their mother's.

But the point... the Jesuits taught me not to stand on some moral, high ground and pass moral judgment on others. The Jesuits taught me, as the Basilians and Benedictine priests before them did... take the burden of moral judgment off your shoulders, and leave it to God to determine who is on solid moral ground with God and who is not. Surely, you are as tired as I am to hear both the Christian fundamentalists and the Islamist extremists using their finite minds and limited intellects to read the infinite mind of God, and then take to the moral high ground, both incredulously proclaiming that: "God is on our side." At times like these, I think that the only way to world "peace" is for all human inhabitants of this world to think of themselves as "citizens of the human race" first and citizens of some patriotic parcel of land or country second, and to think of themselves as "children of the loving, bleeding-heart liberal Jesus" first and members of some organized religion second.

For me, the Jesuit lesson of "non-judgment" was driven home forty years ago on my very first day of law school in 1966... Jewish Professor, Allen Sultan, presiding. As our very first law school class was called to order, Professor Sultan boomed out to no one in particular: "What about homosexuality?" As a 23-year-old Northwest Detroiter, my immediate, knee-jerk response was: "I'll kick their ass." When the question went unanswered, Professor Sultan boomed out another rhetorical question: "What right does anybody in this class have to complain about what consenting adults do in the privacy of their own bedrooms?" That's it! I got it! I understood the point! It was nothing less than an epiphany! Professor Sultan was right. It's not for me to judge or "kick ass." It's up to God, not me, to handle the problem... if there is a problem. At that moment, I felt a great weight slide off my shoulders. For the first time in my life, I felt truly free, unencumbered and liberated by non-judgment.

Working Out My Own Philosophy

"Well," I thought: "So this is law school." Throw out all the pre-conceived notions and all the firmly held beliefs of the past and the philosophy of my parents, the philosophy of the of the Dominican nuns and Benedictine priests at St. Scholastica, the philosophy of the Basilian priests at Catholic Central, the philosophy of the Jesuits in undergrad school and the philosophy of the cracker barrel philosophers from the Hood in Northwest Detroit. Throw out everything I thought I believed in, and throw out everything I thought I held near and dear to my heart, and start all over with a fresh slate, and establish my own value system from the bottom up... a value system that will truly be mine because I'll create it out of the good, the bad and the ugly of the sum total of my past influences and future experiences. That uncertain journey toward such a new order and a new value system is exactly what my Jesuit law school offered me... a rigorous intellectual and emotional journey into the uncharted landscape of new beliefs, new perceptions, new possibilities and new philosophies. And, even if I end up right back where I started before I began, it will be my philosophy of life from the bottom up, and not someone else's philosophy that I just unthinkingly adopted out of some sense of historic or family loyalty.

The first day of law school... lesson number one in my new (yet old) value system: "Don't judge." Don't take a claimed moral, high ground, and look down in judgment on others. Leave moral judgment to God. I was free. I immediately resigned my commission in the "moral police" and terminated my membership in the "moral majority." Thank you Professor Allen Sultan. Thank you University of Detroit Jesuit Law School. Within a week, I again broke ranks with my Northwest Detroit upbringing, and I started my life-long opposition to capital punishment, and started my life-long suspicion of governments and political power bases. From the very first day of law school, I saw the University of Detroit Law School as a training ground for future trial lawyers... a training ground for lawyers with conviction who will stand up to our economic system of "run-away" capitalism where the wealthy 10% have 90% of our resources, a training ground for lawyers who will confront Corporate America and government bureaucrats, lawyers who will stand up to our elected officials in all branches of government and hold a mirror up to those in power so one and all can see if "justice" and "fair play" are winning the battle or whether corruption and injustice are undermining the Rule of Law... lawyers who will hold a mirror up to expose hypocrisies and contradictions like a century of slavery despite the Bill of Right's promise that "all men are born equal." Legal judgment directed toward balancing freedom with security for the benefit of mankind?... yes. But, moral judgment for the sake of judgment itself or superiority?... absolutely not!

For me, it seemed my new-found philosophy of no moral judgment for the sake of vague, ambiguous and subjective concepts of morality took me directly back to the Golden Rule... a rule born out of our Judeo-Christian heritage and best explained by a story from our Judeo tradition. In the story, a gentile approached Rabbi Shami, a strict interpreter of the Torah... kind of a forerunner of our present Michigan Supreme Court majority appointed by Governor Engler.

The gentile presented Rabbi Shami with a proposition: "I will stand on one leg for as long as I can, and, if you can teach me the whole of the Torah while I stand on one leg, I will convert to Judaism." Rabbi Shami picked up a stick and drove the irreverent gentile away. The gentile then came to Rabbi Hillel, a man of love, who was recognized as the kindest, gentlest and sweetest of rabbis. When Rabbi Hillel heard the gentile's proposition, he lovingly accepted the challenge, and, while the gentile stood on one leg, Rabbi Hillel started his full explanation of the entire Torah: "That which you don't want your neighbor to do to you, don't do to him; the rest of the Torah is **mere commentary.**"

Jesuits Are Spiritual Trial Lawyers

Rabbi Hillel's simple message of **what not to do** to others leads directly to the enduring message of **what we should do** for others... a message the Jesuits taught me with the parable of Jesus praising the Apostles for taking care of him in his hour of need:

> "When I was hungry, you gave me to eat.
> When I was thirsty, you gave me to drink.
> When I was an outcast and imprisoned, you visited me... ,"

After which the apostles looked at Jesus incredulously: "Are you bereft of your senses Jesus? That never happened"... to which Jesus replied those famous words: "Whatever you do for the least of these my brothers and sisters, you do for me." **That's it!** That's the **centerpiece** of my Jesuit education. And, that's exactly what Jesuits and trial lawyers have in common. Look out for the underdog, the poor, the common man, the forgotten women, the misunderstood, the downtrodden, the underrepresented, those without a voice and the rest of life's minimalists and unregistered and unwashed masses. Take up their cause with a prayer, a protest sign, a march, a rally, a donation, or with a pen, or just a kind word or gesture, and help them and emotionally or legally protect them from the oppressors whoever they may be. Represent the interests of the underdog and the downtrodden without resort to and without encouraging violence… because violence only begets the endless cycle of "more violence." And, never let "civility," or any other form of "social etiquette," silence or dilute the message of justice. And, remember… many times, those in power merely promote "civility" to advance the cause of the rich and powerful, and to silence or dilute any criticism against them. For, those in power know full well that requiring "civility" and "social etiquette" will surely silence or dilute the voices of the uneducated and the undereducated masses who are rough around the edges with their criticism because they have not learned the facetious art of sarcasm nor the diplomatic way to rail against injustice. In reality, the only form of "civility" that counts is the measure of respect that those in power give to those who have no power.

Now it all makes sense. Even if, at this narrow juncture in the history of mankind, the Jesuits and trial lawyers and their message are cast as politically incorrect, still it makes sense, good sense, not to apologize, but to stand tall in the saddle, and honor a trial lawyer as a "symbol" of Jesuit education and as a symbol of protection for those outside the "loop of power"… those unfortunate masses who endure the burning sting of unregulated capitalism, those who suffer a rending blow from the sword of raw, cold political power, those unfairly shut out by the arbitrariness of government, those bludgeoned by the over-zealousness of law enforcement, those who suffer the unreasonableness of an unmovable insurance industry, those broken economically by the greed of corporate America, or those collaterally damaged by the incessant "influence of corruption" that is brought to bear on our elected officials who are showered with financial gifts from lobbyists and special interest groups out to circumvent the common good and the general welfare of our citizens as they promote the special interest needs of their rich, powerful clientele.

Not surprisingly, it is the establishment groups of the American ruling class-elected officials and their special-interest, lobbyist friends who hate trial lawyers. Why?... because trial lawyers have the power to hold a mirror up to the institutional faces of "ruling class" America, and show the "image-in-the-mirror" to a jury who have the power of "We the People" to hold government, law enforcement, the insurance industry, corporate America, and other members of the "ruling class" of America accountable for their misdeeds and broken promises, or for the shattered lives and demoralized spirits they leave behind as collateral damage and wreckage on their "ruling-class" march to "Progress."

Colin Michael Bryce and Jesuit Social Justice

That's exactly what the Jesuits and their shining star trial lawyer and law professor, Colin Michael Bryce, do at the University

of Detroit Mercy School of Law as they train each new generation of trial lawyers through their "Urban Law" clinics for the poor, for the elderly, for immigrants, and, most recently, their "Project Salute"... an outreach of legal and emotional support for our soldiers coming back from our wars and police

Debra Sandoval-Lauck, Fred Lauck and Professor Michael Bryce

actions across the globe with broken bodies, battered psyches, and spirits overwhelmed with Post Traumatic Stress Disorder.

Vignettes Of Trial Lawyers

Many of the trial lawyers that I have chosen to symbolically represent (as "Alumnus of the Year") are with us tonight. Let me share with you their "triumphs of justice" on behalf of their underdog clients.

LES MARTENS... THE D.J. MAN

First there is Les Martens. Les grew up in Northwest Detroit and went to Redford High School. His family had no money for a  college education so Les was left to figure that detail out for himself. And, figure it out he did, working in the radio business to put himself through Wayne State. While working his way through college, Les met Casey Kasem, of "Top Forty" radio fame. Both Casey and Les dreamed of becoming, and later became, radio voices and broadcasters. Les loves to tell the story of Casey Kasem's father, who came from Lebanon in the Middle East and landed in South America. Casey's father was an itinerant peddler who peddled his wares from South America into Central America, then into Mexico and, finally, into the United States where he eventually opened up his own small grocery market in the Cass Corridor section of Detroit within the shadow of the Wayne State University campus. Casey Kasem's father spoke three languages fluently by the time he landed in Detroit... Arabic, Spanish and English, but he couldn't read or write any language. As Les likes to say: "Old man Kasem was illiterate in three languages."

Les Martens

In the mid 1960s, Les left a successful radio broadcasting career and entered law school, graduating in 1969... the same year I graduated from law school. Shortly thereafter, in the mid 1970s, Les sued "National Lead" to secure pension benefits that National Lead had promised their employees decades before when those employees first hired on, as National Lead began operations in Grand Rapids, Michigan. Then, almost thirty years later, just as those long-term employees started to reach retirement age, National Lead pulled the rug out from underneath them, closed the doors of their business in Grand Rapids, Michigan, moved their entire operation to Ohio, and opened their doors in Toledo... business as usual, but telling their long-time Grand Rapids employees there would be no pensions as promised because none of the employees hit the 30-year vesting mark. After a 13 week marathon trial, Les prevailed and those Grand Rapids employees were paid their promised retirement pensions and benefits.

Two years ago, Les and I obtained an 8.1 million dollar jury verdict in the Oakland County Circuit Court for a journeyman electrician who lost the quality of his life in a construction accident because of the combined negligence of defendants Etkin Skanska, Baker Concrete and Whaley Steel... an accident that could have, and should have, been avoided. Also, recently, Les and I represented a University of Detroit Mercy baseball-scholarship athlete who was shot and injured by a Dearborn, Michigan coward during a verbal altercation in downtown Windsor just across from the Windsor Tunnel. Although the Dearborn assailant was acquitted by a judge in a criminal court in Windsor (don't ask me how), Les and I got a judgment in excess of $350,000 against the Dearborn coward in Wayne County Circuit Court, and, whether we ever collect it or not, the point was made... "words never justify violence." Hooray for the trial lawyers, and hooray for one of the best of them... Les Martens.

DUANE ICE... THE ICE MAN

Next there's Les Marten's law partner, Duane Ice, a tough, "take-no-prisoners," labor lawyer. Duane was a linebacker at Homer High School in Homer, Michigan. He still has that linebacker mentality, and it still serves him well today. I call Duane… "Ice Man" or "Cool Hand Luke." In 2004, I represented Duane's law firm in a three week

trial involving two tough, crusty veteran labor lawyers who claimed they were forced out of the law firm they started ("Miller Cohen") by Duane Ice and the other six upstart, ingrate lawyers I was representing. At trial, the two older lawyers were represented by three separate law firms which included Michigan's number one "Super Lawyer," trial lawyer of the year for two years running. Many storied, local labor leaders testified on behalf of the two older lawyers,

Duane Ice
The "Ice Man"

Harry Lester
United Steel Workers

including the feisty Harry Lester of the United Steel Workers Union who arm wrestled with me over whether he would have to answer my "stupid" questions, and including Flo Walker of the American Federation of State, County and Municipal Employees (AFSCME), and including the likeable, but somewhat confused, Noel Mullet, head of the International Brotherhood of Electrical Workers Local 58, headquartered on Porter Street next to Most Holy Trinity Catholic Church in "Corktown"… the almost 200 year old Irish neighborhood of Detroit.

After a three week "slug fest," the jury began deliberations. The jury deliberated for two days as they considered the older lawyers', Bruce Miller's and Norbert Cohen's, claim for a "four million" dollar verdict against my seven lawyer clients. On day two of the jury's deliberations, the two older lawyers made an offer to walk away from their four million dollar claim if Duane Ice and the other lawyers I was representing would walk away from their million dollar counter-claim. Without batting an eye, my client Duane, "Cool Hand Luke," "The Iceman," took a pass, leaving the case with the jury. Duane then suggested we all have breakfast while the jury continued to deliberate. I had no appetite for breakfast, nor did the rest of the lawyers I represented... hey, we're talking about four million dollars that would have to be paid out of my clients' pockets that was riding on the jury's deliberations. But, Duane "The Ice Man" had just turned down a "You go your way and we'll go our way" settlement offer, opting instead for (as Mick Jagger of the Rolling Stones says): "Tumblin', Tumblin' Dice."

Duane Ice and the rest of my lawyer clients and I went down to the cafeteria in the basement of the Oakland County Courthouse. I stirred a cup of tasteless coffee, and Duane, looking relaxed and peaceful as if he didn't have a care in the world, ordered a full breakfast of bacon and eggs, potatoes, toast, coffee and orange juice. He looked so calm and comfortable... like he was on vacation at some seaside resort getting ready for a day at the beach. As Duane indulged himself with his "one star" cafeteria breakfast, his partners looked on nervously... mostly in silence. Our breakfast (or rather Duane Ice's breakfast) was interrupted by the bailiff who came to the cafeteria to announce that the jury had a verdict. But, Duane wouldn't be rushed as he savored the last morsels of his "one star" cafeteria breakfast. Finally, Duane finished his breakfast, and up to the courtroom we struggled, all of us weary from the ordeal of a three-week trial and from the apprehension of suspended judgment with four million hanging in the balance... what's going to happen to us? The jury marched into the court room, and announced their verdict. The two senior partners, who wanted four million for (as they claimed) being thrown out of their own law firm by my seven young, ingrate clients... got nothing. My clients, Duane Ice and his six law partners, were awarded 1.2 million dollars on our counterclaim. That's my man, "Cool Hand Luke," "The Iceman." Turn down a "walk-away" settlement offer, roll the dice on four million, eat a "Cool Hand Luke," "Iceman," "one star" breakfast, pick up 1.2 million dollars from the jury after which Duane gives the rest of us one of those "of course" looks.

Duane has spent his time as a labor lawyer vigilantly representing the rights of workers. Recently Duane sued three corporations in three different states, including Whitehead and Kales in the State of Michigan, seeking retirement insurance benefits. When the smoke cleared, Duane and the retirees prevailed, and Duane recovered 20 million dollars in benefits for those retirees. Hooray for the trial lawyers, and hooray for "Cool Hand Luke," Duane the "Ice Man" Ice.

STUART ISRAEL

Next there's Stuart Israel, law partner of Les Martens and Duane Ice… another one of my clients in the case I just mentioned. Stuart

graduated from Mumford High School near Curtis and Wyoming in northwest Detroit, taught law school at the University of Michigan and the University of Hawaii, and later joined the Miller Cohen law firm as a labor lawyer. Two months ago, Stuart won a major case against ArvinMeritor requiring ArvinMeritor to live up to their past promise to pay their former employees retirement health insurance benefits.

Stuart Israel

As a result of Stuart's hard work and brilliant representation in that case, 2,900 retirees and numerous widows will now receive the retirement benefits that ArvinMeritor promised them year in and year out while they were working. Hooray for the trial lawyers, and hooray for Stuart Israel.

TOM O'BRIEN AND MICHAEL MORAN

Next there are my University of Detroit Law School classmates... Tom O'Brien and Michael Moran. Michael Moran is the only University of Detroit Mercy Law School graduate ever to land a position as a research clerk in the United States Supreme Court. In the early 1970s, Michael was a law clerk for Justice William Brennan, the diminutive man with the very large heart, affectionately known as "The Great Liberal." Tom O'Brien came by law naturally. His father was a lawyer and judge in the Ann Arbor area, and was one of Ann Arbor's most respected and most loved citizens. When Tom O'Brien and Michael Moran were just barely out of law school, and before they were even 30 years old, they defended Philippino nurses who were charged with the murders of eleven patients at the V.A. Hospital in Ann Arbor... patients who all mysteriously died of respiratory failure around the same time. The trial was national daily news, week in and week out. But, after the trial ended, and, after post trial motions were resolved, and, after the national hysteria ran its course, the cases against the nurses were dismissed. The nurses were freed, and they returned to their families. Hooray for the trial lawyers, and hooray for the young, courageous lions, Tom O'Brien and Michael Moran. I'm proud to have you as classmates from the University of Detroit Law School class of 1969.

Judge Darlene and Tom O'Brien   Michael Moran

RICHARD RASHID... AND A 17 OUNCE POUND

Next there's Richard Rashid... three sport, star athlete at Lansing Resurrection High School who attended University of Detroit

Richard R. Rashid...
Trial Lawyer
Extraordinare

undergraduate school on a baseball scholarship as a free-swinging, left-handed hitting outfielder playing under University of Detroit's legendary baseball coach Bob Miller (a phenom from Redford St. Mary's High School and for the University of Detroit before jumping to the big leagues and becoming one of the Philadelphia Phillies "whiz kids" in the 1950s). Rick Rashid's University of Detroit Titans baseball team of 1965 went further in the NCAA College World Series tournament than any other U of D team in history.

Rick's father, George Rashid, played football for U of D in the late 1930s. He was as good a player as there was. After he tore up his knee, he returned to Lansing and opened a grocery store, and later a bowling alley. Mr. Rashid once told his son Rick: "whenever you weigh out a pound for a customer, don't weigh out an exact 16 ounce pound; weigh out 17 ounces so you are above reproach" ...a lesson well learned for all of us and all future generations, courtesy of Mr. George Rashid, a staunch member of the Greatest Generation.

After Rick Rashid was accepted into the University of Detroit law school in the fall of 1967, his father gathered up every ball point pen he could find, put a rubber band around them, and gave them to his son Rick telling him: "I think you have to write a lot in law school so you'll need these pens"... an act of kindness, love and support from the simplicity-of-heart of one of the Greatest Generation. Rick's father died unexpectedly a week later, and a broken hearted freshman law student had to learn the art of concentration while suffering through the grave depression of the recent, totally unexpected, loss of his father and hero. But, Rick had the legacy his father gave him... a 17 ounce pound, a fistful of pens, and a determination that wouldn't allow Rick to quit. Rick buried his father in the fall of 1967, and tenaciously continued his overwhelming work load in law school in the face of an overwhelming sadness... but with a rich legacy and a compassionate heart

Rick parlayed that rich legacy and compassionate heart into great success as a trial lawyer in Lansing, Michigan. Fresh out of law school in 1970, Rick tried his first civil case ever against big, bad John Collins... the Defense Bar's highly respected and experienced, go-to guy on important, high visibility cases. Rick's truck driver client who hauled material out of a General Motors Plant on a daily basis was accused of stealing from GM, and, even after he was cleared, the GM employees would taunt him as he left the GM Plant: "What are you stealing today?" Embarrassed and humiliated, the truck driver sought legal assistance, but other trial lawyers turned down his case, one after another, until he finally arrived at Rick Rashid's door. In 1971, Rick sued GM for "libel and slander." GM was insured through Royal Globe Insurance Company. Royal Globe retained the John Collins law firm... for the first time ever. The Collins law firm obviously wanted to impress Royal Globe Insurance Company to win them over and keep them as a good source of future business. To do so, Super Lawyer, John Collins, had to publicly beat up the "new-kid-on-the-block lawyer," young Rick Rashid, and Rick's truck driver client. The trial pitted a seasoned, veteran trial lawyer, John Collins, against the upstart, no experience, left handed hitting, local kid, Richard Rashid. John Collins told kid Rashid he had the following option: "take $500 and call it a day, or try the case in the court and get his ass kicked."

Well... you don't threaten a left-handed hitter without it back-firing on you because left-handers' brains are wired differently. Rick, as his non-lawyer father taught him, accepted John Collins' insurmountable challenge, and tried the case against superstar John Collins and surprise... Rick Rashid got a well deserved $30,000 jury verdict for his truck driver client... in 1971 when you could live on $10,000 a year. Right before he retired, the trial judge, at the request of the Defendant GM's attorney, John Collins, took away Rashid's $30,000 jury verdict, and dismissed the case permanently. A few weeks later, attorney John Collins was the master of ceremonies at the judge's retirement party.

But, no one can take away the significant verdict of justice that first time trial lawyer, Richard Rashid, obtained against GM and John Collins. Just recently, Rick Rashid took on another powerful group, the Christian Right Pentecostals, in their own back yard in Charlotte, Michigan, and got a $350,000 plus judgment against a church and a pastor who, in an unchristian-like manner, defamed a church member for being in league with the devil... a verdict that was taken away by the Court of Appeals, but later reinstated by the Supreme Court of Michigan in 2010. Hooray for the trial lawyers, and hooray for the fearless Rick Rashid. He'll give you his father's 17 ounce pound of justice every time.

IRISH JOHN CONLON, ESQUIRE...
WITH BRAMBLES MIKEEN AND JUDGE "TIGER" THORNTON

Next there's my classmate, John Conlon, who started at the University of Detroit Law School with me in 1966. John's father was from Kiltamagh, County Mayo, Knock Parrish on the west coast of Ireland where the soil doesn't yield crops, and where you literally cut chunks of the soil out of the ground and burn it like wood in your fireplace... "County Mayo peat" to warm the cockles of your Irish heart. I wandered about County Mayo, Ireland with John Conlon in 1984 and met his aunts and uncles, and inhaled the sweet fragrance of peat dug up from the earth and burned in the fireplaces of the Irish cottages.

What a pleasure it was visiting with and listening to retired school teacher, Nel Currie, recite poems in "Irish" (Gaelic). Nel's

Irish John Conlon and Kathy Mattison

husband, Brambles Mikeen, was a vagabond, carouser and a hard drinker, and, obviously, a difficult person to count on as a spouse. Brambles had died a few years before John and I arrived in Ireland. The Irishmen from County Mayo referred to Brambles Mikeen as "Brambles the Bog Runner"... a drunk who howls at the moon as he wends his precarious way home over the County Mayo bog-like moonscape, trying to keep his stumbling gait from unceremoniously dumping his unsteady ass into the bog. Despite Brambles Mikeen's underachievement in life, his memory still garnered a facade of respect among the "old timers." Every time someone mentioned the late Brambles Mikeen in conversation at his widow Nel's cottage, someone would instantly pontificate what a great man Brambles Mikeen was, which then evoked an Irish chorus "Tis," "Tis," "Tis," "Tis," and more "Tis-es" following in unison. Given that "Brambles Mikeen the Bog Runner" was no longer among the living, my sense of timing, past tense and logic told me the response should have been "Twas" not "Tis." But, who am I to argue the contradiction of Brambles Mikeen's past and present reputation, or how to express his past tense existence in the present tense "Tis"... especially where I'm only a one quarter Irishman, descending from the Monaghans who emigrated from Fermanagh County, Ireland to Montreal, Canada in the mid 1800s with their descendants thereafter crossing by boat over the Detroit River ("nickel immigrants") seeking shelter in Thunder Bay in Alpena, Michigan, with Catherine Monaghan eventually marrying my great grandfather John McKelvy.

John Conlon's father, Jim Conlon, emigrated from County Mayo, Ireland, and ended up in New York City where he owned and operated various saloons including the infamous "Blarney Rose Saloon" in Manhattan. John's father raised his children in a bar setting without a mother, and, given that bit of history, it's no surprise that John and his brother Tom and I had a confrontation on the very first day of law school in late August of 1966 in the law school's parking lot. I suspect very strongly that John Conlon, like me, also flunked his aptitude test for becoming a lawyer. So, there we were, on our first day of law school, settling disputes through application of the "law of the jungle" in the law school parking lot... just as we were about to learn in the first semester of law school that we were involved in an "affray" – the legal term for our more colloquial and colorful phrases: "throwing down," "a beef," "getting it on," "let's dance," "let's gin" or "throwing hands." We also learned later on that our parking lot confrontation could not be characterized as an "assault and battery" because "mutual consent" to the "affray" precludes the criminal connotation "assault and battery." "Mutual consent" to an "affray" is colorfully captured in the colloquial Irish question: "Is this a private fight or can anybody get in?"

Six years later, at age 29, John asked me to represent him on an "affray" he was having with the United States Army who wanted to extend his tour of duty by two years. When John balked, the United States Army started court martial proceedings against John, issuing an executive order telling John that he had to appear at some military tribunal hearing to be held pursuant to the United States Military Code of Justice beginning promptly at 0800 hours (which I later found out was eight o'clock in the morning). John told me the formal Court Martial proceeding was generated by some adamant, confrontational army official who was throwing his weight around... some guy who obviously flunked his emotional aptitude test also. John suggested that I take up his case against the United States Army in Federal Court. As John explained it, we would "secure" a Federal Court order shutting down the U.S. Army's proposed 0800 hours Court Martial Hearing. John Conlon reminded me of comedian Jackie Gleason's bus driver character, Ralph Cramden, who was great on grandiose plans, but short on the details needed to implement the plan. So, with a lingering question of how two confrontational misfits were going to stop the United States Army juggernaut of JAG (Judge Advocate Corps) officers serving the most powerful country in the world, we began drafting pleadings to obtain a restraining order against the army.

John and I and our secretary, Rita, worked all weekend. John and I filed our pleadings on Monday morning in the United States District Court for the Eastern District of Michigan, located in downtown Detroit. On the blind draw docket system, our case was assigned to the greatly respected and revered federal judge, Thomas Thornton, nicknamed "Tiger" Thornton for his tenacious prowess on the football field in the Boston area and at the University of Detroit for an additional three years while he was attending law school at the University of Detroit.

As I waited for an audience with the great Judge, Thomas "Tiger" Thornton, to present John Conlon's legal pleadings, I knew that I was going to meet a very special person... a legend who I suspect had also flunked his aptitude test on confrontation. Finally, with some trepidation, John and I were ushered into Judge Thornton's spacious and elegant chambers, our petition and temporary restraining order in hand. I introduced John and myself to the solid featured Judge, "Tiger" Thornton, and shook his huge, meaty hand, knowing that I was talking to a legend. My Detroit instincts and my transparency took over as I told Judge "Tiger" Thornton that I knew who he was.

I told Judge Thornton that my first football coach at St. Scholastica was the judge's teammate on the University of Detroit football team, Frank Bowler. I told Judge Thornton that I was a scholarship athlete for the University of Detroit's football team in the early 1960s. We talked about U of D's tough Division 1, NCAA schedule including the Boston College team from his home town. Judge Thornton and I had a great and memorable conversation.

Judge Thornton finally asked what business John and I had before his court. You never get a second chance to make a first impression so I put my best "vouch-for-your-client" foot forward. I explained to Judge Thornton that the U.S. Army was attempting to put a black mark on the budding legal career of my friend, fellow Irishman, fellow University of Detroit Law School classmate and fellow lawyer, John Conlon. Judge Thornton signed the temporary restraining order halting the Army's court martial, and he ordered the United States Army to appear before him and explain why their court martial should not be permanently enjoined. Talk about the awesome, raw power of United States Judges. They are appointed for life, and they hold the power of civilian control over the military... the power to stop the Army of the most powerful country in the world, dead in their tracks. I enjoyed calling the army's court martial tribunal, and telling them that their 0800 hours hearing was off, and Judge "Tiger" Thornton's 0900 hours hearing the next morning was on in the Federal Court for the Eastern District of Michigan, Southern Division... Judge Thomas "Tiger" Thornton presiding. The Army threw in the towel, and John Conlon was honorably discharged, and went on to a great legal career. If you are ever in a litigation fistfight, you can count on John Conlon. He is fearless and articulate. Hooray for Judge "Tiger" Thornton, and hooray for the trial lawyers who flunked their aptitude test on confrontational temperament such as the fearless John Conlon.

THE LAVANS... IRISH REVOLUTIONARIES

Next there is Brian Lavan, University of Detroit Law School Class of 1965. Brian's father, Martin Lavan, came from the same hometown as John Conlon's father, Kiltamagh, County Mayo, but St. Anne's Parish. Brian's father, Martin Lavan, had a personality as fiery as his flaming red hair and as fiery as his relationship with British soldiers who put a price on the head of IRA soldiers like Martin Lavan, Michael Collins, Daniel Sheehy (also a New York Bar owner near Hell's Kitchen), Johnny Rutherford and others. Martin Lavan entered the United States at Ellis Island in 1922, black shoe polish on his flaming red hair and a price on his head back home in County Mayo, Ireland. He identified himself to Ellis Island custom officials as Michael Joseph Muldarig. He got through the Gateway to America, eventually graduated from law school, and began practicing law in Brighton Michigan.

In 1968, *Time Magazine* listed Martin Lavan of Brighton, Michigan, as one of the most "prominent lawyers" in the United States. I had the pleasure of meeting Martin Lavan at a donut shop in Brighton

Irish Revolutionary Martin Lavan and Daughter Mary Elizabeth

in 1971 when I was 28 years old and he was in his seventies. He had a shock of silver hair and wild eyebrows that riveted your attention to his handsome Irish face... a face that ultimately begged the question: "who is this guy and how bad is he?" He noted me with a suspicion born of ages of unfair treatment by the English against the Irish, and born of a natural suspicion of relationships in general... a suspicion and a detachment that was kept alive by the tragic death of his beloved 9-year-old daughter, Mary Elizabeth Lavan, on Valentine's Day 1944.

For me, Martin Lavan was a legendary trial lawyer whose court room performances I had heard about from many others... the same man who knocked down the parking meters in front of his "Lavan" building on Grand River Avenue in downtown Brighton, Michigan with a sledge hammer as city workers were putting them up. I'll bet "even money" that Martin Lavan never had to live with that "too confrontational" label John Conlon and I had to live with throughout our careers, but only because in his hometown of Kiltamagh, Ireland there were no aptitude tests and everyone was a "farmer"... at least by day, and I leave the rest to your imagination. To Martin Lavan, I was just another guy in life... no more, no less. But, Martin Lavan didn't have another year of life to get to know me. The next time I saw this wonderful Irishman, he was all dressed up to go, his last remains neatly attired, reposing in his coffin at the Keehnan Funeral Home in Brighton Michigan. Our lives touched, but just barely, and just enough to tell me I wanted to be a fearless trial lawyer and a force to be reckoned with just like Martin Lavan.

Martin Lavan's brother, Sean Lavan, was a two-time Olympian for the Irish Free State and a medal winner in the 400 meter race in the 1924 and 1928 Olympics. Martin Lavan's son, Sean, inherited uncle Sean's blinding Olympic speed. Sean (the younger) regularly lit it up for Brighton High School on the gridiron. On one such occasion in 1958, Sean (the younger) ran a kick-off back 102 yards, and, as the tumult of the crowd hit its crescendoing peak, Sean kept running through the end zone, right up to the stands, punctuating his touchdown run by handing off the football to his wildly cheering father, Martin Lavan. "Go Brighton!" "Go Irish!" "Go Sean, the Olympian!" and "Go Sean" the Brighton High School tailback with the blinding speed! And long live the tumultuous memory of trial lawyer Martin Lavan from Kiltamagh, County Mayo, Ireland!

Martin's oldest son, Brian Lavan, who is with us tonight, is no slouch, but he was no speed merchant on the gridiron either. Brian

Brian "Wild Man" Lavan ...or is this a Kennedy?

did, however, inherit his father's trial ability and the Irish art of storytelling. Brian was a wild man in his day, but there was no IRA, no English to fight and nothing left to plunder on the open seas so Brian limited his battles to the court-room, and to that general dysfunction that goes hand in hand with the loss of inhibition that surfaces when an Irishman is "under the influ-ence" of the "curse of the Irish." During one such uninhibited moment in the summer of 1972, Brian was driving my 29-year-old self and his 36-year-old self back from Ann Arbor where we had just spent five to six hours toasting the Irish, saluting other patrons and telling our rambunctious stories. The proprietor threw us out at closing time, and there was nothing left to do so we headed back to Brighton. We were traveling northbound on Hamburg Road in Brian's supersized '98 Olds somewhere near the Charles Howell Boy Scout Camp. Since I was never a Boy Scout, Brian was at the wheel, and I was taking a short nap in the passenger seat...

**The Big Crash
Woe Is Me**

when, apparently, Brian took his own short nap. No one can say for sure what happened because I was asleep, and Brian has no recall. What we do know for sure is that Brian's vehicle left the roadway like a rocket, veered eastbound, and crashed into a dense thicket of woods. I awoke (before the era of seatbelts) as my head bounced off the inside of the roof, then off the passenger window, and then right off Brian's head as he was just awaking from his nap. In my dream-like state, I felt like I was in a rodeo, riding a non-stop Brahma bull. Before it was over, Brian hit every tree in that dense thicket, but, thankfully, he sideswiped all of them so we lived to crawl out the windows of his totaled vehicle and tell the story.

We left the steaming hulk of what used to be a car, and walked away from a mystical silhouette of the headlights, fog and radiator vapor. We headed back toward the empty roadway. As we walked in silence, I kept checking my teeth. "How ironic," I thought. My father, with great financial sacrifice, had an orthodontist, Dr. Martinek, put braces on my teeth which I dutifully wore for five years. But, now what did my teeth look like? I was fixated on my teeth. Did I look like a jack-o-lantern? But, hallelujah!... Good news! I found my teeth in their customary sockets. Hooray!... Brian didn't knock my teeth out.

Finally, when we got to the roadway, I confronted Brian: "What just happened, my man?" to which Brian replied without missing a beat: "As Jack Frost said, we took the 'road less traveled'." And so we did, in more ways than one. Brian and I walked and walked, and, finally, a car stopped and gave us a ride to Brian's house where I crashed on Brian's couch, and Brian snuggled up to his wife. I wonder what her thoughts were. As for me, I didn't have any profound thoughts or profound emotions one way or the other. It was just another "day in the life of... " – the usual dysfunction that surrounded me since I could first remember. Although others seem to see these types of incidents and my life as dramatic or perhaps even traumatic, all I knew was that "life was tough," and one hard day just kept evolving and revolving into the next difficult day. As I drifted off to sleep on Brian's couch, my last thought was: "Okay, so today Brian Lavan tried to knock my teeth out by crashing us headlong into the scary darkness of the forest primeval, but I'm still alive. So what's next on the agenda? Tomorrow will tell."

And, quickly tomorrow came. For it seemed like I just laid down and it was already tomorrow, and we were off to the next agenda. As I awoke the morning-after on Brian Lavan's couch, sore and stiff, I saw Brian run through the house in his Reginald Van Gleason III bathrobe down to his ankles, pick the phone up, and call a cab. "Where are we going, Brian?," I asked. "What's the plan, my man?" Brian said that he was "taking a cab to the car dealership to get a new ride." I asked what he was going to do with last night's ride, to which Brian replied: "that car's done, so I'm just going to leave it where it is... probably make a good home for a family of raccoons, and I may claim a charitable deduction for the homeless." I always knew that Brian was a generous guy, but I think I learned more about the psychological phenomenon of "denial" at that very moment than at any time in my entire life. I also learned that very night that I was not cut out to be a drinker. My personality was naturally a little more effervescent and rambunctious than anyone I knew. All alcohol added to my life was an extra layer of dysfunction, a hangover and a loss of energy.

Shortly after that car-crash night, I ran into Brian Lavan in a courtroom in Ann Arbor. Brian was cross examining a witness, and admonishing the witness that he had better tell the truth, or he would face the pain of mortal sin... kind of like theology's counterpart to the law's "perjury." Although witnesses probably have some vague, understated fear of a temporal indictment for perjury, I don't think witnesses have too much concern for some possible, future, spiritual judgment of a mortal sin. Perjury is a "now" thing with consequences for the present, but mortal sin is only about "future" consequences based on the scientifically unprovable assumption that our spirit has somewhere to go after our bodies check out from our earthly home.

JOHN BRENNAN

A close friend of Brian Lavan is attorney John Brennan... a consummate trial lawyer. John Brennan once worked as a letter carrier for my Irish godfather, Jimmy Gribbin, in the Brightmoor Post

Office near Five Mile and Lahser in Detroit. At the same time, John was also going to law school and supporting (then) three children.

My godfather, Jim Gribbin, told me that John Brennan was taking home the post office's reject, wooden boxes for furniture, and using those boxes to construct a dinner table for his family. Through sheer tenacity, John got through law school, passed the bar exam, left the post office, and, with great direction and emotional support from his mentor, Martin Lavan, started his own practice of law in Brighton, Michigan.

John Brennan

Years after my godfather Jim Gribbin retired and lost track of John Brennan, I picked Jim up in my heaterless car on the coldest day of the year in January of 1972 to journey to Brighton, and reacquaint him with his former letter carrier employee… now "trial lawyer extraordinaire," John Brennan, who was then defending Brian Lavan in the Livingston County Circuit Court in front of Judge Paul Mahinski (the judge who swore me in to the state bar on December

Irish Jimmy Gribbin

2, 1969). I'm not saying what Brian was on trial for, but it was not for crashing his '98 Olds and me into the forest primeval on northbound Hamburg Road. Brian was simply on trial for one of those inadvertent failures to pay attention to the details of life… details that an Irishman sometimes is prone to forget or to overlook. In short, it was a political prosecution by long time Michigan Attorney General Frank Kelly's office… another University of Detroit Law School Alumnus of the Year. As Brian Lavan says, it was one of those: "we got the target of the prosecution, Brian Lavan; now let's figure out the crime."

Since I was only sworn in as a lawyer two years before Brian's trial, I was still trying to figure out how to effectively try a case, communicate to the jury and become a "trial lawyer for all seasons." That very cold Saturday in the Livingston County Circuit Court, I saw what I aspired to be… a trial lawyer extraordinaire like John Brennan. John's emotional intensity was the same as mine, but he was experienced and skillful, and he knew how to carry himself in the public eye without upsetting or alarming anyone while, at the same time, still being himself… being true to who he was. John Brennan had a magnetic force, a fearless and confrontational intensity and a "killer instinct" that was slightly subdued beneath a thin layer of tepid "civility." John's natural demeanor was his biggest asset, and it sent an important message to the jury that John Brennan was not putting on an act, and he wasn't fooling around. John was just being his own intense self, and, therefore, the jury could trust him as he showed his true disdain for the charges brought against Brian Lavan and for those who even dared to bring such trumped-up ("exalting form over substance") charges.

By partially subduing his intense emotion beneath a thin layer of civility, John was doing naturally what the great "method actors" of my time… James Dean, Montgomery Clift, Henry Fonda and Marlon Brando did in their careers, and what Josh Brolin (*No Country For Old Men*) does today… partially subdue their own intense emotion, thereby creating an unmistakable "turmoil" and palpable "vulnerability" in the eye of the observer. It is that turmoil and vulnerability that are so compelling, and that create an "energy field" that moves the observer (juror or movie goer) to fully vent the emotion for the vulnerable person in turmoil by taking up their cause to protect them and to take away their turmoil… kind of like the energy field of emotion that compels all of us to take up the fight for an underdog who doesn't know how to protect himself. It's also the same energy that urges jurors to release the pent-up emotions of "quiet desperation" from a lifetime of following orders from the "man"... the "man" who represents the unyielding bureaucracy of officialdom that plagues all our lives.

John Brennan's natural, intense demeanor was the magnet that kept the jurors energized with their eyes riveted on him. John's natural demeanor invited the jurors to partake in his intensity, and give it a full, robust life in the jurors' own emotional lives. John Brennan was the center of that courtroom on that extremely cold January day in 1972 as he exhibited his natural, no-holds-barred courage in standing up to the cops and standing up to the government... a courage that the jurors both admired and trusted. There was no guile. There were no tricks. There was no facetiousness. There were no trial tactics. There was just John Brennan's intensity, his vulnerability, and the subdued turmoil the jury saw in him... a righteous turmoil that was seeking to strike down the injustice of the over-zealous prosecution of Brian Lavan.

It was no contest. John Brennan was killing the prosecution's case and killing Assistant Attorney General, Ed Bladen, who looked like a school yard bully trying to find somebody he could pick on or beat up in the courtroom, anybody... but it was not to be on John Brennan's watch. It was John Brennan and Brian Lavan in control of the court room, and no one from the big, bad Attorney General Frank Kelly's office had a chance.

In an unorthodox move, pushing the edge of the envelope (before that expression became popular), John Brennan called Milford District Court Judge, Martin Boyle, to testify to Brian Lavan's innocence. Judge Boyle was a good looking, no nonsense, yet home-spun guy with a great intellect. He grew up on a farm in Milford, Michigan. He had a tenacious, if not pugnacious, demeanor. He backed down to no one. Judge Boyle hit a home run for Brian Lavan on direct examination by John Brennan. Then assistant attorney general Ed Bladen cross-examined Judge Boyle, smugly asking: "Isn't it true, Your Honor, that ignorance of the law is no defense?" Judge Boyle deftly turned that question around and stuck it in Ed Bladen's heart by responding: "If ignorance of the law proves no criminal intent, then there is no crime." The final result... it was Brennan and Lavan in a runaway, and the Assistant Attorney General, Ed Bladen, had the dubious distinction of going back and telling Attorney General Frank Kelly how he blew the political persecution of Brian Lavan because John Brennan out-lawyered the Attorney General's office by a mile.

What an enduring lesson in lawyering I learned as a 29-year-old young lawyer on that coldest day of January 1972. I contemplated that lesson as Jim Gribbin and I drove home from the courtroom in Brighton to northwest Detroit in my heaterless, ice cube of a car... our vaporized breath condensing on the windows and forming ice on the inside of the windows which I dutifully scraped off every mile. Our only source of heat that freezing cold day was the vigorous post mortem we engaged in as we relived the day's trial and John Brennan's starring, courtroom performance in that trial. Our conversation was so rich that we were able to forget... for the moment... that we were freezing!

The lesson I learned from John Brennan that day... it's alright to be your own emotional, intense and confrontational self in front of the jury, and bring your own true philosophy and commitment to the jurors. Transparency and a partially subdued intensity will win the day, all day, every day, so long as it is presented in a professional, courageous and committed manner. Isn't it strange how life graciously passes on its lessons and its gifts... from Ireland and Martin Lavan and Jim Gribbin to John Brennan and Brian Lavan and then onto me. Hooray for Martin Lavan, the Irish warrior. Hooray for his son, Brian "Lights Out" Lavan. Hooray for his son, Sean "Lights On" Lavan, the breakaway tailback with blinding, elusive speed. Hooray for Jim Gribbin, the very compassionate and humble post office civil servant, and Hooray for John Brennan, the fearless, courtroom gladiator. Thank all of you for your friendship, and thank you for the message that it's okay to be myself. It will not only be enough, it will be more than enough.

"THE CHIEF"... BOB MITCHELL

Next there is trial lawyer, Robert Mitchell. Bob Mitchell grew up in the coal mining town of Youngstown, Ohio. Bob left Youngstown,

The "Chief"
Bob Mitchell
One Skillful Trial Lawyer

and moved to the Detroit area where he ended up as a mortician, bar owner and later... a trial lawyer. I have tried three major criminal trials with Bob Mitchell as co-counsel, including the much publicized jail murder case in the mid 1970s in Recorder's Court. According to the autopsy in that case, the deceased, a 19-year-old inmate of the Wayne County jail, died of a blood clot in the subdural region of the brain. But, the medical issue for the jury was whether the seepage of blood from a dura mater artery into the 19-year-old inmate's brain (which later formed the fatal blood clot) was caused by an anomaly, a ruptured blood vessel that began before he was jailed... or whether it was caused by the defendant's roughhousing in the Wayne County jail. Obviously, a preexisting seepage of blood in the young inmate's brain would have been a complete defense because the young man's fate would have been sealed before he was even locked up in the Wayne County Jail. In an unorthodox move, Bob Mitchell and I called Judge Lawrence Silverman to the stand to testify that the deceased was exhibiting abnormal mental behavior, consistent with an ongoing bleeding on the brain, at the very time that Judge Silverman arraigned the deceased and remanded him to the Wayne County jail where he later died, allegedly at the hands of our clients. It was a wild case in terms of medical causation, and it was enlightening watching Bob Mitchell weave difficult medical concepts into his usual colorful, vernacular presentation.

I have never seen a lawyer who could instantly (and I mean instantly) size up a prospective juror's preexisting beliefs like Bob Mitchell could. Bob had a wide and varied range of experience in life. He was a student of human nature. During jury selection, Bob would disarm a prospective juror with his natural charm, and, after a few short questions, he would smoke out a juror's preconceived notions thereby uncovering a juror's bias and prejudice... all the while the juror, still smiling at Bob's charm, didn't realize, until Bob dumped 'em from the jury panel, that they had just been undressed and their preexisting prejudices uncovered for the world to see.

Watching Bob Mitchell "voir dire" a jury was like watching someone deftly open up an unsuspecting juror's emotional closet with an invisible sword. Bob could tell you in short order whether a particular juror was good or bad for the defense, or good or bad for the prosecution. As I said, Bob Mitchell had an uncanny insight into human nature. However, all these years later, I suspect that what Bob Mitchell was doing all along during jury selection was the same thing that the great Michigan personal injury trial lawyer (and my former client and friend) Albert Lopatin, did... see if he and the prospective juror had the same prism through which they viewed life. As Albert Lopatin once told me: "Fred, you don't need a psychologist to pick a jury; if you like a juror, they'll like you too, so go with 'em, and, if you don't like a juror, that juror won't like you either, so dump 'em." Both Bob Mitchell and Albert Lopatin intuitively knew that, if a juror liked you and you liked them, you were probably both looking at life through the same or closely similar prism so you and the juror were both standing on the first base of mutual respect and understanding from the get-go, and the door was then open to persuade the juror, during the course of the trial, to travel around the base paths to home.

Of the cases that Bob Mitchell and I tried together as co-counsel, the most memorable was the Dewayne McKenzie case we tried in front of Judge John Shamo in Detroit Recorder's Court in 1985. Dewayne McKenzie's father was a hopeless alcoholic who lived with life's misfits in downtown Detroit's Skid Row known as "Cass Corridor." The alcoholic father stayed at the Claridge Arms Apartments at 459 Henry Street in the shadow of Cass Tech High School, just south of the Wayne State University campus. The Claridge Arms was managed by Nel Sweet who later became a dear friend and client. One warm summer night in 1984, Dewayne McKenzie's 55-year-old father and the father's live-in girl friend were drinking, and holding their social hour on the porch steps of the Claridge Arms Apartments (what else was there to do?). Mr. McKenzie ended up in a dispute with another resident, Fred Baker, a local 30-year-old pimp, over some real or imaginary issue of little or no consequence. Fred Baker attacked Mr. McKenzie and unmercifully smashed Mr. McKenzie's face into the concrete steps of the porch, leaving Mr. McKenzie a bloody pulp.

When Mr. McKenzie's 28-year-old son, Dewayne, heard about the incident, his intense guilt for not being able to protect his father and his rage for the beating his drunk and defenseless 55-year-old father absorbed from pimp Fred Baker put Dewayne into emotional overdrive. Dewayne armed himself with a .22 caliber pistol, loaded a blank in the chamber, loaded additional live rounds behind the blank, left his wife and children in Taylor, Michigan, and journeyed to the Cass Corridor to find and confront Fred Baker (what else was there to do?). Dewayne went to his father's Claridge Arms apartment while his father was still in the hospital. Dewayne met up with his father's live-in girlfriend, and got further details of his father's beating. During this highly emotional, dysfunctional conversation (if you could call it a conversation), the girl friend was drinking heavily and toting a rifle around the apartment room when the rifle (you guessed it) accidentally discharged, scaring the hell out of everyone. All the while, Dewayne was waiting patiently for hours at the Claridge Arms Apartments for pimp Fred Baker to show up. Finally, tired of waiting, Dewayne left through the front door foyer of the Claridge Arms Apartments, and, as luck would have it, Fred Baker was just entering the foyer with a bagful of groceries in one arm and one of his working ladies in tow on his other arm.

Dewayne, trapped between two sets of foyer doors and shocked that his intended target was now staring at him "face to face," hyperventilated as he pulled out his .22 caliber pistol. Baker, with a keen sense of "street mentality," sized up what was going down in an instant, threw the bag of groceries at Dewayne, turned on his heel, and bolted out of the apartment building. Dewayne first fired the blank in the chamber, and, with the sonic boom of that blank echoing through the foyer, Baker fled down the steps, hit Henry Street, and sprinted eastbound toward Cass Ave. Dwayne fired a live round at the rapidly disappearing Fred Baker, and, as luck would have it (depending on whether you're the hunter or the hunted), that live round struck Baker in the mid-back, at mid block as he crossed Henry Street. Baker continued running across and down Henry Street. He got halfway to Cass Ave. before he collapsed on the "mean streets" of Detroit's Cass Corridor.

Dewayne sprinted to his car, and made his get-away, escaping westbound on Henry, driving the wrong way on a one-way street. Baker was rushed to the hospital, and he survived only to die of unrelated cancer a couple years later. Dewayne, an avenger posse of

435

one, was later arrested and charged with assault with intent to murder. The father's girlfriend (who had nothing to do with the plan or the shooting) was also charged as an accomplice. Dewayne's cousin, who was asleep at the time in the Yorba Linda Hotel five miles away, woke up just in time to also get charged as an accomplice.

Comical Fred ("I ain't got time for small talk cuz I'm on the way to get a big retainer") Persons represented the innocent cousin who didn't have a clue what happened or why. "The Chief," Bob Mitchell, represented Mr. McKenzie's innocent, live-in girlfriend who also didn't have a clue what happened, but who, drunk as usual, was just sitting around her apartment practicing-shooting live rounds from her rifle into the walls of her apartment, hoping in some vague, indiscernible way that she would get a chance to plug pimp Baker. It was those shots by the girlfriend in her apartment that led to the multiple defendants theory. Hey, I couldn't make this up.

I was retained by Dewayne McKenzie's family with whom I shared somewhat of a "Baker-got-what-he-deserved" philosophy. Judge Shamo's clerk swore in a colorful Damon Runyan, "Cast of Cass Corridor Characters" whom my own Father would instantly label as "a forlorn, moon-for-the-misbegotten bunch who were gypped by their genes." One such witness was "Fat Fred" Glendenning. "Fat Freddie," who was walking his dog directly across the street as the shooting went down saw nothing and heard nothing, prompting Judge Shamo to ask him if he had an "alibi" for not being where he was. Obviously, "hearing no evil and seeing no evil" was the ticket to survival on the "mean streets" of Detroit's "Cass Corridor." The "Russian Roulette," random violence of the streets was dangerous enough. You didn't need any extra enemies gunning for you.

There was also "Crazy Albert," on furlough from the state mental institution, who was on the outside pay phone at mid-block, north of the scene on Cass Avenue and physically unable to see the scene of the shooting, but who swore up and down and sideways that he saw the entire shooting episode… even seeing Dewayne's sleeping and innocent cousin firing a gun. As Crazy Albert acknowledged to no one in particular: "It was great to be of assistance, and to be in the thick of the action, and to be important for a change." Sixty-year-old Nel Sweet, the manager of the Claridge Arms Apartments, brought some semblance of order to this Cass Corridor "chaos of characters" as she prowled the hallway of the court during the trial barking orders to various, misfit witnesses just to keep them from going off on one another. Nel Sweet was strong, but also as sweet as her name. I miss you, Nel. And, I miss our dinners at Carl's Chop House and our Tiger ball games… me in my early forties and you in your sixties, and everyone at the Claridge Arms Apartments thinking you had taken on a younger lover. My lips are sealed, Nel, but my heart is heavy because you left on the midnight train… to who knows where.

Six months before the McKenzie trial, I was in England with John Conlon at a joint seminar for American Trial Lawyers and English Barristers. Talk about smooth, erudite use of language. I saw an English Barrister defend an alleged rapist at the "Old Bailey" in London. The defense was "consensual" sex. When the barrister cross examined the alleged rape victim (prosecutrix), he suggested consensual sex, asking the question: "Madam, let me suggest to you that you extended to my client, shall we say, the maximum in cordiality on a voluntary basis." Wow, did I love that phrasing and that use of the language!… sexual intercourse: "the maximum in cordiality." The English Barrister was on the mark with that "maximum cordiality."

I brought that erudite phrasing all the way across the Atlantic from London's "Old Bailey" to Detroit Recorder's Court, and used it to cross examine the hooker that was on Fred Baker's arm at the time Baker was shot. I attacked her credibility by showing that her profession was that of prostitution. Using my best barrister-inspired phrasing to a "T," I opened with the question: "Madam, let me suggest to you that yours is, shall we say, the oldest profession known to mankind," to which she instantly responded: "No… yours is; lawyers have been screwing people a lot longer than hookers have." There you have it. I think her history is incorrect, but I went down for the count just the same. Even my dear friend and co-counsel, Bob Mitchell, was stifling a laugh until he saw my face, and then he couldn't hold it in any longer. *Touché!* Round one to the witness. And, somewhere in my embarrassment and my uncertainty on how to follow up with my next question, I heard the refrain from my mother's voice and the logic of her eighth grade education: "Don't you ever forget where you came from." That minor embarrassing setback did not alter the outcome of the trial. The judge knew that Baker needed to be put down and that my client, Dewayne McKenzie, was the man for the job. "Not Guilty" all the way around and substantial justice, Detroit style, accommodated the just desserts of everyone. Hooray for trial lawyers, and hooray for one of the best of them… my dear, colorful, "larger than life" friend, Bob Mitchell… who, now in his eighties, is still using his courtroom magic to pick juries and try criminal cases.

A Jury Of… "We The People"

Don't tell me about the McDonald's coffee cup case or those other half-true horror stories that the insurance industry of America likes to drag out to bias would-be jurors through "brainwashing" media campaigns. The trial lawyers I have just introduced to you and their stories are typical of what trial lawyers across the Metropolitan Detroit area, across the State of Michigan and across America do to balance the scales of justice against the awesome power and the infinite resources of the establishment of Corporate America, the Insurance Industry, the Government and Law Enforcement.

And what makes this great "balancing of power" act work? What enables trial lawyers to balance the scales of justice against such an almighty, wealthy, and all powerful "establishment?" The answer in a phrase... **"trial by jury."** And why?... because juries have the ultimate power to hold the rich, famous and powerful accountable for their misdeeds. And therein lies the reason why the "establishment" has a vested interest in doing away with or limiting trial by jury. If the establishment can successfully limit "trial by jury," the establishment of Corporate America, the Insurance Industry, Law Enforcement and the Government will be able to dodge the bullet of their own accountability, and thereby perpetuate their own power, their own wealth and their own control over us with no end in sight. Doing away with or limiting "trial by jury" would give the rich and powerful the god-like attributes of everlasting, infinite control over our universe and our lives without any way for the common man or the forgotten woman to derail the juggernaut of injustice.

Please allow me to explain what I have just said. Trial by jury is democracy in its purest form. The executive branch of government governs by representation. We elect our president, our governor and our mayor, and they exercise the executive power of government as our representatives. The legislative branch of government also governs by representation. We elect our legislators to the Senate, the House of Representatives or the City Council, and they exercise the legislative power of government by passing laws and ordinances as our representatives. "We the People" have a vote in the general election to elect our representatives in the executive and legislative branches of government, but we have no direct participation in the executive or legislative branches of government.

The judicial branch of government, however, is different. In the judicial branch of government, "We the People" participate directly in the judicial process when we are called as jurors to referee disputes between our citizens... civil disputes between our fellow citizens, as well as criminal accusations by the government against our fellow citizens. This direct participation by "We the People" as citizen jurors is the purest form of democracy in the world. And, the beauty of a citizens' jury of "We the People" is that the jury **is not paid** for their vote or hustled or pressured by lobbyists and special interest groups who would offer money and favors to decide a case a certain way. Both the executive and the legislative branches of government are tied into a "good old boys" network with its "culture of corruption" where we tolerate large contributions of money and favors to our elected executive leaders and to our elected legislators by special interest groups and lobbyists who don't give a damn about the common good. In contrast, a citizens' jury of "We the People" sit in judicial judgment without their vote being influenced by lobbyist money or favors, and without their heads being turned by special interest groups whispering in their ears during deliberations. There is absolutely no arguing with the proposition that trial by a citizens' jury of "We the People" is the purest form of uncorrupted democracy in the world.

You cannot over estimate the importance of a citizens' jury of "We the People" in our American society... a society dominated by the economic system of "capitalism." The American citizens' jury of "We the People" is the democratic check and balance against capitalism's accumulation of wealth and political power in the hands of the few... because a citizens' jury has the power to hold everyone accountable, even the rich, famous and powerful... as well as the power to protect those on the lowest rung on the social and economic ladder by insuring no one is set up by our government for political purposes or convicted on insufficient evidence.

In a capitalistic society, ten percent of the people have ninety percent of the wealth while the other ninety percent must share the remaining ten percent. Wealth influences elections in numerous ways.

Therefore, even with elections... in a democratic, capitalistic country like ours, a number far far less than ten percent control the political power. If you doubt that simple fact, just consider for the moment that the economy of America, year in and year out, is created and recreated, balanced and rebalanced by a handful of wealthy people and corporations who use lobbyists to spread their enormous wealth around among our elected representatives to insure that the self serving, "laissez-faire" interests of the American capitalists trump the common good. And consider also that America's reputation worldwide, with our troops tied up for years in Iraq and still pinned down in Afghanistan, was created by the decisions of only a handful of people... some elected, some not. The inescapable conclusion is that, in a capitalistic society like ours where wealth and power are concentrated in the hands of the few, (the "ruling class" of America)... it is absolutely essential that citizens' juries of "We the People," untainted and uncontrolled by the wealthy, the powerful, the special interest groups and their lobbyists, be allowed to function as a check and balance to hold everyone accountable... even (or maybe especially) the wealthy, the powerful and those in political control of our lives. There is no room for doubt or equivocation. In an economic system like capitalism, where a very small minority controls the destiny of the masses, it is impossible to overestimate the value of a citizens' jury of "We the People" to hold everyone accountable, especially the wealthy, the powerful and those politically and economically in control of our destinies as well as to protect the lesser lights of society who may have been wrongfully accused.

Slay The Dragon

The great Lebanese poet Khalil Gibran said that "every dragon gives birth to a St. George who will slay the dragon." Hopefully the

University of Detroit Mercy Law School will give birth to many Jesuit trained, St. George "trial lawyers" who will slay the dragon of injustice and fight the good fight for social justice by preserving our "We the People" right to jury trial. Dean Gordon and Father Stockhausen, if and when you build your brand new law school, complete with new brick and mortar and with the latest in classroom innovation and technology, hopefully, you will continue to infuse the new law school with that low tech Jesuit philosophy of the ages... moral non-judgment, acceptance and inclusion of others and a resounding spirit that jointly echoes the words of a "bleeding heart" Jesus and the mantra of trial lawyers: "When I was hungry... " And, hopefully, those new trial lawyers will fight a pitched battle to preserve our right to a trial by a jury of "We the People."

Although some might accuse me of looking at life through too grandiose a prism, I think fellow alumnus and fellow trial lawyer Rick Rashid of Lansing got it right when he said:

**An Improbable Journey for a
"Dull Normal... "
"Confrontational Kid"**

God sends his Archangels
Down to earth
To battle evil.
Not just his Angels
But his Archangels,
His chief celestial attendants,
His warriors positioned against evil,
Taking on human form
To wage their relentless battle in
this universe.

We are not necessarily Archangels
... but we might be.
We may not be Archangels
... but we could be.
And even if we are not Archangels
... Someday we might be.

CHAPTER 19

Lady Scholastica…
Happy 75th Birthday

St. Scholastica Grade School
Southfield and Outer Drive

From 1928 to 2003... For 75 years, St. Scholastica Grade School educated the youth of the parish at the corner of Southfield and Outer Drive in Detroit, Michigan. Therefore, it was high time to acknowledge 75 years of longevity, dedication, stability, discipline and unwavering focus... all begun 75 years ago by the "Greatest Generation." Happy Birthday, Lady Scholastica!

What a grand celebration. A diamond jubilee mass on October 26, 2003 led by Cardinal Adam Maida. An altar filled with Benedictine Monks, including our own vibrant 90-year-old pastor and spiritual leader, Father Livius Paoli, and including various Bishops in attendance as well as an outstanding choral group directed by the indispensable Betty Rosevear... "This Little Light of Mine, I'm Going to Let it Shine." Wonderful African rhythms and harmonies from the recently arrived Nigerian nuns bearing the offertory gifts. A full church with new parishioners as well as old familiar faces... all of us celebrating at St. Scholastica Church under the auspicious shadow of St. Scholastica grade school, Benedictine high school and the Citadel fortress of the old and venerable Sisters of Mercy, "Mercy College" just across the street. It was an endless parade of nations as now grown-old sons and daughters of Greatest Generation, immigrant parents again sang out old, familiar hymns in joyful reunion and celebration.

Among the early immigrant parishioners, Italians seem to outnumber the others, but the Irish, Poles, French and Germans were well represented. Many of my classmates from the early 1950s were first generation Americans coming from households that struggled with the vagaries of the English language and with supporting families in the new world. The story of the DiBella family is typical. Joseph DiBella from Sicily found beautiful Aquila "Lena" Butera from Calabria, Italy at a party of Italian immigrants in the Detroit area in the early 1940s. Those Italian immigrants, with the same emotional makeup and curiosity as natural born citizens, quickly took to the

exciting American game, "Spin the Bottle." And, as one fateful spin would have it that evening, one side of the bottle pointed to handsome, vibrant Joseph DiBella and the other side to gorgeous Lena Butera, and, out of the cosmic energy from that innocent first encounter, came marriage and

Lena Butera and Joseph DiBella
The Energy of Attraction

the conception of three children: Grace, born in 1942, John born in 1943, and

namesake Joe, born in 1947. Soon afterwards, the DiBellas were raising three children, and living in a single room, sleeping on cots in the back of a grocery store that Mr. DiBella owned and operated at the northwest corner of Biltmore and Mc-Nichols (Six Mile Rd.) in Northwest Detroit.

Just down from the DiBellas lived an Irish family, the McEvoys, who lived in a home that the big bad wolf could have blown down in one puff, but wolves don't mess with the Irish. Cornelius Flynn Sr. from (near) Shannon, Ireland lived a few blocks west on Fenmore. Mr. Flynn supported

The Energy of Conception
Grace, Mrs. DiBella, John and Joe

his family on the modest salary of a Detroit cop… until he died early in 1957. His wife, Julia, from Bohola, County Mayo, Ireland near the rugged, yet gorgeous, west coast of Ireland was one of County Mayo's Dunleavys… famous self-franchisors of the many Dunleavy Taverns in the Detroit area. Near the Flynns lived the Morans whose oldest son, Al, played big league shortstop for those "Amazin'" New York Mets under the legendary Casey Stengel in the late 1960s, and,

445

close by, Johnny "Magoo" McLaughlin and my first grade classmate Bob Green… aka Father Mike, pastor of St. Scholastica, and, now, head of the Benedictine order in the United States. My cousin Mary Lepine lived on Archdale – her grandmother, Kitty McKelvy, and my grandmother, Mary McKelvy… sisters. Next door to Mary lived the Ivory's, across the street, the Pophams, and down the street, the Bostwicks, the Olympic bicyclist, Billy Freund, and Bob Burns who married my younger sister, Jeannie Valentine, and fathered my niece, Patricia Burns, who, in turn, gave birth to my great nephew, Austin Outwater. Nearby lived Jim, John, Marilyn and Michael Schenden whose 80-year-old parents sang and danced at the 75th anniversary.

West of Southfield, on my side of the neighborhood, the Stein-tragers lived on Stahelin with an unobstructed five block view to St. Scholastica School (until the post World War II building boom built up houses everywhere), and nearby them Abbott Leo Cornelli's family and the Hannons, Amos, Valentis, Lewis, Argentas, Saxes, Rosses, Cerittos, Krolls, the Williams with eight boys and the Demers… Detroit Police Sgt. Frank Demers and Eileen Clancy Demers, with their family of four. Ray and Anna Oehler, two original sweethearts, and their four children lived on Greenview, a block south of Knudsen's Bakery and Dempsy's Barbershop.

My family, led by a strong willed, revolutionary, Irish-French mother and a part American Indian "bookie" father, lived in a two bedroom bungalow home on the main drag, Curtis Avenue, with four kids… sometimes three depending on whether my brother, "Michigan Marty," was on vacation in Jackson, Michigan at his temporary, Cooper Street lock-up. Nearby lived the Shankies, Frank Stella, the renown parish and City of Detroit leader, the Bennetts, the Kayes, Neatons, Smiths, Kennys, Bowlers, Gramlichs (Dorthea Gramlich – a long time Dominican nun)… most of whom were there at St. Scholastica Church celebrating the 75th Anniversary.

It was the grandest of celebrations... commemorating St. Scholastica's founding Benedictine Priests including Father Phillip Bartoccetti who left the strip mining, ghost towns of Wichita, Kansas, and came to Detroit in 1928, met with Bishop Gallagher, bought some land in the undeveloped hinterlands of Outer Drive and Southfield in Northwest Detroit, and built St. Scholastica Church and school.

In 1938, when Lady Scholastica was only 10 years old, the newly ordained priest, 25-year-old Father Livius Paoli, son of a chimney sweeper from the northeastern part of Italy (Trent – formerly Austria), came to Detroit. He arrived on the very day of St. Scholastica's ten year anniversary celebration. Sixty-five years later, at St. Scholastica's 75th Diamond Jubilee, this ruggedly handsome 90-year-old priest was still the pastor and spiritual leader for generations of loyal St. Scholastica families.

The stories of strict discipline in the parochial schools are all true. We all received a para-military education as "Christian soldiers," prepared to fight the eternal battle of good and evil with the help of our guardian angels as well as God's Archangels and celestial attendants. But, through all of St. Scholastica's discipline, intimidation and fear there was Father Livius, a **BEACON OF PERSONAL TOUCH**, accepting you as you are, teaching you the fundamentals of football and baseball, giving haircuts, hearing confessions, shoring up your self worth, and, more than anything else, just being there... the constant figure of a gentle, sincere and saintly priest whose presence, even at a distance or in the background, meant "**ALL IS WELL.**"

For some generations, Father Boniface Lucci, pastor from 1929 until his death at Mt. Carmel Hospital in 1957, was "The Man." For other generations, it was Father Leo Cornelli. But, for my generation and many others, Father Livius is St. Scholastica and St. Scholastica is Father Livius, a 100 carat jewel of a figure, the dean of simple Chris-

Fr. Boniface Lucci, OSB

Fr. Livius Paoli, OSB

tian love, peace, non judgment, the "Eight Beatitudes" and the "Sermon on the Mount" – all portrayed in humble fashion in Northwest Detroit by a larger-than-life, spiritual figure for all denominations… a priestly, walking representative of the peace loving, forgiving Jesus of Nazareth.

At the 75th Anniversary mass on October 26, 2003, then 90-year-old Father Livius told us that he would be leaving us soon, but that he would see us again someday in "heaven"… a place he "personally recommended." Father Livius, ever the father figure, then exhorted and pleaded with all of us to keep Lady Scholastica going, going and going after his death.

In a poignant symbol of symmetry, I was at St. Scholastic nine days later on November 4, 2003 for long time parishioner and member of the Greatest Generation, 87-year-old Anna Oehler's, funeral mass. Father Livius and all present heard her son Kenny Oehler echo his mother Anna's same, "last wish" sentiment… that her children remain close after she died – the same wish my mother whispered to me during her last days and the very same "keeping the dream alive" wish Father Livius expressed for his beloved offspring, St. Scholastica Church and School.

I suppose everyone's last wish is to preserve that for which they gave their life's energy. Anna Oehler has no worry. Her four, beautiful children will live out her last wish until the end of their days. Father Livius' last wish to keep his St. Scholastica School and Parish going for each new generation of neighborhood kids in need of an education… is a little less certain. In the face of dwindling religious vocations, and in the face of changing neighborhoods, spiraling tuition and the cost to educate, Father Livius' last wish to perpetuate Lady Scholastica, and give future generations of struggling families the same great education that we had in our "Hood" more than 60 years ago is a precarious wish, dependent upon financial benefactors who are willing to give for no other reason than... the Jesus-like motive to pass on the dream to others they will never know.

Father Livius, true to his word, made his exit on June 22, 2007, at 94 years of age, just three and a half years after his 75th anniversary declaration that he would be leaving soon for "heaven... " a place he "highly recommended." Wouldn't it be great if we could ensure that Father Livius' last will and testament of continuing vitality for St. Scholastica Church and School becomes a reality. But, I must confess, the survival of the Hood remains precariously in doubt as we children of the Greatest Generation wind down and face the loss of our world.

CHAPTER 20

There Used To Be A Ballpark Here

THE CORNER

S ay goodbye! Say goodbye for yourself. Say goodbye for your family. Say goodbye for the living and say goodbye for the dead. The final goodbye… saluting the passing of an era at Trumbull and Michigan Avenue known affectionately among Detroiters as "**THE CORNER.**" The Corner where the "boys of summer" played out. The Corner where the "boys of fall" hung out. The Corner where Detroiters strung out… each passing year for a hundred years – a century of cool Spring days, a century of sultry Summer nights and a century of crisp Fall afternoons.

On those cool spring days at The Corner, the cycle of life renewed itself for every new generation when Ernie Harwell and the "Voice of the Turtle" were again heard throughout the land.

> "For, lo, the winter is past,
> The rain is over and gone,
> The flowers appear on the earth:
> The time of the singing of birds is come,
> And the voice of the turtle is heard in our land."
> (Song of Solomon)

On The Field

On those warm, humid Midwest summer nights at the Corner, the "Bless you Boys" of the baseball diamond fought fatigue, injury and a grueling schedule of games, persevering through the "dog days" of summer, hoping to bring home a pennant winner. On these cool fall afternoons under blue, grey October skies, the burning leaves of autumn sent smoke signals to the Gods of the Gridiron and the Corner erupted into the National Football league's rock'em, sock'em monsters of the midway – Lions, Bears, Giants, Colts, Eagles, Cardinals, Rams, Browns, Steelers, Packers, and Forty Niners giving us biblical archetypes like the "Four Horsemen of the Apocalypse" with "famine, pestilence, death and destruction" and giving us unforgettable gridiron gladiators and Hall of Fame prototypes like Dutch Clark, Hugh McElhenny, Ollie Matson, Frank Gatski, John Henry Johnson, Bill Dudley, Alex Wojciecowicz, Vince (Catholic Central High) Banonis, Charlie Ane, Bobby Layne, Doak Walker, Gil Mains, Jack Christiansen, Karl Karalevitz, Jimmy David, Yale Lary, Lou Creekmur, Joe Schmidt, Dick "Night Train" Lane, Dick LeBeau, Darris McCord, Terry Barr, Alex Karras, Lem Barney, Tom Nowatzke, Charley Sanders, Bruce (U of D High) Maher, Michael (Shrine High) Haggerty, Larry

(Servite High) Vargo, as well as "dignitaries of destruction" from visiting teams: Ray Nitschke, Sam Huff, Dick Butkus, Gayle Sayers, Mike Ditka, Harlon Hill, Norm (St. Mary's of Redford High) Masters, Fred (St. Mary's of Redford High) Arbanas, Ed (Denby High) Budde, Tom (St. Ambrose High) Beer, Danny (St. Anthony High) Currie, Steve (University of Detroit) Stonebreaker, Grady (University of Detroit) Alderman, Leo Nomelini, Joe "The Jet" Perry, Johnny Unitas, Raymond Berry, John Mackey, Tobin Rote, Max Magee, Paul Horning, Fuzzy Thurston, Jim Ringo, Jim Otto, Y. A. Title, R. C. Owens, and Fran Tarketon.

The Hood's Hall of Fame

Bruce Maher
Univ of Detroit High

Michael Haggerty
Shrine High

Larry Vargo
Servite High

Fred Arbanas
St. Marys of Redford
High

Ed Budde
Denby High

Tom Beer
St. Ambrose High

Steve Stonebreaker
University of Detroit

Beginning at the turn of the century and on into the 1900s, we hung out at the Corner with the likes of the Tigers' classy catcher Charlie Bennett, the talented and fiery Hall of Famer Ty Cobb, Sam "Wahoo" Crawford, "Home Run" Baker and Harry Heilman with the American league stars also visiting the Corner to take on our Tigers... including home run king, George Herman, "Babe," the "Bambino,"

Lou Gehrig and Babe Ruth

Ruth and his classy teammate, Lou Gehrig, the "Iron Horse," who saw his 2,130 consecutive game record come to an end at the Corner on May 2, 1939 when he took himself out of the lineup because the insidious effects of amyotrophic lateral sclerosis ("Lou Gehrigs disease") began to diminish his hand eye coordination and strength... soon to ravish his entire body and take his life at an early age. The "Iron Horse" bowed out with class and dignity and with a latter day public address system echoing a crescendoing goodbye at Yankee Stadium: "Today... today, today, I consider myself... myself, myself, the luckiest person... person, person, on the face of the earth... the earth, the earth."

The Detroit News Archives

Charlie Gehringer
Fowlerville, MI
and John McHale
Catholic Central Kid

As the century moved forward into the Great Depression, we stood in soup lines and hung out at the Corner with Charlie "The Gazelle Gerhinger" from Fowlerville, Michigan, Billy Boy Rogell, Schoolboy Rowe, Hank "Never-On-A-Sabbath" Greenberg, Marvelous Marv Owen, Mickey "No-Nonsense" Cochran and Eldon "Submarine-Ball" Aucker. Still later, during and after World War II and the Korean Conflict, we hung out at the Corner with "Prince Hal" Newhauser (two time MVP of the American

League), Art Houteman, Ray (Catholic Central High) Herbert, "Gracious George" Kell, Dizzy Trout, John (Catholic Central) McHale, Virgil (Two-No Hitters in 1952) Trucks, Ray Boone, Steve Gromek, Bill Tuttle, Harry "Suitcase" Simpson, Jimmy Finnigan, Jim Delsing, Frank House, Billy Hoeft, Reno Bertoia (protégé of Basilian priests – Father John Menner and Assumption High School baseball legend Father Ron Cullen), Al Aber, Al "The Kid" Kaline, Charlie "Sunday-Home-Run" Maxwell from Paw Paw, Michigan, Frank "Yankee Killer" Lary, Jim "No-Hit" Bunning (refusing to walk the "splendid splinter," Ted Williams, in the 9th inning with two out, but still getting his American league no hitter, and later a National league no hitter), Ferris Fain, Harvey (University of Wisconsin) Kuehn, Rocky "Don't-Knock-The-Rock" Colavito (or I'll come up in the stands and get it on with you – as he did), "Stormin Norman" Cash (who went up to bat against fireballing Nolan Ryan's no hitter express with a table leg – hey how else are you going to hit it), Manager Mayo Smith and the "Old Announcer" Van "Going-Going-Gone" Patrick.

| Mickey Cochran | George Kell | Ted Williams |

Later, after the Vietnam War, we hung out with Aureillo "The Vacuum" Rodriguez (tragically killed while visiting Detroit in 2003 when an automobile driver had a seizure, jumped the curb and ran over poor Aureillo as he was leaving the El Rancho restaurant on Vernor in Southwest Detroit), Herb "The Curve" Moford, Gator Brown

Denny McLain
31 Game Winner

Billy "Bad Boy" Martin

Mickey Lolich
"Donut Man"

of pinch hit renown, Eddie The Brinkman, Willie "Superman" Horton, Billy "Backstop" Freehan, Dickie "Double-Play" McAuliffe, Denny McLain, baseball's last 30 game winner and two time convicted felon (whom I had the pleasure of confronting and cross examining with my 100 mph fastball in my own ballpark, a courtroom, impaling Denny's endless ego on his own dubious testimony), Manager Billy "Bad Boy" Martin, Mickey Lolich, the World Series Trifecta winner in the 1968 World Series where 31 game winner Denny McLain faltered, and Mickey won three games to take us from the brink (down three games to one) to a World Championship, winning game seven in St. Louis against the unbeatable "Bullet Bob" Gibson.

There was also David "Kung Fu" Rozema who karate kicked himself onto the disabled list during a bench clearing brawl at the Corner, Ron "The Sting" LeFlore, the speedster who came out of Jackson Prison to play centerfield for the Tigers in the 1970s, and who, decades later, was arrested on September 27, 1999 at the Corner as he joined all of the Tiger old timers parading onto the baseball diamond for the last game ever played at the Corner (talk about one of your more elaborate stings – staging a final game, old timer reunion at the Corner with 50,000 extras sitting in the stands masquerading as fans just to nab LeFlore for back child support), Tommy "Blue Collar" Brookens (now Tiger's first base coach),

The Detroit News Archives

Mark Fidrych...
"Talk to me ball"

AP/Getty Images

Jack Morris
"Tough Enough"

Frank Tanana
Catholic Central

Mark "The Bird" Fidrych, the 19-year-old phenom who rocketed to the top, captured our imagination by talking to baseballs and manicuring the pitcher's mound, but who burned out quickly (before the era of pitch counts and limited innings), and then died an early death when his truck slid off the jack and collapsed on him in 2009, Mickey "Does-Anybody-Need-A-Shortstop?" Stanley, Johnny "The Heart" Hiller, Manager Ralph "Kick-The-Dirt" Houk, the ex-marine who managed 3,157 games in the Big Leagues and who just passed in 2010, Steve Kemp, Jason "Strongman" Thompson, Rusty "LeGrande Orange" Staub, Chet "The Lemon Man," Danny Petry, Jack "Tough Enough" Morris (who is in my "Hall of Fame"), Richie Hebner, the left handed grave digger, Mayor "Senor Smoke" Lopez who died an untimely death in an auto accident in Mexico, Lance "Muscle Man" Parrish, Willie Hernandez, (Cy Young winner and American League MVP out of the bullpen for the 1984 world champion Tigers), David "Clutch" Bergman, Frank (Catholic Central High) Tanana, "Tinkers to Evers to Chance" passing the torch of baseball folklore's most famous double play combination to classy Alan Trammell and "Sweet Lou" Whitaker, Darryl "Downtown" Evans, Kirk "King Kong" Gibson – the master of dramatic moments who stole the thunder at the Corner in the 1984 World Series when he drove a Goose Gossage fastball far into the left field upper deck to secure the Detroit Tigers World Championship in five games against

457

the San Diego Padres, Cecil "The Crusher" Fielder, Sparky "I-Won't-Lie-To-You-Now" Anderson, (well... Sparky, were you lying to me

before?), the winning World Series manager in the American League with the Tigers and in the National League with the Cincinnati Reds... and then a hundred years after the beginning, the turn of the century, new Millennium kids who closed out the Corner in its last season in 1999 – Gabe Kapler, Tony Clark, Damien

The Detroit News Archives

Sparky Anderson
"The Skipper"

Easley, Devi Cruz, Matt Anderson, local kid David Borkowski, Jeff Weaver, Doug Brocail, Todd Jones, Gabe Alverez ... players still in search of a nickname. And who will ever forget Rob "The-Last-Home-Run-Hit-At-The-Corner" Fick who, with less than 100 at bats in the big leagues, secured his place in the Corner's history with the roof top shot to right field in the 8th inning of the last ball game ever played at the Corner... September 27, 1999.

At the very top of the Corner's baseball pyramid stand two beloved larger-than-life characters who will forever be the heart and soul of the long, lazy days of summer at the Corner:

broadcaster Ernie "The Voice" Harwell and our forever young, spiritual leader, Al "The Kid" Kaline – the 19-year-old American League batting champion of 1955, Hall of Famer, man for all seasons, the consummate gentleman, athlete, broadcaster, analyst and the Corner's enshrined hero among heroes who patrolled Kaline's "rightfield" corner within "The Corner," running a circle

The Detroit News Archives

Al "The Kid" Kaline   around a circle against everyone else whose athletic talents ever graced the Corner at Michigan and Trumbull during the 20th century... and all of Al Kaline's athletic ability, toughness and daring on display during the Corner's endless summers of our youth for a paltry sum that averaged well under $100,000 a year, while today's untested rookies get a guarantee $400,000 a year minimum salary and early round draft picks get guaranteed millions. As the poet of our generation, Bob Dylan, said: "Oh the times they are a changin."

And, how about those Lions... the Gladiators of the Gridiron who hung out on the Corner when it was outlined against Grantlin Rice's "blue-grey October sky" of football folklore. Each Sunday in the mid 1950s, we watched Chris Carpenter's "Chris' Crew" – Yale "The Blond Bomber" Lary, Jimmy "The Hatchet" David and Karl Karalevitz... mug and destroy receivers and ball carriers who dared venture into the Lion's defensive backfield. We watched Gil "Wild Hoss" Mains, "Texas Bob" Smith, Charlie "Hawaii Five-O" Ane, Dick Stanfell, Lou Creekmur, Doak "Heisman" Walker, Bob (Catholic Central High) Ivory, Leon "Heisman" Hart, Cloyce Box, Hunchy Hornschmier, Dick "Night Train" Lane and his favorite cheerleader Dina "What-A-Difference-A-Day-Makes" Washington, the giant, Lester "Twinkle Toes" Bingeman (but just average size by today's football standards), Dorn Dibble, Jim "The-1953-World-Championship-Catch" Doran, world championship Coach, Buddy "The Psychologist" Parker, Gail Cogdill, "Doctor Dave" Middleton, a three sport, star athlete from the University of Tennessee, Milt "The Plum," Tobin Rote, Carl "Rib Shack" (Fenkell and Livernois) Sweetan, "Superstar" Mel Farr, Terry Barr, Charlie "Too Tough" Sanders, Alex "Bet-Em-To-Win" Karras (who was banished for a season by the Commissioner of Football for betting the Lions to win, spending that off-year tending bar with my mother Jean at Jimmy and Johnny Butsicaris' bar, the Lindell A.C., and my mother was too tough for him), Roger "The Giant" Brown, Wayne Walker, Indiana farm boy, Tom Nowatzke (later unsung MVP in the Baltimore Colts' 1971 Super Bowl V victory over the Dallas

Cowboys), Joe "All-Pro" Schmidt, Tom "The Bomb" Tracy, Pat "The Stud" Studstil, Ron (East Detroit High) Kramer, Darris "14-Years-In-

Ron Kramer
East Detroit High
University of Michigan
Green Bay Packers

The-NFL" McCord, Sam (Michigan State) Williams, Nick (Notre Dame) Pietrosante, Howard "Hopalong" Cassidy, the ill fated Chuck Hughes whose life ran out during a game, laying face down and dead on the "green, green grass of home" at the Corner before 50,000 plus fans, stunned into a deafening silence (never in the history of mankind have so many stood by silently and witnessed a man's final moment on the athletic "Fields of Glory"), Coach Harry "Cowboy" Gilmer and his Western Union messenger Joe Don "The Looney One," and absolutely the sentimental favorite of everyone at the Corner, the ghost of the Lions' glory days and the best high stakes poker player and two fisted drinker to ever play the game of football at anyone's corner... quarterback Bobby "I'll-Take-You-To-The-Promise-Land" Layne who never lost a game (he just ran out of time), and who lived his life in a fast lane hoping to run out of money and breath at the same time and not a minute before.

The marquee at the Corner was diversity 101... Blacks, Whites, Hawaiians, hillbillies, Hispanics, Southern Gentlemen, Yankees, Confederates, Carney Workers, Blue Bloods, Catholics, Jews, Arabs and Baptists – and everyone's security provided for by "Detroit's finest" outfitted in their "special detail" white caps led by my St. Scholastica schoolmate and feisty Irishman, Lt. Ronald Cronin, and, in the era before that, the classy farm boy from Merrill, Michigan, Sgt. Frank Demers, the vice squad man and the leader of the band who put the gay crooner and heartthrob, Johnnie Ray, in the back of a paddy wagon where Johnnie was heard to lament, "The Little White Cloud that Cried" because he couldn't "Walk his Baby Back Home" anymore... all big hits in the 1950s for Johnnie. Just think, the chance of Johnnie getting arrested today because he is "gay" is probably zero, and the chance of any of us listening to my parents' song, the "Gay Caballero," with the same zest my parents had... is also zero.

In The Stands

During the summers and falls, other lesser known Gladiators in the spectator seats entertained the crowds at the Corner with stupendous battles and knock outs. The fans' favorite was Marty "K.O." Lahti, the "King of Fenkell and Livernois Ave." K.O. Lahti always stayed late at the Corner for "last call"... invariably turning out the lights of many a boastful and "beery" challenger. How could we ever forget the British tourist who, after taking in his first American football game, got knocked out by K.O. because he had the singular misfortune of referring to "K.O." as a "bloke." After putting his lights out, an always defensive K.O. asked me: "What's a 'bloke'?" My response: "I don't know... but any man who calls another man a 'bloke' deserves what he gets, K.O." K.O. Lahti and his Damon Runyon trainer, "Peter James" Sullivan, could have moved K.O.'s one round preliminaries from the spectator section at the Corner to ten round main events in the "Ring of Dreams," but, by round two, K.O.'s training regimen of J.B. Scotch would perspire from his forehead into his eyes blinding the whereabouts of K.O.'s fast retreating opponents. K.O. Lahti, my dear brother... you will always be remembered and loved. In death, may you rest in that peace that seemed to have eluded you in life.

Marty "K.O." Lahti
Hard Knocks High

Peter James Sullivan
Catholic Central High

Sometimes at the Corner, you could find K.O.'s life long friend Ducky Dietz, a southpaw from the eastside of Detroit, who fought professionally in the Rocky Marciano stable of fighters. Ducky was the "sandman" who could gently put unruly patrons to sleep with his lightning left hook. You never saw it. They never saw it. No one ever saw it. All of a sudden out of nowhere, someone would just drop and take a short snooze… and you knew Ducky was in the house. Ducky's devastating left hook once found the jaw of Lions Hall of Fame linebacker, Joe Schmidt, and dropped Joe at his own Golden Lion Restaurant. But for his own problematic jaw and some discipline problems, Ducky could have been championship caliber.

Detroit Lion, Joe Don Looney (you could not have picked a more appropriate last name), from the University of Oklahoma was a

AP/Getty Images

Joe Don Looney

hybrid who was emotionally more at home with the brawls in the stands than with the fast-paced, full-throttle collisions on the Field of Dreams. Joe Don (later an underfed elephant trainer in India), will be forever remembered for his inability to break a beer bottle on a concrete curb during an after hours street fight in Detroit. The headlines in the Detroit papers embarrassingly read: "Tough Guy Don Looney Can't Break A

Beer Bottle Over A Curb." On the very next, game-day Sunday, Joe Don sat out the game in full uniform as a measure of discipline to reign in his unruly spirit. At the end of the game, when Lions head coach, Harry "Cowboy" Gilmer, relented and tried to send in a play with Joe Don, Joe told Harry: "If you need a messenger, call Western Union." That was the end of Joe Don at the Corner, but I'm still left with the memory of that grand day I had playing against Joe Don in a college game in New Mexico, with my father in the stands to bear witness to my head-to-head, one-on-one-success against Joe Don

Looney throughout the entire game that very special, warm October Homecoming afternoon in the fall of 1961.

High School Heroics

The Corner's "Field of Dreams" was also home to many high school dreams come true. During the autumns in the 1950s, the Detroit Catholic Central Shamrocks football team played Father ("I never saw a bad boy") Flannigan's Boystown Cowboys from Nebraska. As a grade schooler in the fall of 1955 and 1956, I sat huddled in the stands at the Corner with my family, all of us sick with the Asiatic and Hong Kong flu, as we watched Catholic Central led by number 77, four sport star, Al Moran... later a New York Met shortstop under manager Casey Stengel. When it came to the spoken language, Casey Stengel was a master of linguistic disaster who could stupefy and bewilder the most proficient interpreters of double speak. Casey was the originator of the Yogi Berra malapropism method of communication: "if you come to a fork in the road, take it" or "a verbal contract is not worth the paper it's written on" or, "if you think you're going to hit into a double play, strike out" or "if you fall in love with a homeless woman, don't move in with her." Later in 1958, as a 15-year-old sophomore, I was able to realize my dream and get some playing time for the Catholic Central Shamrocks in the last Boystown game. But, unlike number 77, Al Moran, I was never able to parlay that dream-realized event into a meeting with my linguistic hero of heroes, Casey "Conversation By Obfuscation" Stengel.

Yogi Berra and Casey Stengel "Casey... what the hell we talking about?"

463

Each fall at the end of the high school football regular season, the Corner was host to the "Goodfellow" game... a fundraiser to fund Christmas for poor kids. Each fall, the Catholic football league champion would square off against the Public School champion... always a rousing drama played before 30,000 to 40,000 screaming high school fans. Who will ever forget future Tiger first baseman, John McHale's, high school heroics as Catholic Central defeated heavily favored Hamtramck in the first Goodfellow game in 1938. Who will ever forget U. of D. High School's Dr. Michael Lodish's last minute field goal to beat St. Mary's of Redford 23 to 20 in the 1954 Goodfellow game. Who will ever forget Billy "The Kid" Hennigan and Judge Peter Maceroni rallying the DeLaSalle Pilots from a 20 to 6 half-time deficit to a second-half 26 to 20 victory over big bad Ed Budde's Denby team in 1956. Who will ever forget St. Ambrose's Mike Currie's blast block to free St. Ambrose halfback, Joey D'Angelo, for his swivel-hipped touchdown run with seconds left on the clock to beat heavily favored Cooley High School in the 1959 Goodfellow game (which prompted

Davey Vitali
"Preeminent Blast
Blocker"

the 2009 book "Champions of St. Ambrose"). But, my favorite St. Ambrose "blast blocker" of all time... Davey Vitali, who led St. Ambrose to a 20 to 0 victory over Pershing High School in the 1961 Goodfellow game, and who later blasted me a couple of times when we were teammates at the University of Detroit in the early 1960s.

And others may forget, but I will never forget captaining the Catholic Central Shamrocks and leading them onto the "Field of Dreams" at the Corner before 39,000 screaming fans for the 1960 Goodfellow's game against Denby. And a "thank you" to my right tackle John "Hode It" Lombardi who, as I was looking up into the stands in amazement and gazing into a sea of indistinguishable faces, grabbed my face mask, pulled me directly into his stern gaze and shouted: "Lauck... get your head into the game." And, a long-overdue apology to my St. Scholastica

classmates, John DiBella and Frank Demers, for refusing to acknowledge them as I left the playing field after a bitter 21 to 18 loss to Denby. I walked right by their beckoning voices with embarrassment and tears streaming down my face. Graciousness in defeat was something I learned much later in life, but, DiBella and Demers, I wish I could relive that November 18, 1960 night at the Corner and stop, and spend a special moment with you on our "Field of Dreams." I have very, very few regrets in life, but that is one. Yes, each autumn saw another thrilling high school "Goodfellow" game at the Corner

Lauck gets in-game instruction from Pete Mackert and Coach "Wild Bill" Foley... Goodfellow Game November 18, 1960

with high emotions on visible display. It was a staple of life in Detroit... played out at the Corner of our youth on our "Field of Dreams."

In the spring, both the Catholic schools and the Public schools played their championship baseball game at the Corner. Who will ever forget Northwestern High School baseball star, 16-year-old Willie Horton's opposite field blast with a wooden bat into the upper deck right field bleachers during the Public School championship game in 1959... with his teammate Matt Snorten also hitting one out in left field in the same game. Who will ever forget Catholic Central's Casey Rogowski's almost roof shot blast with an aluminum bat in 1998 in the Catholic League Championship game. My money says Willie Horton's shot was hit harder and further (and with a wooden bat), but you can't take anything away from the awesome blast Casey Rogowski hit far into the upper deck in 1998. And, although others may forget, I'll never forget hitting a shot to the left field wall as a

17-year-old during the 1960 American Legion All Star Game. Hey, I ain't no Willie Horton, but I lit the fuse on that shot.

As a "Brown Insulation" teammate of Willie Horton in the 18-year-old sandlot leagues in 1961, I can tell you first hand that nobody (I repeat nobody) hit them harder or farther than Willie "Superman" Horton. I'll never forget the shot Willie Horton hit off my former Catholic Central classmate, Vince Grainor, in the summer of 1961 at Atkinson field in Detroit. As Vince's K.B. Shell team warmed up, Vince told me he was going to strike out both Willie and me with his "dark one." In the first inning, I was in the "on deck" circle while Willie dug in against Vince. Willie picked up Vince's first "dark one" and launched one for the ages. Vince's "dark one" flew over the left field fence in a nano second. Willie hit Vince's "dark one" so hard it not only flew over the left field fence, but it also flew over the roadway, over the trees, over the Kelsey Hayes parking lot, over all of the cars in the parking lot, over the Cuckoo's Nest and into the wall of the Kelsey Hayes building. If it wasn't for the building ricocheting Willie's blast back into the parking lot, Willie would have launched America's first satellite. Now, Willie "Superman" Horton has a bronze statue of himself in the centerfield stands at the Tigers'

Comerica Ballpark to commemorate not only Willie's Major League heroics for the Detroit Tigers, but, more importantly, his kind and generous nature, and his love of Detroiters and their love of him.

The Next Generation... DiBella Competing at The Corner 1998

I have also lived long enough to see my friend's kids get their chance to play at the Corner. Both Catholic Central's "Italian Stallion" brothers, Nick DiBella and John DiBella, as well as Our Lady of the Lakes' star hurler Sean "The Irishman" Harrington (who later pitched for Eastern Michigan)... had their moments in the sun on the "Field of Dreams" at the Corner.

Historic Neighborhoods

As the City of Detroit hung around the Corner at Trumbull and Michigan, we also met various characters who lived out their

**Mighty Mike Morales
1920**

lives on the periphery of the Corner stadium. Mighty Mike Morales, my daughters Jessie's and Frances' great grandfather from Cuidad Leon, Juanawato, Mexico (may he rest), parked cars on his lot at 10th and Bagley. Mike Morales was not a man to quibble with. You respected him, and he respected you or look out. Don't mistake his kindness for weakness because he will "lower the boom" on you so fast you won't know what hit you. I know because I married his granddaughter, Debra Sandoval... also a certified and registered "boom lowerer."

There was also "Parking Lot Irene," a lovely, pretty lady in her 70s, who parked cars in her backyard just east of the stadium and just across from my "main man" Elmer who covered his own parking lot for years. Elmer was an engaging gentleman with a twinkle in his eye. Elmer took care of my parking needs for a decade at the Corner. Elmer always had my two door Fleetwood Cadillacs (black, blue and later red) running and ready to go with the air conditioning on so nobody's mascara suffered any further humidity damage. I always looked forward to seeing his smiling face. Although, looking back at life, Elmer's smile was probably repressed laughter as he gazed in bewildered wonderment at the oversized caricature I cut at the Corner in my 30s... all the while I was thinking I was "cool." As my father used to say: "Youth will be served." As others might say: "Is anybody as excited about me as I am?"

Ninety-nine year old Sadie Khalil who lived a stone's throw from the Corner went down in 2009... the same year they put the wrecking ball to the Corner. After her husband died early, "Sadie the Lady" raised four sons with the income from her grocery store on Wabash and later Vermont... both in the shadow of the Corner. As a testament to her strength and perseverance, Sadie Khalil later graduated from college with a teaching certificate and taught at St. Francis Cabrini in Allen Park. Sadie's oldest son, Monier Khalil, (may he rest) and her youngest son, Tom Khalil, a former assistant prosecuting attorney in Wayne County, both acquired substantial parking lot holdings over the years at the Corner. Monier's own son, Mikhail Khalil, and his gracious wife, Rose, still operate the O'Blivions Restaurant (formerly the "Devil") just two blocks west of the Corner... still the best lunch in the City of Detroit. Monier's other son, Tom Khalil, ran the Batter's Box Bar and the Phase III souvenir stand with the help of Tom Ritchie while their friend George "the Greek" Vallas, one of the finest and classiest men ever to grace the Corner, was running another souvenir stand on Dee Dee Khalil's parking lot. And, who will ever forget the sneak preview, Monier's two pretty daughters, Sandy and Melanie, got of the three tenors, Pavarotti, Carreras and Placido Domingo from a partially open door into Tiger stadium as they looked over their mother Evelyn Khalil's shoulder. Monier's widow, Evelyn Khalil, a dear client of mine, who lived out much of her life connected to the Corner, emotionally and financially (with substantial real estate holdings in the area), is a classy, fun lovin' lady and a joy to be around as well as the best cook of Syrian food this side of Damascus.

The area around the Corner was surrounded by bars, restaurants, churches and businesses. There was Reedy's bar, owned by Bill Reedy, who was convicted in the drunk driving death of his friend, former

New York Yankee second baseman and former Tiger manager, bad-boy Billy Martin. There was Casey's, Shelly's Place, Nemo's, Max Silk's Deli, Hoot Robinson's, Musial's and the Lager House where my daughters' Grandma, Felippa Jessie Morales Sandoval, would sometimes go "to relax the troubles." The Gaelic League, still an Irish hangout today, is just a stone's throw away, just west of the Corner a few blocks... where the St. Patrick's Day Parade ends its annual traverse after passing by the Corner each year.

The Corner is located in the 200 plus-year-old, Irish neighborhood known as "Corktown"... named after Irish immigrants from County Cork, Ireland. The spiritual center of the Corner is Corktown's Most Holy Trinity Catholic Church... the home of Father Clement Kern (may he rest), one of laborers' staunchest supporters. Holy Trinity is now run by Father Russ Kohler, originally from Monroe, Michigan (Monroe Catholic Central High School). Each Sunday, Father Russ Kohler courageously and boldly stands in the midst of his flock in the Holy Trinity center aisle, and stridently rails against gangs and drugs and their "culture of death." On November 22, 2000, Father Kohler, heralded by the swelling sound of Mariachi music playing to a packed house at Holy Trinity, baptized my beautiful daughter Jessie Valentine Lauck, while his able assistant, Catholic Central's Father "Tunny" Hathaway, baptized my lovely daughter Frances Sandoval Lauck at Holy Trinity on November 8, 2003. It was only fitting that "abuellito" (grandfather in Spanish), Frank Sandoval Jr., saw his granddaughters,

Fr Clement H. Kern
1907-1983
A Staunch Supporter
of Labor

Fr. Russ Kohler
A Staunch Supporter
of Life

Jessie and Frances, baptized in the very same church he attended as a child with Grandmother, Annakaletta Morales, and in the very same "Corktown" neighborhood where he grew up.

A mile away from the Corner, there is Mario's famous old time Italian Restaurant with waiter extraordinaire Nabil serving the Mario table-top salad and the always great Filet with zip sauce. I'll never forget my first visit to Mario's as a 19-year-old in 1962 with my uncle, Marty Montroy, picking up the tab, and my mother Jean so thrilled that her brother Marty was financially successful enough to treat us to dinner at Mario's Italian Restaurant. Hey, without Uncle Marty's patronage, we don't even get downtown… let alone to Mario's. There was also the recently closed landmark, Carl's Chop House, on Grand River (across from the Motor City Casino) still ringing with the ghost of the union chant, "Solidarity Forever"… always a great watering hole both before and after the festivities at the Corner.

Across from Carl's Chop House, was Dunleavy's old time saloon, once operated by the Dunleavys of Bohola, County Mayo, Ireland, and last operated by that wonderful, humorous Irishman and my St. Scholastica Grade School classmate, Don Cronin. Just south and west of the Corner and just west of the Michigan Central Train Depot is "Mexican Town" where Detroit plainclothes cop, Ron Cronin (Don's twin brother), cheated death at Armando's Restaurant

**Chief Ron Cronin
1998**

on Vernor Avenue across from Clark Park… in a shootout with a motorcycle gang member who had just shot another man to death, right in front of a terrified lunch crowd. A shell-shocked, but well trained, Officer Ron Cronin jumped to his feet, and emptied his sixshot .38 caliber handgun at the bad guy. Cronin missed with the first five shots, but killed the bad guy with the last shot. Luckily, no one else was hit. When later questioned about the accuracy of his firearm, a rather defensive Officer Cronin allowed that: "The first five shots were warning shots." Ron Cronin later became Lt. Cronin in Detroit under Police Chief Hart, and, later, "Chief of Police" in West Bloomfield for twenty years.

Just a mile east of the Corner is Greektown with my Greek mother-in-law, Frances Economy Sandoval's, favorite restaurant, "Laikon," with waiter extraordinaire Ilier. But, the Grecian Gardens where my mother Jean waited tables for Gus Calocassides is, like the Corner, also "long gone." And, thank you Gus Calocassides for hooking me up with your Greek buddy, Nick Londes, and getting me a job as an usher for Red Wings hockey games at Olympia as I started law school at the University of Detroit in the fall of 1966. And, my first assignment... guarding the front of the stage for the "Beatles" American Tour. Beatles... ???... whoever they were. Well, I soon found out. Hello John. Hello Paul. Hello George, and Hello Ringo. I'm "Downtown Freddie" from Detroit. "Do you want to start a "Rev-v-v-v-v... olution;" we got enough chicks for an army. And, thank you to Olympia General Manager, Nick Londes, for staying with me, and keeping me on the job after I knocked out Detroit cop, troublemaker and "Stress Decoy," Officer Matusak.

Just across from the stadium on Trumbull, is the Checker Cab, once run by capitalist extraordinaire, Bobby Barnes, whose brother, Basilian Priest, Father Joe Barnes, used to hear my confessions in 1959 and 1960 (such as they were). Just north of Checker Cab on Trumbull is Brook's Lumber Company, home of the most famous baseball catch ever by a building... the spot where Kirk Gibson's monster home run landed after it cleared the right field roof at the Corner flying over Trumbull and landing on the roof of the Brook's Lumber Company. And, just north of the Corner at Harrison and Spruce is the last surviving remnant of the hippie 1960's... "Nancy Whiskey's" Saloon, brainchild of retired cop, Owen McCarthy (may he rest), and his lady

Nancy: "Nancy baby I love you so much more than the rest of my ladies, I'm going to name my saloon after you."

Best And Worst Of Times

The Corner reflected our lives… a tale of one city that has seen "the best of times and the worst of times." The Corner saw drama.

The Detroit News Archives
Celebrating… Detroit Style

The Corner saw elation. The Corner saw tears. The Corner saw peace loving fans enjoying a night out with the family. The Corner saw anarchy and the 1984 World Series national headlines of **Bubba's "Burn-Baby-Burn"** as cars were set on fire and overturned in misguided celebration of the 1984 World Series victory. You say "only in Detroit?" Perhaps.

The Tigers' baseball team lost 100 games at the Corner in some years. The Tigers also won 100 games at the Corner in other years. The Lions' football team sometimes couldn't beat the Little Sisters of the Poor, but, at other times, the Lions were World Champions, like in 1953 on my first visit to the Corner as a 9-year-old with my father. Fighting off the chill of a bleak December day, we watched Bobby Layne connect with Jim Doran on a touchdown pass beating Otto Graham's Cleveland Browns 17 to 16 with 26 seconds left on the clock. Now almost 60 years later, that larger than life victory, at that larger than life Corner, with my own larger than life father remains an indelible memory of… the best of times. But there were many others before and after my time.

There were the pennants and world championships won by the Tigers in the 1930s, 1940s, 1960s, and the 1980s. In the 1930s World Series, there was Schoolboy Rowe throwing aspirin tablets past St.

Schoolboy Rowe

Pepper Martin

Dizzy Dean

Louis Cardinal "Gas House Gang" third baseman, Pepper Martin, who took three huge swings-and-misses, as my 16-year-old father stood in the aisle way behind home plate, selling pop and shaking his head in disbelief at how quick a major league fastball goes 60 feet, 6 inches from the pitcher's hand past Pepper Martin, exploding into catcher Mickey Cochrane's mitt. And, little did my father know then that, 25 years later, his own 14-year-old son would be spending the summer of 1957 with Pepper Martin in Salem, Missouri learning to play baseball and listening to the stories of Dizzy Dean and Daffy Dean and the rest of the St. Louis Cardinal's "gas house gang"... a nickname a sportswriter hung on the Cardinals the day the St. Louis players wore (yesterday's) dirt and sweat filled uniforms when their laundry man unexpectedly "took drunk." Also in the 1930's World Series at the Corner, there was baseball commissioner, Judge Kenesaw Mountain Landis, removing St. Louis Cardinal's left fielder, Joe Medwick, from the game at mid inning before the fans at the Corner killed Joe with a barrage of fruit and bottles for spiking Detroit Tiger third baseman Marv Owen.

World Championships

In the 1940s, there was Prince Hal Newhouser pitching the Detroit Tigers to the World Championship against the Chicago Cubs. In the 1960s, the Tigers were down 3 games to 1 to the St. Louis Cardinals in the 1968 World Series, but hold on... don't count them out.

Down three games to one, Tigers left fielder, Willie Horton, threw out the Cardinals' speedster, Lou Brock, at home plate in game 5 to shift the emotional momentum back to Detroit's advantage while Al "The Kid" Kaline, then an aging veteran, delivered a key base hit to stay alive in game five. That never-say-die attitude of the gritty City of Detroit propelled the Tigers to rally from a 3 game to 1 deficit to win the 1968 World Series in 7 games as Mickey "The Donut Proprietor" Lolich, with just two days rest, out dueled St. Louis Cardinals' mighty flame thrower, Bullet Bob Gibson, in the 7th game of the World Series in St. Louis. The Tigers returned home to the Corner the next day as timeless heroes and world champions: "Bless You Boys of Summer."

AP/Getty Images

Goose Gossage

The Detroit News Archives

Kirk Gibson
1984 World Series

There was the "roar-of-'84" when the Tigers virtually locked up the pennant in the first month and a half of the season with a 35 win and 5 loss start. There was the World Series most valuable player, Alan Trammell, leading the Tigers to that 1984 World Championship. There was Kirk Gibson's 5th game heroics at the Corner when he took the sinister, flame throwing, handle-bar mustachioed, Darth Vader, Goose Gossage, upstairs and downtown. Did any ball ever get out of Tiger stadium quicker than Gibson's upper deck shot off Gossage. Smash – it's gone! Gone from the moment it left the bat. "Let's go" my main man Valentine, 14-year-old "Kid Valentine" Lauck, and the then 40-year-old "old man" sprinted for safety away from the Corner and away from "Bubba's-burn-baby-burn." It's over, Detroit Tigers are the world champs again.

It's good to end on a high note... the roar of '84. Turn off the lights baby. Goodbye seatmate Roma Havens, you wonderful woman. Goodbye seatmate Dwight Havens.

May you both rest, and thanks for your joyous companionship for all those years at the Corner. Goodbye "Flyboy" General Ralph Havens, who went down at the top of his game to an early death. Say good night. That time of life is over. I don't want to stand around and wait for the fat lady to sing. I just want to go to Nemo's or Reedy's or Nancy Whiskey's, put a nickel in the juke box and play Sinatra's "There Used to be a Ballpark Here."

The Corner… Going, Going… Gone

The old familiar Corner was leveled by the wrecking ball in 2009 despite an heroic effort by Ernie Harwell and his "preservationists." And as poet John Donne wrote: "ask not for whom the bell tolls." The bell tolls for all of us hard-scrabble, gritty Detroiters. Just look around. No stadium. No athletic heroics at the Corner. No Corner. No landmark. No emotional home. No sense of history. No jobs. No economy. It's a sign of the times. The Corner is gone, and we've lost our historical and emotional landmark. The same year the ball park went down our spiritual leader at the Corner, Ernie "the Voice" Harwell, announced he was not far behind as he was in the final stages of cancer, awaiting his rendezvous with the "unknown"… a rendezvous that occurred shortly afterward as Ernie took his leave on May 4, 2010 at age 92. Perhaps Ernie will meet up with our beloved departed Corner in heaven. Do Corners and other sacred places go to heaven, or do they just die off as past memories that fade to black over time?

While I ponder these theological questions, I guess I'll just hang around and wander in the deserted landscape that used to be "The Corner." Maybe, I'll get a beer at Nemo's, or maybe a lunch at O'Blivions, or maybe even a mass at Holy Trinity. Maybe, I'll even take in a ball game at "Comerica Park." Comerica Park??? Right now with the Corner lying vacant, I can't even think of "Comerica

Park." And... why should I? Investment bankers like Comerica gave us the Great Depression of 2008 which has left Detroit and our "big three" auto manufacturers in a life and death struggle for survival...

Namesake
Frederick William
Lauck

Anna VanPelt Lauck
American Indian

all some 92 years after my grandfather and name sake, Frederick William Lauck, left St. Louis, Missouri in 1917 with his wife, Anna, and my one year old father, Frederick Valentine Lauck, to come to Detroit and work for Ford Motor Company at Ford's Highland Park plant. My grandfather later claimed his place in history by walking side-by-side with Walter Reuther and Ford's hourly workers on Miller Road in Dearborn on May 26, 1937... a peaceful march that ended up in a fight for their lives on the Miller Road overpass against Ford's goons led by the infamous Harry Bennett and other ex convicts – just so my grandfather and his fellow workers could unionize for fair wages and safe working conditions, as they eventually did, forming the United Auto Workers (UAW) in 1941, shortly after my grandfather's death and a year before my birth. Grandpa Frederick William... I wish you would have lived long enough to see me and touch me with your kind and heroic presence.

Comerica Park? What the hell do investment bankers in three-piece suits have to do with our proletariat, blue-collar baseball park at the Corner where Ty Cobb slid hard, where Hank Greenberg blasted the ball, where Charlie Gheringer fluidly covered the entire right side of the infield, where Al Kaline threw out three runners from "Kaline's Corner" in one game, where pitchers threw it right at your head to back you off the plate, and where the Tigers "never say die" spirit is left to roam... a ghostly memory of times gone by. What the hell do investment bankers have to do with our emotional past at the Corner where we saw the Detroit Lions quarterback Bobby Layne win the

The Detroit News Archives

Bobby Layne

Lions' last world championship in 1957? What the hell do investment bankers have to do with memories of our high school championship teams and our neighborhood characters whose ghost-like memories still roam the now lifeless Corner?

What ever happened to names like "Bennett Park," the Corner's first designation... named after a courageous and unfortunate, but highly respect-ed, turn-of-the-century, Detroit catcher, Charlie Bennett. What ever happened to "Navin Field," the Corner's second designation, named after Frank Navin, a smart financial man with a vision and the courage to pull off his vision. What ever happened to "Briggs Stadium," named after its owner, Walter Briggs, or "Tiger

The Detroit News Archives

Briggs Stadium

Stadium." As with the Detroit Ca-sinos, the monied interests and the power brokers in Detroit made a deal with the Devil, and they trad-ed the charisma and history of our Corner at Michigan and Trumbull and our proletariat ball park of the

"common man"... for the capitalist Comerica's banking money and a new turn of the century stadium where you can check your financial statements while you take in a ball game. We traded our established and respected, memory-filled Corner of a blue-collar ballpark that has served us in the 19th and 20th centuries for the "new kid on the block" with all of the modern day bells and whistles, fountains, merry go-rounds and a ferris wheel at Comerica Park. But, what happened to our tradition? Truly, "more is really less." **THERE USED TO BE A BALLPARK HERE.**

Children of the Greatest Generation… we are winding down and losing our world. So put another nickel in the juke box baby and play Sinatra's "There Used to Be a Ball Park Here." As "The Voice" Ernie Harwell proclaimed on September 27, 1999, during the final act of the last game at the Corner's dramatic stage: **"Farewell"** and **"Goodbye, old friend."**

The Detroit News Archives

Ernie Harwell
"Goodbye, old friend"

As Jimmy Durante said: **"Good night, Mrs. Calabash, wherever you are."** As I said in 2009 when they leveled the stadium: "It's over." And, when it's my turn to go, I hope for a reunion with all of the larger-than-life characters who hung out at the Corner of Michigan and Trumbull in the City of Detroit for over a century… of cool spring days, sultry summer nights and crisp fall afternoons.

CHAPTER 21

You Can't Go Home...
Another Corner Disappears

Once upon a time, the spiritual center of the Hood was the "Holy Corners" at Southfield and Outer Drive... **St. Scholastica** *Grade School on the southwest corner,* **Benedictine** *High School on the southeast corner,* **Little Sisters of the Poor,** *Sarah Fisher home for the aged, on the northeast corner and that unparalleled, architectural work of art,* **Mercy College,** *on the northwest corner.*

Good Friday

Good Friday... April 14, 2006. The day started out with great expectations. My favorite day of the year. The spirituality of the crucified Jesus. "Tre Ore" in my old neighborhood church, St. Scholastica. I still remember fondly Lady Scholastica's 75th birthday party just a year and a half ago, on October 26, 2004 with the ageless, 93-year-old father Livius Paoli on the altar with a well intentioned (but lesser light) Cardinal Maida along side Father Livy. I remember the "after glow" at Mercy College, and standing in the buffet line with my first grade pal John "Pizza" DiBella... his rich baritone voice filling the air with his exuberance: "This little light of mine, I'm going to let it shine... this little light of mine, I'm going to let it shine, let it shine, let it shine, let it shine," and later the crowd chanting to Father Livius: "Give us the blessing Father." "Give us the blessing"... knowing one day, some day, he won't be there anymore (as he has been forever) to shower us with the simplicity of his life's example: "Peace," "Love," "Non Judgment," "Acceptance" and "Compassion"... the only Christian message I'll answer to. "No apology" to the fundamental Christian warriors who believe in hostilities and violence in the name of Jesus.

How did the simple message of "peace" from the Judean carpenter, Jesus, get so bastardized in his name with the likes of Reverend Pat Robertson, evangelist and founder of the "Christian Broadcast Network," calling for America to murder Venezuela's elected president, Hugo Chavez, and later announcing that God cursed Israeli Prime Minister, Ariel Sharon, with a stroke because Sharon was willing to give Palestinians "God's land" to secure peace. That all-punishing, bigoted God of Pat Robertson is not the God I learned of in first grade Catechism at St. Scholastica: **"God is love."**

Caravan Of Memories

Back to "Tre Ore." I was excited. I had not been to Lady Scholastica since Good Friday 2005, and I was anxious and excited to return to my middle class roots, and see my first baseball and football coach, Father Livius Paoli, and to see my grade school classmate, Bob Green, now Benedictine monk, Father Mike, the raw-boned, good looking kid of 63, with the dulcet toned voice... a gifted speaker whose eloquent delivery comes from his transparency and his knack of getting himself out of the way so the Holy Spirit can speak through him. As I say, it was with great expectations that I headed out from

Milford, Michigan with Debra Economos Sandoval Lauck and our girls, 5-year-old Jessie Valentine and 3-year-old Frances. I was again heading home to the old hood to relive some emotional memories, renew some old acquaintances and get in touch with the middle class, spiritual roots that define who I am. I thought I could go home once again. I had no premonition that the old hood had run about as far as it could go. I had no idea the end was probably on the horizon. No doubt, I was winding down in my own rambunctious life. But, it was also soon to become apparent that all of us children of the Greatest Generation were losing our world – a world that was once ours… but no longer.

Upon my arrival into the old hood, I drove through the familiar streets and avenues pointing out everything to my half-listening family. "That's where my man Demers lived on Sunderland"… strangers sitting on his porch, but, what the heck, it's been 45 years since I left the hood in 1961 for the New Mexico Military Institute and the Air Force Academy to throw my competitive spirit into a national setting.

My family's two bedroom bungalow at 18627 Curtis looked pretty good, but a couple of doors away Dennis Fedorinchik's home was gone, nothing but a vacant lot. Down Curtis to Glastonbury and my third grade girlfriend, Diane Zarza's, house. Her father was a Michigan State football star and boxer who strongly suggested to me when I was eight years old that I should hold off dating his daughter until I turned 16. I started out early with a bang, but, by the time I turned 16, I tapered off to a standstill. As far as the opposite sex was concerned, I was an awkward, skinny, pimple faced kid lacking in even rudimentary conversational skills and social graces. I passed Diane's house and headed north to "Kid Gilbert's" house with Joe Poma's house across the street. Joe Poma, the Sal Mineo, good look-ing Italian kid, died young at 19 in an auto accident while he was in the Air Force in Alaska. I'll never forget his funeral procession leaving St. Scholastica with the hearse driving by Joe's childhood home

**Joe Poma
One Last Trip...
Going Back Home**

on Glastonbury, and then on to Joe's final resting place at Holy Sepulcher. That long-ago moment of finality and sadness silently acknowledged, I then drove to John DiBella's house number two on Curtis in the shadow of the Detroit Edison substation, Cornelius Flynn's house on Fenmore next to Dennis Martin, the Perkins, over to Archdale, the Pophams, Billy Fruend (the Olympic bicyclist in the 1960 Rome Olympics), Bostwicks, the Lepines (my mother's first cousin Betty Ann and her kids Kitty, Mary, Mark and John – sounds like a gospel group), and, next door… the Ivorys (John Ivory, a classmate of my father in 1929-30 at Catholic Central number one at Holy Rosary Parish, Harper and Woodward in the New Center area). **"So far so good**," but that was the same refrain heard when the man jumped out of the 30th floor window ledge and flew past the 8th floor, head first… **"So far so good."**

Then over to my Catholic Central High School at 6565 West Outer Drive (now Renaissance High School). Our field house, where we suited up and put on our armor for football practice and for games at the northwest corner of Hubbell and Six Mile (McNichols), was gone, but I could see that special spot on Six Mile Road where my beloved father would park each day, every day, for ten minutes and watch my Catholic Central football practice… just to send a message that I was important to him. Westbound on Six Mile past my Greek father-in-law, Thomas Economos', diner on the south side of Six Mile just east of Greenfield. "So far so good." But, things quickly took an ominous turn.

Westbound on Six Mile, my mini caravan of four continued to the northwest corner of Biltmore and Six Mile and headlong into my memory of the DiBella's first household... cots and mattresses in the back of the grocery story that Mr. and Mrs. DiBella owned. They later moved to the small wooden house just north across the alley... the same house I first visited my first day of first grade in September 1949.

Hurricane Katrina Derails The Caravan

My reverie of fond memories and days gone by collided head on with the reality of two cold, vacant lots where the DiBella's store and home once stood, and the entire Biltmore block from Six Mile north to Outer Drive gone – gone with a cyclone fence surrounding a block-long field of weeds... bereft of homes, bereft of families, bereft of children's voices, laughter and kitchen table conversations, and devoid of life and love, a barren "moon for the misbegotten" moonscape, lacking in any energy, sound or movement. It was an emotional dump, a lifeless landscape that mirrored the remnants of Hurricane Katrina, a poverty of death and disaster moved north from New Orleans to our old Hood in Detroit. *The New Yorker* magazine article rang through my head... Detroit with thirty-three percent of its residents living below the poverty line of minimal subsistence (the amount of food necessary to avoid malnutrition). That bleak City of Detroit statistic of poverty was recently glossed over and hidden by the facade of new freeway concrete as the rich and famous limousined and tuxedoed to the 2005 All Star game at Comerica Park and the 2006 Superbowl at Ford Field in downtown Detroit.

I honestly couldn't tell the difference between this small Biltmore Street strip of Detroit and the photos of war torn Iraq, Palestine or Lebanon. **Poverty... the unrelenting terrorist.** Poverty, like water flowing the path of least resistance, leveling everything in its sight – a tsunami of man's failures with rising waves of hopelessness and despair mocking the unfulfilled words of Jesus: "When I was hungry... when I was thirsty" and replacing those compassionate ideals with the "let them eat cake" philosophy of Fox News and the neoconservatives pontificating their flat-out wrong refrain: "I came from nothing and look at me now." Well, I'm looking, and all I see Bill O'Reily, Sean Hannity, Ann Coulter, Rush Limbaugh and Donald Rumsfield, Carl Rove, Dick Cheney, Alberto Gonzales, and George W. Bush is ignorance, arrogance, misplaced Christianity, a mentality of torture, illusions of grandeur, weak egos and false pride. Well, I better stop. My tone is becoming as judgmental as those American anti-heroes. History will judge George W. Bush and his Machiavellian gang worse than my small condemnation.

Grinding Poverty

My father, Frederick Valentine Lauck, born in 1916, a member of the Greatest Generation and a child of the Great Depression, was a helpless victim of poverty and malnutrition... a kid with little or no chance to live the American dream – an only child, hungry and cold, expending every ounce of his weakened existence just trying to survive on the "mean streets" of Detroit. My father was a living testament to the historical truism that, in a capitalistic society, ten percent of the people own ninety percent of the wealth, while the other ninety percent are left to share the remaining ten percent of society's resources.

My father told me poverty was "grinding"... kind of a relentless, physical dimension that, at first, discourages, then dispirits and then grinds you down, finally demoralizing you as you realize you are not part of the social fabric of society and not part of the establishment, but rather just part of a marginal subculture – an imprecise emotional realization that subconsciously disconnects you from society's values and society's system of law while throwing you headlong into the self-justifying dysfunction of: "It's us against them man... so society's rules don't apply to us." Poverty is the ultimate breeding ground for disconnection, demoralization, anarchy, revolution and terrorism.

Thank heaven, I was one generation removed from the Great Depression, the Dust Bowl, World War II and the Korean War. Bless those strong-willed men and women of the "Greatest Generation" who weathered those storms and survived those bleak, bring-you-to-your-knees times. Thank heaven I had the spiritual refuge of a loving, supportive family and St. Scholastica Parish... that spiritual center of my world that I first connected to in September 1949, and that spiritual center that I still connect to today, 55 years later, just to keep the emotional tsunami of life from sweeping me away. But today, on Good Friday, 2004... a day of surprises was just beginning to unfold before my very eyes.

Reverend Mr. Black

I hurried into Lady Scholastica with the little beauties and Debra... but something is wrong. Something is amiss. A quick glance shows Father Livius in his accustomed position on the altar along with my St. Scholastica classmate, Father Mike, and another priest I don't recognize but, but wait... **where are the people?** Sure the white-flight attrition has been on-going since the 1970s, but a hundred people or more you could usually count on for Tre Ore's Good Friday service. Now, we're down to about 25 people. Is this my beloved "Tre Ore" service at St. Scholastica in Northwest Detroit? Is this another much needed chance to connect to my spiritual anchor and the only form of Christianity I understand... or... could it be... this the end?

I quietly take to the kneeler, and glance around at the worn-out faces of the aged seniors and the still youthful faces of the new order of nuns from Africa. What's happened to Father Livius? His upbeat demeanor and his energized walk were legendary even into his 90th year of life, but, today, he is walking slowly and hanging onto the altar for support. And, who is that priest with the red cap? He must be a Bishop. And so he was… Bishop John Quinn, a handsome, youthful looking Irishman who Hollywood could type-cast to play the role of a bishop, cardinal, pope or even Bishop Fulton J. Sheen, the first Christian television star and the real deal philosopher… not the phony televangelists waiting for your money so they can "rush" their most recent book to you: "Seven Secret Insights on How to Get Rich Selling Jesus"… with a forward by Detroit's own Republican Senatorial candidate, Reverend Keith Butler.

Back to my beloved St. Scholastica and the virtually empty church. As Bishop Quinn stands in the middle of the expansive altar, ready to deliver the homily, I hear the silent refrain from the Beatles' "Eleanor Rigby" who was "buried along with her name, nobody came" while "Father McKenzie was writing a sermon for no one to hear." But, instead of Father McKenzie, I saw Bishop Quinn. He stood up with the strength of conviction, and delivered a sermon fit for a packed Pontiac Silverdome (the same venue Pope John Paul II spoke at to a standing-room-only crowd in the 1980s). Bishop Quinn painted a picture of Jesus as the lamb of sacrifice: "pouring out all of his love and all of his blood" for the sins of the world. Bishop Quinn, to his eternal credit, is no apologist. There was nothing lukewarm about the man. His bearing and demeanor conjured up the strength of Jesus when throwing the money changers out of the temple or admonishing Peter (and his sword of violence) in the garden of Gethsemane while restoring the centurion's ear. Bishop Quinn referred to Mel Gibson's movie, *The Passion*, and the man in the crowd shouting to Jesus: "Why do you think you are the Redeemer?" Jesus did not answer. "What makes you think you are the Redeemer?" Jesus still did not answer. "While you are dying on the cross, the people of Jerusalem are going about their business paying no attention to you." Again, Jesus did not answer.

The parallel certainly didn't escape Bishop John Quinn. While Bishop Quinn was talking to a virtually absent congregation about Jesus pouring out his love and his life's blood on the cross, the whole city of Detroit (and the world) were going about their business with bars and restaurants serving food and alcohol, with boutiques selling the latest fashions, with hardware stores stocking shelves for the onslaught of spring, with golfers seeking those elusive birdies, with business men and women negotiating the terms and conditions of commercial contracts, with rap's violence and tragedies jumping off the radio and imprinting their violent lyrics on the real lives of real people, with the new Christian Crusaders and the Muslim hordes alike killing each other in the name of God and Allah, with President Bush espousing his Christianity in a photo shoot as he enters and leaves church while he sells warfare, suffering, and torture under the guise of global democracy. In reality, George W. Bush unilaterally rejects the principles of democracy and its system of checks and balances and thumbs his nose at the FISA Court's jurisdiction to approve or disapprove of eavesdropping and the intercepting of private communications. And... why? Perhaps to satisfy his need for power and his role as "world ruler"... our benevolent, born-again Christian ruler, George W. Bush, following the message of Jesus: "preemptive strikes, war and death" as over 100,000 innocent Iraqi citizens die from America's preemptive "shock and awe," rained down like "hellfire" on Iraqi citizens who, like us, are just trying to figure out how to support their families and educate their children.

Bishop John Quinn doesn't back down an inch. He keeps reminding the 25 mostly old, bewildered-looking souls that Jesus poured out his love and his blood for us on the cross. The ultimate enactment of the golden rule amid a world in chaos. The sacred heart of Jesus dying on the cross for us... the epitome of a "**bleeding heart liberal**" pouring out his blood and life for mankind. This... the two thousand year old message spoken from the lips of Bishop John Quinn, the ultimate "Reverend Mr. Black, who stood tall in the saddle and carried a Bible in a sack and who could preach hot hell or freezing snow;" "The Reverend Mr. Black who turned his cheek to that lumberjack," reminding all of us that when it comes our time to "walk that lonesome valley," Jesus will be there for us.

It finally dawns on me. **"Thy will be done."** Bishop Quinn cannot command the world or even the city or the parish to listen to him. All he has control of is... his part... his role. And, his part, his role is to stand tall in the saddle and deliver his best sermon, even to a virtually empty church, but knowing full well that **the universe is listening**. The universe hears his positive energy, and the world is the better for his uncompromising dedication. Bishop Quinn plugged it in. He lit it up. He lit up my old Hood and Lady Scholastica and, after "Tre Ore," blessed my beautiful girls, Jessie Valentine and Frances Sandoval Lauck. I don't know who this Irishman Quinn is, but I would like to know more.

"Tre Ore" ended and the gentle eyes of those in attendance met my eyes and the eyes of Jessie and Frances, and they smiled. Bishop Quinn disappeared. Father Livius shuffled off the altar, and my St. Scholastica classmate, Bob Green, now Father Mike, joined the volunteers and cleaned the altar and readied Lady Scholastica for the rest of the Easter vigil. Father Mike, a printer by trade, is left to handle all the overwhelming details of religious celebration, tend to the physical and emotional needs of the aging, dying priests who live in the cold, drafty monastery and... with his left-over time, run the parish. I sought out the music director Betty Rosevear and her fine choir: "Betty, great job as usual." I also gave her silent recognition for her musical role when we buried my mother, Jean McKelvy Montroy Lauck, on January 25, 1989 at St. Scholastica. Little did I know then that Betty was winding down and she would also be gone in two years.

Bombed Out

Jessie Valentine and I did the Stations of the Cross. At 5 years old, Jessie knows all the stations. Jessie and I finished the stations, and walked outside. Glancing northbound as I exited the church, my eyes consciously sought out that classic, architectural work of art, Mercy College, whose architectural style rivaled any European cathedral... a compelling landmark for decades, located right in our Hood on the northwest corner of Southfield and Outer Drive. But, now, shock of all shocks. Say it ain't so! Say it ain't so! Say it ain't so! What do my eyes now behold... just mortar and brick, imploded and lying on sacred ground. The holy four corners of Southfield and Outer Drive are gone. The Little Sisters of the Poor, Sarah Fisher home for the aged on the northeast corner, gone... now a shopping center. Benedictine High School on the southeast corner (the brain child of Father Livius)... closed. Mercy College on the northwest corner, bombed out... leveled and lying in Dresden-like ruins, another victim of the accounting mentality with its hundreds of reasons why "**it isn't feasible**" (great accounting concept) to preserve art. The Taliban blew up Hindu mountain art (Mount Rushmore like) in Afghanistan and the non-Muslim world cried out in protest about the destruction of art. Then, a clueless America quickly goes about "business as usual," and implodes its own national treasures and architectural works of art. I felt the end was in sight, but little did I know then that, four short years later, at the beginning of 2011, the Benedictine monks would withdraw from St. Scholastica Grade School after 82 years, and hand over the only remnant of the Hood's Holy Corners, St. Scholastica, to the Archdiocese of Detroit.

For Whom The Bell Tolls

Well, there is no more denial. The Hood is gone. It is irretrievably lost. Yes, I understand now… **"you can't go home."** Good-bye Hood. Good-bye Lady Scholastica. I'll say my good-byes now while you're still standing. Good-bye to the school and church that I'll always call home. Good-bye to the simple, humble, "Jesus-like Christianity" that I was raised on – the only kind of Christianity I can acknowledge… not the administrative bureaucracy known as "Christianity."

Good-bye to all the families of St. Scholastica. Good-bye Allgeyers, Amos, Angotts, Argentas, Barrys, Beaufaits, Belaisles, Bennetts, Beuhlers, Bonannos, Bowlers, Brogans, Brozeks, Burns, Busleps, Cashens, Cerritos, Cislos, Collins, Cronins, Dacoffs, Davis, Demers, DiBellas, DiPonios, Dizhazys, Dolls, Dopkes, Draws, Dunns, Ergers, Esslers, Fedorinchiks, Ficiones, Flynns, Foleys, Foregs, Fruends, Frundels, Georges, Gerhards, Gibsons, Gilberts, Gleesons, Gorzoneys, Gouges, Gramlichs, Guerrieros, Hankins, Hartfords, Harts, Hedburgs, Hendersons, Hodges, Houles, Hudgens, Hydorns, Ivorys, Katalinas, Kays, Kennys, Klenners, Kosses, Krolls, LaRues, LaTours, Lemires, Lemkes, Lewis, Lindermes, Linds, Loftus, Luthers, Mahoneys, Manzos, Martins, Marxes, Mays, McBradys, McDonalds, McEvoys, McLaughlins, Melodys, Meruccis, Michauds, Mills, Miltons, Monroes, Morans, Mummas, Murrays, Nesbits, Noels, Norgards, O'Flaratys, Ohelers, O'Karmas, Orcutts, O'Sullivans, Parents, Pattersons, Perkins, Petersmarks, Pilons, Platzes, Pomas, Pophams, Quinlans, Quinns, Roses, Rosses, Rotoles, Rutleges, Saads,

Sawayas, Saxes, Schroeders, Seighters, Sevalds, Sheehys, Shendens, Skowns, Soaves, Spaldings, Stecshultes, Steintragers, Stellas, Stevens, Surowiecs, Swierczs, Tamborninis, Uzelacs, Valentis, Vanniers, Versaces, Walls, Whites, Wilhelms, Williams, Wills, Wittbrodts, Youngs, Zarzas, and the rest of those beautiful "Greatest Generation" people who lived with quiet dignity, and who raised, fed and nurtured their families, and went quietly to their eternal reward.

Despite the roll call of the dead, the relocated and the missing in action, despite the dwindling and disappearing flock at Lady Scholastica, despite the last mass by the Benedictine monks on Sunday, January 2, 2011, and, despite the "pave-paradise-and-put-up-a-parking-lot" mentality that has forever changed the Holy Corners of Southfield and Outer Drive, despite all of that... the resilient middle class spirit of St. Scholastica's parish with its simple enduring message of "God is Love" and "Peace be with you" still lives on in the eternal souls and in the great subconscious of those long-gone parishioners for whom the bell now tolls, and still lives on in the minds and hearts of their ever growing descendants wherever they may be – all subliminally touched by the powerful but simple message that "God is Love" and "Peace be with you." Thanks for living that message... Father Phillip Bartoccetti, Father Boniface Lucci, Father Livius Poali, Father Leo Cornelli, Father John, Father Hugo, Father Mike, Sister Marie Ruth, Sister Angeline Marie, Sister Joan Ceciel, Sister Kathleen, Sister Margaret Francis, Sister Matthews, Sister Ricardo, Sister Gertrude Mary, Sister Helena, Sister Josephine, Sister Joan of Arc, Sister Roselyn, Sister Madelyn and all the rest of the followers of those dynamic twins, St. Benedict and St. Scholastica. We have lost the mortared monuments and the historical landmarks of our youth on our path to "winding down... and losing our world," but we can still go home spiritually: **"The Peace and Love of Jesus be with all of us."**

Epilogue...
Eulogies Of
The Greatest Generation

First they taught us how to live...
then they taught us how to die.

Frederick Valentine Lauck

December 15, 1982
Duns Scotus Church
Southfield, Michigan

Reverend Father Harrison and the Basilians, Reverend Father Irbin and the Franciscans... on behalf of my father and my family, I want to thank you for the celebration of this Mass for the soul of my father.

We are gathered here to join in one of the corporal acts of mercy... to bury the dead. Therefore, it is appropriate at this time to say something about the **MAN** we have come to bury. The man is my father, Frederick Valentine Lauck, born in St. Louis, Missouri, on May 11, 1916. He died on December 11, 1982 at age 66 in my home at 3651 McNichol Trail in West Bloomfield, Michigan, sitting in his favorite chair, looking out at the backyard... one last time. In the 66 years between May 11, 1916 and December 11, 1982, he did a lot of living.

This past Sunday while I was at the funeral home, I was summoned to the telephone. A reporter from the *Detroit Free Press* was calling. Since we live in a success-oriented world (or, as I refer to it, a success-disoriented world), it did not surprise me that the *Free Press* reporter inquired about my father's academic and business accomplishments. He asked me where my father went to high school. I told him he attended Catholic Central High School and was taught by the Basilian priests. When the reporter asked me what year my father "graduated," I told him that my father never graduated. My father's education, as many others of the Greatest Generation, fell victim to the Great Depression of the 1930s.

My father was extremely bright and quick-witted, but he never graduated from high school, and definitely never carried his strong intellectual power on his sleeve. My father downplayed, and, at times, outright concealed his far ranging intellectual ability. Feeling somewhat defensive with the reporter, therefore, I rallied to my father's cause, and quickly volunteered that, twenty-five years after quitting high school in the tenth grade to go to work, my father entered the University of Detroit's School of General Education, and earned almost fifty hours of college credits studying philosophy, mathematics and accounting while maintaining a 3.75 grade point average. When the reporter asked me what year my father "graduated" from the University of Detroit, I said to myself: "Here we go again," and I repeated the same refrain: "my father never graduated from any school except Holy Rosary Grade School." I could tell by the tone of the conversation that we really didn't have much of an "obituary" in progress.

The *Free Press* reporter had somehow been informed, however, that my father owned his own business, and the reporter, therefore, turned the conversation to my father's "business success." I told the reporter that my father owned a commercial art studio, "**LAUCK ASSOCIATES**." These words, "Lauck Associates," echoed in my head as I silently reflected upon past telephone conversations I had with my father when I called his office. My father would answer the phone: "Lauck Associates," and I would immediately inquire: "Pa, who are your associates?" But, as luck would have it, every time I called... his "associates" were "out of the office at the present time."

The reporter then asked me: "Where my father's office was located." When I told the reporter that my father had an office in Troy and an office in Southfield, the reporter must have felt we had something to work with now. Based on the two office scenario, there now seemed to be irrefutable evidence of financial and business success in my father's life. But, little did the reporter know that my father's Troy office consisted of a small corner in the library of my own law office where my father loved to hang out, and little did the reporter know that my father's Southfield office was merely a phone number at Bernie Regnier's commercial art studio that greeted all callers: "**LAUCK ASSOCIATES**" with a receptionist to take a message.

The conversation ended. I hung up the phone, and walked back into the funeral home room where my father was laid out in death for the world to see the last remains of my father's earthly humanity. My "emotional response" to that start-and-stop conversation with the *Free Press* reporter:

> "Where in the resume of my father's accomplishments will they touch upon his humanity?"

> "Where in the resume of my father's accomplishments will they touch upon his spirituality?"

Since we are gathered to bury my father, let this be his **"SPIRITUAL OBITUARY!"**

During my father's lifetime, my father achieved the virtues of sainthood. He was not a saint. Far from it. My father was as flawed as any of us, but he did achieve some of the very important virtues of sainthood. During my father's lifetime, he **touched** everyone he met… including all of you who are with us today as we pause to say "Good-bye" to my father. My father opened up his heart, and allowed all of you into his heart to see him and to touch his spirit. My father was spiritually confident and "transparent"… a man without guile, strategy or duplicity. He just opened up his heart and let you in.

During my father's lifetime, he **expected nothing** from others but, at the same time, **greatly appreciated** the smallest of courtesies anyone extended to him. During his lifetime, my father achieved unending **patience**… although, as he admitted to me near the end of his life, "patience" was the most difficult of virtues to acquire. During my father's lifetime, he achieved an ability for **long suffering**, and Lord knows he was no stranger to suffering, having been diagnosed at age 19 with a degenerative, spinal condition known as "ankylosing spondylitis." My father suffered through a lifetime of progressive deterioration of the soft tissue surrounding his spinal vertebrae. He suffered a lifetime of pinched nerves and radiating, sciatic pain followed by the body's eventual bone fusion of his spinal vertebrae.

During his lifetime, my father suffered without complaint. He just didn't let anyone know he was in pain. In the fall of 1981, at age 64, my father was barely making it through life, struggling with "walking pneumonia" and denying the need for medical attention. He was finally hospitalized where the poor people go… North Detroit General Hospital in Hamtramck, Michigan. From his hospital bed, he plotted his own unsupervised release – an unauthorized flight out the second floor window and across the rooftops to freedom… just in case he had an impulse to escape his medical confinement. My father even enlisted me into his plot, making it a conspiracy of two, asking me to "case out" the shortest drop point for his contemplated second floor (unsupervised) rooftop, discharge. But, his escape was thwarted when the hospital voluntarily released him in November 1981, just in time for the Detroit Lions-Dallas Cowboys football game at the Silverdome in Pontiac, Michigan which we listened to on WJR radio on a cool, sunny Sunday... just riding through life, free of hospital confinement, cheering on the Lions' upset victory, and, more importantly, taking in the sights of a beautiful fall day with my father reminding me: "These are the good old days, Lauck" (a man who never called me by my first name).

But, for the rest of 1981, my Father continued to struggle through life, one weak cat... certainly not "good old days" from my perspective. Finally, on New Years Day, January 1, 1982, my father collapsed in his "Satellite" office... the small corner of my law library. He was alone when he went down, and alone when he later came to... who knows how long after his initial collapse. Obviously concerned about his health, my father then drove himself over to the "Golf Dome" in Rochester to hit a few golf balls to confirm that his "lights out" episode was only a meaningless aberration... a minor setback in an otherwise on-going life. Call it "denial," call it "rationalization," but the Spanish speaking people say it best: "esperanza muere ultima," or "hope dies last." Four or five days later, my father went to see his own doctor who, over my father's protest, immediately hospitalized him again in the North Detroit General Hospital where my father was, once again, engaged in a studied attempt to plot his escape – perhaps a primal urge of half-blood Native Americans, like my father, to die on the land of their fathers with the spirits of the ancestors, without fuss or fanfare... not confined to some sterile, hospital setting. But, there would be no escape. My father's weakened condition now trumped his need to fly. He just didn't have the energy to get through the window onto the rooftop, let alone flop his weakened, frail, worn-out, 65-year-old body over the edge to the hard-scrabble ground below.

As my father's heart went into a downward spiral, he claimed that the hospital was poisoning him with drugs: "They're putting gunpowder in my veins." My father refused to take any more of the hospital's drugs. The doctors then tried to twist my arm to force me to get my father to take the drugs. But, as I told the medical staff, it was not my role as a son to force my father to do anything. It was my father's life, and, if he was to die, it was his death and his call… all the way. Acting simply as the "messenger," however, I did relay the doctor's message of my father's "need to cooperate" with the medical staff. After that conversation, my father still refused to take the drugs, and I then relayed my father's "**el paso**" reply to the upset North Detroit Hospital medical staff. And, I stood behind my father's decision. He's the father, I'm the son. "Honor thy father… "

Sensing the need to transfer my father to a real hospital, I got a private room at Providence Hospital in Southfield, Michigan thanks to Medical Record Director, Gail Alder… the "bird heart," as my father called her. The ambulance company showed up to effectuate the transfer to Providence Hospital, but there was still a hiccup. My father, as weak as he was, steadfastly refused to lay down on the gurney, and face the indignity of being carted out of the hospital on his back. He was sick, weak and near death, but he still had a strong self image and a frontier-like need to "die with his boots on."

After a half hour of conversation, my father weakened further, and finally agreed to sit down on the gurney, and there he sat for a half hour with everyone waiting for him to eventually collapse into a supine position. It was one of life's poignantly, ridiculous moments – a 65-year-old man, out of gas, almost out of life, dressed in a suit and tie and overcoat, with his trademark fedora on, looking dazed ("stop the fight, my man's defenseless"), sitting in a precariously, upright position on a gurney... everybody in a holding pattern waiting for the next move. On the surface, it was one of life's more humorous events. Exhaustion, vulnerability and human dignity were all vying for control. Finally, exhaustion conquered dignity, and my father collapsed onto the gurney, and he was carted out of North Detroit General for transfer to a real hospital.

My father no sooner arrived at Providence Hospital, and was placed in the Intensive Care Unit, and I no sooner got home to crash, when I received the call. My father's vital functions were shutting down, and the Code Blue button was pushed in a frantic effort to beat back death. As the doctors at Providence said, my father was suffering from "digitalis poisoning" from the medication at North Detroit General... confirming my father's intuitive belief that North Detroit General was indeed poisoning him with medication ("Gun powder in my veins). Thank heaven I let my father make the call on whether he would or would not comply with the request of the North Detroit General doctors to take more "digitalis." I wasn't smart. I didn't have any special knowledge. I was just loyal and influenced by the fourth commandment: "Honor thy father... " But, my father was intuitively aware that he was, indeed, being poisoned.

After a ten day sojourn in a spiritual "twilight zone" where an intense battle was waged between timeless antagonists, life and death, and after my father's own grandiose dreams repetitively captured one of the Dallas Cowboy football players, holding the "jawbone of an ass," beckoning my father to leave his hospital bed and fight (later described by my father as himself beckoning himself to fight to live), my father finally rallied, and his fragile life triumphed over the compelling grip of death... but just barely. My father was eventually transferred from the intensive care unit to "step-down" intensive care. I drove over to Providence Hospital one more, endless time, but this time in a celebratory mood. The greatest man I have ever known had won the fight, and his remaining life had conquered his impending death... at least for the moment.

As I silently stepped into the doorway of my father's new, step-down, critical care room, unseen... I saw the back of the great doctor, Na'il Basmaji M.D., a very warm-hearted, but tough Armenian doctor educated in Iraq by the Jesuits. Dr. Basmaji was standing behind my father, stethoscope in hand, reaching around my father's back with both arms, monitoring my father's heart tone and rhythm. I fell silent and motionless... unnoticed. My father was in the middle of a conversation, telling the great doctor Basmaji to hurry up with his exam because, as my father said: "I gotta get out of here and get to Toledo, Ohio tonight." "Fat chance of that," I thought, just eavesdropping at the door. Dr. Basmaji, stifling a laugh at the ridiculousness of my father's suggestion, responded: "What are you going to do in Toledo, Fred?" "I got a date with Blaze Star at 8:00," responded Fred. As I'm thinking about the ridiculousness of my father dating an ancient burlesque star from the Gypsy Rose Lee era, Dr. Basmaji hugged my father from behind, laughing loudly while proclaiming: **"Lauck, you really know how to live!"** Little did I know then that I was not only standing at the threshold of the hospital room, but I was also standing at the threshold where "mortality" meets "immortality"... "Lauck, you really know how to live!"

The scene in that hospital room went from ridiculous to ludicrous, but it hit me as I heard an echo of immortality replay in my mind... "Lauck, you really know how to live." "Lauck, you really know how to live." "Lauck, you really know how to live." That's it! That's my father's epitaph! Through the pain, through the poverty, through the hunger and malnutrition of his early life, through the hard times, through the lack of opportunities (the fate of many of the Greatest Generation as they started out as childhood victims of the Great Depression), and through all of life's numerous disappointments, grievances and unfairness... through it all, my father lived life to its fullest. He never got cheated out of life's spectrum of emotions. He lived and felt all of life's emotions, and, in the process, he stayed a loving, gentle soul and a humorous, raucous, entertaining story teller, philosopher and loyal friend who would sweep you up in his charisma, and take you for a ride along his merry, minstrel, carousel way of life... laughing all the way:

> "A walking contradiction,
> partly truth and partly fiction,
> wearing yesterday's misfortunes
> like a smile."

A month later, my father was released from Providence Hospital. It was now February 1982... the week after the San Francisco 49ers Superbowl victory over the Cincinnati Bengals in the Silverdome in Pontiac, Michigan. The discharge diagnosis: "cardiomyophathy" and "two years to live." But, for my father it was: "Let's get out of this joint," turn on the radio and listen to Willie Nelson's *On the Road Again*... as my father headed full speed forward toward his May 11, 1982 sixty-sixth and final birthday.

Ten months later, on December 10, 1982, my 12-year-old son Frederick Valentine and I met my father at one of his favorite spots, the Normandy Bar on Second Ave. at the Grand Boulevard... less than a mile from the rented flat my father grew up in as a kid on the southwest corner of Piquette and John R. My father was very weak that night, but he had an appetite... reassuring for the moment. He insisted on picking up the tab. With the waitress hovering over him like a mother hen, my father counted out 26 one dollar bills, including his usual generous tip, leaving him without any money. The waitress gave him one of those "Oh, Fred" looks: "Fred, you can just sign the bill and put it on a tab," after which my father reassured her without missing a beat: "My parole officer only lets me counterfeit one dollar bills so it's okay"… another humorous event with a certain sense of logic carrying the moment. But, it was so like my always generous father… to pick up the last tab of his life.

I left the Normandy Bar that very cold, damp December 10th evening and walked my 66-year-old, frail father to his car. Smiling our good-byes, I drove off with 12-year-old "Kid Val"… both of us with buoyant spirits as "Red Neck Girls" by the Bellamy Brothers played on the radio. With a driving, rhythmic song in our ears, we were about to fly off down the entrance ramp of northbound John C. Lodge Freeway at the Boulevard… when I was struck like a bolt out of the blue. My father and I had a rule. We never drove off without making sure that both of our cars started, and we were both on our way. I didn't follow the rule that night. I didn't see my father start his car or get underway. So I aborted the freeway entrance, turned off the radio, retraced my steps and drove five blocks back to the Normandy Bar parking lot. There sat my father in his cold and unresponsive car… alone, helpless and too weak to even get out of his car. Wow! I thought. I just averted disaster and, perhaps, hypothermia for my father. I immediately arranged for a tow truck to tow my father's car to my mechanic, and then my father, "Kid Val" and I headed out of the parking lot to spend that last-of-life, December 10, 1982 night at my home in West Bloomfield.

On that last night and in those last early morning hours of his life, my father sat in my bedroom, shifting around in a Lazy Boy chair trying to get comfortable, and trying to get some sleep in a sitting position. Severe mid-back pain (the heart) kept him from getting into bed or sleeping on his back or on his side. I spent time trying to comfort him as those dark, emotionally frazzled, early morning hours dragged on. All the time I was with him, my father was worried that his stifled groans would awaken "Kid Val" sleeping in the adjoining bedroom. He wanted to make sure that his grandson and namesake, Frederick Valentine Lauck, got enough sleep for his 12-year-old hockey game, the next day, Saturday, December 11, 1982. My father was also worried that I was not going to get enough sleep. My father insisted that he was alright, and that I should go back to bed. On the last night of his life, suffering through the dark hours of that long, arduous night, he carried his cross, **cheerfully** and **uncomplainingly**, all the time worrying about others along the wayside.

After a few hours sleep, I awoke to find my father still in pain. I called Dr. Basmaji, who phoned in a Tylenol prescription. I picked up the pain pills from the drug store, knowing that having a plan, any kind of a plan, was the only way I could hold off my sense that I was "failing," "failing," "failing." I returned home, got a couple pain pills in my father, and then left to take kid Val to the hockey arena for a team photo. I dropped Val off, and then returned home again to check on my father. I had left my front door open so that, in my absence, the West Bloomfield fire fighter who was moonlighting as a curtain man could hang my new curtains for my big Christmas party that night. While I was on the "to and from road of life," the curtain man arrived and found my father sitting in his favorite chair, looking out at the back yard... lifeless. When I arrived home, two West Bloomfield police cars were in the driveway, and, with a crescendo of adrenaline, I intuitively knew: "It's over." Damn it! Damn it! Damn it!

As I entered the house, I brushed off the police officer's physical restraint and his second hand version of what happened, and I went directly to the living room and spotted the unfamiliar... a cheap, plastic sheet covering something on the floor. I lifted the plastic cover they put on top of my father's now eternally, lifeless body, and looked straight into the vacant and distorted face of my father's death. He was gone, and, in the end, it appeared that it was mercifully quick. Hopefully, the pain pills I got in him comforted him in his final hours on that cold, bleak December 11th day of death. The Desmond Brothers undertaker showed up, put what was left of my father on a stretcher... this time with no complaint by my father. Death has no dignity. The Desmond undertaker went off down my street, eastbound, with the last earthly remains of my father. His life done, I stood in the road on that cold, lifeless, gray December day, my only companion... the "finality" of death.

But, my father's legacy lives on. My father was a poor kid who never lost the sense of who he was or where he came from. From the bleak days of his childhood living in abject poverty and hunger during the Great Depression, to his middle class success of buying a two bedroom bungalow home in Northwest Detroit for $11,000, and putting his kids through Catholic schools... through it all, he lived life to the fullest, and constantly entertained his friends and family with his art work, his music, his poetry, his humorous story-telling, his generosity and his uncanny ability to paint a picture of life that was humorous, grandiose and dramatic. The glass was not only half full. The glass sang, danced, wept and sparkled with an energy that was larger than real life, an energy that gave off a luminous light of joy and love... and all this charismatic energy on a low key, limited financial budget.

On December 15, 1982, my father was buried at Holy Sepulcher Cemetery with two symbols that capture his life... a $275.00 particle board casket, just like the ones they bury the Jesuit priests in, and a grave marker bearing the Latin inscription "**Vixit**": "He lived!" Or, as Dr. Basmaji said to an audience of two Laucks: "Lauck, you really know how to live." And, Lauck, thank you for that very important message... you don't have to be rich to really live and enjoy life. You just need to have the right spiritual attitude. And, more importantly, thank you for giving me the message... I could be somebody.

During my father's lifetime, he achieved total **courage**. He was not afraid of life. He was not afraid of death. He was not afraid of anything. His attitude... "There's nothing you can do to hurt me." My father was a product of the Great Depression. He was a man touched by poverty, hunger, malnutrition and suffering, and he never forgot the plight of the poor. He always reached in his pocket, and gave the "down and outers" some of his limited bankroll. My father had no **false pride**. It simply didn't matter whether his clothes were less than stylish. In fact, he preferred a poor man's wardrobe. He felt more comfortable not standing out. It didn't matter whether his clothes were color coordinated... although, ironically, in his line of commercial art work, he knew everything about coordination of color, pattern and fabric, as I found out when he color-coordinated my selection of "trial lawyer suits" at Chelsea in Wyandotte, Michigan when I started out practicing law on my own in 1976. But, my father's **pride** was in his own spirituality, and not in any material impression or facade.

Perhaps my father's biggest achievement was his absolute **faith** in the existence of **God** and his total, absolute and unequivocal faith in the existence of **eternal life**. When my father survived his "Code Blue" experience in Providence Hospital in February, 1982, I later discussed his near death experience with him, and asked him, point blank, whether he thought there was a God. His immediate response: "Absolutely!" I then asked him if he thought there was "eternal life." His response: "When we die we are all part of the Great Subconscious of Mankind." Ever the trial lawyer, I followed up my cross examination with: "Are we just part of the 'Great Subconscious of Mankind' because we were born and have lived life, or are we also aware, after our death, of being part of the Great Subconscious of Mankind?" Again his immediate response: "Both!"

My father, Frederick Valentine Lauck, had an **indomitable spirit** and **unconquerable soul**. Life could not defeat him. He took everything life gave him, and he was still standing, "bloody but unbowed." Death takes all of us, but life could not defeat him. That is the essence of the **man**. This is his obituary.

When I was a young kid, 10 years old, my father, while wiping away tears I could not understand then, read a poem to me that I would like to share with you... **"IF"** by Rudyard Kipling:

> If you can keep your head when all about you
>   Are losing theirs and blaming it on you;
> If you can trust yourself when all men doubt you,
>   But make allowance for their doubting too:
> If you can wait and not be tired by waiting,
>   Or, being lied about, don't deal in lies,
> Or being hated don't give way to hating,
>   And yet don't look too good, nor talk too wise;
>
> If you can dream – and not make dreams your master;
>   If you can think – and not make thoughts your aim,
> If you can meet with Triumph and Disaster
>   And treat those two imposters just the same.
> If you can bear to hear the truth you've spoken
>   Twisted by knaves to make a trap for fools,
> Or watch the things you gave your life to, broken,
>   And stoop and build 'em up with worn out tools;
>
> If you can make one heap of all your winnings
>   And risk it on one turn of pitch-and-toss,
> And lose, and start again at your beginnings,
>   And never breathe a word about your loss;
> If you can force your heart and nerve and sinew
>   To serve your turn long after they are gone,

And so hold on when there is nothing in you
    Except the Will which says to them: "hold on!"
If you can talk with crowds and keep your virtue,
    Or walk with Kings – nor lose the common touch,
If neither foes nor loving friends can hurt you,
    If all men count with you, but none too much.
If you can fill the unforgiving minute
    With sixty seconds' worth of distance run,
Yours is the Earth and everything that's in it,
    And – which is more – you'll be a Man, my son!

YOU ARE A MAN, MY FATHER

Good job, Pa.

Well done, Pa.

Good life, Pa.

Godspeed, Pa.

Jesus Christ, St. Basil, St. Francis, Father Clement Kern, and Father Solanus Casey, take my beloved father into your loving arms and enjoy him in eternal life as we have enjoyed him on this earth.

Frederick Valentine Lauck
1916-1982

Jean Montroy Lauck

January 25, 1989
St. Scholastica Church
Detroit Michigan
Father Livius Paoli officiating

My mother was born on October 18, 1914 and died at high noon on January 21, 1989 at age 74. The passing of every soul carries with it a "message" for those who remain. Let me share with you the message in my mother's death – a message of the inevitable losses along the road that leads to death and the enduring message of "love" that walks side by side with those losses... a message of "love" that triumphs over those losses and even death itself.

On October 18, 1914, my mother arrived on the cold, windswept plains of northern Minnesota in the small town of Tower. She was the second youngest of ten children born to Charles Montroy and Mary McKelvy. The youngest, the baby of the family, Charlene Montroy LaTour, is with us today. Charlene is also the mother of ten children, many of whom have come from faraway places to be with us today.

My mother began experiencing life's inevitable losses at two years of age. Her 17-year-old brother, Sherwood Montroy, was killed

Sherwood Montroy
An Abbreviated Life
1916

in a logging accident. As was the custom then, Sherwood was laid out in the parlor of the family home... a boarding house which my grandmother, Mary McKelvy, and my grandfather, Charles Montroy, ran for the strong, young, daring lumberjacks who were cutting down the great, virgin forests of northern Minnesota for wealthy lumber barons. As a 4-year-old, my mother vividly recalled the bright copper pennies that were placed on her lifeless brother's eyelids to hold them closed as a wooden coffin peacefully embraced 17-year-old Sherwood's battered body in the parlor of the family home.

Shortly after Sherwood's death, my mother's family moved from the stark, but beautiful Minnesota wilderness, and landed in the bustling City of Detroit... just as the 20th Century motor car giants were making their mark in the world, in a city that would later be known as the "Motor City." My mother's large family moved into a rented duplex at 254 Marston in the Boulevard Center area of Detroit... just north of Grand Boulevard and a few doors east of Woodward Ave. My mother Jean attended Holy Rosary Parish Grade School at Woodward and Harper near what used to be Medbury Park, now the I-94 Freeway. She met my father at Holy Rosary Grade School.

As life evolved, my mother continued to suffer losses. She lost her own mother, Mary McKelvy Montroy, on June 20, 1931 at the relatively young age of 52. I remember my mother telling me about her own mother's death, and how her mother must have suffered because there was no air conditioning to aid her mother's breathing and no modern medical support to help her mother during her mother's long, last moments. As my mother told me, right before her own mother drew her last breath, she talked of beautiful visions, and asked where the beautiful music was coming from… certainly a pleasant entrée beckoning her on to eternity.

The losses continued. My mother lost her oldest sister, Katherine, the so-called "beauty of the family"… although I fail to see how

Mary McKelvy Montroy

anybody could be more physically attractive than my own mother. According to the *Detroit Times* newspaper, Katherine died on July 4, 1939 at "age 36 in a charity ward at Receiving Hospital," a victim of alcoholism and a brutal beating at the Dixie Hotel at 143 E. Vernor in downtown Detroit… where the hotel night clerk merely ignored Katherine's groans as she faded away into the darkness of that long, last night of her life. Next, my mother's sister Corrine died on January 18, 1952… after a hard life with the drink and dysfunction (God love her). Next, her sister Mary Josephine died in New England in 1964 of breast cancer. I remember telephoning Aunt Jo in 1964 on a pay phone just outside Fenway Park when my University of Detroit football team journeyed to Boston to play Boston College. Her voice was pitifully weak. A short time later,

Katherine Montroy, 1916

she was gone. Next my mother lost her brothers

Jack and Larry Montroy, both of whom played football at Notre Dame in the mid 1920s under the legendary Notre Dame coach, Knute Rockne. Her brother Jack Montroy died in Chicago of throat cancer and her brother Larry died of emphysema and alcoholism in California. In 1976, my mother lost her beloved brother, Marty Montroy, who died of emphysema in San Diego, California. Marty was so very good to my mother. In 1974, her brother Marty flew her out to southern

California… where he had settled after his second escape from the "Bowery" of alcoholism. I had flown my mother out to San Francisco and down to Carmel in 1969. She loved California, and she was so delighted and felt so loved when her brother, Marty, later flew her out to San Diego for a sight-seeing tour from San Diego to all points north of Orange County, up to the artist colony in Solvang, California.

Fourteen years ago, at age 60, my mother's losses became even more personal and more dramatic. She was diagnosed with emphysema after years of non-filtered cigarette smoking. My mother started smoking cigarettes at a time when both Hollywood and the medical profession glamorized cigarettes, and at a time when the corporate tobacco manufacturers failed to disclose the known dangers of cigarette smoking to the public. The tobacco companies' motto was: "Just hook 'em on nicotine, and let the good times (and the profits) roll." It was only in 1965 that the cigarette manufacturers were forced to disclose the dangers of cigarette smoking by putting warning labels on cigarette packs. By that time it was too late. Many of the Greatest Generation, including my mother, were irretrievably "hooked" on the highly addictive drug nicotine, and had already suffered irreversible lung and heart damage by their supposed "harmless" addiction to nicotine. But, that is the story of corporate fraud, betrayal and government complicity that I will leave for another day.

At first, my mother's losses with emphysema were gradual. In her early sixties, she had to quit working as a waitress. She just didn't have the energy or vitality she used to have. Then, she was unable to go out of the house and socialize like she used to. She was noticing shortness of breath upon slight physical exertion. Next, she lost the ability to drive a car. I remember surprising her with a new car on St. Patrick's Day 1984, kelly green ribbon wrapped around it, and my mother thinking I lost it… driving around on St. Patrick's Day with a green ribbon on my car. Then, she lost it when she finally figured out the "surprise"... it was her green ribbon on her brand new car. And, I also remember the very regrettable mistake I made, devastating my mother, by giving her car to her grandson Valentine in 1987 so he had wheels to drive to and from Plymouth, Michigan to Catholic Central High School. Although my mother could no longer drive, she was not emotionally ready to part with the car, nor to accept the "inevitable message" the loss of the car meant.

Next my mother lost the ability to go out to restaurants for dinner. I remember one of the last times out to a restaurant. On Valentine's Day in 1986, my son Valentine and I took her out to dinner at Joe Muer's on Gratiot in the Eastern Market area of Detroit. It was only appropriate that on Valentine's Day she should spend time with her grandson, Valentine. It was also appropriate that I should be taking my mother out on Valentine's Day since my mother was my original sweetheart – the woman who taught me to ice skate, to swim, to dance, and to survive life, including the emotional intensity needed to play full throttle, bang-bang, collision football... as she would patrol the sidelines of my St. Scholastica Grade School football games reminding me to "knock someone down!"

Mother
Jean Montroy Lauck
Ever The Teacher

She was also the mom who hailed a taxi cab to take us to the circus and to the fair when we had no car. The good looking mom that strange men in crowds would fight over as they rushed to open a door for us. The mom who told the world how great I was, but who emotionally leveled me, one on one, just to accent the lesson of humility, and to remind me of the ever-ongoing mission of life... there's always "more to do." At the Joe Muer's Valentine dinner, I used a wheelchair to wheel the now-older Jean Lauck into Joe Muer's restaurant. She didn't take to the wheelchair idea at all. She wanted to walk, and maybe even knock someone down on the way, but the distance was too great, and the wheelchair, thankfully, accommodated her shortness of breath. It was a memorable Valentine's dinner... great food, great ambience and better company, including my mother's tableside visit with the proprietor, Joe Muer. Thanks for making her feel special, Joe.

The last time my mother went out to dinner was in 1986 when my St. Scholastica, grade school friend, Fred Saxe, came to town from California. My sister, Mary Katherine, was going to drive my mother downtown to meet Fred Saxe and me at the Roma Café in Detroit. My

mother didn't have any out-to-dinner clothes but, with compromised lungs, she didn't have the physical stamina or the breathing ability to go shopping. My sister Katie, in her usual ingenious way, solved the problem by going to Saks Fifth Avenue, buying $500 to $600 worth

A Moment of Levity

of clothes, bringing them into the house and hanging them in my mother's bedroom... creating my mother's own personal "Saks Fifth Avenue" wardrobe room. My mother made her selection, the rejected garments were returned to Saks, and off we all went to dinner at the Roma Café. In her usual fashion of generosity, my mother used her limited Social Security allotment and picked up the tab... tip and all. It cost my mother a lot more than it would have cost Saxe or me. But, my mother's emotional lift from still being in the game of life and picking up a tab was... "priceless."

About two and a half years ago, in October of 1986, my mother almost died. Thereafter the pace of her losses began to accelerate. When she came home from the hospital, she was no longer able to cook for her family. I remember seeing her try to cook, leaning over the stove to open up her lungs for more air. She wouldn't let anybody know that she was struggling to breathe. She pretended like she was merely cooking and tending to her food. But, her cooking days were over.

Eventually, my mother lost the ability to sit at the kitchen table and visit. As you know, my family grew up in northwest Detroit in a small, two bedroom bungalow. The kitchen table was our "middle class," social hour and cultural center. But, 10 years ago, after I parlayed some "roll-of-the-dice," personal injury cases (in the law business) into some financial gain, I was able to move my mother into a new home in Livonia, Michigan, with an attached garage, a small kitchen and a family room... side by side. My mother loved to hold her social hour at that kitchen table, and look out over the kitchen, the family room and out through the sliding glass door into her picturesque back yard. As my mother's Irish relatives might say: "Jean... was in her element!" But, as my mother's emphysema progressed, she lost the ability to even sit in her favorite spot in her home and look around at her trusty surroundings. In 1986, a couple of years before her death, she became homebound and confined to bed.

In the fall of 1986, after another near death experience, my mother's life long friend Jim Gribbin drove in from Cedar, Michigan in the Leelanau Peninsula to be with my mother. Jim and my mother used to exchange books as both were avid readers. The books that Jim Gribbin left with my mother in the fall of 1986 went unread, however, because, by then, my mother had lost even the ability to read.

In June of 1988, my mother almost died again. She had a breathing attack and stopped breathing. She passed out and my sister Katie held her in her arms waiting for death to come. Katie waited for about 45 minutes, but my mother didn't die. Katie figured she had to do something. So an ambulance was summoned, and my mother was taken to St. Mary's hospital. Again, it was a rough road, but somehow

Mother Jean survived and returned home. When she returned home, however, the losses began to accelerate again… at an alarming pace. Mother Jean lost the ability to get up and go to the bathroom. Then she lost the ability to use the bedside bathroom. Then she lost the ability to watch television. Mother Jean, ever a revolutionary, loved to watch the Iran-Contra hearings, highlighting wrong-doing by the executive branch of the government as President Ronald Reagan and his cabinet surreptitiously thumbed their collective noses at the U.S. Congress… so they could secretly arm the Contra revolutionaries in Central America to take out Daniel Ortega, the leader of Nicaragua. She waited for the televised hearings to bring down President Reagan, his cabinet members, Oliver North and the rest of those "pious" rascals. After a day of Iran-Contra hearings, it was on to the "weather," and then her favorite late night comedian: "He-e-e-e-er's Johnny" Carson. The weather came on everyday at 6:14 p.m. on Channel 4. She constantly reminded me that the television had to be on Channel 4 at 6:14 p.m. so that she could use her remote to usher the T.V. weatherman into her bedroom to give her the next day's temperature and humidity predictions… just so she could determine how difficult it would be for her to breathe the next day.

Eventually, Mother Jean lost the ability to feed herself. She also lost the ability to turn over in bed and the ability to adjust her position in bed. She couldn't even reach down and pull up a cover if she was cold. She couldn't take a cover off if she was too warm. This sad state of affairs continued for about the last 6 months of her life.

Finally, about a week ago, on Monday January 15, 1989, she became very difficult to arouse. It was practically impossible to get her medication in her. She was not eating or drinking. By then, she had lost everything she had except the ability to expend all of her strength and energy in simply laboring to breathe in and out. I said a rosary at her bedside last Thursday and Friday. As I watched her in her twilight zone existence, she was unconsciously using all of her body energy and strength to simply breathe. Watching this poignant scene of survival, I recalled the words of Rudyard Kipling in the poem "*IF*" –

"If you can fill the unforgiving minute
With sixty seconds worth of distance run,
And if you can force your nerve and heart and sinew
To serve you long after their time has come,
Till there is nothing left within you
But a voice that says hang on – hang on."
Hang on, hang on, hang on.

My mother was a living example of those words. And, therein lies the contradiction of life and death. My mother was ready to go to her Maker long before she actually died. She was ready to give up her body, and leave this "vale of tears" long before death, mercifully, overtook her. So, why the great struggle to "hang on?" I don't know the answer. I can only guess. Perhaps the answer lies in the words of the great poet and playwright, William Shakespeare... we are all "**creatures of habit**." That's why we teach our children to acquire good study habits so that they will have no choice, but to study correctly as a "creature of habit." That's why we train professional boxers so strenuously... so that when the fighter gets knocked down in the fifth round, he is able to rise to his feet, as a "creature of habit," and finish the fight, never remembering the knockdown or the rest of that round or even the sixth, seventh, eighth, ninth, or tenth rounds. The fighter's mind was disengaged, but the fighter carries on as a "creature of habit"... the discipline of the gym paying off at a time when his mind was seemingly disengaged from his body. The reason I guess my mother was still hanging on with only the ability to breathe left in her was that... like a "creature of habit" and the "fighter" that she was, she continued to fight long after her body had served her and long after her time had come.

To say that my mother was a fighter is a comical understatement. My mother was the most vocal champion of the underdog I have ever known. She railed and fought against corporate America, bureaucrats, capitalists and those generally in charge of our lives. She fought for the poor. She fought for the little man and the neglected woman and those forgotten or abandoned by society. She even brought them home for dinner, as we kids wondered: "Who the heck is this misfit?" And, if any of her children were threatened, my mother would fearlessly rally to our side. I remember the summer of 1966 when, as a 23-year-old, I had a dispute with some (my way or the highway) cop just outside the Saxe Club on McNichols (6 Mile) near Woodward Avenue, in Detroit. I was being treated unjustly, and Mother Jean came to my defense, and we both ended up in jail at the Woodward-7 Mile Road precinct. I remember my mother in a lock-up cell across from mine staring daggers at me. John DiBella, one of my mother's pall bearers, was with us, and he also ended up in jail and handcuffed with the key broken off in the lock. My mother and I were released, but DiBella can't get un-handcuffed, so he's staying with the cops until the locksmith from downtown gets there. Nothing was going right that night.

Mother Jean was vulnerable by nature but fierce by necessity... especially when one of her own was under attack. Mother Jean was a competitor and a fighter by necessity, and, even though she only had an eighth grade education, she schooled me well on the fearless temperament a trial lawyer must have to cross examine the rich, the powerful, the ever-expanding throng of courtroom experts and intellectuals, the cops, the power brokers and anyone who is a member of the "ruling class" of America. As a "creature of habit," my mother was a fighter who fought during her entire life, and, as a "creature of habit," she fought during her dying experience right up to the long-over-due end of her life.

Last Saturday, January 21, 1989, a little after noon, I came over to my mother's house to help my sister Valentine change mother's position in bed and to say another rosary. When I came in, I knew it was over. I could see it written all over my sister Valentine's face... a sense of peace and relief. I went to my mother's back room. The only thing that my mother still had left, the ability to breathe, was now mercifully gone. She rested in quiet repose. She had died 10 minutes before I got to her house. I wondered if, like her mother before her, she had heard the "beautiful music"... usher her into eternity. I approached her peaceful remains. I placed my forehead on her forehead, and, through my tears, I pleaded: "Go Momma – Go Momma." Get out of your old, worn and tired body. Get out of this room that has been your prison for the last two and a half years. Get out of this house that has served you well, and go on to your eternal reward. Don't even look back. Fill your new lungs with the air of eternity and run, run, run, and let your beautiful, dark hair of youth again flow through the gentle breezes of life. "Go Momma – Go. Go. Go." I was her cheerleader in death like she was my cheerleader in life... right over here on the fields of St. Scholastica where she used to cheer me on while I played football and baseball when our celebrant, Father Livius, was my coach. As her cheerleader, I knelt and said my last rosary with her as she rested, quiet and still. Just the two of us. One there... and one gone... no more cabs to catch for a ride to the circus or the fair, just the peace of relief and the finality of death.

So that's it – life and its losses, and, finally... death. Little by little and year by year, we lose everything we have until, finally... we lose our life. But, the real message is not in the losses or even in death itself, but rather the way in which my mother handled those losses and her impending death... with patience and strength. She taught me it takes a ton of patience to die. With patience and strength, she handled each and every accumulating loss that she met on her march to Calvary. Mother Jean handled each and every loss leading to her death without ever letting the losses or even her impending death demoralize her or break her spirit. How you do that, I don't know… yet.

In addition to being a "fighter," my mother must have intuitively known that to fight death was the necessary preoccupation or distraction that keeps us from being demoralized, and that allows us to "live in the moment" and get mileage and quality out of what remains of our last years, last months and last moments of our life. Sure, she was discouraged at times, but she absolutely refused to allow her losses and her impending death to demoralize her or break her spirit, and darken the days and the moments of life she still had left. It is an important message for all of us who will, one day, take the same relentless march to the hereafter that Mother Jean just finished. As we go through life, everything will be okay so long as we do not lose our spirit. Therefore, one of the messages of my mother's death is to face all losses and even death itself with patience and without letting our spirit break, knowing that, perhaps, the preoccupation in the fight to live is all that we have "control" over… even though the loss of that battle is inevitable.

But… the "greatest message" that comes out of my mother's death and her long battle against death is… "**LOVE**." For it is "love" that fills the voids of the losses that inexorably usher us out of life and into death. And, when I talk about love, I am talking about you, my dear sister Mary Katherine, or as mother called you "Katie." And, when I talk about love, I'm talking about you, my dear sister Jeannie Valentine, or, as mother called you, "Vallie." You two girls were splitting sick vigil shifts with me… each of us taking two days and three nights at a time. One of her children was with Mother Jean 24 hours a day, 7 days a week for the last two and a half years of her life. Personal lives were put on hold as the voids of our mother's losses were each filled with "love" from her children. We took up our mother's losses. We carried them for her, and filled in those losses with our love just as she did for us when we were helpless infants and children. You girls cooked for her. You fed her. We gave her her medication. We kept her spirits up. We were her arms and legs. We were up in the middle of the night while she was experiencing difficulty in breathing. Many times, Katie and Vallie, you got in bed behind mother Jean, and placed your breasts against her back, and gave her the rhythm of your breathing, helping her through the long, dark nights. But, more importantly, we created a world for our mother. When she was a shut-in, and, when impending death locked Mother Jean in her back-bedroom prison, we were her hands and feet as we connected her to the outside world from her cloistered bedroom. We also gave her the news of the day, and spoke to her of days gone by, and relived interesting and happy events with her that kept her afloat emotionally.

When I talk about love, I'm talking about you, Valentine, her grandson... the gentle giant. When you came into her room, your broad shoulders filled the doorway. You came in with gentleness and cheerfulness. You greeted your grandmother with: "Hello, Mama Lauck," and then you embraced her or held her hand... even if she might have criticized you the day before, as she could do. Valentine, you always came in fresh.

When I talk about love, I'm talking about you Patricia Burns, her granddaughter. You were cheerful and more than willing to help your grandmother at all times. When I talk about love, I'm talking about you John DiBella, her pall bearer. You came over to my mother's house, and spent two hours talking to my mother shortly before her death. Your positive influence of love and friendship was so strong on her physical and spiritual well being that she called me right after you left that night, and told me to get her car back to her because she was cured... and ready to drive.

When I talk about love I'm talking about you, Carolyn Van Winkle, who cooked food for my mother, and even cooked the last meal

523

she ever ate. When I talk about love, I'm talking about you, Sam Hoot, my dear brother-in-law. You know the Laucks are very philosophical, deep thinkers who like to talk, but Sam… you are a genius. You don't just talk. You are a man of action, an engineer, and, whenever anything in the house needed to be repaired, Sam you were there… "Sammy on the Spot" to cheerfully do it. Out of love, Sam, you maintained the air conditioning unit to ease my mother's breathing. Out of love, Sam, you maintained the oxygen equipment. Out of love, Sam, you cut the grass and trimmed the lawn – each of mother Jean's losses leading to death always filled with love… yours and everyone else's.

When I talk about love, I'm talking about you, Wanda Webb De-Ponio, who would drop everything you were doing, and drive from West Bloomfield to Livonia to help my sister Katie with some crisis she was handling for my mother. When I talk about love, I'm talking about you, Cass and Leo Stoner, who sent my mother messages and get well wishes. When I talk about love, I'm talking about you, Helen Ivory, who sent flowers and visited and consoled my mother. When I talk about love, I'm talking about you, John Lombardi, and your mother Grace. John, your mother Grace came over and visited my mother regularly, talking to my mother through my mother's bedroom-window connection to the outside world… as your mother Grace took her daily walk through the neighborhood. When I talk about love, I'm talking about you Charlene, her sister, who came and visited with her. On Thursday, a little more than a week before her death, you had a two hour visit with her, and even poured a little beer for her to drink.

So the message of my mother's death is not just the fight to live, the patience to die and the acceptance of losses and death, but it is about the love which fills the voids of all of the spiraling losses that lead to death. My mother died at her own home, the old fashioned way, surrounded by love as she mercifully faded off to the abundance of perpetual and eternal life.

Even after my mother lost the only thing she had left, the ability to breathe, there was more love. All of you are here out of love for my mother and my family. My mother's sister Charlene and her family have driven from afar. Sis and Martha LaTour, my mother's nieces, drove from Atlanta, Georgia. Charles LaTour, my mother's nephew, drove from Washington D.C. to be here. Bobby LaTour, my mother's nephew, drove from South Haven, Michigan to be here today. Jeanne Marie and Paul LaTour drove with their mother Charlene from Lansing to be here. John Conlon, my law school classmate, drove from Kalamazoo, Michigan to be here. I have a difficult time getting up on Sunday to think about driving to church, and yet all of you are driving from all parts of the country to be here today. More love... love that, even in death, fills the last void left by the loss of breathing.

And, suddenly... it dawns on me. I remember when we were grade schoolers in the first grade right over here at St. Scholastica School. Do you remember?... Helen Ivory. Do you remember?... John Amo. Do you remember?... John DiBella and Frank Demers and Jerry Surowiec and Jimmy Sheehy. Do you remember our catechism class? Do you remember the first page of our catechism book?... "Who is God?," "God is Love." Yes, "God is Love," and, now, after all her mounting losses, there is nothing left of my mother that remains but love... the spiritual attraction that binds universe and "the subconscious of mankind." Therefore, my mother must be wrapped in love, one with God. Let me share with you what the great Apostle Paul had to say about love:

> "Though I speak with the tongues of men and angels, and have not love, I am as sounding brass or a tinkling cymbal. And though I have the gift of preaching and understand all the mysteries, and have all the knowledge, and though I have faith so strong that I can move mountains, if I have not love, I am nothing. And though I give away everything that I am, and give myself but do it in pride, not love, it profits me nothing.

"Love is patient and kind, never jealous or envious, never boastful or proud, never haughty or selfish or rude. Love does not demand its own way. It is not irritable or touchy. It does not hold grudges, and will hardly even notice when others do it wrong. It is never glad about injustice, but rejoices wherever truth wins out.

"If you love someone, you will be loyal to them no matter what the cost. You will always believe in them, always expect the best of them, and always stand your ground in defending them.

"All the special gifts and powers from God will someday come to an end, but love goes on forever. There are three things that remain – faith, hope and love – and the greatest of these is love." 1 Corinthians 13:4-8, 13

When my mother would have difficulty breathing, she would have us pray with her: "Lamb of God who takes away the sins of the world, have mercy on me." Momma – it is done.

"Lamb of God, who takes away the sins of the world, have mercy on us." "Lamb of God who takes away the sins of the world, grant us peace."

Jean Montroy Lauck
1914-1989

James Edward Gribbin

Holy Rosary Church
Lake Leelanau, Michigan
September 18, 1997

"A friend is gone, our hearts are in pain.
He left last night on the midnight train."

Ask not for whom the bell tolls. The bell tolls for thee... as in all of us.

On Sunday, September 14, 1997 at 4:00 p.m., the bell tolled for 86-year-old Jim Gribbin. His lovely bride, Mary Wilson Gribbin, was at his side. She reported that his breathing became irregular and shallow. At 4:00 p.m., Jim took one last breath, opened his eyes and surrendered his spirit to the Lord. Mary saw a lone tear silently, slowly... drift down Jim's face.

My name is Fred Lauck. I am 54-years-old. I have known Jim Gribbin for 54 years. In the early days of my life, when I was carrying my Gene Autry cowboy guns on each hip, Jim called me "Tex," "the Gunslinger" and "Two Gun." He later called me by my family nickname, "Snack." Still later, he just called me "Lauck," not Fred, not Fred Lauck... just "Lauck."

Before Jim's children, Mary Elizabeth Gribbin, Jamie Gribbin, his namesake, and Sarah the "Bear" Gribbin... were born, Jim was my second father. I had a wonderful father on my own, but to have a second father like Jim Gribbin was a double blessing. In an age when many children have no father at home, I was blessed with, not one, but two wonderful fathers to cheer me on, to nurture me, to show me compassion, ideals, wisdom, and to subtly direct me to value life, embrace life and fill each "unforgiving minute" (as Rudyard Kipling says) "with 60 seconds worth of distance run." As a kid, Jim and Mary had me over to their house for dinner on numerous occasions

Fred, Jim, Molly and Chrissy 1953

where I had the momentary luxury of being an "only child" and, afterwards... to the movies for cowboys and Indians with Gene Autry, Randolph Scott, Hopalong Cassidy, Tex Ritter and Roy Rogers. Jim also took me to the fields surrounding the Capuchin Monastery in Northwest Detroit so he could run his beagles, Molly and Chrissy, and, afterwards... Mary to welcome us back home for dinner. In 1950, Jim stood beside my sister Jeannie Valentine and became her godfather. In 1954, Jim stood behind me at St. Scholastica Church in Northwest Detroit, and, facing the bishop, Jim put his hand on my right shoulder, sponsoring me for confirmation. I took Jim's name for my confirmation. So you see Jim Gribbin... my name is not "Lauck." My name is Frederick William **JAMES** Lauck.

After Jim's children were born, Jim spent his fatherly time and energy with his own children. After Jim's children were raised and graduated from St. Suzanne's Grade School and Bishop Borgess High School, Jim retired as a Postal Inspector with the United States Post Office and moved up to Cedar, Michigan near Traverse City in the gorgeous Leelanau Peninsula. But, despite the four hour drive, I stayed in touch with Jim, visiting him regularly in Cedar over the years.

In 1980, when I was 37 years old, it began to dawn on me... that Jim was not only a loyal, supportive, life-long friend, but that, in his own right, Jim Gribbin was a **most unique man** and an interesting philosopher. Therefore, in 1980, I started a "Jim Gribbin" file, keeping all the correspondence between Jim and me, some of which I will share with you later. For now, though, let me share with you a collage of Jim's character and personality. First and foremost, Jim Gribbin spoke his truth directly and in straight forward fashion. He was a man without guile, duplicity or manipulation. A humorous example of Jim's straight forward approach was captured in his recent trip to his local post office in Cedar, Michigan. When Jim came out of the Cedar post office, a lady pulled up and double parked alongside Jim's vehicle, blocking Jim's exit. When the lady exited her vehicle, and headed into the post office, she hurriedly told Jim: "I'll only be a **MOMENT**," to which Jim replied: "Madam, this is my moment... so please remove your impediment from my moment."

Jim came from very humble beginnings in Turtle Creek, Pennsylvania, one of many children born to Irish immigrants. Jim's early struggles to survive led him to a passionate belief that all of God's children were entitled to the basics of food, shelter and medical care. Therefore, government and political parties across the world and the "establishment" in general were all fair game to Jim... if they could not, or would not, deliver those basic services to the world's citizens. In an August 21, 1991 letter, Jim wrote:

> "If a strong man comes forth (the man on horseback)... who knows what might happen? The leaders of our nation are lacking. Prisons cannot be built fast enough. **It's like searching for a cure for typhoid instead of cleaning up the polluted well water.** The only cure is to get people to work, develop their pride, etc. There are plenty of jobs out there. Roads and bridges to be built, homes and cities to be restored, water systems to be cleaned – but no, let's have some new tanks and bigger guns."

This from a man of the "Greatest Generation" and a decorated World War II veteran who fought his way across Europe against the Nazi scourge.

Jim was a most spiritually supportive and generous friend, and, like many Irishmen, he had a "superstitious influence" in his brand of Catholicism. In a September 22, 1989 letter to me, Jim wrote:

> "Now about my health – it could be better. I don't worry about it, but I'm covering all of my bets with contributions to the Capuchins, Father Solanus Casey Guild, Holy Trinity, St. Jude, Friends of the Elderly (Hancock, MI). In short, I'm touching all bases."

Jim's generosity and Irish superstition blessed my family as, at least once a year, I would receive a mass card for my deceased parents from Jim that came from Hermosillo, Mexico, the hometown of Jim's daughter-in-law, Amalia. In his youth… in the 1940s, before Jim married, he wandered down to Acapulco, Mexico and lived amongst the indigenous people, and, I suspect, Jim's relationship with those very humble, very Catholic, and very superstitious Mexicans convinced him that prayers from Mexico were more powerful than prayers from the United States. Same God, for sure, but a God more willing to listen to "Los Pobres"… "the poor of the earth with whom I will share my poems," ("Guantanamera… Guajira, Guantanamera" written by Cuban exile, Jose Marti, shortly before his death, and sung over a hundred years later by the Weavers, Pete Seeger and, later in the 1960s, by the Sandpipers).

As an Irishman, Jim had an insatiable love of language, a keen wit and great sense of humor. In an April 14, 1991 letter, Jim complained that the mass cards I had purchased for his special intentions weren't working because he hadn't hit the lottery yet. In the same letter, Jim wrote: "Both of us know happiness is overrated because it can't buy money." And, one of Jim's favorite Irish toasts:

"May God bless the hearts of those who are our friends.
May God turn the hearts of those who are not our friends
so that they become our friends.
For those who refuse to have their hearts turned,
may God turn their ankles,
so that we know our enemies by their limp."

But, for all his compelling humanity and personality, what stood out the most?... Jim's "gentleness" and "compassion." Jim cared for every human being and every animal on this earth. An insight which gives you a flavor of Jim's gentleness and compassion can be summed up in a one-page story that Jim wrote in June of 1980 about an abandoned Volkswagen Beetle that had been stripped by thieves and marauders, and unceremoniously dumped over the bank of the Rouge River in Northwest Detroit and left to die... alone.

Death Of A Volkswagen

It began in June (1980). A V.W. Beetle was shoved over an embankment of the Rouge River, rolled over two or three times before coming to rest – all four wheels on the ground.

I observed what happened to the V.W. on my daily walks with my poodle Rosie. The V.W. had not been damaged too much by its tumble. It had, of course, been stripped – engine, radio, battery, seats were gone, but, strangely enough, the rear window and side windows were intact.

The next time I saw the car those windows had been smashed, and the poor little Beetle had been rolled over again two or three times. It was now resting on its top. The wheels were still on but I could see that the tires were of no value.

It was a week before I next saw the V.W. I had developed a certain respect for that little bug. It could stand abuse for certain. It had been rolled over a few more times – each time getting nearer to the river. Somebody had taken two by fours and beat the fenders and top until the body was a mass of dents. The wheels were gone.

On my next visit, I saw troubled young men each brandishing a stout piece of wood, strangely beating on the frame. They only stopped battering the Beetle for a beer break. I called to Rosie and got out of the area. If these vandals could get such pleasure out of beating a car, just imagine what they would do to me and my little dog.

The indignities were not over yet. On my next outing, I saw that the body, or what remained of it, had been torched. A considerable amount of fuel must have been used, for the grass and weeds in the immediate area were burned. The V.W. was now dead, but it went out the hard way. Hitler would have been proud – not of the German engineering, but of the Huns who persistently and steadfastly destroyed something good.

Jim Gribbin – June 1980

As you may know, before his death, Jim had been hospitalized with congestive heart failure. After a week, Jim was released from the hospital and was sent home. Jim was having a rather difficult time at home. He had no energy. He was sleeping 23 hours a day. During this time, Jim asked Mary to "call Lauck." I talked to Mary, and we were both confused. Mary indicated that Jim really didn't want to see anybody. I assumed, therefore, that Jim just wanted Mary to update me on his health. When my beloved friend, Debra Sandoval, overheard my conversation with Mary, she became enraged... indicating that both Mary and I were missing Jim's message: "Fred, Jim asked for you! Don't let logic or uncertainty cloud the issue. Jim asked for you... period; you have no choice but to go to his bedside." Therefore, On Friday, September 12, 1997 at 5:30 p.m., right after I finished a grueling three hour cross-examination to expose the biased and flawed opinions of psychologist, Charlene Kushler, in the Livingston County Circuit Court, I drove up to Traverse City, arriving about 11:00 p.m. Debra and I spent the night in a hotel. The next morning I drove to the Northport Hospital at the northern tip of the Leelanau Peninsula. Jim was in a room by himself with a window overlooking a beautiful scene of trees, Lake Michigan and the Manitou Islands. Jim's eyes were closed. I approached Jim, and put my hand in his hand as if to shake hands with him. I also clasped his hand with my left hand. Jim never opened his eyes – "Lauck, you're here." The question was answered. Jim sent for me. Debra was right. Her spiritual interpretation of rather ambiguous information was right on the mark.

I sat with Jim for a half hour and talked to him, not fully realizing that the sand in the hour glass of his life would run out in twenty-four hours. As I was helping Jim sit on the edge of the bed, his hospital gown opened up, exposing him. I frantically reached to pull the curtain around his hospital bed when Jim told me: "Don't bother... I'll walk down Woodward Avenue like this." In retrospect, I can see that Jim was telling me: "Don't bother Lauck, I came into this world naked and unashamed, and I'll go out naked and unashamed."

During this, my last visit with Jim, he surprised me by telling me that he "didn't think he was a good enough father." I pondered that statement for a moment, and then I responded that the role of a father (or any parent) is, in large part, simply to "**be there**" for their children. I said that for the most part it probably doesn't matter whether you teach your children, instruct your children or direct your children. The primary role of a father or any parent is simply to nurture your children by "being there for them," encouraging them and shoring up their confidence and self image as they struggle through life... trying to find out who they are and how to be true to themselves. I told Jim the absolute truth. Jim was reassured.

Jim was always there for his children, day in and day out, week in and week out, month in and month out, year in and year out and decade in and decade out. Jim needn't have any regrets for his role as a father. Jim, still struggling with some guilt surrounding his role as a father, replied that at least he never beat his children. He then hesitated, backed up mentally, and finally put his finger on an incident that, obviously, still bothered him: "I take that back, Lauck; one time I did hit my son Jamie when we were in a restaurant." Jim said that 7-year-old Jamie was carrying on so Jim took Jamie by the hand: "My man, come with me." Jim told me he took Jamie into the bathroom of the restaurant and spanked him **one time** on the butt **ever so lightly** as he demonstrated to me three times on the rail of his hospital bed. Jim said a tear came down Jamie's eye when he asked Jamie: "if he was going to be a good boy?..." to which Jamie replied: "Yes."

The story of son Jamie wasn't about physical discipline. It was about "vulnerability"... the vulnerability Jim still saw in Jamie's eyes those many years ago across the miles of life. I can't help but see the symmetry about the tear coming down Jamie's eye and the lone tear coming down Jim's eye as Jim drew his last breath at 4:00 p.m. September 14, 1997. I am left to wonder whether Jim, at the time he drew his last breath, was still preoccupied with son Jaime's "vulnerability" from the tear he saw come down son Jamie's cheek... or, perhaps, Jim was just sad to be leaving us.

But, when I was at Jim's hospital bedside in Northport, Jim seemed to have eventually diffused the energy of that "yesterday's guilt," and the story about son Jamie marched off in another direction to a humorous conclusion. Jim told me that when Jamie came back to the table in the restaurant, Jamie ordered his meal from the waiter, specifying that he wanted a beef patty with no bun, mashed potatoes with a hole in the middle and gravy in the hole, but that he didn't want the gravy to escape from the hole and touch his other food. Jamie also told the waiter that he wanted some peas, but he did not want the peas to touch the mashed potatoes. When Jamie was finished, the waiter replied: "That's what I like... a man who knows what he wants."

As all of you probably know, Jim had a special relationship with each of his children. He greatly admired you, his oldest daughter, **Mary Elizabeth Gribbin**. He admired your intellectual ability, your work ethic and your scholastic achievement. Jim understood the power that comes from knowledge and education, and Jim greatly admired you, Meggie, for your hard work and persistence that earned you a Ph.D. Jim himself was a high school graduate, but, like many others of his era, any opportunity for a higher education fell victim to the Great Depression. Still, Jim Gribbin was one of the brightest and absolutely one of the most well-read men I have ever known. The combination of Jim's great analytical ability and his voracious appetite for the written word gave Jim a better command of world politics than any other man I have ever known. He was my teacher. I was his student.

Sarah... "the Bear," you are your father's daughter. You have his personality. You have his strength and independence. It is not difficult to imagine that there was a potential for sparks when two strong, independent thinkers like Jim and Sarah Gribbin discussed an issue. Sarah... your daughter Chloe was the absolute light in Jim's eyes for the last five years.

Jamie... you are your father's one and only son. That says it all. During the last half hour of your father's life, besides telling me interesting stories about you and sharing his residual guilt with me, Jim also told me that he was so proud that you had now taken up  "serious reading," and were well on your way to "self education." Jim was so pleased that you were reading "Truman"… a folk hero to a hard working "Greatest Generation." Jamie, your son Jimmie has your father's good looks, which he will carry with him through life. As they say: "You never get a second chance to make a first impression," and young Jimmie's "Hollywood looks" will open some doors, giving Jimmie an enlarged opportunity to

Kid Jimmy Gribbin
Age 21

show he has substance… and is more than just a pretty face. More importantly, however, at age 11, grandson Jimmie has the same compassion for the underdog that his grandfather, Jim Gribbin, had for the 86 years of his life.

In his November 14, 1990 letter to me, Jim fully disclosed the compassionate side of his nature:

> "We – you and I, Lauck – we'll always miss our loved ones. We are softies. As your father would say, Lauck – 'we are bleeders.'"

In my "Jim Gribbin" file, the very first piece of paper you see is John Donne's poem, *For Whom the Bell Tolls*… a copy of which daughter, Sarah Gribbin, also found in Jim's wallet after his death. Let me share this poem with you:

> "No man is an island, entire of itself;
> Every man is a piece of the continent,
> a part of the main;
> If a clod be washed away by the sea,
> Europe is the less,
> as well as if a promontory were

as well as if a manor of thy friends
or if thine own were;
Any man's death diminishes me
because I am involved in mankind;
and therefore never send to know
for whom the bell tolls;
It tolls for thee."

I have never understood John Donne's poem in clearer fashion. Jim's compassion was the hallmark of his character. Jim has died, and the world has lost the compassion of Jim's nature. Therefore, those of us who knew and loved Jim Gribbin, and those who have never even heard Jim's name have suffered a loss. But, we can turn this loss into a gain for our world. If each of us will take up Jim's compassion, and put it on our back like a fine garment, and walk out of this church and into the world with Jim's compassion, we will honor Jim's memory and keep Jim alive in us, and make the world a better place to live... all because our spiritual mentor, Jim Gribbin, once lived on and roamed through this earth, cloaked in the gentle garment of compassion.

Jim, you kept the faith. Jim, you ran the good race. Jim you claimed the laurel wreath of victory and eternal life. We all salute and applaud your 86 years of life and everything you stood for and everything you did. Godspeed, Jim Gribbin... until we see you again.

And So It Ends

I walked outside. I stood a few feet removed from the steps of the front door to Holy Rosary Church, at the top of the hill that the church was built on, looking far and away at the undulating landscape of Lake Leelanau, Michigan. It was a most pleasant, balmy fall afternoon... a colorful red and gold, autumn day in the Leelanau Peninsula. I watched the black hearse carrying off the last remains of Jim Gribbin.

Death and tears come in threes. One silent tear traced my cheek as the hearse disappeared at the bottom of the hill, and then reappeared ascending the next hill, and then disappeared again at the bottom of the next hill, and then reappeared again and disappeared again, and reappeared, disappeared, reappeared and disappeared, smaller and smaller, until… finally, the hearse bearing Jim Gribbin's last mortal remains disappeared all together, converging into the straight line of the horizon. It was over… Jim was gone. But, his spirit of compassion remained behind on that gorgeous fall afternoon in Lake Leelanau – a spirit of compassion still vibrantly alive in the hearts and minds of Jim's admirers… those for *whom the bell has not yet tolled.*

Irish Jim Gribbin
1911-1997

And Now
Mary Gribbin is Gone

November 15, 2001

There never was a time when Jim and Mary Gribbin weren't there. There was a time when they were single, and there was a time when they were married. There was a time when Jim and Mary worked, and a time when they retired. But, there was never a time when they weren't there. There was a time when they partied hard, and a time when they mused and reflected upon life, religion, politics and law. But, there was never a time when they weren't there. There was a time without children, and a time when they raised a family at old St. Suzanne's parish. But, there was never a time when they weren't there. There was a time when Jim and Mary were young and carefree, a time when they were middle aged, and a time when they were growing old gracefully. But, there was never a time when they weren't there.

No matter what the time, what the season or what the reason, Jim and Mary were always there from the time I was born, through the time of my childhood, through the time of my youthful exuberance, through the time of my middle age until, finally, I too was (not so gracefully) growing old. There was never a time when they weren't there. But, now they are gone, and a silence of disbelief is deafening. I have lost a part of myself. How could such a vibrant, interesting couple who were always there, day in and day out, year in and year out... now be gone? When Jim was gone, we still had Mary to visit, to tell stories to, and to travel around the Leelanau Peninsula with, but now they're both gone. Jim and Mary Gribbin gone? How could it be?

I remember waking up on the couch one Sunday morning at my wood frame house at 19011 Patton Ave. in Detroit, Michigan in 1945, at 3 years of age, wondering who scooped me up and spirited me out of my "kid bed"... and why. My curiosity overtook me, and I ran to the upstairs attic to find my "kid bed." What I found was Jim Gribbin fast asleep, half off and half on my kid bed... a victim of too much liquid exuberance the night before. I physically opened Jim's eyelids, asking him: "Jim Gribbin, are you in there?" I also remember playing cowboys and Indians with Jim... he called me "Tex" and "Two-Gun!" I remember how attractive Mary was with her ever present, gentle femininity. I remember Jim and Mary coming to my football games, boxing matches, wrestling matches and baseball games at St. Scholastica and at Catholic Central, and, later, my courtroom matches as I became a "trial lawyer." I remember Jim and Mary making my son Valentine part of their family. I remember visiting Jim's aunt, Ethel Gribbin, at her Burlingame, Linwood apartment in Detroit in the late 1940s and early 1950s, and then in the 1960s at Carmel Hall for the aged on Woodward Avenue when she was 87-years-old... her telling me she had lived too long and was ready to go, and, go she did, shortly thereafter. I remember staying overnight on Grandmont Street in Detroit with Jim and Mary before their children were born, and running the beagles "Molly" and her pup "Chrissy" on the grounds of the Passionist Monastery, St. Paul of the Cross, on Schoolcraft Rd. in Detroit. I remember Mary's flirt with death in the 1970s (perhaps Hodgkin's), and how it changed her priorities, increased her spirituality, and ushered her into a full fledged, non judgmental, free thinking, "liberal" way of looking at her world. Anybody for a joint?

I remember a Friday following Thanksgiving in 1971 at the Gribbin dinner table partaking in Mary's famous onion stew... me with an overwhelming heartache of rejection and depression shared with no one, and my father yelling to the priesthood in general – "Get up on the cross," shared with everyone, and Mary and Jim roaring with laughter. I remember visiting with Jim and Mary on Thanksgiving 1982 with my father so sick he could barely struggle into their house through the front door... and then greeting Jim and Mary at the Desmond Funeral Home two weeks later as we buried my father, and then greeting them again seven years later in January 1989 when we buried my mother next to my father at Holy Sepulcher Cemetery in Southfield, Michigan.

Through it all, Jim and Mary were always there, including right up to the end... my visits to Cedar, Michigan in the Leelanau Peninsula, punctuated with rousing conversations and debates on Christianity, Catholicism, the Pope, Unions, Labor, politics, law, medicine, philosophy, the American Civil Liberties Union, Human Rights Watch, the rights of the "Common Man" and the "Forgotten Woman," Social Justice, the Irish, the British, the Famine, Donegal, Northern Ireland, and on and on filled with howling laughter and songs. Those precious, social interactions were rambunctious, joyful, stimulating and uplifting, but always tinged with the sad recognition that we've lost so many old friends and family members along the way. But, at least we still had each other... for the moment. Then, in 1997, we lost Jim Gribbin, my confirmation sponsor and my confirmation namesake, James, or, as the Irish would say, "Seamus." Now, in 2001, we've lost his dear wife and my dear friend, Mary Wilson Gribbin. Say it ain't so.

I last saw Mary at St. Joseph Hospital in Ann Arbor in August of 2001. We conversed with an alphabet board. Despite her infirmity,

I could tell how pleased she was to see my old familiar face. I don't think she saw my guilt for not visiting her sooner or more often, or, if she did, she gently covered my guilt in non-judgment and forgiveness. The next thing I knew Mary was gone… the World Trade Center crashed in ruins on 9/11, and our lives had changed forever. Jim and Mary were always there … always, always, always, but now they are gone. But, the memories… "Rich," "Rich" and "Richer."

Mary and Jim Gribbin
1953

Charlene McKelvy Montroy LaTour

December 30, 1999
Resurrection Church
Lansing, Michigan

This is the second time in three months that we have gathered together to say good-bye to a LaTour. On September 13, 1999, we said good-bye to 46-year-old Paul LaTour... son, brother, cousin, uncle and friend. Today, with only thirty-six hours left in the 20th century, we gather again to say good-bye to Charlene McKelvy Montroy LaTour... **our 83-year-old matriarch** and my mother Jean Lauck's younger sister.

ALL-ABOARD!! ALL-ABOARD!! Before the 20th century ends, let's borrow a page from America's royalty, the Kennedy clan (as they buried Robert Kennedy), and take a train trip on the "Charlene Express." First stop Ireland... the Emerald Isle with wild, rolling scenes of Celtic beauty. Let me take you back in time, 150 years ago, to the late 1840s and the early 1850s. The "Charlene Express" journeys through the mystical Irish countryside, careful not to run over any wee people, leprechauns or unicorns who occasionally come out of nowhere, and dart across the tracks.

The windows of the "Charlene Express" are clouded by the passage of time, and our view out to the Irish countryside is somewhat obscured, but there is no mistaking the beautiful rolling hills of the Emerald Isle... Tipperary, Galway, Sligo, Donegal, Dingle Bay, Andie's Island, Cliffs of Moher, Ring of Kerry, River Black Water, River Shannon, Gap of Dunloe, Castle ruins, Bantry Bay and Killarney  lakes. But, let not the beautiful Irish landscape blind you to the harsh reality of starvation. In mid-nineteenth century Ireland, the wee people, leprechauns, unicorns and the "lilt of Irish laughter" have disappeared. On the sides of the tracks and on the sides of the roadways, all we see are hollow eyed, starving Irish men, women and children, their gaunt, hopeless faces and expressionless eyes searching for food... anything... anything they can eat. They are starving.

Tens of thousands of Irish have starved to death because of the potato famine while the world stood by and just looked on... forgetting the spiritual message of Jesus: "When I was hungry, when I was thirsty... God help their poor, suffering souls, but, perhaps, we can reach out and save Charlene's grandparents, John McKelvy and Catherine Monaghan. The "Charlene Express" stops for an imaginary moment in time to pick up and save a most appreciative young laddie, Johnnie McKelvy, and a young lassie, Catherine Monaghan... as off we ferry over the Atlantic Ocean to the promise and abundance of America. For the "Charlene Express" is truly a magic train that time-travels over land, over water, and through the air. We land on the eastern seaboard of the United States and Canada and begin anew the land journey, as we set out for the great Midwest. During the course of our journey, young laddie, Johnnie McKelvy, and young lassie, Catherine Monaghan, have grown up strong and physically striking. They have fallen in love, married and settled down in Eau Clair, Wisconsin where, in 1878, their first child, Charlene's mother, Mary McKelvy, is born on November 12, 1878... **122 years ago.**

Keep your seat. The "Charlene Express" is on the move again. We journey northward through the beautiful countryside of Wisconsin, through hundreds of fresh water lakes and through the beautiful Wisconsin Dells, crossing over the Minnesota border, into the breathtaking virgin forests of Minnesota that lay between rolling land that funnels the southbound currents of the Missouri River and the great Mississippi. We reach the Canadian border and travel northeast into the province of Ontario and into the city of "Port Dover," Ontario. The immigration of Charlene's French grandparents is lost in history, but in Port Dover, Ontario we find Charlene's French grandparents, John Montroy and Josephine LaMothe. We arrive in Port Dover, Ontario just in time for the birth of Charlene's father, Charles W. Montroy, born March 27, 1870... **130 years ago**.

The "Charlene Express" moves on with a rich legacy of Irish and French ancestors, each born to bloom in the sun, fade under the cover of night and rest in the bosom of Mother Earth at journey's end. Somewhere around the border of the United States and Canada, Charlene's mother, Mary McKelvy, meets and falls in love with Charlene's father, Charles Montroy. Ten children are born into that Montroy-McKelvy embrace... some in the wilderness of Canada and some in the pristine wilds of Minnesota. Staying a step ahead of minimum survival, the Montroy-McKelvy family locates and relocates in various small cities in Minnesota including Hibbing, Duluth and Tower (where my mother Jean was born in 1914). The "Charlene Express" arrives in Virginia, Minnesota on June 3, 1916 just in time for the birth of our strong-willed child of survival, Charlene McKelvy Montroy... the last of the ten Montroy children.

Charlene's early childhood is spent in Minnesota... **a child of wonder** trying hard to establish roots of life and bloom in the frozen north land of Minnesota. During her lifetime, Charlene shared with me some of her childhood wonders... the cold, long, harsh, mostly sunless winters of the Minnesota wilderness, the great Lake "Superior," frigid, arctic air that her lungs rebelled against, taking her breath away, the bone chilling crunch of frozen snow under foot, walks down narrow pathways with snow shoveled up on either side of her, well over her head, and the undeniable weight of depression and hopelessness that insidiously found pathways into her family's psyche as the endless winters of Charlene's youth stubbornly refuse to give way to an earth trying to move back toward the "sun of life"... at the end of May and the beginning of June. Charlene saw her world of wonder through her eyes of wonder and through the eyes of wonder of nine older brothers and sisters.

Charlene bore first hand witness to the ebb and flow of survival as her father, Charles Montroy, and her mother, Mary McKelvy Montroy, ran a boarding house for loggers. As a child, Charlene stood in awe as she looked at the strong muscled bodies of hard working and hard drinking, live-for-today, die-tomorrow lumberjacks. Charlene had her first glance at death in 1918 as the decimating flu pandemic killed a multitude of millions worldwide – before the discovery of antibiotics that might have saved those that survived the initial onslaught of

Sherwood Montroy
An Abbreviated Life
1916

viral infection... only to die in the second wave of bacterial infection. At age 2, Charlene's oldest brother, 17-year-old Sherwood Montroy, died in a tragic logging accident as he worked side by side with the lumber jack nomads who scaled up and cut down the 100 to 200-year-old giant trees of Minnesota's, virgin forests. Charlene remembers Sherwood's battered body lying in repose in the parlor of their home in Minnesota. But, Charlene was ever the **child of wonder**, and her wonder triumphed over her early memory of a brother's death and the accompanying hardship and emotional depression it visited upon her grieving family. The "Charlene Express" moves on.

After the tragic death of her brother, Charlene's parents uprooted the family, walked away from the Minnesota wilderness, left the pain of the "loss of a child" behind, and started anew. Charlene and her family landed in the (just beginning to rev it up) Automobile Capital of the World... Detroit, Michigan. The family moved into a rented duplex at 254 Marston just north of the Grand Boulevard, in the first block east of Woodward. As a young girl in the city of Detroit, Charlene saw a whole new world of wonder for her eyes to behold... arriving just in time to see the industrial revolution of Henry Ford's, dollar-a-day assembly line and the daring, high wire acts of iron workers walking steel beams in the sky, erecting the Fisher Building and the General Motors Building on Grand Boulevard. As Charlene looked up to the sky each day from the Woodward Avenue path she took to and from Holy Rosary Grade School, she saw the City of Detroit grow from a small town to a large city, Motown... "the Motor City."

But, just like Minnesota, Charlene's childhood in Detroit was brief... as Charlene felt the brutal effects of the Great Depression which struck her reality in October of 1929 at age 13. Charlene knew first hand what it was like to do without. Charlene knew hunger... thankfully, however, not the same kind of relentless hunger that brought starvation to tens of thousands of Irish during the great potato famines. Still, during the 1930s in the city of Detroit, there were thousands of hungry and homeless souls victimized by the "Great Depression," standing in "soup lines" or walking aimlessly around the City of Detroit, gaunt and weak, with rumbling pain in their stomachs and anxiety in their eyes. Charlene's father, Charles Montroy, was, luckily, one of the more fortunate... employed, as he was, working, on and off, on the iron-ore carriers, plowing through the Great Lakes. Charlene's father was a cook on the boats, journeying from Lake Superior through the Soo Locks at Sault St. Marie, down into Lake Michigan to Chicago, while at other times, from Lake Superior, through the Soo Locks down into Lake Huron, down the St. Clair River, into Lake St. Clair, the Detroit River, into Lake Erie, through the Welland Canal, and on into Lake Ontario to Toronto. As the poet-song writer, Pat Dailey sings:

"Mother Michigan, Father Superior…
Runnin down from Mackinac
To Sault Ste. Marie.
Blue water Huron…
Down to Lake Erie-O
Falls to Ontario…
And runs out to sea."

Charlene felt the loneliness caused by the absence of a father who was gone most of the time… waging the battle of economic survival. At age 15, Charlene was reacquainted with death as she buried her 52-year-old mother in 1931. Later, at age 23, Charlene buried her 36-year-old sister, Catherine Montroy Weadock, who was beaten to death in downtown, Detroit on July 4, 1939. But, through it all, Charlene stayed strong and carried on, overcoming sadness

Mary McKelvy
Montroy

Katherine Montroy
1916

and grief. Through all the tragedy and loss, Charlene learned to recover, to emotionally bounce back, and again dance, sing, laugh and nurture that great sense of humor that served her so well during her long life. I've seen the old photos of a young Charlene, and I've been entertained by my mother with stories of yesterday... as my mother Jean and sister Charlene ran through the streets of their youth, the two youngest of ten children. Before Charlene was your mother, LaTour kids, she was a young, vibrant redhead running free and wild and living off the energy of her wonder and her **great sense of humor** – a legacy that Charlene leaves for us... the same childlike wonder and sense of humor that Charlene hung onto as a child and as a young woman to overcome grief, hardship, suffering and death. The "Charlene Express" moves on.

Charlene met and fell in love with Chuck LaTour in the mid 1930s. They were married and moved to Lansing, Michigan to start a family. Charlene and Chuck raised ten children in a house at 718 Fairview in Lansing... a house barely big enough to raise two or three children, and a house, I'm sure, the "Big Bad Wolf" would have looked at as "easy pickin's." Out of necessity, Charlene balanced love with large doses of discipline. Charlene did not believe in spoiling a child. She was the typical "non-doting," Irish mother, a strong-willed woman who raised her children with a firm hand... telling them there is always more to accomplish because "time waits for no one!" Charlene taught her children a strong work ethic, and all of her children secured work outside the home as soon as they were old enough which, in those days, was age 9. I still remember Charlene's son, Tom, and I collecting old newspapers "door to door," wrapping them up, tying them together, and putting them in the LaTour stuffed, wooden garage so that we could later sell those papers to recyclers for a couple of pennies to the bundle. Charlene taught her children to work for and appreciate anything and everything they had in life.

In 1947, Charlene's 77-year-old father, my grandfather, Charles Montroy, known as "Good Time Charlie" among his drinking buddies,

"Good Time Charlie" Montroy and Charlene Montroy... Age 16 1934

came to live with the LaTour family in Lansing, and run out the remaining months of his life. "Good Time Charlie" had little money except for his end-of-month, Social Security stipend. Most of the time, "Good Time Charlie" would stay put at the LaTour home, dealing with his infirmities, behaving himself as a model citizen, and biding his time until his Social Security money arrived at month's end. Eureka! When that pension check arrived, good-bye LaTour household. It was time for "Good Time Charlie" to get loose and get out on the prowl. He bathed, put his drinking pants on, and headed off to the "beer garden" as they called them in those days. Eventually, Charlene's husband, Chuck, had to go find "Good Time Charlie" Montroy and bring him home... not an enviable task, because *Sir Charles* was never in the mood to return home to his Fairview Street confinement. When Chuck arrived at the premises of distilled spirits, "Good Time Charlie" could see the handwriting on the wall, but he wasn't going back without a fight, often telling his five foot, five inch son-in-law, Chuck LaTour: "I don't take no direction from you... you sawed-off S.O.B." Charles Montroy died in 1947 in Lansing at Sparrow Hospital of a stroke at age 77. Charlene was 30 when she buried her 77-year-old father.

Five years later, tragedy struck. In 1952, Charlene's 7-year-old son, Jimmy LaTour, drowned on the Canadian side of Lake Huron... a parent's worst nightmare... little Jimmie floating face down in his red bathing suit. He was buried out of Ted C. Sullivan Funeral Home in northwest Detroit... the "Mass of the Angels." I was 9-years-old and devastated as I knelt at the kneeler with my 36-year-old father peering into the small, white casket holding my dear cousin Jimmie's last remains. But, what must my Aunt Charlene and her family have felt? In what was probably Charlene's greatest hour of tragedy and loss, Charlene, her husband Chuck and all of the LaTour kids hung together those tragic days... bound by love and an overwhelming (how do you possibly cope) depression, counterbalanced by the need to survive and carry on. To their eternal credit, the LaTour family stayed strong and survived the grief of losing a young child and brother... and became the stronger and the more compassionate for surviving life's greatest ordeal.

Charlene's kids grew and flew... scattering across the country: California, Florida, Maryland, Oregon, Las Vegas and Georgia. Charlene's youngest son, Paul, however, stayed home and became Charlene's constant companion after her husband Chuck died in the early 1980s. Even though all of Charlene's other children were widely (and successfully) scattered throughout the United States, Charlene still held her family together emotionally and spiritually with a strength and love that conquered the "miles of separation." And, kind of like a female version of her father, "Good Time Charlie," who wouldn't stay tied down, Charlene traveled to family reunions, baptisms and weddings throughout the United States. I remember attending Tom and Barbara LaTour's wedding in San Francisco in November 1989, right after the October earthquake. I especially remember the reception at Tom LaTour's hotel-restaurant, "Splendido," with Charlene dancing with all of her children at the same time, the matriarch of the family surrounded by her children, everyone dancing to the same beat. I nudged a slightly inebriated sister Katie standing next to me. Katie asked: "Time to bounce?" "No, Katie, time to take a mental photograph of this matriarch dance of love, and lock it in your mind forever."

Just this summer, Charlene and her family went to Chicago for the baptism of Charlene's great-grandson, "Baby Jack"… grandaughter, Tracy LaTour's, and Eric Dallingher's new son. I had the privilege of driving Charlene, her daughter Sis (Kathryn), and my brother, K.O. Marty, from Chicago to Lake Forest, Illinois for the baptism of "Baby Jack." What a great time to visit with Charlene. In the twilight of life, Charlene maintained her sense of humor as her spirit still sang and danced… moved by love of family, and determined not to give in to advancing years and infirmity. Charlene held her family together across the miles with her (won't be denied) spirit, love and determination. **Love and determination** is the legacy that Charlene leaves us, for Charlene knew, as a survivor of life and grief, that love and determination conquer all… hardship, suffering and death. The "Charlene Express" moves on.

During the past couple years of her life, Charlene struggled to maintain her health, and, with great strength, determination and the support of her family, Charlene was able to make numerous recoveries from the brink of extinction. In December of this year, the slow, now-running-out-of-gas "Charlene Express" moved to Sparrow Hospital, Room 427. On Sunday, December 12, 1999, I came to see Charlene. I visited with Charlene and her daughter, Martha. Charlene was very weak, and I knew that the "Charlene Express" was approaching its final destination. During a conversation that bleak December day, she told me that her son Tom had flown into town from San Francisco a few days before, and spent hours with her at the old homestead at 718 Fairview in Lansing. Since Tom is a CEO of the Kimpton (boutique) hotels and restaurants throughout the United States, I was anxious to find out what great restaurant Tom took his mother, Charlene, to. Charlene's eyes lit up as she told me that her son Tom didn't take her out, but that Tom cooked dinner for her… their last visit, just a couple weeks before Charlene's death.

On Saturday, Christmas Day, December 25, 1999, a listless "Charlene Express," barely able to chug along, moved again, but... for the last time. Charlene was moved from Room 427 at Sparrow Hospital to Room 825. For reasons I still don't understand, I drove to Lansing, unannounced, that Christmas Day 1999 to see Charlene at Sparrow Hospital. When I entered the hospital room, I saw my LaTour cousins, Sis, Martha, Bobby, his wife Kathy, Jeanne Marie, and the youngest of 10 children, Annette. I told them to leave the hospital, and go celebrate Christmas, and that I would spend some time with Charlene. I spent five hours with Charlene on Christmas Day... my Christmas present to myself. The first couple of hours were smooth, and I was able to say a rosary while watching over Charlene.

After a couple of hours, Charlene woke up and was clinging to the sides of the bed, and I could see that she was having difficulty breathing. I had been through these, difficult-to-breathe episodes in the past with my own mother, Jean. Therefore, I wanted to make sure that Charlene received immediate respiratory dilation treatments to ease her breathing. I was looking for the call button for the nurses' station when I accidentally tripped the "code blue" button. Now, a medical swat-team charged headlong into the room with everyone yelling: "Who called code blue?" "Who called code blue?" "Who called code blue?" In fear, my 58-year-old self immediately reverted to childhood denial... "Oh, nothing." I just looked at my shoes. I didn't say a thing. If they would have directly asked me, I would have told them that I mistakenly pushed the "code blue" button, but they didn't directly look at me and ask me, and I didn't volunteer anything, and, besides, it was good to see a fully-alerted, medical team helping my Aunt Char regain a breathing rhythm. Derrick, the inhalation therapist, a giant, but compassionate and kind man, took over and eased Charlene's breathing. He had to use the vasal dilator solution to relax Charlene's respiratory system and open up her airways. He worked a fairly long time to make sure that Charlene was stable. After he left, saintly Nurse Shenling (from Taiwan) and I watched Charlene hold the sides of the hospital bed, and lean forward with her chin on her chest so that she could expand her lungs and breath easier. For an hour and a half, Charlene resolutely held to that position.

Charlene's strong survival instinct had instinctively taken over, and she was "holding on"… "holding on." After an hour and a half, Charlene's breathing became more measured and relaxed, and Charlene slid down on the soft pillow the family had brought from home. As she laid down, to my surprise, she stuck her trembling hand through the railing of the bed. I held her hand as she whispered in my ear: "It takes a long time to go." She then told me that I had been good to her, and she thanked me for everything I had done. Obviously, I felt guilty because I had done very little… other than an occasional visit in Lansing to take her out to dinner, but Charlene, a child of the Great Depression and a member of the Greatest Generation, was ever appreciative of the littlest of courtesies extended on her behalf.

The family, led by my sweet, feminine cousin, Martha, had shouldered the burden, and cared for Charlene as Charlene had done for her when Martha was a child. Martha lived with Charlene, and had been her daily visitor at the hospital. Before Martha went to work, at her lunch hour, and after Martha left work, she visited her mother at the hospital, and took care of Charlene's every need. Before I left the hospital on that Christmas Day December 25, 1999, I told Charlene that I had said a rosary for her, and that I asked her deceased love ones, her husband Chuck, her sister Jean, her son Jimmy and her son Paul to intervene on her behalf, and help her reach a peaceful end. I also told Charlene that all of her children were doing very well, and that they all had good, long lives ahead of them. Charlene then fell into a deep sleep as I thought about the significance of the rosary I said, recalling the words: "Pray for us sinners now and at the hour of our death Amen," as well as the words from the Our Father: "Thy will be done." Charlene's oldest child, Charles, called from Chicago and I told him "**ALL IS WELL.**"

After Charlene fell asleep, I talked to Nurse Shenling, and asked her if she could get Charlene's doctor on the phone. She was somewhat hesitant since it was Christmas Day, but she did call Dr. Batka. When I spoke to Dr. Batka, I was also somewhat hesitant as I worried about crossing a family boundary on Christmas Day, but Dr. Batka was a great man who loved and respected Charlene, and who had been helpful in keeping her alive for many years. Dr. Batka agreed with my non-medical assessment… the time had now come to change the medication. I was there and watched with relief as Charlene was put on a more powerful medication that insured that for the next three days of her life she would not suffer a single breathing difficulty. Charlene fell asleep, stayed asleep, and three days later, on December 28, 1999, drifted off peacefully to eternity and the land of her ancestors as the "Charlene Express" came to a gentle rolling stop in the station of last destination, after 83 full years of hard charging ride by the Charlene Montroy "La… Tour Express."

Farewell dear Charlene. You're gone and we will miss you, but your legacy will live on in us. In a phrase, your legacy is to "**LIVE THE FULLEST LIFE POSSIBLE.**" Live life like Charlene lived it. Live life with **child-like wonder**. Live life with a **great sense of humor**. Live life with a great **enthusiasm**. Live life with a great **appreciation**. Live life in a **truthful** fashion, direct and head on. Live life with **love and compassion**. Charlene's zest for life reminds me of the saying that "everyone dies, but not everyone lives." Charlene's zest for life and her enthusiasm is captured in the old sports writer Grantlin Rice's poem *Alumnus Football…* " When the great scorer in the sky comes to mark against your name, it matters not whether you won or lost, but how you played the game." And, how that diminutive Charlene played the "Game of Life"... a consummate major leaguer with the stamina and heart of a lion.

Charlene is gone, but that powerful, dynamic wisp of a woman lives on in all of us. We will miss her company and her joyous spirit, but we will **honor her life** by living life to the fullest as she did. L-I-V-E, L-I-V-E, L-I-V-E... live life to the fullest through both triumph and disaster, and, more importantly, live life to the fullest through the incessant drone of common place, every day life.

SING, DANCE, LAUGH, L-I-V-E
SING, DANCE, LAUGH, L-I-V-E
SING, DANCE, LAUGH, L-I-V-E.

Thank you dear Charlene for your legacy. You have run the good race, and you have fought the good fight, and you will wear the laurel wreath of victory for eternity. Your work is done, dear Charlene. We'll take it from here, and we'll restore and reappoint the "Charlene Express" and let it run again, fueled by the legacy and energy of your life, and we will let the "Charlene Express" transport us through a life of **SONG, DANCE** and **LAUGHTER**... as we **LIVE, LIVE** and **LIVE**... like you, dear Charlene.

Charlene Montroy
LaTour
1916-1999

Joseph DiBella

November 3, 1997
St. Robert Bellarmine Church
Redford, Michigan

My lifelong friend, John DiBella, asked me to say a few words about the passing of his father, Joseph DiBella. It is a great honor to be standing before you and speaking about our beloved friend, Joseph DiBella.

My name is Fred Lauck. I have been a friend of Mr. DiBella for 48 years. I first met Mr. DiBella in 1949 when I was 6-years-old. I started St. Scholastica Grade School in Northwest Detroit with Mr. DiBella's son, John, in September 1949. On the very first day of first grade, John met me after class and asked me to be his friend. I said, "Yes," and John invited me to his house. So, off we trudged on our little first grader legs, southbound on Southfield Road to Six Mile, left hand turn, eastbound to Biltmore, ending up at the DiBella grocery store, and later into the DiBella wooden frame home just across the alley from the grocery store.

On that magical first day of first grade in 1949 at the DiBella household, I met John's sister Grace, a second grader, and John's little brother Joe with his long, black, curly hair. Joe was so pretty, I thought he was a girl. But, I found out that baby Joe was a 2-year-old boy, and woe be to anyone who suggested cutting baby Joe's long, dark curls... so said John's beautiful, Italian mother. At a glance, I knew John's mother was one of the most beautiful women I had ever seen... as she still is today. Finally, I met John's father. Even as a 6-year-old, I knew in a moment that Mr. DiBella was a **kind, upbeat, accepting** and **sweet** man. In an instant, I took a liking to Mr. DiBella.

Being in the DiBella household that day was a one-of-a-kind experience… watching and listening, as the great zest and energy for life that the DiBella family had, bounced from floor to ceiling, wall to wall, small room to small room, exiting out the roof like heat escaping from an uninsulated home on a cold day in winter. The atmosphere in the DiBella household was electrically charged… wind and fire. There was never a dull moment. As I visited amid a crescendoing din in that first generation Italian household, my 6-year-old brain sensed: "somebody is going to whack somebody," and there may be some bloodshed. Eventually, however, I realized it was business as usual… just hanging out in a highly energized, highly emotional, Italian household aka "The DiBella Family."

John DiBella and I spent the ensuing eight years together attending St. Scholastica Grade School in Northwest Detroit nurtured by the Dominican nuns of the Adrian order and the Benedictine priests from Italy. We were there for first grade, First Communion, first fights, first girl friends, first dances, first embraces, the magic of pursuing girls for first kisses and, finally, our first graduation in 1957. Our St. Scholastica classmates, Jack Gilbert, Frank Demers and Neil Flynn, who shared all those "larger-than-life" first memories with John DiBella and me, are also with us today… as, in a larger sense, we honor the "wind and fire" DiBella family and bury their patriarch, Joseph DiBella.

Let me share a **collage of snapshots** located front and center in my memory… a collage of a very loveable man that all of us join together to honor and bury today. Mr. DiBella was a new world, Italian immigrant with a huge heart and an entrepreneurial spirit that he poured into his own grocery store on the northwest corner of McNichols (Six Mile) and Biltmore in northwest Detroit. Whenever Mr. DiBella delivered groceries to our household, the entire atmosphere of our home also became electrically charged with the "wind and fire" of Mr. DiBella's, bubbling-over charisma. Mr. DiBella's love of life and his joyful spirit was "infectious." My mother and I would both watch Mr. DiBella carry his box of our groceries up to our house and into the kitchen as his handsome, smiling, Italian face lit up… filling our household with joy. Joseph DiBella was, indeed, a special, charismatic man with an all-embracing love of life and love of God's people.

Mr. Joseph DiBella and
Father John DiBella
1953

After Mr. DiBella sold his store and became a UAW blue collar worker at General Motors, the family moved to the northwest corner of Curtis and Southfield Road right next door to the Detroit Edison substation. It was there, at that Curtis "Boulevard" (as John called it) home that I first saw Mr. DiBella's own father, John DiBella, when he came over from Sicily and lived with the DiBella family for about a year. And, it was then that I saw, first-hand, the respect that Mr. DiBella accorded his own father… the early lessons of kindness and acceptance in 1949 followed by later lessons of "respect" in the early 1950s.

I also remember visiting the DiBella household when Tonino Fama, a fellow Italian, would visit on family day, Sunday. Tonino came from Italy… alone. He had no family or friends in the area. So… Tonino would visit the DiBella household on most Sundays. John and I would both watch and giggle as Tonino and Mr. DiBella sat side by side in a small, two-seater loveseat where they had to crane their necks away from one another to even see each other. John and I both thought it odd that they would sit so close. Looking back, it was apparent that Tonino was a lost soul in America who needed a little bit of family life in the new world, and that physical closeness of Mr. DiBella to Tonino was part of that "Italian style" family life. On Sundays with Tonino, there was food for all. Even though my mother was an excellent cook, she could not match Mrs. DiBella's Italian style cooking. I always looked forward to eating a meal at the DiBella household, especially the rigatoni pasta and the exuberant ripping-off a piece of bread from the loaf ("Let it rip")… and sharing the DiBella's love of family with all at the table. Mr. DiBella was a man of unconscious love. In addition to the early lessons in **kindness, acceptance and respect**, I also learned something about love from Mr. DiBella.

As the years moved on, John and I headed off to high school… John to Benedictine, while I headed down the road to Catholic Central High. I remember sitting in the new football stands at Benedictine High School in 1960, the fall of my senior year, watching a Benedictine High School football game on "Father-Son Day." Mr. DiBella was wearing a football jersey with the name **"DiBELLA"** written across the back in bold, black & white lettering. He was so proud that John was playing "American" football for Benedictine High School, and he beamed with joy as he vivaciously conversed with the other Greatest Generation fathers whose sons were on the gridiron playing American football. I had a difficult time watching the game. The action in the stands was more captivating than the game-time action on the field. I was riveted to Mr. DiBella, watching his joy and pride as he socialized with the crowd, laughed with everyone and lit up the spectator section with his magnetic charisma. You could tell at a glance that Mr. DiBella was comfortable… a foreigner who now felt like he belonged to America and its ritual of American football. Mr. DiBella didn't see much of the game, but he sure was the proudest and most social of all the fathers on that warm, sunny fall afternoon of football in 1960 in northwest Detroit… just a couple short blocks removed from the old grocery store that was home and livelihood for Italian immigrants and their three kids, all under 5-years-old, sleeping on cots in the back of the store next to the alley-way.

Another snapshot. When we were juniors in high school, John and I got a little rambunctious and found ourselves in the embarrassing position of having to explain the inexplicable… the "flight of the errant watermelon" into the side of the cop car. During the conversation, John's Italian "wind and fire" personality convinced the police officers that they should take us over to the 16th Precinct for further conversation and investigation. When we got to the 16th Precinct, we explained the misunderstanding to the desk sergeant. Since I was 17 years old and an adult in the eyes of the law, the Sergeant thought it easier for all concerned to let me walk out of the station to drift off into the darkness of the early morning hours. But, since John was only 16 and a juvenile in the eyes of the law, John had to remain until a parent picked him up. In the dark and alone at 2:30 a.m. (yet very happy not to be staying overnight as a guest of the City of Detroit taxpayers), I headed out of the 16th Precinct police station at Grand River and Six Mile and disappeared under the cover of night. I headed eastbound on Six Mile Road until I got to Outer Drive, where I took a left-hand turn going northbound toward my home. As I was walking around the Outer Drive curve, now heading eastbound again, I saw poor Mr. DiBella drive by, aroused from a deep sleep, both hands and his chin on the steering wheel, staring straight ahead with a blank look of interrupted sleep. I didn't have the need to face him, so I turned away, concealed by the dark of night, and kept on walking. Later, the next day, I knew I had to face the music. When I saw Mr. DiBella, he let me know that my actions fell short of his expectations, but immediately thereafter he let it go, forgave me and invited me into his house to eat. In the past, I had learned about **kindness, acceptance, respect and love** from Mr. DiBella. That day I learned about "**forgiveness**."

More snapshots. In the recent past, when Mr. DiBella's health was still good, Mr. DiBella, Mrs. DiBella, John and I would go to restaurants for lunch. We'd go to Mario's Eastside Restaurant or we'd go to Ernesto's Italian Restaurant in Plymouth. Although I was ready, willing and able to buy lunch, Mr. DiBella always insisted on treating me to some of the great Italian lunches we shared. As a child and as a young man, I had learned about kindness, acceptance, respect, love and forgiveness from Mr. DiBella. As an adult, I learned about **generosity**... on a limited budget.

Also, as an adult, I was most fortunate to accompany Mr. DiBella as he revisited past, familiar days-gone-by... this time watching his grandsons, John and Nick DiBella, play football and baseball for Catholic Central on state championship teams. Whenever you got to the Pontiac Silverdome and Catholic Central was playing, you had to search out Mr. DiBella because, in tribute to his days as a grocer, he always had a box of groceries... just in case anyone got hungry. Mr. DiBella must have been hungry in Sicily, but he wasn't going to be hungry in America, and none of his friends were going to be hungry either. It was American football with an old world, Italian picnic with olives and cheese and fresh Italian bread and some Italian sausage thrown in. Recently, I saw Mr. DiBella at a joint party for his 83rd birthday and his grandson Michael's graduation. He looked absolutely wonderful. He was tanned and peaceful looking as he sat in a chair and enjoyed his family, including his grandchildren and his great-grandchildren... insisting, as usual, that everyone eat: "Manga, manga."

A year ago, I drove over to John's house. When I came in the house, Gracie DiBella O'Brien called with a worried tone. She had been calling her father's home, and there was no answer. She was very concerned that something was amiss. John and I jumped in the car, and drove over to Mr. DiBella's house in a controlled panic. Son Joe, who had also received a telephone call, was coming from the opposite direction in his own state of controlled panic. Both cars met head-to-head at the side door of Mr. DiBella's home, and, like a swat team of three, we barged into Mr. DiBella's home... fear in our eyes, expecting the worst. Mr. DiBella was sitting in his favorite chair watching a college football game on television, and, somewhat indignantly, he questioned us: "What's-ah all-ah the commotion-eh about!" When John told his father that we were worried because phone calls went unanswered, Mr. DiBella asserted the role of a parent asking why he couldn't watch the football game in peace... uninterrupted by a phone that never stops ringing. Mr. DiBella then invited us to stay for the game. Obviously, Mr. DiBella's knowledge of American football had grown quite a bit since thirty some years ago when he was watching his son John play for Benedictine High School on "Father-Son Day."

In the recent past, Mr. DiBella had been in failing health, and had been in and out of the hospital. Whenever I visited him in the hospital, he was always courageously cheerful and upbeat. On his 84th birthday in June, I was at his home and spoke with him. He was in a hospital bed in the bedroom. When I suggested that he must be rather discouraged with his inability to get around, he looked at me with those big, beautiful, Italian eyes, and gave a smile, saying: "Whaddaya gonna do?" During the days of Mr. DiBella's failing health, his wife courageously stood by him and cared for him through it all – **Mrs. DiBella**... a stout hearted champion who **always had Mr. DiBella's back**.

As I watched those who gathered around Mr. DiBella in his last days of life, I saw all the love that he gave to his family return to him ten-fold. I saw the great love, admiration and respect that his children had for him, the great love, admiration and respect that his grandchildren had for him and the great love, admiration and respect that his great-grandchildren had for him... Mr. DiBella's living example of love effortlessly flowing and running down through each connecting generation.

More snapshots. At the funeral home, I was talking to Eva and Tony Palella. Tony is a conversational expert on healthy eating habits. Tony gave me a nutritional recipe for long life. Thereafter I went up and knelt at the casket and looked at the roman-straight-jawed face of Mr. DiBella, and I thought to myself: "The real secret to long life and joy and happiness is the **ZEST FOR LIFE** that Mr. DiBella had." If you want a long life, embrace life like Mr. DiBella did, run with it, dance with it, even cry with it, but never stop embracing life. When Mr. DiBella was in his fifties, the doctors, lamenting Mr. DiBella's heart problems, told him he didn't have long to live. Those same doctors went to their eternal reward long before Mr. DiBella ever did. Mr. DiBella was a symbolic pallbearer for the "pessimism" of the medical profession, burying the pessimistic doctors and their gloomy prognosis side by side, R.I.P. doctors... while Mr. DiBella lived on and on and on. Mr. DiBella's zest for life is something we all should embrace first, and, then, if there is any time left over, we can discuss Tony Palella's nutritional recipe for long life.

Great-granddaughter, Ashley Chiado, approached her grandfather's casket in the funeral home. She tried to speak to Mr. DiBella: "Papa, wake up," as she wondered what happened to her vivacious, zest-for-life grandfather. Ashley was told that Papa had died, had gone to heaven and was with the angels and Mary and Jesus. Ashley seemed to accept that explanation... at least for the moment, as she walked away. Later, little Ashley came back to the casket and asked: "Papa, when are you coming back from heaven?" "Papa" is not coming back from heaven dear Ashley, but we will all see him again one day, somewhere over the rainbow... when we meet him in heaven.

Although sadness and grief come with death... today, tomorrow and the rest of our days should be a celebration of life, the same celebration Joseph DiBella lived out for 84 long, beautiful, love-of-family filled years. Mr. DiBella has given us living examples of kindness, acceptance, respect, love, zest for life, courage, love of family, and, most importantly, **forgiveness** and a philosophy of **non-judgment**. Let's take those great qualities that Mr. DiBella showed us during his lifetime, and put those attributes in our hearts and souls, and walk out of this church with a part of Joseph DiBella's vivascious "wind and fire" spirit alive and well... in our own spirit. That way, Joseph DiBella will continue to live through us... as we are kind to another, as we accept, respect and love one another, and as we pass no judgment upon one another, and as we always forgive one another. Let us follow in his large spiritual footsteps, and fill our hearts with the breath of life, dancing and singing and vivaciously expressing our joy and our love. Joseph DiBella... you are a special man.

You fought the good fight; you ran the good race; you claimed the laurel wreath of victory and you have gained eternal life. We salute you, Joseph DiBella, and everything you stood for. Godspeed, dear friend Joseph DiBella, until we all see you again... somewhere over the rainbow.

Joseph DiBella   Lena Butera DiBella
1913-1997   1920-2010

Frank Sandoval, Jr.

October 14, 2004
Holy Trinity Church
Corktown, Michigan

Welcome everyone. On behalf of the family of Frank Sandoval Jr. and on behalf of Frank's sister, Delores "Lola" Zavala, I welcome all of you to celebrate the "life and times" of Frank Sandoval Jr.

Frank Sandoval was born on June 15, 1935 at home in Detroit, Michigan... right here in Corktown. 1935 was the height of "hard times"... the Great Depression as well as the legacy of the Dustbowl on the Midwest plains. "Brother can you spare a dime?" was the refrain heard from a popular song of the era. Times were tough in the mid-1930s in Detroit and across the nation. "Welcome, young Frank Sandoval. You are going to have to be a strong spirit to negotiate your way through these bleak economic times." And, a strong spirit... he became.

Frank Sandoval Jr. was a child of mixed blood, descended from the Spanish Conquistadors and the Aztec Indians of Old Mexico. But Frank Sandoval broke ranks with his heritage. Although he served in the Korean War, he was not a warrior by nature. He was not a conquistador, a conqueror nor a colonizer. He did not believe any of God's children should be conquered or dominated by any other group or race. He was a follower of Jesus... a man of peace and a man of gentleness. In this, the first decade of the 21st century... as Christians and Muslims alike are making war, killing and maiming one another while pontificating that: "God is on our side," Frank Sandoval Jr. would say: "Don't worry about God being on your side; worry about you being on the side of God."

Frank Sandoval Jr.'s first months of life were challenging. He fought to survive. Frank was born premature... an infant who rallied to live, nurtured to life on goat's milk. For the most part, Frank was raised by his mother, Phillipa Jessie Morales Sandoval... a strong-willed woman who, out of necessity, was up to the task of raising her oldest son, Frank Sandoval Jr., her daughter, Delores, and the youngest of the family, John Sandoval. Just two years ago Frank Sandoval stood in this church, right where I am standing and spoke at his 88-year-old mother's funeral:

"She was my mom."

"She was my world."

Frank Sandoval was also raised by an extended family. His grandfather, Napoleon "Mike" Morales, was born in the State of Juanawato, Mexico, City of Leon. Grandfather Morales taught young Frank

**Mighty Mike Morales
1920**

Sandoval Jr. discipline by letting him know that his actions always carried consequences. Frank's grandmother, Annakaletta Torres Morales, taught a very young Frank Sandoval Jr. to recite the rosary... right here in this very church, Holy Trinity, some 60 years ago. Ironically, and in tribute to his grandmother, Annakaletta, it was the rosary and other prayers she taught Frank that comforted him as he lay on his death bed a few days ago:

Holy Mary Mother of God, pray for us sinners, **now** and at the **hour of our death.** Amen

* * *

Thy will be done on earth as it is in heaven... and forgive us our trespasses as we forgive those who trespass against us and lead us not into temptation but deliver us from evil. Amen.

* * *

Glory be to the Father, and to the Son and to the Holy Spirit, as it was in the beginning, is **now** and **ever shall be**, world without end. Amen.

The hallmark of Frank Sandoval's personality was a compatible mix of **devotion** and gentle **humor**... devotion to Jesus and family and a humorous acceptance of the weakness of the human condition – which prompted Frank to tell me in Puerto Vallarta, Mexico in 1998 that he attends mass daily at Our Lady of Guadalupe Church because: "I am a sinner, Fred."

Frank loved a good story, loved to laugh and loved to "rip it up." There are so many Frank Sandoval stories of humor and poignancy, but time permits me to only highlight a few: his escape attempt at our Casaladera Condo in Puerto Vallarta, at age 65, wrestling with a locked door to the outside world, refusing to give up, scaling a brick wall and finally dropping 10 feet onto a concrete slab, landing on an incline and rolling into a crowded taxi stand... all after his daughters tried to confine him to quarters for a night of rest ("Sir, sir, are you alright?"... "Madam, do not call attention to me, I'm trying to escape on foot, and I don't need a cab"); **and**, in another incident at the same Casaladera Condo, which recalls a scene from the Tennessee Williams play, *A Streetcar Named Desire*, as Frank plaintively called out in the still of a ("South of the Border") night to his good looking, church-going, damsel-of-the-night friend staying at the Mesa Delmar Hotel across the street: "Stella," "Stella," "Stella"; **or**, in an at-home-in-Michigan incident, sliding his "driverless" Trans Am "muscle car" off the lazy, arching freeway exit in Novi, Michigan, then disappearing from the "driverless" car into the dark of the night on foot; **or** his charitable delivery of free bags of groceries (accompanied by his young grandson, Jimmie McElroy) to a damsel in distress... an errand of mercy with Frank entering the damsel's house to confront three "shiftless," beer swigging, couch potato con-men who sure appreciated the free groceries; **or**, in another incident of misplaced trust, Frank, at age 19, being talked into enlisting in the U.S. Army as part of a Detroit Recorder's Court "Buddy System" plea bargain so his brother, John, could avoid lock-up, but Frank ended up freezing to death on the frozen tundra of Korea, alone, without brother John... who lost the benefit of his plea bargain when he got caught in another "caper," after Frank and John both enlisted, but before they reported to active duty.

Another one of Frank's stories that bears repeating, centers on Frank's army service in Korea. Homesick and endlessly chilled to the bone, Frank got word that a bus load of "Michigan" soldiers were coming in to his base in Korea. What they said was "Michigan," but what Frank heard was "Michigan Avenue." Frank was so excited to see who was coming in from the Hood that he went to the bus destination a couple hours before the "Michigan" soldiers arrived and waited in anxious anticipation. Finally, the bus arrived, and, as the Michigan soldiers bounded off the bus, Frank ebulliently asked: "You're the guys from "Michigan," right? Where are you from?" with Frank growing more confused with each answer:

Pelston (Where the hell is Pelston?)
Dowagiac (? – what?)
Marquette (? – what?)
Niles (? – what?)
Baraga (? – what?)

Finally, Frank blurted out in frustration: "I thought you guys were from 'Michigan'." The soldiers replied in unison: "We are," then asking Frank what part of Michigan he was from... "Michigan and Trumbull," "Corktown, Michigan," Frank blurted out, with a 19-year-old Frank Sandoval Jr. now beginning to appreciate that Michigan Avenue is just one of many Hoods in the Great Lake's State of Michigan.

But, the episodes that Frank found most humorous and heartwarming, and that probably connected Frank to a family he didn't

Frances Economy and
Frank Sandoval
1968

quite have growing up, happened right in his own home (on Newberry, near Junction and Vernor in Southwest Detroit) as his wife, Frances Economy Sandoval (may she rest), conspired with "the kids" to jump Frank. The kids and mother would "lie in wait" to get the jump on Frank, and then humorously pummel him into submission on the living room floor while Frank cried out for mercy: "No, Fran!" "No, Fran!"... "Help!"... "Help!" Frank passed that humorous legacy on to me. Many's the night that Frank's daughter Debra and his granddaughters,

Jessie Valentine Lauck and Frances Sandoval Lauck, pummeled me into submission on the living room floor while I screamed: "Uncle!" "Uncle!"… "I Give!" with 2-year-old Frances and 4-year-old Jessie so very excited and proud that they could bring the big, scary father down into a submission hold. But, I must confess, things sometimes got out of hand when an overly aggressive 2-year-old Frannie started with the "head-butting" and "putting the boots" to me.

Frank Sandoval was a man of overwhelming generosity. When he came to your house, you held your breath… "what the heck is he bringing into the house today?" Was it a musical instrument, a computer, a Nordic track, an exercise bicycle…? Frank was a poor kid growing up, always working two jobs, but he was going to make sure (just like my own father) that his friends and family were going to get the material advantages in life that he never had. Frank's generous sharing with others is legendary.

In the mid 19th century… Cuban exile, Jose Marti, wrote a simple poem, "Guantanamera." One hundred years later, his poem was musically scored and sung by the "Weavers," Pete Seeger and, later in the 1960s, by the "Sandpipers." The song is about a sincere man from the land of the palm trees who, before dying, wants to share his poems with the world. The song captures Frank Sandoval's love of art, music, and his generosity of spirit:

> "Con los pobres de la Tierra
> Quiero yo mi suerte e char."

Translated
> "With the poor people of this earth
> I want to share my fortune."

Like Jose Marti, the Cuban exile, Frank Sandoval's fortune was not financial. Frank's fortune was spiritual and soulful. Frank always gave away whatever material possessions he had, but the best gift Frank gave all of us was himself – the spiritual gift of just "listening": listening to family, listening to friends and even listening to strangers and sending out the spiritual message to all of us that "we count," that we are important, that Frank is interested in us and that he loves us... with an irrepressible Frank Sandoval Jr. finally choosing the right moment to break away from the seriousness of life and illuminate the moment with his immense sense of humor, born out of his immense humanity. Just being around Frank Sandoval was an open invitation to live all of life's emotions. Feel what you will... Frank won't judge it.

Frank Sandoval was diagnosed with gall bladder cancer in October 2003. He quietly and courageously fought a year long battle against cancer. But, Frank was ever the optimist. While Frank was undergoing chemo therapy, he was hobbled by a bad knee and he needed surgery... a knee surgery that would give him much more mobility, once he beat back the cancer. Everything was just a temporary setback to the courageous, non-complaining, strong man. And, although he was hobbled with a bad knee and undergoing chemo, he was still working at Ford Motor Co.... 42 years as a blue collar, UAW, hourly employee at the Wixom Plant... still on his feet eight to ten hours a day, five to six days a week until the cancer left him no alternatives. In July of 2004, Frank had to stop working and clear out his locker at Ford's Wixom Plant. His 42 year run was over. What a sad day... at least from my perspective. Can you imagine the emotional upheaval, the sense of loss, the sense of helplessness and the sense of resignation as Frank cleared out his locker, turned and walked away, after 42 years at the Wixom plant... recognizing that his own end was near. But, Frank never complained, and never shared the poignant, overwhelming emotion of the moment, when, for the last time, he closed the door of his cleaned-out locker... after a 42 year run. Frank's stoicism saw him right through to the very end of his life.

On September 11, 2004, one month before Frank died, he attended the wedding of his grandson, Doug McElroy, and his wife, Julie Connick McElroy. I drove him home from the wedding... as we left the "night life" celebration of youthful energy to the younger generation. During that ride, I thought to myself... I never heard this man complain, ever. He reminded me of my own father... another strong, stoic, non-complaining sweetheart of a man. But, I am different than Frank Sandoval Jr. and my own father, Frederick Valentine Lauck. As a matter of choice, I decided as a kid I wasn't going to be a strong, silent type. I decided as a kid that I was going to follow in my mother's footsteps, and allow my emotion to be seen and heard. For me, the bottling up of life's emotion did not seem to be a healthy, lifestyle choice. So, if something bothered me, I was going to be heard. I was going to let it out. To this day, if you want to know if something is bothering me, all you have to do is stand next to me for a moment as I communicate my emotion to the world.

On the way home from Doug McElroy's wedding, I summoned up my cross examination courage, and asked Frank why he never complained. He thought for a minute and then responded: "Why would I embarrass myself?" I'm not quite sure what he was saying, but one interpretation might suggest that I have been embarrassing myself for the last 61 years. But not to worry. No embarrassment in the ride home that night, for, as Frank Sandoval lived life, he allowed everyone to be themselves, and he passed no judgment on others. Everyone was unique and accepted and included in Frank's world without moral judgment... with Frank leaving judgment up to God. In our ever expanding world of judgmental "exclusion of others," Frank Sandoval Jr. was a transparent, breath-of-fresh-air "acceptance of others." Maybe seeing himself as a "sinner" (as Frank would say) kept him from passing judgment on others.

On Sunday, October 3, 2004, one week before Frank died, Father Russ Kohler, pastor of Frank's lifelong parish in Corktown, "Holy

**Fr. Russ Kohler
A Loyal Friend to
Those in Need**

Trinity," came to Frank's "Trailer on the Pond" in Wixom, Michigan, and blessed Frank's recent marriage to Guadalupe. Frank was gaunt and weak and probably hadn't eaten a decent meal in two or three weeks. Lupe was dressed in a wedding gown, and Frank was dressed in a tuxedo. Frank barely had the strength to get out of bed, and there he was dressed in a tux, standing on wobbly legs, and participating in the blessing of his marriage. What a poignant moment... bittersweet, but filled with Frank Sandoval's never-say-die attitude. In his last week of life, in a weakened condition, Frank Sandoval opened his "Trailer on the Pond"... and his heart to everyone. Frank then sat in his chair and visited with lifetime friends, his best friends, Jessie Medina (the giant... both physically and emotionally), Indian Charlie Minear (a.k.a. "Chief Day") and Salvatore Garcia. What a precious moment. Four guys from the "Hood"... as colorful a group of characters as you'll ever see, anywhere. The faces and bodies all decidedly older, but the spirits... the same as the old days when they were growing up and running full-tilt through the Hood in Southwest Detroit. But, those days were gone, and... the end was near.

One week later, on Sunday, October 10, 2004, I saw Frank at 6 o'clock in the evening. He was in his bedroom lying in a hospital bed next to his own bed. He was propped up in a semi-sitting position. His eyes were closed. His life was measured in hours. He was gaunt, but the pure beauty of the man's face could not be denied. The Aztec cheekbones sitting up high and proud, the prominent forehead, the wide-set, soft eyes and the strong jaw line. His breathing was not labored as much as it was measured. He would take a breath, and a short time later he would exhale with a sigh. He did not have the strength to talk. There was no conversation, no stories, no humor and no interaction… although the doctors would probably say Frank could hear those attending to his final moments. As I looked at Frank that evening, all there was to see was the man's soul clearly visible beneath the last remnants of a lingering, fading facade of a body that had completed its mission on earth. It reminded me of the poem "*If*" by Rudyard Kipling:

> "If you can fill the unforgiving minute
> With sixty seconds worth of distance run
> And hold on when there's nothing left within you
> But, the will that says hold on – hold on."

It was a poignant moment that none of us will truly understand until our turn comes. Out of respect, I knelt at Frank's feet, and said parts of a rosary. I then held Frank's hand, and told him he was my brother, my best friend and that I loved him. Frank and I parted company that evening of October the 10th, 2004, for the last time… on this earth.

I left and took his grandchildren, 4-year-old Jessie Valentine Lauck and 2-year-old Frances Sandoval Lauck home. At 5:00 a.m. the next morning, I awoke and noticed lights on in the house. Debra must be home. If daughter Debra is home, father Frank is gone. I knew Frank's ordeal was over… "Holy Mary, Mother of God, pray for us sinners. **Now and at the hour of our death. Amen.**"

The last time I saw Frank Sandoval was at 6:30 p.m. on Sunday, October 10, 2004 as his life was measured in hours. Later that night, his life was measured in minutes, and then in moments as Frank drew his few last breaths. At the very end, his sister Delores put a candle in his hand. All of his children were with him. He squeezed the candle, taking his last few breaths. At 11:15 p.m. he exhaled one last time and breathed no more. A great man was gone... He **fought the good fight** with two parts fight and one part resignation, and, through his year long ordeal, he accepted without complaint: **"Thy will be done."**

At 5:00 a.m. in the solitude of darkness and within hours after Frank Sandoval Jr.'s great spirit left us, I went to the "great room" of my home, alone, and looked out the window, east bound toward Frank's home. I saw a bright crescent moon with an even brighter star above it. Frank's soul was let loose in death, no more to be tied to this earth by the bonds of gravity or human struggle. Fly Frank, fly. Soar Frank, soar. You earned your wings. You fought the good fight. You ran the marathon of life, and you filled "each unforgiving minute with sixty seconds worth of distance run"... a marathon run of love, kindness, acceptance, forgiveness, humility, humanity and humor.

God Bless Frank Sandoval's children. There is a special place in heaven for those who accept the challenge of caring for a parent's last needs. Frank's children were with him each step of his journey, comforting Frank and learning from him each day, right up to his last breath. What comfort there must be to have all his children with him each step of the way on his last earthly journey into the great unknown of eternity:

Linda Sandoval Hinojosa Smith... you flew in from Arizona when your father told your siblings that one of his flock was missing. You spent the last two weeks of your father's life with him. God Bless you Linda.

Phyllis Sandoval... you flew in from Arizona and stayed day and night with your father for the last months of his life. God Bless you Phyllis.

Joanne Sandoval Berry... you who worked seven days a week – ten to fourteen hours a day caring for your father. You put everything else on hold to be with your father on his last journey. Always remember the boost to your confidence your father gave you when he became your swimming coach, and urged you to overcome self doubt, and excel to new heights and possibilities. Your father wants you to live each day with that confidence he brought home to you.

Diana Sandoval Kirschner... I'll never forget your gentleness with your father. You held his hand and gently caressed his forehead in his last moments. Your father loved your soft, compassionate heart.

Debra Sandoval Lauck... although you are the youngest of the Sandoval girls, you are the leader. If there was ever a problem or a question, your father looked to you, knowing you could solve it. What a great show of respect when you bathed your father after his death. Debra, I will never forget your last words over your father's grave:

> "My father never complained. My father never said, 'Why me?' My father never cursed his fate. Those of us left behind should learn from my father. Although our life seems to be filled with turmoil that provokes our anger and emotional upset, those everyday incidents of life are not really important enough to take away our emotional peace."

Frank Sandoval Jr. and Debra Sandoval
Puerto Vallarta Mexico
1998

Frank Sandoval... your father's namesake, your father's only son... you were always your father's "**pal**." Now, pal Frank, you are the last male standing in the Frank Sandoval Jr. family... with all its tension, with all its craziness, with all its humor, with all its loyalty, with all its strong opinions, with all its generosity and with all its love. Frank, you are your father's son much more than you know. I know you will follow your father's example and truly appreciate the unique qualities in all of your sisters.

My daughter Jessie, Frank Sandoval Jr.'s 4-year-old granddaughter, **Jessie Valentine Lauck**, summed it up when she spoke at her "Abuelito's" graveside as the doves flew off:

> "He was a very special man.
> He brought a lot of joy to the world."

Jessie Valentine Lauck and her Abuelito
Frank Sandoval Jr. 1935-2004

Buena suerte, mi amigo. And... Frank Sandoval Jr. says to all of us: "Buena suerte, mi hente. H'asta Luego."

Phyllis Jessie Morales Sandoval

Holy Trinity Church
Corktown
April, 27, 2002

Grandma Was a Noble Spirit

She was born in the Aztec Canyon of Laredo
Her pockets lined with the dreams of a child
Unaware of the Indian blood that made her,
She felt accepted… for a while.

But the pockets of childhood empty into reality,
A nameless face.
She accepts her place with stoic grace
And, begins life unlisted on the social registry.

The canyon couldn't hold her.
A stirring in the air… an urge,
From the trees, a restless breeze, a surge
And, off she flew with the crow and the blackbird.

She landed among the smokestacks of industry
A child of God, in need of ministry.
She felt the cold shoulder of anonymity
And fought hard to hold onto her identity.

Over the years she won the love of those around her,
And in a world of discontent
She gave a much needed respite
To close-knit misfits and other broken wings who found her.

The raven-haired child has turned to gray.
Her youth belongs to another day.
Saying her goodbyes, before she dies…
And, leaving the world more enlightened along the way.

Her memoirs are the souls of sadness brightened,
Her legacy the countless lives she's lightened,
Her trademark… each wrong forgiven without reservation;
Her destiny… the moon, the stars and the constellations.

Don't weep when she's gone.
Instead, stand and applaud for her cause
And sing her song.
And remember as you look above
The intuition of her humble mission
Came simply from her vision of love.

Phyllis Jessie Morales Sandoval
1914 – 2002